T0312780

More praise for *A Wealth of Well-Being*

"This book is full of relatable stories and real wisdom about the relationship between money and life. It infuses the often dry topic of finances with something all too rare: humanity."

—Christine Benz,
Director of Personal Finance and Retirement Planning, Morningstar

"Statman, a renowned financial and behavioral scientist, takes aim beyond financial well-being—he targets *life* well-being. His arguments are smart, wise, practical—with the added advantage of being right! Statman weaves all of life domains into a whole—family, friends, health, work, education, religion, even society. Financial well-being is the start, but life well-being is the destination. I plan to buy *A Wealth of Well-Being* for my wife, kids, partners, and clients. This book will make you richer—richer in ways far more important than money."

—Theodore R. Aronson,
Co-CEO AJOVista

"There are few people in the world better situated to help us make better decisions about our financial well-being than Professor Statman. He has already taught us what investors really want. Now, more importantly, he is teaching us how to make better decisions about our life well-being."

—Barry L. Ritholtz,
Chairman and CIO of Ritholtz Wealth Management,
Host of *Masters in Business* podcast

"In gripping chapters on such subjects as parents and children, education, and even religion, Statman demonstrates both money's importance and its limitations. Financial advisors will give better and more thoughtful advice, understanding the fundamental importance of family ties and attachments to the community."

—George A. (Sandy) Mackenzie,
Author of *The Decline of the Traditional Pension*,
Founding Editor of *The Journal of Retirement*

"Few people understand the evolving nature of financial planning better than Meir Statman. Ultimately, it's not about investing, or even about money; it's about enabling us to live authentic and fulfilling lives that reflect who we are and what we value. That's why, all over the world, financial planning is morphing into holistic life planning. Anyone wanting to succeed in this exciting new profession should read this inspirational book."

—Robin Powell,
Journalist, Author, and Editor of *The Evidence-Based Investor*

"Aspects of well-being are not only explained, but are also then tied to life circumstances, making it easy to relate personally to the many stories told and learn from them. This is a wonderful book for ordinary people, never mind academics."

—Don Ezra,
Former Co-chair, Global Consulting, Russell Investments,
Author of *Happiness* and *Life Two*

"I wish my parents had the opportunity to read *A Wealth of Well Being*; finances created stresses to other parts of their lives that were simply irreconcilable. Meir's ability to take complex behavioral economic theory and distill it into practical life advice is second to none, with idea after idea to help readers create and improve their own model for personal well-being. *A Wealth of Well Being* should be required reading for all financial advisors."

—Alex Potts,
President Emeritus, Buckingham Strategic Advisors

"As humans, we know that wealth and its quantitative nature underlies well-being, but we also know that well-being depends on the qualitative nature of family, friends, health, education, religion, and more. As financial professionals, however, we are tempted by our knowledge of math and modeling to focus on wealth and its quantitative nature. In *A Wealth of Well-Being*, Meir integrates quantitative and qualitative in a holistic approach, guiding us, even financial professionals, to reflect on our well-being and enhance it."

—Eduardo Repetto,
CIO, Avantis Investors

"Targeted at both financial professionals and general readers, Statman's book encourages a deeper understanding of how financial and life well-being are integrated in domains such as family, health, and education, guiding readers toward greater financial and life well-being in all its domains."

—Robert Powell,
Editor-in-Chief of *Retirement Management Journal*,
Host of *Exceptional Advisor* podcast

"Yet again, Meir Statman has written a book that could well be called "revolutionary," offering a holistic approach to behavioral finance. Clients will see themselves, their joys and sorrows, in the book's many studies and life stories, and bind themselves more closely to their advisers."

—Jean Brunel,
Managing Principal of Brunel Associates,
Author of *Goals-Based Wealth Management*

"Meir's book is a must-read for those of us fascinated by the intersection of finance and psychology that is behavioral finance. His amazing insights continue to enlighten wealth advisors as he helps us guide clients to life well-being, beyond financial well-being."

—H.F. "Rick" Pitcairn II,
Chief Global Strategist, Pitcairn

A WEALTH OF WELL-BEING

A WEALTH OF WELL-BEING

A HOLISTIC APPROACH TO BEHAVIORAL FINANCE

MEIR STATMAN

WILEY

Copyright © 2024 by John Wiley & Sons, Inc. All rights reserved.

Published by John Wiley & Sons, Inc., Hoboken, New Jersey.
Published simultaneously in Canada.

No part of this publication may be reproduced, stored in a retrieval system, or transmitted in any form or by any means, electronic, mechanical, photocopying, recording, scanning, or otherwise, except as permitted under Section 107 or 108 of the 1976 United States Copyright Act, without either the prior written permission of the Publisher, or authorization through payment of the appropriate per-copy fee to the Copyright Clearance Center, Inc., 222 Rosewood Drive, Danvers, MA 01923, (978) 750-8400, fax (978) 750-4470, or on the web at www.copyright.com. Requests to the Publisher for permission should be addressed to the Permissions Department, John Wiley & Sons, Inc., 111 River Street, Hoboken, NJ 07030, (201) 748-6011, fax (201) 748-6008, or online at http://www.wiley.com/go/permission.

Trademarks: Wiley and the Wiley logo are trademarks or registered trademarks of John Wiley & Sons, Inc. and/or its affiliates in the United States and other countries and may not be used without written permission. All other trademarks are the property of their respective owners. John Wiley & Sons, Inc. is not associated with any product or vendor mentioned in this book.

Limit of Liability/Disclaimer of Warranty: While the publisher and author have used their best efforts in preparing this book, they make no representations or warranties with respect to the accuracy or completeness of the contents of this book and specifically disclaim any implied warranties of merchantability or fitness for a particular purpose. No warranty may be created or extended by sales representatives or written sales materials. The advice and strategies contained herein may not be suitable for your situation. You should consult with a professional where appropriate. Further, readers should be aware that websites listed in this work may have changed or disappeared between when this work was written and when it is read. Neither the publisher nor authors shall be liable for any loss of profit or any other commercial damages, including but not limited to special, incidental, consequential, or other damages.

For general information on our other products and services or for technical support, please contact our Customer Care Department within the United States at (800) 762-2974, outside the United States at (317) 572-3993 or fax (317) 572-4002.

Wiley also publishes its books in a variety of electronic formats. Some content that appears in print may not be available in electronic formats. For more information about Wiley products, visit our web site at www.wiley.com.

Library of Congress Cataloging-in-Publication Data is available:

ISBN 9781394249671 (Cloth)
ISBN 9781394251759 (ePub)
ISBN 9781394251742 (ePDF)

Cover image(s): Courtesy of the Author
Cover Design: Wiley

SKY10068654_022924

To Navah, my wife, and Barbara and Ruth, our children

Contents

physicians, business owners, police officers, or plumbers. And we do that by spending, saving, and investing.

The domain of finances is crucial in well-being on its own. Moreover, the domain of finances is crucial because it underlies all other well-being domains. We need finances to support ourselves and our families. We need finances to maintain our own health and that of our families. We need finances to pay for education. We even need finances to experience and express our religion.

Chapter 6: Widowhood and Divorce   81

Widowhood and divorce often diminish people's finances and well-being, but not always. Widows and widowers experience loss and grief in different ways, and communication with people who have not experienced widowhood is often awkward.

Divorced people experience lower well-being than married ones, but divorce does not necessarily diminish well-being. Indeed, divorce generally enhances well-being by dissolving unsatisfying marriages.

Chapter 7: Parents and Children   91

Parenting is expensive. Insufficient finances are prominent among reasons leading couples to remain childless.

Parents enhance the well-being of children by the utilitarian benefits of food, shelter, and education. Children reciprocate with utilitarian support as necessary when parents grow old, providing money and care in their parents' homes or their own. And parents and children enhance the well-being of one another by the expressive and emotional benefits of security, support, and love.

Chapter 8: Elderly Parents, Grandparents, Siblings, and Pets   115

Filial loyalty is practiced in the United States more than preached, evident is the prevalence of the "Sandwich Generation" of parents stressed financially and emotionally as they care for both young children and elderly parents. Grandparenting usually enhances well-being. The well-being of grandparents to at least one grandchild is higher than that of grand parents with no grandchildren.

Close sibling relationships in childhood enhance well-being long into middle age. Yet sibling relationships are often difficult, diminished by rivalry. Pets are family members to many pet owners, enhancing the well-being of those who describe themselves as pet parents, as others describe themselves as children's parents.

Chapter 13: Religion 227

Religiosity measured by frequency of attendance at religious gatherings enhances well-being by more than religiosity measured by private religious acts and beliefs, such as prayer. Members of many religious communities support one another with money and care when needs arise. When tragedy strikes, such as the sudden death of an infant, parents who attend religious gatherings receive support from fellow members, and that support restores well-being.

Chapter 14: Society 235

Societies vary in well-being and governments vary in enhancing it, yet finances underlie what governments do. Government finances involve well-being trade-offs among citizens. Both liberals and conservatives care about fairness in income and wealth distribution, but their values are different, affecting government finances. Liberals tend to define *fairness* in terms of equality, favoring policies that redistribute income and wealth from the wealthy to those in need. Conservatives tend to define *fairness* in terms of equity, preferring that individuals and private organizations help those in need.

Chapter 15: Conclusion 263

Few are fortunate enough to enjoy well-being in all its domains. Life well-being calls for applying well-being medicines from one domain to heal well-being injuries in another. Well-being medicine from an ample finances' domain can heal well-being injuries of a disabled child in the family domain. And volunteer contributions in the domain of work, helping families with disabled children, can heal well-being injuries further.

Preface

A few years ago, I was speaking at an investment conference about saving, spending, financial well-being, and life well-being. I noted the reluctance of many people possessing abundant financial well-being to spend some of their ample savings on themselves, their families, and their communities, thereby enhancing their life well-being by more than they sacrifice in financial well-being.

People approached me after my presentation, describing the critical need to curtail spending and increase saving, the hazards of giving adult children money without asking them to pay it back, and the recklessness of widows splurging irresponsibly soon after their husbands die. One stood aside, waiting until the others had left.

She said, "I burst out crying when you said, 'It is better to give with a warm hand than a cold one.'" Indeed, she had tears in her eyes when she spoke to me. It turned out that she had lent her son some $27,000 for college tuition and now insisted that he pay her by the agreed schedule. The mother had more than enough savings to forgive the loan without imperiling her financial well-being, but she reasoned that paying by schedule would benefit her son, increasing his future financial well-being by teaching him financial responsibility. Yet the son was financially strapped now, at the beginning of his career, lacking even money to buy his girlfriend an engagement ring, and his mother's demand soured their relationship.

Financial well-being comes when we can meet current and future financial obligations, absorb financial setbacks, and keep driving toward financial goals, such as adequate retirement income. Life well-being comes when we live satisfying lives, full of meaning and purpose.

I often note that the biggest risks in life are not in the stock market. If you want real risk, I say, get married. And if you want more risk, have children. People laugh because the point is obvious. Yet that point is regularly lost when we speak about financial well-being, neglecting life well-being. I was motivated to write this book by reflecting on my own financial and life well-being and those of others. We need financial well-being to enjoy life well-being, but it is life well-being that we seek.

Life well-being has many domains, including those of family, friends, health, work, education, religion, and society. The domain of finances has a special place among the domains of life well-being because it is important on its own and because it underlies all other domains. We need finances to support ourselves and our families, paying for food and shelter. We need finances to maintain our own health and that of our families, paying for the services of physicians and hospitals. We need finances to pay for education that would qualify us for well-paying and satisfying jobs, careers, and vocations. We even need finances to experience and express our religion.

The woman in my story could have increased her son's life well-being and her own by forgiving the loan, sacrificing some well-being in the domain of finances, but gaining in the domain of family more than she had sacrificed. I hope that this is what she did that day.

This book is addressed primarily to financial professionals, enriching their knowledge and adding to their contributions to their clients, and to financial academics, enriching their scholarship and adding to their contributions to their students. Yet this book is also addressed to all people who strive to enhance their life well-being. All will learn from research by scholars in many fields, including finance, economics, law, medicine, psychology, and sociology, and all will learn from writers, journalists, and ordinary people of wide-ranging experiences.

I was reflecting on my own financial and life well-being as I was listening to that woman. I was born in 1947 in a displaced persons camp in Germany to Holocaust survivors, and we came to Israel in 1949. Navah, my wife, and I were students at the Hebrew University of Jerusalem when we were married in 1969.

A few months before our wedding, my parents traveled to meet Navah's. After dinner Navah and I were excused to go for a walk, and our parents set down to business. Business meant deciding how much each set of parents will contribute to support the young couple, helping with a down payment on an apartment. My parents were far from wealthy, and Navah's parents had even less, but as I learned later, Navah's mother said to her father, "Whatever Meir's parents offer, we will match." They borrowed some of the money from relatives and repaid it later.

I graduated from the Hebrew University with a B.A. in economics and statistics and an M.B.A., and got a job as a financial analyst at a large company. The job enhanced my life well-being for a few months and then diminished it. As I would say later, projects lasted longer than my interest in them.

One morning I got up, called work to say that I will not be in, and Navah and I traveled to Jerusalem where I remembered a library that had a catalog of American Ph.D. programs. It also had a catalog of scholarships available to foreign students. One institution wrote back to say that it could not tell by my name whether I am a man or a woman, but I should know that this is an endowment of a sorority, awarding scholarships only to women. In time, Navah applied and received a scholarship that paid most of the tuition for her master's program.

Navah and I had sufficient means to live as students when we arrived in New York City to study at Columbia University. But at some time during the application period, I was concerned that we would have to forgo our plans because we would not have sufficient means. I asked my father for a loan. "I wish I could lend you money," said my father, "But you have a younger brother and sister, and they would also need support when they are married. I do not have financial means beyond that."

Life well-being is constrained by life's circumstances. All people and families have points of pain, diminishing life well-being, whether poverty, a disabled child, a difficult marriage, or an early death. Our family is not exempt. Barbara, our older daughter, lives with bipolar illness. Her illness was not diagnosed for years, during which we were told that her difficulties stem from family dynamics. It seemed that the only question yet to be answered was whether blame lies with Navah or with me. We let our anguish seep into our marriage, diminishing our life well-being in that domain, beyond diminishing it in the domain of children.

We enjoy greater life well-being now, as Barbara's situation is stable. She says "I love you" at the end of every conversation. Navah continues to enhance the life well-being of many people living with mental illness and their families as a volunteer at the National Alliance on Mental Illness (NAMI). We are fortunate to have an ample finances domain, able to support Barbara without constraining our budget, and we are even more fortunate in the domain of family as Ruth, Barbara's younger sister, loves and supports her.

I see the need to explore life well-being and enhance it in my own experiences, in the experiences of financial professionals and their clients, and in the experiences of professors of finance and their students.

Some years ago, a financial adviser I know called to ask for my advice. His young son had just experienced a psychotic break. He and his wife were shocked and bewildered. I invited them to our home for a conversation with my wife and me. We described our identical shock and bewilderment years before, offered our empathy, and shared with them what we have learned from our experiences and those of others.

That adviser now cares for many clients living with mental illness and their families. Some people living with bipolar illness may spend recklessly when in manic states. The adviser described a client admitted for psychiatric care who requested the custodian overseeing his funds to remove his adviser so he can withdraw a large sum of money. When his manic state subsided, the client was surprised at what he had done, and reinstated the adviser. Concerned about recurrence, the client has designated a trusted person to evaluate his requests before proceeding.

I teach investment courses in our graduate programs. I teach the usual content of such courses, including portfolio theory, asset pricing theory, and market efficiency, but I also help my students explore links between financial well-being and life well-being. My students share their stories of saving, spending, investing, wants, financial well-being, and life well-being with one another and with me, and I share my stories with them. In the process, I enhance my students' life well-being and my own.

One assignment presents an alphabetical list of 10 wants answering the question "Why is wealth important to you?" including "Buying the things I really want," "Educating my children," "Helping the less fortunate," and "Providing financial security." I ask my students to rank the wants by their importance to them and explain their rankings. I also ask them to comment on the postings of two classmates.

One wrote: "Providing financial security is right at the top of my list. It's not just about me; it's about my family's journey and their struggles after the Vietnam War."

Another wrote: "Am I too selfish or unethical if I place helping the less fortunate as the last thing that I prioritize in life?"

And yet another wrote: "Fourteen years ago, prior to the birth of my son, I would have put buying things for myself as my main goal. Now, my mind is centered on my son."

In another assignment I ask my students how they manage their savings and spending. Do they find it hard to refrain from spending even when they know they shouldn't spend? If they are in a relationship, how do they resolve differences about saving and spending? What have they learned from their parents about savings and spending?

One student wrote that he is about to be married. His fiancée wants them to combine their finances but he prefers to keep them separate. "What do you think, professor?"

In this book, I share with you what I have learned about financial well-being and life well-being. I hope that my words will help you reflect on your financial well-being and life well-being, and enhance them.

Introduction

Life well-being, the center of this book, is composed of three parts: experienced, evaluative, and meaning, described by psychologists Andrew Steptoe and Arthur Stone, and Nobel Laureate economist Angus Deaton.[1]

Experienced well-being, also known as emotional or hedonic well-being, refers to our momentary emotions such as happiness, sadness, and anger. *Evaluative well-being* refers to our satisfaction with our lives. *Meaning well-being*, also known as eudemonic well-being, refers to our assessment of the meaning and purpose of our lives. *Life well-being*, as used in this book, is about all the parts of well-being. In what follows, I use *well-being* as a shorthand for *life well-being*.

Steptoe and coauthors measured experienced well-being by asking people about their emotional experiences, with adjectives such as *happy*, *sad*, and *angry*. They noted that negative adjectives are not simply opposites of positive adjectives. Instead, each kind contains unique information about a person's emotional state. Therefore, experienced well-being is composed of two dimensions, positive and negative, that point in imperfectly opposite directions.

The researchers measured evaluative well-being by Cantril's Self-Anchoring Scale, also known as Cantril's ladder. It asks: "Please imagine a ladder, with steps numbered from 0 at the bottom to 10 at the top. The top of the ladder represents the best possible life for you and the bottom of the ladder represents the worst possible life for you. On which step of the ladder would you say you personally stand at this time? On which step do you think you will stand about five years from now?"

Meaning is an orientation to something bigger than oneself. People enjoying high-meaning well-being agree with statements such as

"I understand my life's meaning," "I have discovered a satisfying life purpose," and "I have something to contribute to society."

The three parts of well-being are distinct by cognitive reflection. Experienced well-being can be reported directly, requiring no cognitive reflection, whereas evaluative and meaning well-being require cognitive reflection, including aggregation over time and comparison with self-selected standards such as our lives today compared to our lives a decade ago, our lives compared to the lives of others, and our lives compared to our aspired lives.

Differences between experienced and evaluative well-being are evident in Finnish people's reactions to the top place of their country in the World Happiness Report, six years in a row.

Finns acknowledge their high evaluative well-being, praising their country's strong social safety net. A Finn who has also lived in the United States noted that Finns, unlike Americans, have no big worries in life. "I am retired, getting a pension which is about 70% of my last salary, and I'll get it till I die. . . . I still pay relatively high taxes, but all education is free also through college. . . . I have had two hip replacement operations with hospital stay, total cost to me about $600."[2]

Yet Finns also acknowledged their low experienced well-being, characterizing themselves as quite gloomy, a little moody, or not given to unnecessary smiling. Indeed, when a leaked video of Sanna Marin, Finland's 36-year-old leader at the time, showed her dancing energetically and singing with friends, some Finns suspected that she was high on drugs.[3]

Julia Wilson-Hangasmaa, a 59-year-old woman, immigrated to Finland from Zimbabwe three decades before. Zimbabwe ranks 144th, in the World Happiness Survey, better only than Lebanon and Afghanistan. Wilson-Hangasmaa appreciates the freedom Finland provides all people to pursue their dreams without worrying about meeting basic needs, but when she returns to Zimbabwe, she is struck by people's exuberant joy. "What I miss the most, I realize when I enter Zimbabwe, are the smiles."[4]

Differences between meaning well-being and experienced well-being are striking in the experiences of mountain climbers. Economist George Loewenstein described the experience of Maurice Herzog, the first man to climb an 8,000-meter peak. Herzog lost several fingers and parts of his feet to gangrene, surely diminishing his experienced well-being and likely his evaluative well-being, but the ordeal enhanced his meaning well-being. The ordeal, wrote Herzog, "has given me the assurance and serenity of a man who has fulfilled himself. It has given me the rare joy of loving that which I used to despise. A new and splendid life has opened out before me."[5]

Some people are willing to trade experienced well-being for meaning well-being. Ample finances provide John Craig the funds for high experienced well-being, including the mansion where he was interviewed by sociologist Michele Lamont. Yet he seeks to enhance his meaning well-being. "To keep the pace up to generate a lot of income gets wearing," he said. "We live in a high-ticket town. I got caught up in the big house and the high lifestyle. . . . Now I have become more conscious and aware of what is important to me." To redefine what is important to him, he is reading *The Road Less Traveled* by M. Scott Peck, a book aimed at helping readers attain meaning well-being.[6]

Others trade future evaluative and meaning well-being for present experienced well-being. Many find experienced well-being in smoking, excessive spending, or fleeting relationships, but these often detract from future evaluative and meaning well-being. Fred Jones, an elderly man, never married, had six children by four different women, yet maintained close ties with only one of his children. "I played and played and played until I played out," he said. "I wasn't smart enough. I thought I was gonna be healthy, happy, and vigorous and everything else for a hundred years at least. Then I got caught—nobody here to take care of me, and it's all my own fault."[7]

COVID-19 led some to reconsider their well-being, assigning less weight to day-to-day experienced well-being and more weight to evaluative and meaning well-being. Yet it led others to renewed appreciation of experienced well-being. Dennis Littley, a retired chef, has been eating well at home but looked forward to the simple pleasure of sitting at the patio of his favorite restaurant, drinking a dark beer, and eating "a really, really good cheeseburger," pleasure made possible now by his COVID-19 vaccination.[8]

The third generation of behavioral finance

Life well-being is also at the center of the third generation of behavioral finance, a generation preceded by standard finance and the first and second generations of behavioral finance. Standard finance describes people as computer-like "rational," immune to cognitive errors such as overconfidence and emotional errors such as excessive fear. Rational people aim to increase their wealth and its utilitarian benefits, mostly consumption, and are able to strike it perfectly.

The first generation of behavioral finance described people as bumbling "irrational," aiming at increasing their wealth, as in standard finance, but hampered from striking it perfectly by cognitive and emotional errors, such as overconfidence or excessive fear.

The second generation of behavioral finance described people as "normal," people like you and me, neither rational nor irrational. Normal people aim for expressive and emotional benefits in addition to utilitarian ones, and are sometimes willing to sacrifice some wealth and its utilitarian benefits for them.

Utilitarian benefits are the answer to the question: what does something do for me and my pocketbook? Expressive benefits are the answer to the question: what does something say about me to others and myself? Emotional benefits are the answer to the question: how does something make me feel?

Watches offer an example of the three kinds of benefits. Expensive watches diminish well-being by the utilitarian costs of high prices, but enhance it by the expressive benefits of high social status and display of refined tastes, and by the emotional benefits of beauty and pride. Indeed, it is impossible to explain the wide ranges of watch prices, from $10 to more than $1 million, without considering their expressive and emotional benefits.

The third generation of behavioral finance also describes people as "normal," but is explicit in describing life well-being as people's overall want. This generation broadens its lens to see people as whole persons and show them in the domain of finances, but also in the domains of family, friends, health, work, education, religion, and society.

The special place of the domain of finances

The domain of finances has a special place in life well-being because it is important on its own and because it underlies well-being in all other domains. We need finances to support ourselves and our families, paying for food and shelter. We need finances to maintain our own health and that of our families, paying for the services of physicians and hospitals. We need finances to pay for education that would qualify us for well-paying and satisfying jobs, careers, and vocations. We even need finances to experience and express our religion.

Doug Lynam used to be a monk. Now he is a financial adviser. "For too long," he wrote, "religion and money have been held separate, as if the very existence of one sully the other. But the cold hard truth of modern life is that we need money . . . even monks. I discovered this fact the hard way when our community went bankrupt."[9]

The domain of finances is often overlooked or downgraded by both ordinary people and scholars. "To me, well-being means balance between work, friends/family, my relationships, and my health," said Jean, a 31-year-old American woman interviewed by BlackRock. "Each of these things definitely factors in, with maybe my relationships being the most important part."[10]

Jean did not mention finances among the domains underlying her life well-being. And even when mentioned, that domain does not rank high. One survey found that the domain of finances ranks no higher than the domains of family, work, and health.[11] Another found that it mattered little, much less than the domains of family, friends, and health.[12] Still another found that it ranks last.[13]

Yet a BlackRock survey of Americans reveals that 55% percent of them ranked finances as the major source of stress in life, followed at some distance by stress over work, health, family, and social life.[14] Indeed, high perceived financial well-being, measured by low stress over present finances and high security over future finances, is a key predictor of life well-being, comparable in magnitude to the combined effects of high job satisfaction, good physical health, and solid supporting relationships.[15]

1

Financial, Social, Cultural, and Personal Capital

Life well-being is enhanced by four kinds of capital: financial, social, cultural, and personal. Financial capital consists of income and wealth. Social capital centers on social networks of people supporting one another by acceptance, trust, and cooperation. Cultural capital encompasses knowledge of the many aspects of the culture of a group, ease of interactions with fellow members of that group, and comfort of adherence to the group's values and practices. And personal capital includes physical and mental features, gender and sexual orientation, race, and nationality. Each kind of capital is associated with utilitarian, expressive, and emotional benefits and costs, and each varies by social class.

Social class—elite, working class, and poor

Law professor Joan Williams noted that the term *middle class* has become too broad to designate social class.[1] Almost nine out of 10 people see themselves as members of the middle class.[2] Instead, she classified people by social class into elite, working class, and poor. The social classes differ by financial capital, measured by income and wealth, but also by education, employment, preferences, and attitudes, reflecting social, cultural, and personal capital.

The elite are the professional and managerial class, consisting of families with incomes in the top 20% and at least one member who is a college graduate. Working-class families are those with incomes above the bottom 30% but below the top 20%, and also families with higher incomes but no college graduates. And poor families are those with incomes at the bottom 30%.

Well-being divides between social classes and within them have expanded during the decades. Well-being was stable among the white members of the elite between the 1970s and 2010s, while declining among white members of the working class and poor. Well-being among Black members of the working class and poor was fairly stable, while increasing among Black members of the elite.[3]

Respect enhances well-being by expressive and emotional benefits, and disrespect diminishes it. Respect and disrespect vary by social class. Economists Richard Reeves and Isabel Sawhill noted that most Americans said that they were "treated with respect all day yesterday."[4] But they also noted that respect did not extend to all, especially people of color and those without college education. A man interviewed by Pew said: "It would be nice to live according to my being rather than my blackness. I will never know how a totally worthwhile life will feel because of this."[5]

The expressive and emotional costs of disrespect are evident in Stephanie Land's story of her life, "Maid: Hard work, low pay, and a mother's will to survive." She described paying for groceries with food stamps, suffering the expressive and emotional costs of stigma as other customers eyed her shopping cart judgmentally. One older man said loudly "You're welcome!" as if he is the one who had paid for her groceries.[6]

The elite members of the 1% can be comforted by the utilitarian benefits of their wealth, yet their well-being is diminished by the expressive and emotional costs of disrespect by the 99%. Sam Zell, a wealthy real estate investor, likely a member of the 0.001%, argued that the 1% deserve great respect from the 99% because "The 1-percent work harder, the 1-percent are much bigger factors in all forms of our society."[7]

Indeed, the expressive and emotional benefits of respect enhance well-being by more than the utilitarian benefits of wealth. College students rated how respected they felt in their group and how much they respected the other people in their group. They were also asked about their family income and their own well-being. Feeling wealthy, without also feeling respected, does not enhance well-being.[8]

Members of the working class resent disrespect by members of the elite, such as lawyers, doctors, and teachers. Author and political activist Barbara Ehrenreich recalled how her working-class father countered that disrespect by disrespect, calling lawyers shysters, doctors quacks, and professors phonies.[9]

Financial capital

Financial capital consists of income and wealth and their utilitarian, expressive, and emotional benefits. These benefits are evident in the words of Divya, a 33-year-old American woman interviewed by BlackRock.[10] "My financial status enabled us to purchase this home that is well out of reach for many individuals in my age group and place in life. I felt proud that my family could make the decision to purchase this type of home. . . ."

This home provides Divya utilitarian benefits as shelter, expressive benefits as an emblem of high social status, "well out of reach for many individuals in my age group and place in life," and emotional benefits in pride "that my family could make the decision to purchase this type of home. . . ." Moreover, financial capital underlies all of these benefits. Divya said: "My financial status enabled us to purchase this home. . . ."

Ample finances enhance both evaluative and experienced well-being, documented by psychologist Matthew Killingsworth.[11] He measured evaluative well-being by answers to the question: "overall, how satisfied are you with your life?" And he measured experienced well-being by answers to the question: "how do you feel right now?"

Killingsworth found that higher income enhances evaluative well-being at all levels of income, confirming a conclusion reached earlier by Nobel Laureates psychologist Daniel Kahneman and economist Angus Deaton. But he overturned their other conclusion: that experienced well-being ceases to increase once annual income reaches $75,000.[12] Instead, he found that higher income enhances both evaluative and experienced well-being at any level of income.

Killingsworth noted that Kahneman and Deaton asked people to recall yesterday's experienced well-being, yet a gap likely exists between yesterday's experienced well-being as recalled right now, and yesterday's experienced well-being, as experienced right then. Instead, he measured current experienced well-being by smartphone answers to the question "how do you feel right now?"

Higher income enhances experienced well-being by increasing positive feelings and diminishing negative ones. Higher annual income in the range below $80,000 is associated with higher positive feelings in four out of the list of five: confident, good, interested, and proud. It is associated with lower negative feelings in the entire list of seven afraid, angry, bad, bored, sad, stressed, and upset.

Higher annual income in the range above $80,000 is associated with the entire list of five positive feelings, including inspired, and lower negative feelings in four of the seven negative feelings: bad, bored, sad, and upset. This implies that higher income, from low to moderate, enhances experienced well-being mostly by reducing suffering, indicated by lower negative feelings. Higher income, from low to moderate, also enhances experienced well-being by greater sense of control, measured by answers to the question: "to what extent do you feel in control of your life?" and greater financial security, measured by answers to the question: "did you have trouble coping with regular bills during the last 15 days?"

Killingsworth found that higher income enhances both evaluative and experienced well-being, not ceasing at any level of income. Nevertheless, the magnitudes of well-being increments associated with income increments are lower when income is higher. For example, the difference in well-being between a family with a $20,000 annual income and one with triple that, $60,000, is about the same as the difference in well-being between a family with a $60,000 annual income and one with triple that, $180,000.

Social capital

Social capital centers on social networks of people supporting one another by acceptance, trust, and cooperation. Social capital can be narrow, consisting of family, or broad, encompassing people in a county or country.

The effects of social capital are evident in decisions to flee after fatal road accidents. Accidents are not planned and decisions to help or flee are made under great emotional distress and time pressure, thus providing a test of the role of social capital. Analysis of fatal accidents involving pedestrians in U.S. counties shows that greater social capital is associated with lower probability of hit-and-run.[13]

The social capital of the elite usually consists of broad but weak social networks, such as managers they can contact for leads to jobs or professors they can approach for advice on placing their children at their preferred universities. Investments in social capital are higher in occupations, such as management and law, where they can yield greater benefits.

An experiment using LinkedIn data found that relatively weak ties in a broad social network were more helpful in finding jobs than strong ties in a narrow social network.[14] A reader of an article on the LinkedIn experiment provided an example. "I was laid off after a 30-year career with a big well-known company. Thankfully, LinkedIn exists and I have kept networking despite rarely looking to make a move. I got multiple interviews and a great job after six or so weeks of looking."

Social networks among the working class and poor usually consist of a tight group of extended family, friends, and neighbors who watch children when parents must be away, or provide a loan for an urgent trip to visit an ailing parent. Sociologists Jonathan Morduch and Rachel Schneider described Tahmid Khan, an immigrant from Bangladesh working as a fruit vendor in Manhattan. Tahmid loaned $1,500 to a cousin who had lost two months of income after Hurricane Sandy damaged his shop, $400 to a friend of his wife, and $2,000 to another friend who urgently needed to visit his ailing mother in Bangladesh.[15]

Psychologist Dacher Keltner and coauthors contrasted the social capital of the elite and lower classes, noting that the greater resources of the elite reduce their need to rely on others. "What wealth and education and prestige and a higher station in life gives you is the freedom to focus on the self," said Keltner. Wealthy people don't read other people's emotions as well. They hoard resources and are less generous than their resources allow.[16]

The lower classes, however, must rely on others. "If you don't have resources and education, you really adapt to the environment, which is more threatening, by turning to other people," said Keltner. "There's always someone there who will take you somewhere, or watch your kid. You've just got to lean on people."

Journalist Esau McCaulley provided an example of the workings of social capital in the working class during his childhood. His mother worked the late shift at a Chrysler plant—from 2 to 12 p.m., six days a week. Friends and neighbors drove him and his siblings to and from school. When available, aunties, cousins, and grandmothers watched them in the evenings. "Oversight of children is patched together, and favors are bartered to get through each week." This did not strike McCaulley as odd because it was common among all the children he knew.[17]

Extended family is at the center of the social capital of the working class. Sociologist Annette Lareau describes Wendy, a child in a working-class family, whose life is interwoven with those of her extended family. Wendy's best friends are her cousins Rosie and Rebecca, who live a short distance away. She enjoys her daily visits to her maternal grandparents, who live within walking distance. Wendy's grandfather often picks her up after school, and on Easter Sunday morning, Wendy calls her grandmother and sings "You Are My Sunshine."[18]

Lareau contrasted the social capital of the working class with that of the elite, describing Garrett, a member of an elite family, who chooses to join a scheduled soccer game rather than attend a family celebration of a cousin's college graduation. "Soccer is more of a priority. Isn't that right, Garrett?" says Garrett's father, as Garrett nods in agreement.[19]

Social capital contains boundaries set between those included in a social group and those excluded. Exclusive behavior is displayed as discomfort by the excluder and perceived as disrespectful or snobbish by the excluded. Sociologist Michele Lamont quoted an elite man displaying exclusive behavior toward people outside his social group by "being reserved, being quiet, not really openly discussing things, or being very formally courteous, not having much to do with you because I have no time or use for you and I try and send signals in that way." That man displays inclusive behavior toward fellow elite members by making them feel "comfortable," giving up "fronts," and interacting as "human beings."[20]

Cultural capital

Cultural capital, a concept introduced by sociologist Pierre Bourdieu, consists of knowledge of the many aspects of the culture of a group, ease of interactions with fellow members of that group, and comfort of adherence to the group's values and practices.

Sociologist Daniel Laurison described the role of cultural capital at a television-production firm. Employees at the firm wore all kinds of casual clothes, but some casual clothes, such as tracksuits, were consistent with their cultural capital of studied informality, whereas others were not. One employee, a man who grew up in a working-class family, always stood out, wearing tracksuits inconsistent with that studied informality, perhaps because he failed to comprehend it or perhaps because he was unwilling to adopt it. He left the firm not long after joining it.[21]

Better cultural fit between managers and their companies is beneficial, extending managerial tenure. Companies' stock prices increase when information indicates high cultural fit within them. In contrast, companies that hire culturally disruptive managers suffer lower future market values and performance.[22]

Breastfeeding is part of the cultural capital of the American elite. Sociologist Elizabeth Currid-Halkett noted that 17% of American college-graduate mothers breastfeed exclusively through a baby's first six months, whereas only 9.3% of those without a college degree do.[23] Ample financial capital makes it easier for elite mothers to apply their cultural capital by quitting full-time employment, facilitating breastfeeding. This ease is illustrated in the words of Rebecca Thompson Hitt, founder of The Consciously Parenting Project, rejecting doubts about the benefits of breastfeeding. "Once I became a mother, I quit my day job and only took on jobs that I could do while putting my baby first. . . . There is nothing more important than my children and our relationship. Nothing."[24]

Cultural capital varies across societies. Currid-Halkett noted that breastfeeding is not part of the cultural capital of the French elite. "For French women, the badge of postpartum status is losing weight quickly and looking sexy again." This contrasts with the American mold of tent dresses justified by preoccupation with breastfeeding.[25]

Personal capital

Personal capital includes physical and mental features, gender and sexual orientation, race, and nationality. It also includes education, health, and religion, which are explored in the chapters that follow.

Physical features

Beauty provides utilitarian, expressive, and emotional benefits. Beautiful children enjoy greater popularity at school and wider friendship networks, and beautiful adults are more likely to be invited to join organizations and informal gatherings, expanding their social capital.[26,27] Beautiful borrowers are more likely to get loans, pay similar interest rates, yet default more often.[28]

Beautiful managers of stock funds attract greater investments into their funds than less beautiful ones, despite earning lower returns. Beautiful managers are also more likely to be promoted. This is especially true among funds available on FinTech platforms where managers' photos are accessible to investors.[29]

And taller people enjoy higher benefits than shorter people, evaluating their lives more favorably, more likely to enjoy positive emotions, and less likely to suffer negative ones.[30]

Mental features

Extraversion and cheerfulness are personality traits associated with high well-being whereas neuroticism and depression are associated with low well-being.[31] Personality as teenagers predicts midlife well-being. Women who were more extraverted as teenagers enjoyed higher well-being in midlife. In contrast, both men and women who were more neurotic as teenagers suffered lower well-being in midlife.[32]

Optimism is associated with high well-being. BlackRock surveys reveal that people enjoying high well-being tend to agree with the statement "I am optimistic about my future."[33] Optimists live longer. The most optimistic women lived an average of 14.9% longer than their more pessimistic ones, and the most optimistic men lived 10.9% longer than their more pessimistic ones.[34]

Optimism hastens recovery from cardiovascular surgery and diminishes chronic pain, diabetes, and carotid atherosclerosis.[35] Yet the power of optimism is limited. No study has found that optimism aids in cancer remission.

Emotional intelligence, the ability to recognize and manage our own emotions and understand and influence the emotions of others, is associated with high well-being. Yet well-being is not associated with cognitive intelligence, the intelligence measured by IQ tests.[36]

Gender and sexual orientation

Gender and sexual orientation offer well-being advantages and disadvantages. Gender inequality diminishes well-being in liberal countries, especially among women. Yet it has little effect on well-being in conservative countries.[37]

Deviations from stereotypical gender roles diminish well-being among both men and women. Writer Norah Vincent explored these by presenting herself as a man, "Ned," for 18 months with a new wardrobe, shorter haircut, and an extremely tight sports bra. She found that men suffer as much, if not more, from gendered expectations. Men who do not conform to masculine stereotypes are called pansy, sissy, fag, and queer.[38]

Legal scholar Douglas NeJaime noted that the debate about religious freedom in the context of same-sex marriage obscures the central role of sexual orientation. Same-sex relationships constitute lesbian or gay identities, and religious objections arise largely from objections to such identities.[39]

Transgender and gender non-conforming people looking for housing suffer discrimination. They are 27% less likely to be shown additional areas of an apartment complex, 21% less likely to be offered financial incentives to rent, 12% more likely to be told negative comments about the apartment and the neighborhood, and 9% more likely to be quoted higher rental prices than people who are not transgender and who conform to typical gender standards.[40]

Bisexuals also face considerable discrimination from both heterosexual and gay and lesbian groups. Bisexuals reported significant levels of employment discrimination, including inappropriate jokes, sexual harassment, and diminished access to fringe benefits.[41]

Race

Some personal capital, such as being Black, counts as a liability more often than as an asset. Law professor Meirav Furth-Matzkin sent 19 testers, Black and white women and men, to return unworn clothing items without receipts to stores in Chicago.[42]

Sellers granted white customers more concessions beyond formal policy, and granted Black customers fewer store credits or exchanges. White customers whose requests for credits or exchanges were denied were almost 30% more likely to be allowed to speak to a manager than Black ones. And among those who got to speak to a manager, white customers were 14% more likely to be granted concessions than Black customers. The disadvantages faced by Black customers are known as "Shopping while Black."

Discrimination against Black hosts is evident in vacation rentals. The race of hosts is disclosed on Airbnb but not on HomeAway. Black hosts receive lower ratings on Airbnb than the same Black hosts receive on HomeAway. An experiment replicating these findings found that the race of hosts affects the ratings they receive, and another experiment found that people stereotypically expect Black hosts to perform worse than white hosts.[43]

Discrimination against Asian Americans spiked at the start of the COVID-19 pandemic. Airbnb users with distinctively Asian names suffered a 20% decline in guests relative to hosts with distinctively white names.[44]

Nationality

An American interviewed by Pew said "I feel very, very fortunate. Being a middle-class American is like winning the planetary lottery. People lose sight of that."[45] Citizens of unstable and poor countries such as Venezuela and Honduras are willing to trek many miles over dangerous terrain to enter the United States, and citizens of poor and unstable countries such as Afghanistan and Syria are willing to risk life on rickety boats to reach Europe.

Citizens of rich countries enjoy extensive travel freedom across the globe, whereas citizens of less-developed nations suffer stringent visa controls. The effects of nationality on travel freedom and well-being are evident in interviews with citizens of Serbia and Israel who have acquired a second passport from a European Union country. Passengers continuously monitored the way they were treated by border control authorities, comparing their travel freedom to that enjoyed by citizens of nations that they perceived as culturally similar. They suffered shame when their treatment fell short of their expectations and enjoyed pride when treated better than comparable others.[46]

Combinations of financial, social, cultural, and personal capital

Combinations of financial, social, cultural, and personal capital among the elite make it easier for their children to find career sponsors who can fast-track their careers. Elite parents provide their children valuable cultural capital in information and a sense of ease, and sponsors build on it by providing the organization's cultural capital. Gatekeepers to elite careers, likely members of the elite, tend to misperceive this cultural capital as evidence of talent or merit.

A combination of the four kinds of capital underlies the career advantages of children of the Norwegian elite over children of the working class who bump against the "class ceilings."[47] Children of the elite are able to accept desirable but unpaid internships, pursue promising but risky career opportunities, and resist exploitative employment. They are also able to buy residences in cities such as Oslo, London, Paris, and New York, which are too expensive for children of the working class.

The four kinds of capital are generally aligned, but not always. The financial capital of Leon Cooperman, a hedge fund manager, is surely aligned with the elite, and his social capital is likely aligned with it, but his cultural and personal capital are not.

Cooperman is richer than most hedge fund managers, yet heavyset, with a lumbering gait, and according to the affectionate description of a fellow hedge fund manager, "wearing clothes that qualify him as the worst-dressed billionaire on planet Earth."[48]

The four kinds of capital are also not aligned in the lives of adjunct instructors at many colleges whose education, knowledge, and tastes reflect the cultural capital of the elite, yet whose financial capital is aligned with that of the working class or poor. One wrote: "I live in what the Victorians would have referred to as 'genteel poverty.' I come from a respectable middle-class background, and I have two college degrees. Unfortunately, my work as an adjunct college instructor means that I have little income and reside in the lower class in economic terms."[49]

Moreover, the four kinds of capital can be in conflict. High financial capital can diminish social capital. A wealthy man described getting little sympathy from others when his sister got sick and died after many tests and no definitive diagnosis. "I couldn't believe how many people, instead of saying 'I'm sorry for your loss' said something like, 'my father died last year but we didn't have the finances that you do. Maybe now you understand what it's like for the rest of us who don't have the money.'"[50]

And a working-class man described his awkwardness in the company of people with substantial financial capital. Several wealthy families in his church have gorgeous homes they often open up for gatherings. He appreciates their generosity, but is discouraged from inviting them to his middle-class home because, "Well, I know our house just isn't as nice as theirs."[51]

2

Financial Capital

Marissa Lopez, a 31-year-old single mother of three, completed some college education and is certified as a medical assistant.[1] Yet she has been working for a temp agency in hospitals and doctors' offices during the last seven years because she cannot find a full-time job. Speaking to sociologist Sarah Halpern-Meekin and coauthors, she said: "Sometimes I'm able to get 40 hours a week. Other times I'm lucky if I get 8 hours a week."

The domain of finances is important in well-being on its own. High incomes enhance both experienced and evaluative well-being. Moreover, the domain of finances is important because it underlies well-being in all other domains.

It is difficult to enjoy well-being in the domain of family when finances are inadequate to support a mother and her three children. And it is difficult to enjoy well-being in the domain of work when employed by a temp agency, dependent on inadequate wages earned in work hours that vary from week to week.

British families coped with diminished finances in the time of COVID-19 by cutting spending, dipping into savings, and borrowing from banks and friends. The burden of coping reduced their well-being by an equivalent $313–$4,388 of annual income.[2]

Many financial concerns are similar among people of all countries, but some are different. Concerns among Americans include the burdens of student loans, cost of housing, inequality, and stagnant wages. "I think it is harder to achieve financial health now than it was for our parents' generation," said Mike, a 33-year-old American man interviewed by BlackRock, "because we entered the job market in the middle of the 2007–2008 financial crisis and it's been an uphill battle to get to where we are today."

Britons are concerned about the cost of housing, childcare, and tuition, likely decreases in pension benefits and increases in pension qualifying age, and the uncertainty induced by Brexit. "I feel if you can't get on the property ladder it hinders your chances to achieve this financial health and owning your own home is a big step towards this," said Tracey, a 51-year-old British woman.

Mexicans are concerned about the country's poor economic and political environment, taxes, unstable currency, inflation, and corruption. "I am worried about the political environment in Mexico, the impunity, and the corruption," said Orlando, a 43-year-old Mexican man. And Rosa Celia, a 61-year-old Mexican woman, said, "I am worried about some aspects such as the inflation increasing every day. This is affecting our salaries, pensions, or any other income."

And Chinese are concerned about housing, medical care, education, jobs, inflation, volatile financial markets, and inequality. Many noted that people in their parents' generation were less susceptible to losses in Chinese financial markets because these markets were not as open back then, and available investments, such as savings in banks and government bonds, were less risky. Moreover, they noted that people in their parents' generation were poorer on average than people today, but they were equally poor, whereas today's open economy and financial markets foster great inequality and competition for money and social status. "In our generation, there are too many temptations, intense working competition, insufficient medical and education resources," said Lei, a 29-year-old Chinese man.

Utilitarian, expressive, and emotional

Ample financial capital enhances our well-being by utilitarian, expressive, and emotional benefits. Meredith, a 31-year-old American woman interviewed by BlackRock, illustrated these benefits, comparing her financial situation during her college days to her situation today. All throughout college she made $7 an hour, which was enough to pay for drinking on the weekends and going out with her friends. She knew she was poor, but it didn't matter because all her friends were also poor.

Meredith's well-being is higher now that her savings exceed those of people in her social comparison group: "Every time I see articles stating that most Americans don't have enough in savings for a six-month emergency fund, I feel a LOT better about myself because I easily have that, and more."

The wealthy, owners of extravagant financial capital, enjoy utilitarian benefits unavailable to owners of mere ample financial capital.

Documentary filmmaker Abigail Disney, an heiress to the Disney fortune, acknowledged these benefits. "If you move up from coach to business to first class, you won't want to go back to coach. And once you've flown private, wild horses will never drag you through a public airport terminal again."[3]

The wealthy also enjoy expressive and emotional benefits beyond those available to owners of mere ample financial capital. As Disney continued, "I've never been much of a materialist, but I have wallowed in the less concrete privileges that come with a trust fund, such as time, control, security, attention, power, and choice. The fact is, this is pretty standard software that comes with the hardware of a human body."

Well-being is enhanced when the three kinds of benefits are in balance. "Regarding the need for wealth, it is definitely better to accumulate as much as possible," said Qiang, a 40-year-old Chinese man interviewed by BlackRock. "However, the need for wealth should not become a form of burden. It is something that cannot be overly pursued or ignored."

And Michael, a 71-year-old American man, said, "I've seen people pursue [wealth] as a goal and screw themselves. You can't exist without money but achieving wealth was never a goal. Living a good life and being happy was more important."

Some possessions, such as houses and cars, require much financial capital whereas others, such as sunglasses, handbags, and baby carriers, require relatively little, but all enhance well-being by utilitarian, expressive, and emotional benefits.

Houses

The utilitarian benefits of houses are evident in a large-scale program in Mexico, replacing dirt floors with cement floors. The program enhanced the well-being of children by fewer cases of parasitic infestations, diarrhea, and anemia, and higher cognitive development. And it enhanced the well-being of homeowners by lower rates of stress and depression.[4]

Houses in developed countries such as the United States offer utilitarian benefits to some offshore buyers as safe havens for illicit wealth. These utilitarian benefits are evident in a premium paid by these buyers.[5] American houses are prominent as safe havens for Chinese buyers, and demand for them is especially great when economic stress in China is high. Prices of houses in American cities preferred by Chinese buyers have increased faster than prices of houses in similar neighborhoods in less preferred American cities.[6]

The expressive and emotional benefits of homeownership in comfort and peace of mind and their contributions to well-being can dwarf their utilitarian benefits as investments. An American man noted that he doesn't think of a home as an investment. He loves it for its comfort and peace of mind. "We lived in the same house for 45 years, bought it for $59,000 in 1975 and sold it for $505,000 in 2018. Good financial investment? I doubt it, but it was a home where we raised four children. That was a good investment . . . in our family.[7]

Yet homeowners' expectations of enhanced well-being by homeownership are often exaggerated. A comparison of expectations of well-being increases five years after buying houses to realized well-being increases five years later indicates that people overestimate the well-being increases that come with homeownership.[8] Indeed, the well-being of female homeowners is no higher than that of female renters, perhaps because female homeowners tend to spend more time on housekeeping and less time on enjoyable activities, such as active leisure.[9]

Haunted houses diminish well-being by expressive and emotional costs. Prices of Hong Kong apartments drop by 20% when they become haunted. Prices drop by 5% among apartments on the same floor, 3% among apartments on the same block, and 1% among apartments on the same estate.[10]

And Singaporeans pay more for houses with lucky addresses, illustrating their expressive and emotional benefits. The price premium on larger apartments with lucky addresses on top floors is especially high because these housing features are highly visible emblems of wealth.[11]

Sometimes the wealthy, such as Warren Buffett, the CEO of Berkshire Hathaway, enjoy expressive and emotional benefits by subverting the usual ones. Living in a modest house when able to afford many mansions says, I'm too smart to be fooled into buying a mansion when a modest house serves me well. "I'm warm in the winter, I'm cool in the summer; it's convenient for me. I couldn't imagine having a better house."[12]

Cars

Cars enhance well-being by the utilitarian benefits of reliable transportation. Gerald, a 32-year-old American man interviewed by BlackRock, described his joy on the day he bought a new car. "It [removed a] lot of stress and worry in my life because I wasn't worried about what would happen when I was driving for work." Cars also enhance well-being by the expressive and emotional benefits of high social status and pride. An inexpensive car elevates one's social status and adds pride where few own cars. Qiang, a 40-year-old Chinese man, enjoyed these benefits. "Even though it was the cheapest model in [my city], I really felt happy that day."

Expensive cars like a BMW or Porsche elevate social status and add pride where car ownership is common. Suzanna, a 59-year-old American woman, said: "When my husband turned 50, he decided that he really wanted to buy a BMW. We had never owned such an expensive car but I knew that this was really important to him. . . ." Paul, the previously mentioned 70-year-old American man, noted his desire to move up from his Subaru to a Porsche, prompting Helene, a 56-year-old American woman to exclaim: "Wow. And we just moved 'up' to a Subaru!" BMW's design chief wants each of his cars to be a conversation piece, providing expressive and emotional benefits beyond their utilitarian transportation benefits. "We don't make automobiles that are utilitarian machines you use to get from point A to point B. We make cars moving works or art."[13]

Desire for expressive and emotional benefits drives many in the lower-middle-class to buy cars expressing membership in the middle-middle-class, and many in the middle-middle-class to buy cars expressing membership in the upper-middle class. This desire is evident in the preference of buyers with low credit scores for prestigious cars, a preference that often leads to sad outcomes in loan defaults and further declines in credit scores.[14]

Buying cars on credit has taken root in Russia during recent decades, as bank loans for otherwise unaffordable cars have become common. The desire for cars is evident in the observation that the average price of new cars financed by car loans has grown faster than the average income of car buyers. Buyers of expensive cars sacrifice the utilitarian benefits of other purchases, including those satisfying basic needs.[15]

Debt in the form of a car loan is often inevitable when cash is insufficient, yet joy accompanies paying off that debt. "When I got the title in the mail, it felt great that I actually owned it 100% in my name and not the bank," said Katie, a 28-year-old American woman interviewed by BlackRock. "I worked hard to pay it off and now I have the title in hand. I felt empowered after making that final payment online to pay it in full. It was a memorable event."

Nursing covers and handbags

Some emblems of high social status are expensive, such as houses and cars, providing expressive and emotional benefits to their owner by being conspicuous to all. Other emblems are less expensive, providing expressive and emotional benefit by being inconspicuous to all but particular target groups. Sociologist Elizabeth Currid-Halkett illustrated signaling high social status by elite mothers to their target groups of fellow elite mothers with products such as Baby au Lait designer nursing covers, Ergo and Baby Bjorn baby carriers, and cloth or compostable diapers. She noted that the "nursing cover itself is not expensive or even overtly conspicuous; rather it is a material sign of an often expensive and time-intensive mode of parenting."[16]

Both high-priced and low-priced sunglasses and handbags are less likely to display clear brand markers than mid-priced products. Cheaper handbags displayed fewer logos or brand-related patterns than mid-priced handbags, but handbags costing more than $600 had as few logos or brand-related patterns as the cheapest handbags. Marketing scholars Jonah Berger and Morgan Ward found that working-class consumers prefer explicitly marked products which are widely recognizable as status symbols. Consequently, elite consumers prefer subtle markers that differentiate them from the working-class, and thus, facilitate communication with others in-the-know.[17]

Still, luxury handbags can impose expressive and emotional costs if they induce the impostor syndrome, making owners feel inauthentic. The imposter syndrome caused a 70-year-old Manhattan Upper East Side woman to carry a basic canvas bag, leaving her luxury handbags in her closet.[18]

Financial capital and financial capital relative to others

Whether the average well-being of people in developed countries remains flat or continues to rise as average incomes increase is a matter of debate. The "Easterlin Paradox" is the finding that average well-being in developed countries ceases to increase as average incomes increase. Yet there is no debate that the well-being of individuals within a country is lower when their incomes are low relative to incomes of others in social comparison groups. People suffer low well-being when they fail to keep-up-with-the-Joneses. As Richard Easterlin himself noted, "Individuals assess their material well-being not in terms of the absolute amount of goods they have, but relative to a social norm of what goods they ought to have."[19]

An old joke describes the difference between Americans and people in the former Soviet Union. When Americans see a beautiful house at the top of a hill, they say, "I wish to have a house like this." But when people in the Soviet Union see such a house they say, "I wish to see this house burn down." Yet Americans, like people everywhere, enjoy expressive and emotional benefits when watching decreases in the financial capital of members of their social comparison groups.

Journalist Alina Tugend described Ellen, a woman feeling a mix of curiosity and envy as she watched friends spend lavishly on vacations, cars, and home renovations. Ellen was relieved, like the Soviet man in the joke, when she found that her friends' lavish spending was financed by debt, eventually forcing them to sell their house and move to a rented apartment. "I did feel very vindicated," she said.[20]

The effects of social comparison groups on well-being are evident among people whose neighbors form their social comparison group. An increase in neighbors' income reduces a person's well-being by as much as an equal reduction in that person's own income.[21] But an increase in neighbors' income does not affect the well-being of people who do not socialize with their neighbors, thereby not considering them as their social comparison group.

People have some leeway in selecting their social comparison groups, but not much. People can avoid their neighbors as social comparison groups by not socializing with them, but they cannot avoid their co-workers. People have multiple social comparison groups that are context-specific. Family members form one social comparison group, coworkers form another, and the identities of social comparison groups are largely transmitted across generations.[22] Comparisons to coworkers, people in the same occupations, and friends, have the greatest effect on well-being. Moreover, people tend to compare themselves upward, to those who earn more, diminishing well-being.[23]

Inconsistencies are common between perceived rankings in different social comparison groups such as neighbors, friends, or broader society. People whose rankings, relative to neighbors or friends, are low compared to their ranking relative to the broader society suffer lower well-being.

Distance from others, social disengagement, and diminished meaning in life explain how ranking inconsistencies undermine well-being.[24]

Income inequality compels many low-income people to pick up their pace by purchasing goods that are conspicuous and signal high social status. These purchases are often financed by costly loans, furthering inequality.[25] Spending on luxury goods in China increased when urbanization, mobility, and openness increased the intensity of social group comparisons.[26] Neighbors of people who won lottery prizes increase borrowing, and some suffer consequent bankruptcies.[27] Conversely, people feel free to slow down when they see members of their social comparison groups fall behind. Neighbors of bankrupt Singaporeans reduce their spending.[28]

The toll of relatively low financial capital leads people to calibrate utilitarian, expressive, and emotional benefits and costs, and trade off each against the others. "I realize I've chosen paths in life that are fulfilling, personally enriching, but don't bring enormous wealth," said Jeffrey, a 60-year-old American man interviewed by BlackRock. "I worked with a corporate president once who got a $7-million bonus on top of a ridiculously large salary. What do you do with an extra $7-million? I temper my wants . . . I never wanted to live out in the suburbs where there was a keeping-up-with-the-Joneses."

The toll of relatively low financial capital also leads people to downgrade the importance of money in their lives. Thinking that money is unimportant improves the well-being of low-income people, whereas thinking that money is important improves the well-being of high-income people.[29]

Adrian, a 35-year-old British man interviewed by BlackRock, noted that his well-being increased when he stopped listening to other people or judging my level of success and happiness by the consensus definitions, "which ironically meant that I stopped thinking and began living." Moreover, the toll of relatively low financial capital leads people to focus on intrinsic attributes, centered on personal growth and interpersonal relationships because, unlike extrinsic ones, centered on financial capital, they cannot be compared to those of others.[30] My accomplishments of personal growth are neither better nor worse than yours. You can get a "Best Father" mug from your children, and so can I. It is more difficult to gain well-being by extrinsic attributes. Either I have more financial capital than you or you have more than me.[31,32]

Journalist James Parker described sitting at a London café, staring at his mug of tea. "I took a despairing slurp from my mug, then put it back down. As I did so, the side of my hand touched the Formica tabletop, and I felt the radiant heat from where the mug had been resting a second before." The radiant heat sent Parker a message. "One day, you'll be able to simply appreciate what's in front of you. The tea, the café, London, the little lens of warmth on the table. One day, this will be enough." "Set your aspirations high," wrote Parker, "strive for excellence, but lower the bar and keep it low. Extend forgiveness to your idiot friends; extend forgiveness to your idiot self. Make it a practice. Come to rest in actuality."[33]

Yet it is hard to withstand the damage that relatively low financial capital inflicts. Anne, a 53-year-old American woman interviewed by BlackRock, made a list of things to do: "Eat healthy. Read the Bible. Attend church. Thirty minutes or more of exercise per day. Don't compare yourself to others. . . ." Still she added, "The hardest goal for me would be to not compare myself to someone else. It would help if I would review this list each morning as a reminder."

Transparency about income and wealth can diminish well-being or enhance it. Tax records in Norway have been public since the nineteenth century, but access to them was difficult before 2001. One had to appear in person at a tax office and submit a formal request to see someone else's income. In 2001, however, the Norwegian media digitized tax records and created websites that placed every Norwegian one click away from finding the income of every other Norwegian. Online tax lists became extremely popular, sometimes more popular than YouTube, and were used mostly to snoop on friends, relatives, and social contacts, rather than identify tax cheats. Users could build lists of the highest and lowest earners among their Facebook friends or maps displaying the incomes of everyone in a neighborhood. The Norwegian media called it "tax porn." Transparency enhanced the well-being of the Norwegian wealthy while diminishing that of the poor. The gap in experienced well-being between wealthy and poor increased by 29% and the gap in evaluative well-being increased by 21%.[34]

The well-being costs of transparency are evident in a study by Nobel Laureate economist David Card and coauthors. They made salary information transparent to a subset of University of California employees by informing them about a new website listing the salaries of all university employees.[35] Subsequently, all employees were surveyed about their job satisfaction and job search intentions. Workers who had learned that their salaries are below the median of their coworkers suffered well-being declines, expressed in lower satisfaction with their jobs and salaries, and higher likelihood of searching for new jobs.

Still, well-being declines by transparency can lead to enhanced future well-being if lower satisfaction with jobs and salaries prompts people to negotiate higher salaries or look for new jobs. Sara Swenson, a 39-year-old vice president of product development, got a 50% increase in salary after speaking with coworkers about their salaries and learning when to ask for a raise and how much to ask for. A conversation of Bailey Koch, a 25-year-old employee of the Minnesota State Senate, with her team members revealed that her salary was lower. She quit when her request for a raise was denied and found a new job as a digital-communications strategist at a labor union.[36] Pay transparency can also reduce the gender gap. Canadian laws allow public access to the salaries of faculty members if they exceed specified thresholds. The laws reduced the gender pay gap between men and women by approximately 20–40%.[37] And transparency can enhance well-being by reducing status-enhancing spending. People facing income transparency show a lower preference for status-enhancing spending than people facing income privacy because they do not need to signal their income by spending.[38]

Some among the wealthy embrace transparency to boost their well-being. Indeed, many Russian oligarchs seem to find it impossible to refrain from ostentatious displays of their wealth. "What is an oligarch without ostentation?" asked sociologist Brooke Harrington. "For many Russian oligarchs, the answer is nothing. Oligarchs need not only to be filthy rich, they need to be seen as such."[39] More often, however, the wealthy refrain from ostentatious displays of their wealth, aware of its power to elicit resentment among those with less. A survey of exceedingly wealthy families described their "secret fears."[40] Some said they have lost the right to complain about anything, fearing that complaints would make them seem ungrateful. Others noted that their vast wealth burdens them with expectations of lavish gifts at holidays, disappointing those who receive mere expensive gifts. "We try to be as sympathetic and open-minded as possible. But if we listened and responded to everyone's request, we would spend 30 hours a day."

The secret fears of the wealthy elicit little empathy and much resentment among those with less. One wrote, "No one is disputing that the rich have their own problems. But these are not real problems. A real problem is significantly damaging your life . . . like poverty, paralyzing illness, death of a loved one." The wealthy alleviate their secret fears by socializing with fellow wealthy and signaling their wealth discretely to fellow wealthy who understand their concerns and empathize with their fears. "I am always working towards financial stability and increasing my wealth, but it's not something I talk about and certainly don't boast about this," said William, a 47-year-old British man interviewed by BlackRock. Indeed, ostentatious displays of wealth are regularly met with derision, diminishing well-being. The pejorative terms *nouveau riche*, *parvenu*, and *bling* describe people who display their wealth and boast about it. In Chinese, *Tuhao* is a pejorative term for the newly rich, analogous to *nouveau riche*.[41] The wealthy prefer euphemisms such as *comfortable* or *fortunate*.

Envy, *gluckschmerz*, *schadenfreude*, and *freudenfreude*

Envy is a common human experience, forbidden by the Ten Commandments but not extinguished. Envy of people in our social comparison groups diminishes well-being by expressive and emotional costs. "Facebook envy" is the feeling that overcomes us when we see our Facebook friends "eating lobster salad on sailboats off Nantucket or learning so much about Joyce in Dublin with an Oxford don as a paid personal guide."[42] Young people are especially susceptible to envy, and levels of envy fall as people grow older. Moreover, envy does not act as a useful motivator. Greater envy today is not associated with future economic success, but it is associated with slower growth of future well-being.[43] Potential envy inhibits us from giving gifts superior to our own possessions. Instead, we give inferior gifts that preserve our well-being.[44]

Gluckschmerz is pain at another's good fortune, diminishing well-being as envy does.[45] We feel little *gluckschmerz* when a student we barely know wins a prestigious award, but the sting of *gluckschmerz* is painful when a student in our social comparison group wins it, and that sting is searing when our best friend wins it. A woman wrote to Dr. Andrea, an advice columnist, "My sister and I are best friends and yet every milestone she has—work promotions, buying a house, getting married, having a child—I think I am happy for her but it stings so bad. I want to be able to enjoy her successes, but I always compare things to my own life. . . . Why am I this way? And how can I tone it down?"[46]

Schadenfreude, pleasure at another's misfortune, enhances well-being.[47] That pleasure is expressed in every language. The Japanese say: The misfortunes of others taste like honey. The French speak of *joie maligne*, delight in another's suffering. The Danish talk of *skadefryd*, and the Dutch of *leedvermaak*. In Hebrew, joy at other people's catastrophes is *simcha la-ed*, and in Mandarin, *xIng-zai-lè-huô*.[48]

Freudenfreude, the joy of another's good fortune enhances well-being, but it is difficult to feel. Psychologist Juli Fraga told the story of Eugenie George whose heart sank when she heard that her friend passed a financial counseling exam she had failed weeks earlier. "My inner child got upset," recalled Ms. George, but she overcame her envy and called her friend to congratulate her. She was surprised to find that *freudenfreude* enhanced not only her friend's well-being, but also her own. "I congratulated her and told her she inspired me."[49]

Others, however, noted that it is easy to feel *freudenfreude* when the success is that of "friends, family, anyone." What is difficult is to feel it when the success is that of "a competitor in a narrow and difficult field in which one's own life, ambition, and future are invested."

Present financial capital and aspired financial capital

Our aspired financial capital is generally proportional to our present financial capital. Those with meager financial capital aspire to moderate financial capital, those with moderate financial capital aspire to ample financial capital, and those with ample financial capital aspire to extravagant financial capital that would make them truly wealthy. Meredith, the 31-year-old American woman with moderate financial capital, described her aspirations for ample financial capital, short of extravagant. "Wealth to me is something I'll never have. I think I'd use the term *financial stability* to describe my own goals of living comfortably with the occasional indulgence."

Many with meager financial capital strive to reach their aspiration for moderate financial capital by playing the lottery. They prefer lotteries with relatively low prizes that can provide moderate financial capital, perhaps in the tens of thousands, rather than ones that can provide extravagant financial capital in the many millions. They do not tend to buy more lottery tickets when lottery jackpots increase from moderate to extravagant.[50] The story of a 64-year-old man who won $50,000 in the Maryland Lottery by the numbers of his mother's birthday illustrates this general finding. The man's astonished wife felt numb when he told her they had won $50,000. "I still didn't believe it," she said. The couple has moderate plans for their winnings. "I want my kitchen done," said the wife, perhaps adding a renovation of the basement and living room to the list.[51]

A diamond rush in South Africa attracted people aspiring to escape desperate poverty. They rushed to a small village in KwaZulu-Natal by a rumor that a herdsman had found in its soil clear stones resembling diamonds. Sbusiso Molefe, a 41-year-old man who had lost his job at a textile factory, was subsisting on government subsidies totaling less than a quarter of his former salary, unable to provide to his three children staples like beef, milk, and butter. Two days of heavy digging had yielded four stones "I'm feeling desperate," he said. "We are just hoping. If they are real diamonds, it means we are winning."[52]

Some novice stock market investors in the time of COVID-19 spoke as if they aspired for extravagant financial capital, but in truth, they aspired to no more than moderate financial capital. Den Kovacs, a 25-year-old IT professional, hoped for profits that would pay his $7,000 credit card debt. "I want to put myself in a position where I'm not sitting in debt like that," he said. "It's hurting my credit score, and I want to be able to move somewhere else." Indeed, short-term unsecured debt, such as credit card debt is associated with depressive symptoms and lower well-being.[53] Joe Ballent, a 32-year-old physician assistant, aspired to pay for his upcoming wedding and a down payment for a house. "I feel like there's a lot of people who have never been able to get ahead. I took on six figures of debt [for graduate school] and worked two jobs before school, but now I can't afford a house?"[54]

The aspired future financial capital of people with extravagant financial wealth also tends to be proportional to their present financial capital. Sociologist Marianne Cooper described Bob Newman, unable to feel secure even with $25 million cash in the bank. "I don't know why," he said. "I mean, it's hard to spend $25 million. . . . But when you throw in the emotional insecurity about really wanting to be financially secure . . . I'm not sure I felt that until I had $30–$35 million."[55] Some with financial capital exceeding $35 million still do not consider themselves financially secure, aspiring for more. For that, they say, they would need on average one-quarter more wealth than they currently possess.

One, heir to an enormous fortune, said that Christianity matters most to him, and his greatest aspiration is "to love the Lord, my family, and my friends." He added, however, that he would need $1 billion in the bank to feel secure.[56]

And many wealthy do not consider themselves wealthy because they compare themselves upward, toward wealthier ones. Sociologist Rachel Sherman quoted Helen, a former banker married to a lawyer with an annual income exceeding $2 million and assets more than four times that. "I feel like we're somewhat in the middle, in the sense that there are so many people with so much money. They have private planes. They have drivers. . . . And, you know, we don't have that luxury in that way."[57]

Gaps between present and aspired financial capital diminish well-being especially where they are impossible to close. This is evident in India, where people are assigned to castes from birth. Gaps between incomes of people in middle castes and incomes of people in high castes are immensely large in the state of Punjab, despite similar levels of education. People in middle castes suffer low well-being not only relative to people in high castes, but also relative to people in low castes who are resigned to their low positions.[58]

Many Americans hold the middle class only tenuously. Median lifetime earnings of men who entered the labor market in 1983 is lower by 10–19% than those of men who entered the labor market in 1957. Median lifetime earnings of women who entered the labor market in 1983 is higher by 22–33% than those of women who entered the labor market in 1957, but that increase is relative to the very low median lifetime earnings of the 1957 group.[59] Responding to an article about middle-class people feeling economically insecure, a college graduate with a full-time job, modest lifestyle, and careful watch over his finances, wrote "I am 35 years old. When my father was my age, he had a home, a full-time job, spectacular benefits, two children, and a wife who was able to stay home most of the time." Some readers however pushed back, blaming "a middle class with an appetite that exceeds its income . . . we ripped out Formica to put in Corian, then upgraded to granite which doesn't look as lovely as the quartz countertops and glass tile backsplashes that are currently all the rage."[60]

Differences in financial capital among Chinese widened from 1990–2000, leading to a general decline in well-being despite a general increase in financial capital.[61] Those lagging behind reacted by spending more, especially on conspicuous luxury goods, so as to "keep-up-with-the-Wangs."[62] Increases in financial capital boost well-being, but these boosts tend to diminish over time by adaptation, as people grow accustomed to their higher financial capital. The well-being of extremely poor people in Latin America increased substantially when they received better housing, but 60% of that increase was gone after eight months.[63] Adaptations to changes in financial capital tend to be faster than adaptations to changes in financial capital relative to social comparison groups. People's well-being fully adapts to changes in financial capital after four years, but adaptations to changes in financial capital relative to social comparison groups take longer.[64]

3

Saving and Spending

"There needs to be a good balance between well-being now and peace of mind for the future," said Orlando, the previously mentioned 43-year-old Mexican man. "I think you need to know how to manage your finances in a way that you can enjoy what you like today, but knowing you have built a solid economy for the future."

A good balance between saving and spending enhances well-being now and in the future. In turn, well-being enhances that balance. People enjoying high well-being expect longer lives and are therefore careful in balancing saving and spending.[1] Barbara, the previously mentioned 28-year-old British woman, considered that balance as she contemplated dipping into her retirement savings: "After thinking about it and doing further research, I realized it was not a good idea and would be terrible for me in the long run." Yet a good balance is hard to strike. Tony, a 55-year-old British man, recalled the words of a British magnate, "I've written books on the subject, cheque books." Many conclude, later in life, that they had failed to strike a good balance. "When I was young, I wasted my money on things that covered only a few needs but were mainly entertainment rather than essentials," said Carolina, a 35-year-old Mexican woman. "I think that pressure from friends was one of the barriers to good financial management. You want to be fashionable, have the most modern cell phone, brand name clothes, the best computer, etc."

People are irked when they see others fail to maintain a good balance between saving and spending, especially when such failure imposes costs on others. Harleen, a 32-year-old British woman, described a conversation with a coworker who earns a good salary, but for the past 16 years she and her husband have taken the approach of "life is too short, enjoy it while you can." As a result, after several consolidated loans, multiple maxed credit cards, and being on the brink of bankruptcy, they applied for a government program to help pay back some of the debt, and have the rest written off. As Harleen listened, she sensed bitterness in her coworker's description of her struggle to pay her children's $100 monthly dance school fees. "I was extremely angry by this response, and tried to offer support that every family had 'additional' outgoings, and that this was a luxury." The coworker was aggravated by this comment, and Harleen did not push further, but she walked away from the conversation thinking "You shopped like mad for years without a care, now you resent others for spending their hard-earned cash."

Framing, mental accounting, and self-control

Good balance between saving and spending requires competent use of the tools of framing, mental accounting, and self-control. We frame money into mental accounts, such as for utility bills, food, and entertainment, and use self-control rules to prevent us from dipping into one mental account, say for food, for spending on entertainment.

John, a 30-year-old British man, learned these tools from a mentor. "Example, create three jars for your savings and put x amount of money into each one . . . for bills, social, and investments. This has helped me become more aware of my in-goings and out-goings spending patterns." And Karen, a 60-year-old British woman, learned them from her brother who has an account into which he puts the money he makes from freelance journalism for extra spending money on his hobby. "I might do the same, but as a weekend-away fund."

John and Karen are members of the *stable* group, members of the working-class and elite who earn adequate incomes steadily throughout their working years and use these tools effectively to save enough for adequate retirement spending. Other people are members of the *precarious* group, consisting of two segments, *low-earners* and *high-spenders*. High-spenders are mostly members of the elite who earn more than adequate incomes during their working years but spend all of it and more, failing to save. Low-earners are members of the working-class who strive to save, but their low and unsteady incomes place them precariously close to poverty.

Meredith, the previously mentioned 31-year-old American woman, observed differences in balancing saving and spending by watching her parents. Her father is a member of the high-spenders precarious group, whereas her mother is a member of the stable group. Her parents had wildly different approaches to money and it was a huge factor in their divorce. "My mom saves EVERYTHING and my dad spends everything." They're around 70 now and Meredith can see who's living a better life. "Spoiler alert, it's my mom." Luckily, she takes after her mom.

Members of the stable group, like Meredith and her mother, save mostly in retirement savings accounts, such as an IRA, 401(k), and 403(b), aided in self-control by automatic enrollment and employer contributions matching their own. Indeed, fat retirement accounts, not expensive houses or luxury cars, separate the stable group from the precarious high-spenders.

Scarcity adds to low-earners precariousness, illustrated by the consequences of a mismatch between water-bill due dates and social security paydays.[2,3] Monthly water-bill due dates in Jerusalem are randomly assigned, and therefore, can occur just before or after social security paydays. Economists Momi Dahan and Udi Nisan compared the likelihood of late payments by low-income families when they receive their social security benefits a day after the water-bill due date to the likelihood by similar families when they receive their benefits a day or more before the water-bill due date. The small liquidity shock suffered by families receiving their social benefits a day after the water-bill due date inflicts a decline in well-being in addition to an increase in interest charges and late payment penalties.[4]

Evictions from rented houses are common among low-earners, contributing to a cycle of poverty. Evicted tenants usually face economic problems long before evictions, in lower earnings and higher financial distress. Evictions exacerbate their problems, increasing homelessness and hospital visits, including mental health related visits, further reducing earnings and access to credit.[5]

Members of the upper end of the stable group derive greater well-being from spending on experiences, such as vacations and concerts than from material goods, such as shoes and clothing, likely because their ample resources let them afford both. But members of the lower end of the stable group derive greater well-being from buying material goods which provide practical benefits, last longer, and bring their children a sense of belonging among peers.[6]

Some people are wealthy, at the very top of the stable group. Willa, described by sociologist Rachel Sherman, was born to wealthy parents, and now she and her husband earn $2 million annual income and live with their children in a $5 million brownstone in New York City.

"We were joking the other day, when we played the Powerball," said Willa. "And it's like, nothing would change. You know? I mean, we're happy with this house. You know. We have everything that we need. Our life is not going to change if we win the Powerball."[7]

Others ascend to the top of the stable group by high income and prodigious savings. Authors Thomas Stanley and William Danko called them the "millionaires next door." They are professionals, such as doctors, lawyers, and accountants, and business owners, such as welding contractors, pest controllers, and owners of mobile-home parks.[8]

People learn to balance saving and spending mostly from parents, generally following in their footsteps. The propensity to default on personal loans is more than four times higher among people whose parents default. The link between financial troubles of parents and children exists mainly because parents transmit financial attitudes and behaviors to their children.[9]

Most parents are conscientious about transmitting financial attitudes and behaviors that foster a good balance between saving and spending. Tracey, a 51-year-old British woman, described transmitting these to her 24-year-old son, a low-income law student with a serious girlfriend and a desire to buy a house. Yet, she said, when he is paid each month, he forgets himself and goes out to expensive restaurants. "I explained to him that even though he needs to enjoy himself whilst he is young, he needs to think ahead and plan, otherwise he will never achieve his goals. I hope he has taken this on board."

"My parents always taught us to be savvy with money," said Naren, a 55-year-old British man. "They worked so hard in factories, often working seven days a week to keep us clothed and gave us a good living that it ensures you do not forget the hardships that they faced and squander money." Yet Tina, a 55-year-old British woman, walks in a direction opposite to her parents'. "My parents were greedy and always in debt, it taught me a valuable lesson." She does not get into debt and neither do her children. "Living beyond your means is not worth it, it causes stress, unkindness and bitterness and ruins relationships around you."

Friends and neighbors help one another balance saving and spending by sharing information, such as about food expenditures. "Very recently our best friends were talking about how little they spend on food each month, and it came as quite a shock to my wife and I," said Ashley, a 32-year-old British man. This prompted them to sit me down and discuss budgeting for the first time. They agreed to reduce their costs by using Aldi supermarket for large purchases and their local Tesco supermarket for fresh fruit and vegetables, foregoing the more expensive Marks and Spencer. Friends and neighbors also help one another balance saving and spending by sharing information beyond food expenditures, such as about mortgage refinancing. People are more likely to refinance their mortgages if neighbors within 50 meters have recently refinanced.[10]

Debt is often inevitable when savings are insufficient for buying a house or a car, yet attitudes toward debt vary. Gender, income, and educational attainment among Germans separate a larger group of emergency debtors from two smaller groups of debt refusers and debt pragmatists.[11] Debt attitudes among Swedes determine indebtedness as much as education, risk-taking, and financial literacy.[12] And debt, whether housing debt or non-housing debt, is associated with low well-being among Chinese, decreasing life satisfaction and increasing stress.[13]

People are eager to reduce their debt. A study of people who gained windfalls in the form of natural gas shale royalty payments found that they repaid 33 cents of debt per dollar of windfall, and people with low credit ratings repaid much more debt than those with high credit ratings. Debt repayment preceded purchases of durable goods, such as refrigerators, especially among people who were financially constrained before receiving their windfalls.[14]

People in low-income countries, such as Indonesia, regularly rely heavily on kin and social sharing networks to balance saving and spending. Insufficient rainfall increases both transfers sent and received, reducing vulnerability of spending to rainfall fluctuations.[15] Some people in high-income countries, such as the United States, also rely heavily on kin and social sharing networks to balance saving and spending. Americans accumulate substantial credit card debt as they provide financial assistance to their relatives in need. This is particularly prevalent in low-income groups and in African-American communities, in which needs are especially high.[16] The benefits of sharing networks come at a cost, as pressure to share savings deters some people from working. More generally, higher kinship sharing intensity diminishes economic development.[17] Factory workers in Côte d'Ivoire were provided blocked saving accounts that shielded savings from sharing. The accounts mitigated the effects of sharing on working.[18]

Some methods of limiting sharing are more ingenious than blocked saving accounts, and more indigenous. When Rolf Engelbrecht, an

American missionary, first arrived in Guinea, West Africa, he was amazed to see "ruins" of old mud brick houses standing around in villages and across the countryside. He soon learned that these are savings accounts. "You see," wrote Engelbrecht, "in Guinean culture it's like this: If you have any cash on hand and your relatives find out about it (which they almost certainly will), they are entitled to come over and 'ask for help,' meaning a financial handout." Since Guineans feel socially obligated to comply with relatives' requests, it becomes very hard to save up money for special projects "like buying a wife, building a house, or hiring some-one to carve a dugout canoe for you." The solution is to open a savings account by laying a foundation to a house. Bricks are added whenever cash comes into the household, making it out-of-bounds to hungry relatives. But the process is so slow that sometimes substantial trees grow in the middle of these works in progress.[19]

Deficient self-control

Self-control is hard to muster and some fail to muster it at all. Indeed, deficient self-control, reflected in impulsivity, lack of organization, and preference for living for today, increases the incidence of financial dis-tress more than deficient education or financial literacy.[20] Sociologists Jonathan Morduch and Rachel Schneider described the difficulty of exercising self-control in the lives of Becky and Jeremy, members of the low-earner precarious group. Becky's words reveal their precariousness. If the main earner in her household stopped working she couldn't go for more than a month without borrowing money. She would never be able to retire. Her children would have even fewer opportunities than she has. And her financial well-being is mostly out of her control.[21]

Becky and Jeremy opened a savings account to accumulate a rainy-day fund but failed to maintain it. "It's tough for us. I don't know why," Becky conceded. "The discipline for us to not dip into that rainy-day fund—for entertainment or something fun—is too much." Instead, they built a rainy-day fund composed of toiletries, frozen pork chops, and boxed cereals. "You can't buy movie tickets with eight tubes of toothpaste."[22]

The combination of poverty and deficient self-control is evident in the life of 29-year-old Ashlee Reed, described by sociologist Sarah Halpern-Meekin and coauthors. Reed works at Head Start, a program for young children, but not in the summer. "My goal usually, even though I don't ever make it, is to have enough money saved up for summer," before she receives her first unemployment benefits check. It takes four weeks for that check to arrive, too long for her savings to last.[23]

Online lending platforms can help precarious low-earners overcome financial setbacks, thereby decreasing bankruptcy filings. But deficient self-control leads many into debt traps, increasing bankruptcy filings. Availability of the online lending platform of Lending Club increased bankruptcy filings by approximately 8%.[24] "Buy Now Pay Later" (BNPL) is a FinTech innovation that provides consumers with easy access to credit for specific retail purchases. But BNPL induces greater spending, increasing overdraft charges and credit card interest and fees and worsening financial health.[25]

Precarious low earners use a range of self-control devices to help them save. Morduch and Schneider described Janice, a woman wary of the traps of payday loans. Payday lenders require borrowers to submit signed checks in the amounts of the loans plus interest, dated for the following payday. "It's like an addiction if you have a checking account," said Janice. "You borrow $60 and you pay back $75. If you borrow $200, you pay back $250. But what if you then don't have the $250?"[26] Janice bolsters her self-control by refraining from ordering a new box of checks when the earlier one was empty. She bolsters her self-control further by keeping her savings at a bank with limited opening hours 35 miles away. The bank offers an ATM card, but Janice cut it in two on the day it arrived. "I have to really, really need the money before I go get it."[27]

Mortgage payment schedules serve as self-control devices, increasing savings. One part of mortgage payments covers interest and the other adds to savings in the form of home equity. Mortgage payments are especially effective at increasing savings because they do not crowd out other savings such as in 401(k) accounts. People generate the money necessary for mortgage payments and other savings by working more and spending less.[28] Self-control can be augmented by outside control or replaced by it. Parents impose outside control over adult children. Morduch and Schneider described Robert, a precarious low-earner who hands his earnings over to his mother. "She's like Fort Knox. . . . She's impossible to break into."[29]

More often, parents impose outside control over young children. The young daughter of Ruth, a 38-year old British woman interviewed by BlackRock, asked for some money to go with her friends for a milkshake and a sausage roll for lunch. Ruth gave her a five-pound note but told her that she wouldn't be getting anymore for the rest of the week. "She pulled her face and said that wouldn't be enough." Ruth suggested she had lunch at home before she left. "Her face pulled even further to this suggestion!" Soon after, the daughter asked for money for an ice cream. Ruth suggested she take the dog for a walk of at least 30 minutes for ice cream money. "Eyes rolled and huffing and puffing, she did this only to return 10 minutes later." Ruth reset the clock back to 30 minutes and her daughter returned at the correct time just as the ice cream van arrived.

Average weekly allowances for children in American families is now $30.[30] Yet four in five parents who give an allowance expect their children to do chores for it, about five hours a week on average. Most parents give allowances to teach children financial responsibility, and most children spend it on outings with friends, digital devices and entertainment, or toys. Only a few place portions of their allowances in saving accounts. Automatic enrollment of employees into retirement saving plans augments their self-control, increasing savings. Savings of civilian employees of the army in the Thrift Savings Plan increased by 4.1% of annual salary four years after enrollment, with no added financial distress.[31] Governments and institutions also engage in outside control, strengthening self-control or weakening it. A restriction of access to payday loans reduced liquor sales.[32] But an expansion of operating hours of liquor stores led to higher alcohol consumption, greater use of consumer credit, and higher rates of default.[33]

The tax authority offers a self-control device in overpayment of taxes followed by tax refunds. Morduch and Schneider described Becky and Jeremy's method. Each month, Jeremy pays more taxes than he owes, not listing his four children as dependents. But when he and Becky submit their tax forms at the start of the year, they list their children. This method, combined with the Earned Income Tax Credit (EITC), produces a $7,300 tax refund in March, a substantial sum relative to Jeremy's $35,000 of paychecks that year.

The Earned Income Tax Credit is a line that separates the precarious low-earners from the poor who generally do not work, surviving on welfare from government agencies, charity organizations, and family. That line is thin, often crossed over, yet it matters greatly to members of both groups because of the expressive and emotional benefits of earnings, and the expressive and emotional costs of the stigma of welfare.

Concern about the spending habits of the poor is often exaggerated, imposing on them constraints that diminish well-being unnecessarily. One common constraint consists of providing in-kind food assistance rather than cash. A study in Indonesia replaced in-kind rice with approximately equivalent electronic vouchers redeemable for rice and eggs at a network of private providers. Voucher recipients received higher-quality rice, and increased consumption of eggs.[34] Indeed, precarious low-earners use most of their tax refunds to pay bills and debts, stockpile goods, buy durable goods such as refrigerators, and fix cars. Still, the modest portions of the refunds that are spent on what the general public might perceive as frivolous are of great symbolic importance to members of that group. A dinner out at a sit-down restaurant instead of a fast-food joint, or a dream birthday party for a child struggling in school.[35]

Sociologist Sarah Halpern-Meekin and coauthors described Debra McKinley, a 28-year-old waitress, who promised Lacey, her older daughter, that she would treat her to "the best seafood restaurant in America" for her birthday if she passed the fourth grade. But the best seafood restaurant in America is not in Boston. It is not even in Massachusetts. Indeed, Lacey's dream dinner was at the Red Lobster restaurant chain, and the closest location is in Connecticut.[36] Lacey kept her end of the bargain, and the family of four, together with another carload of relatives, were on their way to Connecticut. Debra struggles to remember the exact price of that Red Lobster meal. The only price she knows is that Lacey spent $68 on her meal and ate every bit of it. "I know that she had a good birthday. . . . I didn't have good birthdays [as a child]. Because of that . . . I try my hardest to give [my girls] anything that I've ever wanted and could not have."

Excessive self-control

Deficient self-control turns us into spendthrifts, spending too much and saving too little. But excessive self-control turns us into misers, saving too much and spending too little. Excessive self-control is as prevalent as insufficient self-control. The relation between patience and well-being is hump-shaped. Too little patience diminishes well-being, but so does too much patience.[37]

Sociologist Rachel Sherman described Nicholas, a wealthy man whose spending style tilts toward excessive self-control, and his wife whose spending style tilts toward insufficient self-control. Nicholas creates small spending barriers for himself and his wife, choosing hotels away from the beach on beach vacations and avoiding hotels where "they massage your toes.""All of her questions [about spending] are like, 'Can we afford it?'" said Nicholas, encapsulating their different spending styles. "And I'm always like, 'It's not a question of can we afford it. The question is, do we need it?'"[38]

A perceived enhancement of well-being by excessive self-control can come from distortion of the meaning of choice. Excessive self-control can override personal preferences in favor of external norms.[39] A reader responding to an article about saving and spending described these norms: "I'm saving now because good, admirable, upstanding people sacrifice their current standard of living to save, save, save for the future." Indeed, people are likely to borrow at high interest rates in emergencies rather than dip into their savings when they believe that dipping into savings is what irresponsible people do.[40]

Proficiency at framing, mental accounting, and self-control helps people save for retirement but impedes them in retirement when it is time to set these aside and enjoy the fruits of their savings. One extremely wealthy man, a retired insurance company executive, wrote in response to an article I wrote in the *Wall Street Journal* about saving and spending:[41] "I've struggled with boundary issues between income and capital. I've actually taken on a couple of board of director assignments so that I feel justified spending for what I consider extravagant."

The "Big-Five" personality traits are extraversion, agreeableness, openness, conscientiousness, and neuroticism. Conscientiousness is the trait most closely associated with self-control. The retired insurance executive went on to write:"The points on conscientious saving hit the nail on the head. I grew up as one of nine children of Depression-era parents. They always stressed education, achievement, savings, and marital happiness over satisfying urges for material things."

Some people are good at avoiding distortions of the meaning of choice. A reader wrote:"I am deriving pleasure from assuming the strategy of 'I am through saving. Now I am spending it.' Judiciously, to be sure, but nevertheless with a view to obtaining satisfaction." He and his wife have made some long-desired renovations to their home, plan to schedule at least two major overseas vacations a year, supplement their children's financial needs when their children need it and when they can see the results. He devotes more time and money to charitable work, continues to exercise at a local athletic club, now free thanks to Silver Sneakers, reads more, and indulges in his love of classical music. "All of this gives me significant satisfaction." Another wrote: "I learned from my mom that the greatest joy in life is giving to your family. She would give something to all her six children, their spouses, the grandchildren, the great-grandchildren and all their spouses on their birthdays, anniversaries, St. Patrick's Day, Valentine's Day, and for no reason at all. If you want the closest thing to eternal life, try this." Others, however, are not willing to change their meaning of choice and tilt away from excessive self-control because they derive expressive and emotional benefits from saving and expressive and emotional costs from spending. As one wrote: "What if the enjoyment is in the saving, and the pain is in the spending?"

Prior life experiences can induce excessive self-control and poor balance between saving and spending. People who have lived through times of high unemployment show persistent pessimism about their future income and spend much less than others, even though their actual future income is unrelated to their past experiences. Their frugality enhances savings and wealth, but it does not enhance well-being.[42] A reader described her late husband, reared by extremely thrifty parents who survived the Great Depression and World War II and accumulated a very comfortable nest egg through hard work and frugality bordering on miserliness. "They passed on to him their fiscal philosophies and my husband absorbed them like a sponge." Once he died she was amazed to discover how much money they had. "I shall have to work very hard to spend all of it, but I plan to give it my best effort."

Journalist Paula Span described Nancy Canu, a 92-year-old woman who takes multiple medications for heart failure, and joint pain makes it hard for her to walk more than a block. Renee Turner, her 37-year-old granddaughter, moved into her home five years ago to care for her, gradually taking over household tasks such as shopping, cooking, cleaning, doing the laundry and paying the bills, and also administering her grandmother's medications, driving her to doctors' appointments, staying nearby when she showers and helping her up the stairs. "It wasn't a question," Ms. Turner said. "I wanted to be here for her." Still, she added, "it's become my full-time job."[43]

Yet a reader in her 60s wrote "I feel for the granddaughter featured in this article," sharing her story of caring for her 87-year-old mother who suffers increasing dementia. She loves her mother and is happy to care for her when she is in town, but she would like to enjoy some travel after more than 40 years of full-time work. Yet her mother refuses to dip into her savings to hire a home health aide when her daughter leaves town, insisting that her grandchildren step in or that her two daughters coordinate their travel so they are not gone at the same time. "She is frugal to a fault and will never willingly pay for even part-time help or move into an assisted living facility. . . . My mother's stubbornness, extreme frugality, and expectation that family members will provide all of her care seems to be quite common."

Common concerns about running out of money are valid among many members of the stable group, as current membership does not assure continued membership. Journalist AnnaMaria Andriotis described Alysse Hopkins, a 43-year-old lawyer who represented clients in foreclosure cases and personal-injury lawsuits until March 2020, earning about $175,000 along with her husband, enough for paying a mortgage, two car leases, student loans, credit cards and other costs of raising two daughters. Her work dried up as COVID-19 halted many foreclosures and closed courts. Unemployment benefits have helped, but their savings cannot sustain $9,000 in monthly debt payments. "It frustrates me to not be able to earn a living," she said. "I have a law degree, almost 20 years of practice."[44]

Concerns about running out of money might, however, be exaggerated among members of the stable group with substantial savings who are retired or close to retirement. "Florida's retirees are famous for lining up at oceanside diners for the 'Early Bird Special' discounts. But what compels retirees in general to economize?" wondered economist Mariacristina De Nardi and coauthors. They noted that "While the savings of singles tend to fall with age, those of retired couples tend to increase or stay constant until one of the spouses dies."[45]

Pursuit of personal pleasures ebbs as people enter their "no-go" 80s. Older people spend less, in large part because physical limitations make them less able to spend and because they are less inclined to spend for personal reasons. Spending at age 84, adjusted for inflation, is 23% less than it was at age 62 among college-educated American couples. Spending on movies, theater, opera, and concerts declines by more than 50% between the ages of 60 and 80, whereas spending on hearing aids, nursing homes, and funeral expenses increases by more than 50%.[46] A reader illustrated these observations: "Lots of people lose a spouse and do not travel or vacation much because they are by themselves. They have enough money but just do not go anywhere or do much. They have lost their best friend and have not found a second life after losing their spouse. So, they sort of mope around and just do not do much. It is really sad." This reader tried to help people in this situation, but was met with little success. "We lose not only spouses, but friends; couples we used to dine or travel with. Same-sex individual friends we used to golf or shop with. Suddenly we're left to do those things alone, or not do them."

Home equity is the primary source of wealth for many older adults, especially for those relying entirely on Social Security for their income. Dips into home equity, such as by reverse mortgages, can reduce poverty in old age. A public reverse mortgage program in Korea increased income by approximately 20% among people 65-year-old and older, and the program was especially effective among those with the lowest incomes. The added income from reverse mortgages reduced poverty rates among older adults from 41% to 31%.[47] Yet many homeowners are reluctant to dip into their home equity, striving to leave their houses to their children. This is sadly evident among lower-income older adults who choose to forgo prescribed medicines despite having home equity that can be used to pay for them.[48]

Homeownership has deep meaning for Robin Valentine. Unlike her late mother, who was unable to leave any money to her children, Valentine plans to leave her house to her three children. "I told my children, 'If anything happens to me, and you don't want to stay here, that's fine. Take the money and put it towards your home.' It's more than just me buying this house and living in it. It's for me to leave a legacy."[49]

Excessive self-control among young people

Excessive self-control in saving and spending is usually practiced by older people, but it is also practiced by young people who join the FIRE movement—Financial Independence, Retire Early, advocating saving 50–75% of income while working, to retire in their 30s or 40s. Mindy and Carl, a young couple who joined the FIRE movement, retired with $4.3 million. They recalled a time when their daughter bought the most expensive item on a breakfast menu, resulting in a $99 bill. That bill caused little damage to their wealth but it imposed much anxiety.[50]

Many FIRE adherents fail to strike a good balance between saving and spending in the present and future, assigning excessive importance to saving and the future. Jeffrey, the previously mentioned 60-year-old

American man, described a classmate who joined the FIRE movement. "[He] worked his tail off between the age of 22 and 32, worked a bazillion hours a week, retired at 32. But he lost his 20s." Jeffrey prefers a better balance between saving and spending: "One shouldn't float through life, but I find a determined quest for some goals can be limited and limiting and you miss the voyage along the way." He wants to be reasonably happy in what he does in the present, have enough money to enjoy life along the way, and be able to save and invest enough along the way to have a relatively comfortable retirement. "I want time to pursue new interests, more time to spend with my wife, and the ability to visit the kids and possible grandkids at will." Indeed, some FIRE adherents, including Mindy and Carl, come to regret their supposedly farsighted choice of extreme frugality, as time diminishes guilt over past indulgences but increases regret over missed pleasures.[51] "We don't want to just keep throwing money on the pile and keep being cheap," Mindy said. "I do look at everything based on how much it costs, and I don't need to. I shouldn't." "We've identified that we probably live sub optimally," Carl explained. "If something truly makes you happy, you should spend money on it. . . . And there's stuff we've postponed or we think about money too much, and at this point, we probably shouldn't."

The COVID-19 pandemic persuaded some to clean their financial house, aiming at financial independence, FI, rather than at the more radical FIRE. "The pandemic made me realize how fragile our security really is," said Traci Williams, a psychologist in her 30s working at an Atlanta hospital. She was pleasantly surprised when she examined, for the first time, the balance of her retirement savings account at the hospital, but was concerned about $30,000 in credit-card and car debt. She figures that she will reach her $1 or $1.5 million financial independence number by her 50th birthday if she follows her financial plan. "I love being a psychologist, so I don't want to stop working then," she said. "But when I reach a point where I won't need a paycheck to support myself and my son, that will give me more options."[52]

In another *Wall Street Journal* article, I offered the following statement, asking readers whether it is true or false. The price of a venti latte at Starbucks is a bit more than $4, amounting to approximately $500 a year if you drink 10 lattes each month. If you are 25, the $500 from just one year's worth of lattes would compound to a bit more than $5,000 in the 40 years until your retirement at 65, if you save it in an account yielding 6% annually. So, it is best that you forgo lattes. True or False?

I answered "False."

Sure, for some people this may make sense. But not as a rule. The price of a box of 240 diapers is approximately $46, amounting to about $500 a year if you use 11 boxes to diaper your baby each year until they are toilet-trained. Yet few would advise you to wait and have your baby at 65. "Whether lattes or diapers, ask yourself whether $500 at age 25 would serve you better or worse than $5,000 at age 65." I added: "Listen to my mother's advice: 'Spend money, but don't waste it.' Don't make saving a virtue and spending a vice."

Some readers agreed. "I especially liked the counter-intuitive point about the value of spending $500 a year on lattes when you are 25 versus spending $5,000 on something else when you are 65." More disagreed, many vehemently. "Make your latte at home and save the cash—overconsumption is the enemy of personal investment!!!"[53] This man's attitude is common among older people, berating younger ones for too much spending and too little savings. But, as journalist Isabella Simonetti noted, people in their 20s today struggle to save and are tired of being lectured about it.[54] She described 22-year old social worker Shea German-Tanner, who tries to save even if only $50 per month, but often finds it impossible on her $40,000 annual salary. She has only $600 in her savings account and has not started saving for retirement. "I feel like the older generation is constantly pushing you to do stuff like they did when they were in their 20s, but it's not even comparable to when they were in their 20s." An older reader offered comfort and perspective. "I spent my entire twenties working and going to graduate school . . . your 20s are a time to invest in yourself. My multiple degrees helped me land a secure job and I started seriously saving for retirement and buying a house when I was 35 years old. Being poor when young is normal unless you are born a trust fund baby. Relax, learn, enjoy life."

4

Investing

Wise balance between saving and spending enhances well-being, but it is not enough. Wise investments and investment behavior enhance well-being further. Foolish investments and investment behavior can fritter away substantial savings, diminishing well-being.

Wise investment behavior can be simple. Add to your investments when savings are available, and withdraw when you need to spend, such as for tuition, down payment on a house, or retirement expenses. People, however, are susceptible to misinformation and a range of cognitive and emotional errors that mislead them into foolish investment behavior. Wise investments can also be simple, overcoming intimidation of the kind voiced by Mary, a 38-year-old American woman. "I've been interested in investing in stocks but I'm clueless as to how and where to start." Clues about stocks and other investments can be obtained and investment knowledge can be acquired. Here, too, people are susceptible to misinformation and errors that mislead them into foolish investments.

Prospects of riches and prevention of poverty

I often note, with obvious exaggeration, that we want two things in life—prospects of riches and prevention of poverty. Prevention of poverty provides utilitarian benefits in adequate consumption, and expressive and emotional benefits in financial independence and freedom from fear. Prospects of riches provide utilitarian benefits in ample consumption, and expressive and emotional benefits in high social status and pride.

Investors can start, and perhaps finish, with a simple portfolio satisfying the two wants. The portfolio consists of three broadly diversified low-cost mutual funds or their corresponding exchange traded funds (ETFs), a total world stock fund, a total bond fund, and a money market fund. A total world fund is composed of shares of thousands of companies in North America, Europe, Pacific, and Emerging Markets, a total bond market fund is composed of Treasury bonds and bonds of thousands of companies, and a money market fund is composed of Treasury bills alone or in combination of short-term securities of hundreds of companies. These three mutual funds and corresponding ETFs are available from a number of mutual fund companies at annual fees of 0.10% or less, and they are also on the menus of many retirement saving plans. Some investors might choose to replace the total world stock fund with a combination of a total U.S. stock fund and a total international fund. Others might choose to replace some or all of the stock fund with individual stocks. Some might choose to replace the bond fund with individual bonds. Others might choose to add investments in real estate, commodities, or cryptocurrencies.

A wise portfolio can be built to balance prospects of riches and prevention of poverty. The money market and bond funds can be placed in a mental account satisfying prevention of poverty, perhaps with portions of the stock fund, and the rest of the stock fund can be placed in a mental account satisfying prospects of riches.

People balance the preventions-of-poverty and prospects-of-riches mental accounts by the relative weights they assign to the two wants. In general, the prevention-of-poverty mental account of young investors consists mostly of their potential earnings during their working years, what economists call human capital. This implies that young people might choose to place all or almost all their portfolios in the prospect-of-riches mental account, allocating it to the stock fund. Older investors with less human capital might choose to allocate more to the money market fund or bonds of their prevention-of-poverty mental account, including Social Security benefits, and perhaps pensions, is insufficient for the prevention-of-poverty task. Older investors with wealth substantial enough to provide prevention of poverty might choose to continue to allocate all or almost all their portfolios to stocks, expanding their prospects-of-riches mental account for their own benefits later on in life, or for the benefits of family and community.

Some shy away from investing in stocks or bonds because they are concerned that investment losses might hamper satisfaction of wants for prevention of poverty. They prefer money market funds or bank saving accounts that exclude potential for losses. Drafting a letter to his adviser, Paul, the previously mentioned 70-year-old American man, wrote: "I realize my relationship has not changed with you over time, and unless you give me some type of guarantee I will not lose my initial investment if I invest, it will probably not change in the future." Yet he noted the downside of neglecting satisfaction of wants for prospects of riches: "The only real disappointment I have is that I passed up some investments that have proved to be very good investments."

Excessive pessimism about business conditions and unemployment rates hampers some low-earners, deterring them from purchasing homes, cars, and durable goods.[1] Excessive pessimism also deters them from investing in the stock market and drives them to sell whatever stocks they own in market slumps. Low-earning Israelis sold stocks held in tax-advantaged accounts in the March–April 2020 COVID-19 related market slump, sustaining tax penalties in addition to losses incurred by selling at low prices. In contrast, higher-income people refrained from selling at the time and gained as the stock market rebounded.[2]

People who allocate substantial portions of their portfolios to money market funds expose themselves to the likelihood that their low returns, even in the absence of losses, would fail to satisfy wants for prevention of poverty, let alone prospects of riches. Stock and bond may inflict losses and fail to satisfy wants for prevention of poverty, but they are less likely to do so because they offer higher expected returns. As Victor, a 25-year-old Mexican man, noted: "I am afraid of losing my assets, but I think that if you risk nothing, you gain nothing."

Bill, a 52-year-old American man, described the differences in circumstances and knowledge between his generation and that of his parents and parents-in-law. "Both my parents and my wife's parents have saved money for retirement and both have pensions to support them in retirement. However, they did not understand the stock market and have never really benefited from investing the way that my generation has." Bill's parents and those of his wife are lucky to have pensions that pay their bills in retirement, but pensions are receding, and younger people do well to accept potential losses in stocks, bonds, and other investments as a necessity, not a luxury.

Some who invest in stock and bond mutual funds and ETFs do not consider themselves investors. Meredith, the 31-year-old American woman, is one. "I technically am an investor through my retirement account," she said. "I check it monthly to see how my account is doing, but I don't really get into the details of it." In fact, Meredith is an investor, not only "technically." Meredith is employed at a college that provides retirement saving accounts to its employees. Such accounts, usually invested in stock and bond mutual funds, are common in American colleges and universities, funded by contribution of both employer and employee. Meredith is embarrassed about her lack of stock market and other financial knowledge. "I would love a guide to investing in the stock market, which is still a pretty big mystery to me. I'm good with my own money, but the financial world is definitely still "the unknown." I basically need a dummy's guide. . . ." Yet Meredith needs not be embarrassed. She invests for good reason: "My reason for investing is to help my future self," and checks her retirement account "just to make sure I'm on track." She is likely to satisfy her wants for prevention of poverty, and perhaps, even her wants for prospects of riches, even if she knows little about the stock market.

Satisfying prospects-of-riches slowly or quickly

A diversified portfolio, such as the three-fund portfolio, can satisfy wants for prospects of riches, but only slowly. A concentrated portfolio can satisfy these wants fast or squander satisfaction of both prospects-of-riches and prevention-of-poverty. A reader of an article I wrote in the *Wall Street Journal* noted the upside of diversification. "Getting rich slowly has seemed to work for a lot of folks, getting rich quick for a slender few." And a fellow reader noted the downside of concentration. "You can get poor just as quickly!"[3]

Abandoning fast satisfaction of prospects-of-riches wants has an extra benefit in freeing time for better uses. Another reader noted that most people in the accumulation phase of their lives are also raising young children and trying to build their careers and do not have the time to perform the day-to-day study necessary for attempts at fast satisfaction of prospect-of-riches wants. "Diversification and mutual funds are boring but work for most people."[4] Yet another reader described working with a man who was a full-time computer specialist but also an amateur investor. He beat the market for two years but was spending so much time at home researching investments that it annoyed his wife. "She told him 'The small amount of extra money you're making is hurting our marriage, and you're not spending enough time with the kids.' And that was the end of that."[5]

Still, many are not ready to settle for slow satisfaction of prospects-of-riches wants. "Diversification will of course mitigate the losses from your bad picks," wrote one reader, "but it will also strictly limit the rewards from the good picks." Another noted that diversification "ensures that your money is never concentrated in the best-performing assets, but diluted in lower performing assets." Some claim great satisfaction of prospect-of-riches wants by concentrated portfolios. One reader wrote: "I 'diversified' into AAPL [Apple] for the third time in '98—bought 100 @ $20.25—added 80 @ $150 about 8–10 years ago—held all of it until last week. Sold an investment of $14,000 and change for $1,901,000—including many years of dividends along the way." But another reader countered: "Gamblers only brag about their winnings. P.S. I don't believe you." And another noted: "One of the problems with overconfidence is [investment amateurs] usually don't accurately keep track of the whole score. . . . We have a bias to remember our winners, not necessarily our loser picks." Indeed, analysis of data from an X-like investor social platform, shows that investors are more likely to post about their better-performing stocks, and their followers are more likely to buy the posted stocks.[6] A study of amateur investors, members of the American Association of Individual Investors (AAII), found that they had overestimated their own investment returns by an average of 3.4 percentage points relative to their actual returns, and they had overestimated their own returns relative to those of the average investor by 5.1 percentage points.[7]

Other investors shun diversification because they strive to satisfy prospects-of-riches goals such as early retirement, unlikely to be satisfied by diversified portfolios. One wrote that he had abandoned his widely diversified portfolio several years ago and invested substantial amounts in individual stocks, striving to retire early. "In the first two years, I made some great choices in mega-tech, fintech, solar energy, and PC gaming. . . . I've hit a few home runs and all my blunders were small. Mission accomplished. I am now retired ahead of plan." Yet he added, "I will be the first one to tell you it was 98% luck and 2% skill. I'm amused by all the stories of the new Robinhood savants who think they have it licked." His plan is to get back to something much more conventional and diversified. "I don't want to mess up . . . I'm not rich, but close enough. Don't be greedy."

Still others shun diversification because they crave the stimulation of investment gains and are ready to pay with the pain of losses. Yong, a 43-year-old Chinese man interviewed by BlackRock, described the stimulation of gains. "In May 2015, the stock prices were soaring and I felt like my wealth was increasing 10% each day." But Fangfang, a 37-year-old Chinese woman, described the pain of losses. "The stock market this year [2018] isn't great. All the high earning investments collapsed in an instant." And Zihan, a 34-year-old Chinese man described the effects of losses on his well-being: "Three years ago, the investment of P2P companies worsened, almost 90% of my capital was lost. At that time, my quality of life plummeted." Indeed, a decrease in stock prices increases antidepressant usage by investors.[8] And others shun diversification because they enjoy investing as a hobby, like fishing, reluctant to forgo its expressive and emotional benefits. One wrote, "I have been an active investor for 19 years, mainly because I like investing" He has beaten the market in 13 out of 19 years but has no illusions that he can keep this up. "In terms of time spent, it might have been better to do other things, but as noted, investing is a hobby, like fishing, and I don't follow sports."[9]

Wants for expressive and emotional benefits of investing as a hobby are evident among Dutch investors who agreed with the statement "I invest because I like to analyze problems, look for new constructions, and learn" and the statement "I invest because it is a nice free-time activity" more than they agreed with the statement "I invest because I want to safeguard my retirement."[10] These wants are also evident among German investors who trade often because they enjoy it.[11] And they are evident among the quarter of American investors who said that they buy stocks as a hobby or because it is something they like to do.[12] Other investors forgo diversification because they are misled by cognitive errors into believing that it is easy to beat the market, exceeding the mediocre returns of diversified portfolios. "Look at it this way," wrote one. "Start with ten funds to choose from" and "weed out at least half of the managers as poor performers. . . . Now select the 'average' from among those left . . . and you'll end up in the top quartile and beat the market." Another, however, noted the cognitive error of hindsight. "Do you drive your car by looking through the windshield or the rear-view mirror?"

Responsibility for choices adds the emotional sting of regret to the cognitive error of hindsight. We feel that sting as we contemplate, in hindsight, how much better off we would have been if we had chosen the mediocre diversified portfolio instead of what turned out to be a bottom concentrated portfolio. Hindsight and regret are useful teachers, teaching us to avoid choices likely to turn out poorly. Their lessons, however, take time to sink in. William, the previously mentioned 47-year-old British man, illustrated the practice of "averaging down" as balm for the sting of regret. The price of a particular stock he held for many years plummeted. "It was extremely distressing as I had also advised my parents of this share and they had invested some money. . . . I also increased my holding and now my average is lower." Regret is also induced when we know, in hindsight, that choices we had contemplated but refrained from making resulted in gains. Paul, the 70-year-old American man, had a discussion with relatives about a marijuana company. "They felt it had a bright future and were willing to risk some of their money to buy their stock," but he felt it was too risky so he did not invest in it. As it turns out, they bought the stock at about $0.30 per share. It now sells for $1.20. "I probably should have listened to them."

Framing errors also lead investors to shun diversification. One investor advocated gaining superior returns with concentrated portfolios by acquiring investment skills necessary for picking good investments and avoiding bad ones. "It's vital to know investing's and finance's language, how to read a financial statement, have run a decent-sized business, understand how to value a business, are disciplined and patient and understand the qualities that separate great businesses from good."

This investor joins many in framing wise investment picking as playing tennis against a training wall. Picking wise investments, however, is properly framed as playing tennis against a professional on the other side of the tennis net, perhaps Novak Djokovic. Investment amateurs play against investment professionals, perhaps ones with inside information or better ability to combine public information into superior assessments. It is a folly for physicians, professors, or plumbers to believe that they can acquire in their free time the information and skills investment professionals acquire and deploy in their day jobs. As Zihan, the previously mentioned 34-year-old Chinese man, correctly noted, "When managing assets, first of all, I am not a professional, and the investment information is asymmetric. Obviously, it is a trap."

Granted, very good tennis amateurs might beat middling tennis professionals from time to time. Luck helps. This is even more true in the investment game because luck helps in investing more than it does in tennis. Lucky investment amateurs, however, become overconfident in their investment picking skills, encouraged to continue picking. Over time, their returns are more likely to lag than lead diversified portfolio returns.

Amateur investors who mistakenly believe that they are able to pick winning investments also expose themselves to fraud. Victims of fraud are disproportionately better educated single young men.[13] Victimization reduces well-being by decreases of wealth and its utilitarian benefit, and it reduces well-being even more by the expressive and emotional costs of foolishness.

Penny stocks, stocks that sell for pennies or fractions of pennies, have always tempted investors with prospects of riches. More often than not, however, they offer these prospects to fraudsters. In the perennial "pump and dump" scheme, fraudsters buy heaps of shares of an obscure company, pump them with positive information that pushes up their prices, and dump them on naïve investors who hope for prospects of riches and find themselves closer to poverty. Journalist Matt Phillips tells the story of SpectraScience, a San Diego medical equipment company that had not disclosed financial results since its quarterly loss in late 2017, its 12th in a row. The price of its shares soared 500% before collapsing.[14]

Cognitive decline poses dangers to older investors, as financial skills peak at age 53.[15] That danger can rob older investors of their judgment, often without much warning, potentially ravaging a lifetime of hard-earned savings. Some investment companies work to mitigate these dangers by detecting signs of decline and informing designated family members.[16]

Staying true to our values

A commercial for Ave Maria Catholic Values mutual funds shows white pills forming a nest egg, then a question mark, and finally a skull and bones. The announcer says: "You worked hard to build a nest egg, but do your investments match your values? Many mutual funds invest in companies that support abortion, Planned Parenthood, and pornography. We screen out these companies so you can put your money where your faith is." Now we see white clouds against a blue sky and an image of a cross and open book, as the announcer says: "Ave Maria mutual funds—Smart investing and Catholic values."

More recently, after the U.S. Supreme Court overturned *Roe v. Wade*, Alinea, an investment app, saw a great desire among young adults to invest in companies that support reproductive health. "When the news came out, one of the community members created a pro-abortion-rights playlist," a basket of stocks of companies that were supporting the cause, said Eve Halimi, an Alinea cofounder.[17]

Values come from families, religions, education, cultures, and life experiences. "Although I was raised secularly for the most part," said an education consultant, "my core values come from my family's religious tradition, that is, that Jewish people believe in social justice." Her grand-father emigrated from Eastern Europe when he was 14. He was one of the founders of a major local union and then went on to start his own business. "When I was a teenager," she continued, "I was doing some work for him when there was a strike at his business, and he told me I couldn't cross the picket lines. My mother said, 'You have to go to work and help him,' but my grandfather said, 'You can't do that.' Those are the experiences and the key framework that led me to emphasize feminist and workers' rights in my investing."[18]

Investors vary in combining investments with values and willing-ness to forgo utilitarian benefits for expressive and emotional ones. On average, investors are willing to forgo some portions of their invest-ment returns to stay true to their values. Yet about a third of investors are unwilling to forgo any portion of their returns to stay true to their values. Democrats, women, and higher-income investors are more will-ing to forgo portions of their returns to stay true to their values than conservatives, men, and lower-income investors.[19]

A banker is among investors who are ready to separate investments from values and unwilling to forgo investment returns to stay true to his values. He works in corporate finance, making bank loans to corpora-tions. "We finance tobacco companies, defense contractors, gaming and casino companies, all the sins certainly. . . . When I go to my grave, will I regret making those loans or investments? I don't think so. I think there's certainly a difference between one's moral life and one's profes-sional life."[20]

Investors willing to forgo portions of their returns to stay true to their values still worry about the size of the foregone portions. As a financial adviser said, "Even socially responsible investors want to retire someday." "For our church, investing according to socially responsible principles is more a matter of integrity than making a major difference," said an official of the Church of the Brethren. He occasionally sees arti-cles on "sin" funds that invest primarily in stocks of tobacco, alcohol, and other "sin" companies, advising people to separate their investments from their values, using profits from "sin" funds to support good causes. "That argument seems completely backwards to me because the money is already out there supporting bad things." Yet he added "People from the church ask us fairly regularly whether we give up anything in terms of returns by narrowing the focus of our portfolio [by excluding companies inconsistent with our values]. Often, it's phrased just that bluntly: "How much does it cost me to invest with you and exclude those things from my portfolio?"

5

Dating and Marriage

Dating, weddings, and marriage, can enhance well-being greatly. Yuxuan, a 30-year-old Chinese man interviewed by BlackRock, described high well-being while dating. When he was dating his wife in university, they didn't have extra money to travel, to buy clothes, or go for casual dinners out, "but we were still very happy and enjoyed each other's company. That is happiness to us—to be together every day!" Na, a 36-year-old Chinese woman, described high well-being on her wedding day, "receiving congratulations from friends and family. I had all the attention for the day and all the conversation topics were about me. I felt a lot of love and was very touched." And Jane, a 59-year-old American woman, described high well-being long into marriage: "My husband and I had a mini getaway for his birthday. . . . It was relaxing, and gave me a feeling of well-being because I let the world slip away, leaving just my husband and I with no worries, just good conversation." Spending time with a spouse enhances well-being, often worth the cost of synchronizing work schedules. On average, couples are willing to forego 17% of their hourly wage to convert an hour of childcare from private to joint, and 10% to convert an hour of leisure from private to joint.[1]

Links between marriage and well-being go both ways. High well-being enhances the likelihood of marriage, and marriage enhances well-being. People who get divorced are distinct not only in low well-being during marriage but also in low well-being before marriage.[2] Women's positive emotional expressions in their college yearbook photographs are associated with greater likelihood of being married at age 27 and greater marital satisfaction at age 52.[3] Well-being in marriage spills over from one partner to the other,[4] and the size of health gains from marriage is remarkable, as large as the health gains from giving up smoking.[5] High marital quality, reflected in low stress and high harmony, enhances well-being, and low marital quality diminishes it.[6] The likelihood of divorce is higher when partners' well-being is lower.[7]

Respect between spouses enhances well-being. A man interviewed by Pew said: "[My wife and I] don't always agree on everything, but we care enough about each other and respect one another enough to find good compromises, overlook faults, or make individual sacrifices."[8] Disrespect between spouses diminishes well-being more than respect enhances it. A 26-year-old soon-to-be divorcée said: "Perhaps what was most hurtful was the idea that this was happening with someone I thought I loved, and who I thought loved me. . . . Eventually, that bitter taste starts to linger, then it becomes completely sour until you can't deal with it anymore."[9]

Marriage enhances well-being in same-gender marriages as it does in mixed-gender marriages.[10] A wedding column told the story of Luke Kalat and Justin Conner, a same-gender couple who married more than a decade after they were attracted to each other.

"We just started talking, it was just the most open, honest conversation that I'd ever had," said Mr. Kalat, recalling their first conversation. "It just kind of dawned on me that this is the man I'm going to marry," said Mr. Conner. Mr. Kalat was a bit nervous when he joined Mr. Conner and his family at Thanksgiving, having never met a boyfriend's family before. But he was relieved to find that Conner's family received him with open arms.[11]

Another wedding column told the story of Stephanie Schulter and Halle Bauer, a same-gender couple who had their first date at the Coney Island Polar Bear Plunge. Not long after, they were on a canoe that flipped. Ms. Schulter "immediately came over to me," Ms. Bauer said, "picked me up by my shirt to make sure I was above water and paddled us both to shore. . . . I remember returning from that trip . . . and being like, I think I'm in love with this person." They married four years later.[12]

Marriage enhances the well-being of both men and women but it enhances the well-being of men more than of women.[13,14] This might be because the burden of chores and childcare falls mainly on women, and men benefit more from the social support by women.[15,16] Relationship quality, however, tends to affect the well-being of women more than of men.[17] "Women in South Korea are on strike against being baby-making machines," wrote author Hawon Jung.[18] South Korean women find it hard to escape gender norms, "whether in pregnancy guidelines to arrange clean undergarments for your husband before labor, or the days-long kitchen drudgework for holidays like the Chuseok harvest festival." And even in dual-income families wives spend more than three hours daily on chores and childcare, whereas their husbands spend less than an hour on them.

Marriage enhances well-being especially in middle-age, when well-being tends to be lowest,[19] indicating that marriage may help alleviate the causes of the mid-life dip in well-being and that the benefits of marriage are long-term. Having a spouse enjoying high well-being is associated not only with longer marriage but also with longer life.[20] Indeed, psychologist Olga Stavrova found that the well-being of a spouse was more closely associated with a partner's mortality than the partner's own well-being. People whose spouses enjoyed high well-being at the beginning of Stavrova's study were less likely to die during the following eight years than people whose spouses suffered lower well-being at that beginning.

Well-being in marriage is associated with behaviors that affect health, including diet and exercise, and people whose spouses practice active lifestyles are also likely to practice active lifestyles. "If your partner is depressed and wants to spend the evening eating chips in front of the TV," said Stavrova, "that's how your evening will probably end up looking, as well." Behaviors that affect health underlie some of the lower mortality among married people than among singles during the COVID-19 pandemic. A study of 46,450 people in 67 countries found that married people are more likely to comply with COVID-19 protective measures than single people. This marital gap in compliance is especially high among men.[21]

The high well-being accompanying marriage is long lasting because, unlike tangible aspects of our lives, it is not diminished by social comparison. Well-being increases when our income rises from $100,000 to $150,000, but it is soon diminished when we learn that colleagues earn $200,000. But high well-being accompanying marriage is not diminished when we learn that our married colleagues also enjoy high well-being because well-being accompanying intangible aspects of our lives defies social comparison.[22]

Well-being in marriage can often withstand great adversity. Responding to an article about caregiving, a man wrote, "For nearly 20 years now, I have been the sole caregiver for my wife, who is totally and permanently disabled from a stroke she suffered." He is a virtual prisoner in his own home and now, at 66, is certainly not living the retirement life he had imagined. "But my wife does not suffer from dementia or incontinence. She knows who I am, and most importantly knows what we mean to each other. That goes far in compensating for the losses."[23]

Search for marriage partners

American expectations of marriage have changed over three eras, identified by psychologist Eli Finkel.[24] In the first, lasting from the colonial period until about 1850, newlyweds expected no more than satisfaction of material needs. In the second, extending until about 1965, newlyweds also expected love. Today, in the third era, newlyweds expect self-discovery and personal growth in addition to love and satisfaction of material needs. These expectations are difficult to fulfill, and well-being is diminished when they are not.

Universities are sites of learning, places for acquisition of knowledge that would serve as the foundation of good-paying jobs and careers. But universities also serve as "marriage markets," as economists call them, places where people meet, date, and consider preferences, resources, and market conditions as they search for marriage partners. Other marriage markets include online dating sites and workplaces, and matchmakers, friends, and family, who act as facilitators, linking people to potential marriage partners.

Susan Patton, who graduated from Princeton University more than three decades before, offered marriage market advice to current Princeton women. "Forget about having it all, or not having it all, leaning in or leaning out—here's what you really need to know that nobody is telling you," she wrote. "For most of you, the cornerstone of your future and happiness will be inextricably linked to the man you marry, and you will never again have this concentration of men who are worthy of you. . . . Find a husband on campus before you graduate."[25]

The story of Lynn Hamilton, told by sociologist Pamela Stone, illustrates Patton's advice and also the pull of the traditional social norms of breadwinner and homemaker.[26] Hamilton met her future husband at Princeton when they were both 19-year-old undergraduates. She thought that, with almost identical credentials and comparable skills, their combined income would be sufficiently high to obviate any need for either to work "killer jobs." It turned out, however, that both were working killer jobs. "And I kept saying, we need to reconfigure this. And what I realized was, he wasn't going to." So, Hamilton quit her job to become a homemaker.

The pull of the traditional social norms in the search for marriage partners is evident in preferences displayed in online dating sites. Women looking for men place twice as much weight on men's incomes as men place on women's incomes. This is true whether women's own incomes are high or low.[27]

The pull of the traditional social norms is also evident in the tendency of single women to shy away from choices that are likely to enhance their careers when they imply traits, such as ambition, that are valued in men but might lessen the marriage prospects of women. Single women in an MBA program asked for lower salaries, expressed lower willingness to travel, and reported lower readiness to work long hours when they were aware that their classmates, especially single men, will observe their preferences.[28]

And that pull is evident in a popular Indian matchmaking website, where profiles of women who signal desire to work after marriage receive almost 22% less interest from men than those of women who have never worked. Women signaling willingness to give up work after marriage face a lower penalty.[29] Both men and women prefer marriage partners who are similar to them by age, ethnicity, and religion. Single women shy away from divorced men, whereas divorced women prefer divorced men. Both men and women with children prefer partners who also have children. And men and women without children shy away from those with children.[30]

Preferences vary by culture. A study of matrimonial ads in Canada, France and India from 1950 to 1995 shows that stated preferences for high income in an ideal partner have fallen sharply in favor of personality traits in Canada and France, especially after the late 1960s. In India, however, income remains the top criterion. Still, income matters even in Canada and France. Demand for personality traits rests on satisfaction of the demand for ample income.[31]

Differences, such as in wealth, worry marriage partners. An article about the joys and discontents of wealth quoted a man: "I am worth $3 million so I'm not super-rich. However, I do worry about affection; whether my wife married me for me or for my money. She brings it up quite a lot."[32] And differences in wealth worry parents of potential marriage partners. A mother of a daughter set to receive millions in royalties from her share in a large oil field wrote to ask for my advice. Her daughter has a well-meaning, bright boyfriend, but he has close to nothing. Will her marriage be stable?

Interfaith marriages are common now in the United States, yet marrying within a faith is still most common. A Pew Research Center survey found that 7 in 10 married people share a religion.[33] The proportions of people cohabiting with or married to partners of their own religion are high among American Hindus, Mormons, and Muslims, and lower among Jews, mainline Protestants, and religiously unaffiliated people.

The story of Myra Farooqi, a young Muslim Pakistani-American woman, and a young Hindu Indian-American man illustrates the often-insurmountable barriers to marriage between people of different religions and ethnicities. Farooqi met the man on Dil Mil, a dating app for South Asians, despite filters she set to avoid heartbreak by excluding all non-Muslim and non-Pakistani men. When Farooqi told her mother about her relationship, her mother asked "Is he Muslim?" When she said "no," her mother shrieked. "Is he Pakistani?" When she said "no," her mother gasped. "Can he speak Urdu or Hindi?" When she said "no," her mother started to cry.

The mother softened when Farooqi described how happy she is in her relationship, and the man's pledge to convert to Islam. But when the man told his parents he was thinking of converting, they broke down, crying, begging, and pleading with him not to abandon his religion. In their final conversation, the man said "I will never convert to Islam, not nominally, not religiously." And Farooqi said "Then that's it," knowing that she had lost the man she thought she would love forever.[34]

Some men and women trust their parents to know their preferences and select marriage candidates. This is especially true where arranged marriages are common, such as in India and China, and among Orthodox Jews in the United States. Linda Hirschel, an American Jewish Orthodox woman, described being matched to her future husband in an arranged marriage, a *shidduch*. She became Orthodox when she was 24, and went on a few *shidduchim*. "Eventually, I was introduced to Mr. Right. Our story went like this: We met on a Friday night, we went out three times that week, and we were engaged by the following Friday. Three months later we were married, and this year we will celebrate 30 years."[35] Hirschel described the benefits of arranged marriages. "*Shidduchim* work because the parents provide the filter, the idea is that our kids don't have to kiss a lot of frogs before finding their prince or princess." As a mother, she tries to find marriage partners who share her family's principles and goals, who will commit themselves to the marriage, and who will help raise children with those same principles and goals.

The arranged marriage of Mina Shankar and Aditya Radhakrishnan is likely to be as successful as that of Hirschel and her Mr. Right. They met at the suggestion of their parents, who managed their children's accounts on BrahminMatrimony.com, a marriage-oriented website for people of

Indian descent. "They were just trying to help me out," Radhakrishnan said of his parents. "I said, I'll keep an open mind." And Shankar said: "My mom is the one who introduced my sister-in-law to my brother, and they've been married 10 years now. . . . My mom obviously has my best interests at heart." Their first date ended in a kiss. "It was just really easy to communicate with him," said Shankar, "I felt like I already knew him." "I think at the end we were both pleasantly surprised," said Radhakrishnan. They were married a year later.[36]

Not all attempts at arranged marriage are as successful as those of Hirschel and her Mr. Right or Shankar and Radhakrishnan, but a woman of Indian descent dismissed the notion that arranged marriages are forced marriages. "My parents met and spoke before their wedding day in India and were asked whether they each saw a future with the other." She agreed to a date with Raj, arranged by her parents. She really wanted something to work out between them, to get married and make everyone happy. "But as we talked after brunch that day it was more apparent that a romance between Raj and me wasn't in the cards." She would have had to bend her career-oriented, passionate, food-loving, world-traveling self if she were to marry him.[37] The woman's parents understood, trusted her judgment, and let the subject drop. "I gave their way a chance and that was enough for them. . . . All they want for me is security."

Parents' perceptions of marriage and their preferences are often different from those of their children, even when parents have their children's best interests at heart. Postponed marriage in China's major cities is common now, but parents' expectations of traditional gender roles persist. Unmarried women in their late 20s are called "leftover women," facing parental pressure to find a marriage partner. Interviews with young, single, Chinese, white-collar professional women in Beijing show differing perceptions and preferences of parents and daughters on marriage, romantic relationship, and gender role, as well as daughters' aspirations for autonomy and independence.[38]

Sometimes, however, parents do not have the interests of their children at heart, and arranged marriages descend into forced marriages. Indian parents with many daughters often rush the older daughter to marry a man of low education and occupation, to allow them sufficient time to marry off her younger sisters. As a consequence, older daughters leave school earlier, and are handicapped by lower literacy.[39]

Moreover, Indian parents sometimes distort the choice of spouse, sacrificing love between the couple for services to them. When Indian parents are involved in the choice of spouse, sons are less likely to marry college-educated women or women who develop careers.[40] Similarly, parent matchmaking in China is associated with less marital harmony between the couple, more submissive wives, and a stronger belief in support from sons to elderly parents.[41]

Bans on child marriage enhance female educational attainment and employment. A study of more than 250,000 females from 17 low- and middle-income countries found that raising the minimum legal age of marriage to 18 increased age at marriage, age at first birth, and the likelihood of employment.[42] Still, some marriages are forced. A large proportion of women in the Kyrgyz Republic marry by *ala kachuu*, sometimes characterized as staged or ritualized elopement, but more likely to be forced marriage. Couples in *ala kachuu* marriages turn out to be far less similar than other couples, a dissimilarity inconsistent with its characterization as a staged or ritualized elopement. And *ala kachuu* marriages diminish the well-being of women.[43]

"Shotgun marriages" in the United States are not as forced as *ala kachuu* marriages, but they are hardly free. Writer Merritt Tierce was a college student on her way to Yale Divinity School. If she had notions of having children or being a wife, they existed in a vague haze of a distant future. Then, when she was 19, she got pregnant. Tierce conceded to her parents' pressure to keep the baby and marry the father of her son, and they had a daughter before they divorced. The children turned out well, but Tierce has misgivings about her practices of raising them. "I was shut down and withdrawn and in pain and exhausted. . . . I wanted to go to grad school, so I could have feelings of accomplishment and contribution and confidence and curiosity."[44]

Marriage-market conditions in the search for marriage partners

Marriage-market conditions can strengthen or weaken the positions of prospective marriage partners. Market conditions changed in France following World War I, as the ratio of women to men increased by the high military mortality during the war. That high ratio strengthened the position of men in the marriage market and weakened that of women. As a consequence, men were more likely to marry than women, out-of-wedlock births increased, and men were less likely to marry women of lower social classes.[45]

On the opposite side, the one-child policy in China and the preference for sons combined to increase the ratio of men to women, strengthening the position of women in the marriage market and weakening that of men. Families with sons responded by accumulating more wealth than families with daughters, and owning additional residential real estate.[46] Fangfang, the previously mentioned 37-year-old Chinese woman, illustrated that response. "In the future, when children grow up, the cost of marriage and raising children is too high, but my child does not need to worry. I have a house ready for him when he gets married in the future. . . ."

The relative position of American women in the marriage market weakened when competition from China eliminated jobs in American women-dominated manufacturing industries, such as leather-goods. Marriage rates increased, as women perceived marriage as more likely to lead to economic security than single motherhood.[47]

Marriage-market conditions also affected dowry payments in the Indian marriage market. The proportion of Indian marriages that included dowry payments doubled between 1930 and 1975, and the average real value of payments tripled. The increase in dowry was due to modernization that strengthened the positions of men possessing skills made more valuable by modernization.[48]

Anti-dowry laws introduced in India in 1985 have some sad effects. The new laws greatly reduced dowries, but also led to increased domestic violence against women. Children born to mothers affected by these laws are shorter and have fewer years of completed schooling. This is likely because of domestic violence against mothers and lower family wealth caused by lower dowries.[49] In China, it is the groom providing dowry, and insufficient dowry also has sad effects. "My wife told me a story about her classmate," said Zihan, the previously mentioned 34-year old Chinese man. "During her wedding, the groom did not give enough for the dowry, resulting in his mother-in-law treating him quite unkindly ever since."

The role of finances

Marriage is now about more than material resources, but these resources continue to underlie it, and the resources of the poor are meager. When the usual mishaps of life occur, a car repair or a knee injury, the poor are more likely to suffer unemployment, eviction, and destitution. The poor are also less likely to have control over their work schedules and less money for childcare. And when they find time for conversations with spouses, they are likely to arrive at them feeling emotionally depleted by other stressors, and the topics of conversations are often pointed—how to budget their little money, and how to get affordable childcare. The poor know that there is no such thing as "poor but happily married," that marriage among the poor is likely to end in divorce, and that divorce is the ultimate loss of face. It is better not to marry than marry and divorce.[50]

Sociologist Victor Tan Chen noted that until a few decades ago those without college degrees were much more likely to be married by age 30 than those with college degrees. Now, however, only half of women without a college degree are married by their early 40s, compared to three-quarters of women with a college degree. He pinned the decline in rates of marriage among those without college degrees on the decline of well-paying jobs available to them, a decline that impedes stable relationships. Indeed, marriage is now a central component of income inequality, allowing married college graduates to pool their incomes. Chen quoted a 51-year-old man formerly employed at a car plant in Detroit, whose marriage crumbled during three years of almost constant unemployment. "I've got no money and now she's got a job," he said. "All credibility is out the tubes when you can't pay the bills."[51]

Financial stability and housing security are crucial determinants of family structures. Financial distress increases a married couple's probability of divorce by 4–8%.[52] At the other end, a study of winners of substantial lottery prizes in Sweden indicates that increased wealth increases the likelihood of marriage and reduces the likelihood of divorce. Increased wealth also increases male fertility.[53]

Poor young men and women search for marriage partners and hope to parent their children in a marriage. Moreover, when their children are born outside marriage, most poor young men say they want to marry the mothers of their children. Yet marriage does not usually follow children's birth, and relationships between couples tend to unravel quickly, in large part, because poor men lack the financial, job-related, and behavioral resources necessary to sustain a marriage.

Sociologists Kathryn Edin and Timothy Nelson offered the story of Bear and Amber, a poor young couple, as an illustration of the complex dynamics whereby a sudden pregnancy, a strong desire for children, lofty standards for marriage, and palpable mistrust set almost insurmountable barriers to marriage.[54] Bear and Amber, who barely knew each other before conception, suddenly discover, once the baby is born, that they do not share the same values and priorities. Caring for a baby creates in Amber certain financial, job-related, and behavioral expectations to be fulfilled by Bear. Amber now expects Bear to be a conscientious job-holder, fully accountable to her. Yet Bear was never a conscientious job-holder, and he resists being accountable to Amber. Moreover, Bear did not choose Amber as his wife. He ended up with Amber because a baby was on the way.

The lofty marriage standards of Bear and men like him call for a marriage of absolute trust and commitment, a marriage that will not waver when real-life challenges appear, whether it be drug addiction, a prison term, or a job loss. These lofty standards make actual relationships profoundly unsatisfying. "Plain Jane must suddenly compete with the contender for the Miss America prize." Ironically, higher marriage standards are much of the reason for today's lower rates of marriage among the poor. Many poor men who would have met the standards of the 1950s and 1960s do not meet today's standards.

Poor women consider marriage a luxury, aware of the meager resources of potential marriage partners, but they consider children a necessity, placing the mother-child relationship at the center. Therefore, poor women might be willing to have children by men unsuitable as marriage partners. They hope that their relationships with the fathers of their children might improve when children are born, but know that they will keep the children even if their relationships with the fathers unravel.

Still, there is more to declining marriage rates among people lacking college education than declining job prospects and wages. Changes in social norms also matter. Economists Melissa Kearney and Riley Wilson explored the consequences of "fracking booms" on rates of marriage. They confirmed that the fracking booms were associated with increased wages for men lacking college education, yet they found no increase in marriage rates. This might be because changes in social norms removed some of the stigma of single motherhood and out-of-wedlock childbirth.[55]

Men and women of the elite, unlike the poor, take for granted that their finances will be adequate and material needs will be satisfied. They expect to marry someone with the financial, job-related, and behavioral resources necessary to sustain a marriage. Confident that they will find such a person, they delay marriage until they complete schooling, establish careers, and enter cohabitation as trial marriages. They place the husband-wife relationship at the center, and consider children as a possibly desirable complement. Sarah Barton, a 34-year-old elite woman had lived with her now-husband for several years before they married, as did her siblings. "[My parents] didn't like that or approve. But for my younger cousins and family members I strongly encourage it."[56]

When members of the elite commit to long-term partners, they have financial resources and support that let them focus on emotional support and connection, make compromises, and get help when they face difficulties. This reduces likelihoods of breaking up, and increases likelihoods of finding new partners if they do break up.[57] The birth control pill afforded female members of the elite the opportunity to postpone marriage and continue from college into graduate professional programs. The proportion of women in such programs increased substantially just after 1970, and the age at first marriage among female college graduates began to increase around the same year.[58]

Members of the elite can also afford to postpone marriage because they can afford in vitro fertilization (IVF). Israel's 1994 adoption of free IVF provides a natural experiment for how fertility time horizons impact women's marriage timing and other outcomes. The policy change was followed by a substantial increase in average age at first marriage. This shift appears to be driven by both increased marriages by older women and by younger women delaying marriage. Age at first birth also increased.[59]

Conflict resolution

The well-being benefits of marriage are especially great when spouses are best friends, supporting each other.[60] An older couple described their relationship with a smile, "one limps and the other is a walking stick." Still, conflicts arise even among best friends, and a walking stick is not always offered.

Psychologists John Tierney and Roy Baumeister described constructive strategies couples use when behaviors of spouses bother them. "Let it slide and hope things improve, or explain what bothers you and work out a compromise." They also described destructive strategies. "Sulk.

Say nothing, emotionally withdraw from your partner, or head for the exit. Threaten to break up, or start looking for another partner."[61]

Constructive strategies improve relationships by only a little, but destructive strategies damage relationships by a lot. "When you quietly hang in there for your partner, your loyalty often isn't even noticed. But when you silently withdraw from your partner or issue angry threats, you can start a disastrous spiral of retaliation."

In their studies of thousands of couples, psychologists John Gottman and Robert Levenson found that contempt is first among factors that tear couples apart, diminishing well-being and signaling the end of relationships. In contrast, kindness, generosity, and gratitude, bind couples together, enhancing their well-being.[62] "We tend to overestimate our efforts [in] a relationship and underestimate the amount of work our partner is contributing," said psychologist Allen Barton.[63] Gratitude is a guardrail against the common tendency to take for granted the contributions of a partner.[64]

Venting anger at a spouse may be cathartic, but it damages relationships and diminishes well-being. Scheduled meetings to discuss disagreements heal relationships and enhance well-being. Rhaina Cohen, a podcast producer and editor, described the transition from venting to meeting in the relationship with the couple Liz and Tom.

"Showing anger in dramatic ways was clearly part of our back-and-forth," said Tom, describing the early part of their relationship. Now, they write down their grievances and wait to discuss them in meetings scheduled every three months. Waiting drains painful momentary emotions and facilitates cooperation and creativity. Liz and Tom set norms for their meetings and established rules of engagement. "Don't shut down the other person's observations. . . . Prepare to hear criticism, admit your faults, and be grateful for your partner. Commit to working on the relationship for the long haul, and accept that change might come in baby steps."[65]

Failures of kindness, generosity, conversation, and compromise strains marriage and diminishes well-being, evident in the story of Meredith, the previously mentioned 31-year-old American woman. "A time when I wasn't feeling good was when I first moved from Boston, where I'm from, to Oregon." She and her husband were going through a rough patch in their marriage and adjusting to having to take care of a dog. "I felt like I couldn't talk to him at all because he'd grown up with pets and just couldn't understand what my problem was. Overall, communication was poor and it just wasn't a good time for either of us." Differences in the absence of compromise continue to diminish Meredith's well-being now that her husband has left his full-time job for school. "This affects our budget in two ways: one, we're now living on one income, and two, we're now having to pay tuition on top of our normal expenses. AND ON ONE INCOME." Meredith explained the problem to her husband. "Basically, when we have these conversations, it's me explaining that even if he charges lunch at Taco Bell on his credit card . . . it's me paying for it." So far, her explanations have not sunk in. "It's usually just me talking and him apologizing. It sucks, honestly. . . ."

Financial fidelity

Financial infidelity, hiding spending and debt from a spouse, is likely more frequent than sexual infidelity, and it too can damage relationships. A survey of marriage partners found that 40% said they had engaged in financial infidelity and 85% of them said that it damaged their relationship, ranging from angry conversations to divorce.[66] Jessica Matthews, a financial adviser, divorced her husband when she discovered that he was hiding more than $30,000 in credit card debt. Now she shares her experience as she guides her clients.

Joint financial accounts can forestall financial infidelity by disclosure and outside-control, supplementing self-control or replacing it as each partner must justify spending to the other. A joint bank account induces partners to buy basic goods, as each needs to justify spending to the other, whereas separate bank accounts tempt them to buy luxury goods.[67]

Danny, a 43-year-old American man interviewed by BlackRock, described the benefits of disclosure and outside-control in his marriage. A few months before, his wife confessed that she had failed to manage her personal finances. Over the past three years she had amassed a $10,000 credit card debt. Initially, Danny was angry, but following a conversation with his wife, they agreed that he would handle all their finances. "We decided to give her a weekly cash allowance, which seemed sad . . . but necessary."

Couples that combine finances in joint bank, credit-card, and investment accounts enjoy higher well-being and accumulate more assets than couples that keep their finances separate.[68] Yet outside-control by joint finances is not always benign, sometimes used by one partner to control the other. Sociologist Rachel Sherman described Stephanie, a member of a wealthy couple, complaining that her husband buys gourmet food and wine for his friends but restricts her spending on necessities for their child and household.[69]

Moreover, lack of trust deters many couples from combining their finances. And lack of trust is sometimes justified. Writer Naomi Jackson defined *vex money* as "money stashed on your person or in a secret place such as your brassiere, a bank account, or your grandmother's Bible, to be spent only in case of emergency, when a once stable situation suddenly turns vexed—usually but not always because of a man."[70]

Jackson observed few happy marriages in her Afro-Caribbean immigrant community. "There were whispers about outside women and illegitimate children, clucked tongues about men who gambled away both their own earnings and their family's savings." She was taught that it was better to remain married even in the face of profound betrayal, but she also understood that it is not wise to depend on a man unable or unwilling to provide for his family. "Vex money is the manifestation of our unwillingness to trust."

A white woman from an upper-class background was astonished to find that her experience is similar to that of Jackson. Her mother had to flee her abusive and wealthy husband who withheld money from her and their children as a divorce tactic. "There is security in having the funds for emergencies."

Another white woman who grew up in a poor to lower middle-class family quoted her mother: "Don't ever rely on a man. If you want something, get it yourself. First, get a good education because no one can take it away from you." That advice served her well after her divorce.

And another wrote "In my European German Jewish community, we had the same thing but it was called a *knipple*! I guess women having to keep some money for themselves in a secret place is a long tradition."

Differences over financial behavior

Age, ethnicity, and religion are easy to ascertain before marriage, but financial behavior, especially behavior related to saving, spending, and risk attitudes, are harder to assess. Nevertheless, partners are generally able to ascertain financial behavior somewhat. Many couples in stable marriages have similar credit scores indicating similar propensities for spending and saving,[71] and often, married partners generally possess similar risk attitudes before marriage, rather than converge their risk attitudes during marriage.[72] Still, some people often marry partners whose financial behavior is different from their own because each fails to anticipate the effects of marriage on behavior and outcomes. When we are hungry, we might be more inclined to buy more food at the grocery store than when we are sated. And when we are in love, before marriage, we act as if we expect to be in love forever.[73]

"In couple relationships, discussing finances is often considered taboo," noted marriage and family researcher Matthew Saxey and coauthors. Yet emerging adult couples face some unique financial challenges that may lead to poor financial communication and relational risks. Saxey and coauthors found that early financial discussions in romantic relationships can improve relationship quality, but they can also create financial conflicts. Yet, overall, their findings suggest the sooner emerging adult couples discuss finances, the better.[74]

The relationship between April, a 31-year-old American woman interviewed by BlackRock, and her husband is falling apart over money. "When I was a kid, I was naïve," she said. Her parents and grandparents were very generous. When she got married in 2008 the reality of money hit her hard. She had just graduated college, her fiancé lost his job, and her father's retirement savings account had crashed. "Fast forward 9 years . . . my husband has lost 5 jobs in 9 years . . . bled through a significant amount of our savings more than once. . . ."

April prefers to keep some of her money in an individual account. Sharing her philosophy on money with a friend, she spoke about "how women who work deserve a kitty . . . to treat themselves to something—a massage, manicure, pedicure, etc." Her friend did not agree, arguing that all dollars go into a joint account. "It was interesting to me that we didn't see eye to eye on this."

Bargaining power matters. The share of spending on wives' beauty goods is higher and the share of spending on alcohol is lower when the relative education and potential wages of wives are higher. And stronger wives' bargaining positions in couples with children is associated with higher investment in children, reflected in higher budget share on books, stationary, and school supplies.[75] Bargaining also takes place between employed husbands and homemaker wives. Danielle, an inheritor of a family fortune and former banker interviewed by sociologist Rachel Sherman, is bolstered by her previous employment. "When asked 'what do you do?' I say 'I'm at home, I'm not working. I'm a retired banker.'"

Still, she felt guilty about spending "vanity money." "Earning your own money is validating. Somebody's paying you for what you're doing." She and her husband have calculated what it would cost to replace her domestic labor. "It's a sizable amount. . . between babysitting, tutoring, house-cleaning, cooking—what does that add up to in people hours?. . . it's a bunch of money." Danielle pays herself a salary for her work, drawn from her investments, which she uses for family and personal expenses.[76]

Masculinity and femininity, breadwinner and homemaker

Much of what is going on in marriage today is still rooted in the traditional social norms of masculinity and femininity, breadwinner and homemaker. By these social norms, husbands are breadwinners, providers of income, and wives are homemakers, caring for home and children.

Some educated young adults reject these traditional social norms in favor of equal marriage whereby each marriage partner is equally breadwinner and homemaker. Yet the pull of traditional social norms remains strong.[77] "Marriage proposals are stupid," argued writer Caroline Kitchener, "This is no way for two grown humans to make a major life decision."[78] The American ritual of the marriage proposal calls for a man to take a woman to someplace romantic and surprise her by getting on one knee, popping the question, and presenting a diamond ring. That ritual then calls for the woman to cry and immediately say "yes."

The traditional social norms adjust somewhat when husbands become stay-at-home dads, but not entirely. Stay-at-home dads increase their childcare and housework on weekdays, but not on weekends.[79] Sociologist Rachel Sherman described Patricia Lambert, an elite woman, acknowledging that her husband made it possible for her to stay home. He was making enough money that they did not have to have her income. "I don't want to not be grateful and aware of that. We really had a choice, and most women don't. And I see that in my sister-in-law who is a nurse."[80] Sherman also described Melissa Wyatt, another elite woman, who noted a business metaphor her husband uses to justify their traditional division of labor after she left her job upon the birth of their first child: "He's revenue and I'm operations."

The social norms of husband as breadwinner and wife as homemaker are under stress and well-being is diminished when wives out-earn their husbands. Such husbands are more likely to use erectile dysfunction medications than other husbands, even when differences between earnings are small. And both husbands and wives use more insomnia and anxiety medicines when wives out-earn their husbands.[81] Indeed, aversion to a wife out-earning her husband reduces the likelihood of marriage. And, if married, this aversion reduces the likelihood of a wife's employment and her income if employed, and increases the likelihood of divorce.[82]

Still, husbands swallow their pride, preferring a wife that out-earns them when they earn too little to support the family. Sociologist Victor Tan Chen spoke to a 54-year-old former factory worker who said that her husband's resentment about her frequent temporary layoffs spilled over into fights over money and eventual separation. "Anytime I got laid off, he got pissed," she said. Husbands out-earned by their wives reduce their distress by inflating the earnings. They report higher earnings to census surveyors than their employers report to the Internal Revenue Service. And wives reduce their discomfort and that of their husbands by deflating their earnings.[83]

A report about these findings elicited many responses, mostly insisting that their well-being is not affected by the relative earnings of husband and wife.[84] A man wrote that he is proud of his wife for earning more than him. "She has worked diligently and consistently improved her education so all her earnings are well deserved. A marriage is teamwork and if we, the home team, win then we celebrate together." Others, however, echoed the finding that well-being is diminished when wives out-earn their husbands. A woman wrote: "My dad was a peaceable man but when my mom happened to mention that she was bringing in more income . . . he'd lose his cool so quickly I couldn't really believe that he was the same guy." Her mother learned not to bring money issues out into the open, at least not when her father was unemployed or underemployed. If her father was satisfactorily employed, meaning out-earning her mother, he would be highly accommodating to her mother and did not care how the money was spent. "But you don't kick him when he's down."

Wives generally strive to assuage the fragile egos of husbands they out-earn. Sociologist Rachel Sherman noted that such wives go out of their way to recognize their husbands' contributions, more than husbands do for their wives. Yet wives retain primary responsibility for their homes and children, even if they bring into their marriage greater earnings or inheritance.

Sherman described Miriam, a wife earning an annual $1.2 million income from long hours of banking work, 10 times the income of her husband. Yet her husband has the priority job in the family because his ego was more wrapped up in his job than hers. She was the one who stayed home with the kids when the nanny was sick. "I think there's a gendered thing that happens, where women who work also are the CEO of the house, and the men just work."[85]

Assuaging a husband's ego is more difficult when household income is low. Sociologist Marianne Cooper described the escalating fight between Laura Delgado and her unemployed husband, Vince, when he bought a new truck. "When he was really depressed about not being employed, what did he do? He went out and bought a truck. I mean, c'mon, a truck, with oversized wheels . . . that we couldn't afford—that says masculinity."[86]

By traditional social norms, husbands are also assumed to possess greater financial knowledge than wives. Female identity hinders wives' contributions to financial decisions, whereas male identity promotes resistance among husbands.[87] Sherman described Ellen who noted that men want to invest the money so they can "have their footprint" on it.[88]

Well-off millennial women, those with at least $250,000 in investable assets, tend to defer to their husbands on investing even more than female baby boomers do. Among millennial women living with male partners, 54% percent of those surveyed said they defer to their partners on investing rather than share that responsibility or take the lead, compared with 39% of boomer women.[89]

Some of the differences in finances between elite families and working-class or poor ones likely stem from the fact that finances in elite families imply investing, whereas they imply budgeting among working-class and poor ones. Sociologist Marianne Cooper described Malinda, a working-class woman, carrying responsibility for her family's budget. Owen, her husband, explained that his check from work goes right to cover their expenses. And so, a lot of times when he wakes up and gets ready to go to work and, and it's the third of the month and Melinda would say, "When is the money coming in? 'Cause I gotta do this, I gotta do this,' so she's absolutely the one to [budget]."[90]

Cohabitation

The well-being benefits of cohabitation can be equal to those of marriage, especially in cultures that accept cohabitation, all dependent on trust, communication, and styles of conflict-resolution.[91,92] Indeed, writer

Mandy Len Catron argued that the well-being benefits of cohabitation exceed those of marriage. "When my partner, Mark, and I talk about whether or not we want to get married, friends tend to assume that we are trying to decide whether or not we are 'serious' about our relationship. But I'm not expressing doubts about my relationship; I'm doubting the institution itself."[93]

Catron accepts her married friends' point about the intangible well-being benefits of marriage in feelings of belonging and security but notes the costs of these benefits. She described the work of sociologists Natalia Sarkisian and Naomi Gerstel who found that marriage weakens other social ties. Married people are less likely than singles to socialize with friends and neighbors, visit or call parents and siblings, or offer emotional support and pragmatic help. "It isn't the circumstances of married life that isolate," wrote Catron, "it's marriage itself." Yet evidence indicates that the well-being benefits of marriage are generally higher than those of cohabitation.[94]

The well-being advantage of marriage over cohabitation comes from marriage's greater stability, reflected in feelings of belonging and security noted by Catron. Sociologists Bradford Wilcox and Laurie DeRose noted that marriage increases stability by elaborate wedding rituals, norms of commitment, fidelity, permanence, and distinctive treatment by family and friends. In contrast, the very freedom and flexibility that makes cohabitation attractive, make it less stable. Wilcox and DeRose found that almost half of cohabiting American college-educated mothers break up with their partners before their child turns 12, whereas less than one-fifth of mothers who were married when the child was born do so. The same is true in Europe. Children born to cohabiting couples are about 90% more likely to witness their parents' breakup by the time they turn 12 than children born to married parents[95]

Moreover, psychologists Scott Stanley Galena Rhoades found that couples who cohabitate before marriage were more likely to see their marriages end than those who did not. This is especially true for those who started cohabiting before being engaged.[96] Reasons for moving in together matter. People who reported that their top reason for cohabiting was in testing their relationship or in finances were more likely to see their marriages end than those who did so because they wanted to spend more time with their partner. Also, those who have had more prior cohabiting partners were more likely to see their marriages end.

6

Widowhood and Divorce

Betty Rollin is an author and former television news correspondent. She is also a widow. A friend assumed that Rollin had moved on, more than a year after she had lost her husband. "Apparently, the correct amount of time is a year or so," said Rollin. "Apparently, I wasn't doing the recovery thing right."[1]

Rollin offered a few pointers to friends of widows: Don't disappear after one sympathetic email with your widowed friend. Don't tell sad stories about your other widowed friends. Don't assume that all widows have overcome their grief in a year or so. Don't assume anything about widows' finances. "My Christian friends sent flowers; my Jewish friends sent food. Food is better."

Joseph Chuman, a widower of six years, balked at the designation of "prolonged grief disorder" as a mental disorder in the *DSM-5*, known as psychiatry's bible. Grief is not "an emotional state that one passes through to emerge on the other side as one was before," he wrote. "Grief is transformative, and I am not the same person I was before my beloved wife died."

In the first several months after his wife's death, he was consumed by overwhelming emotions. With the passage of time, he was able to regain his normal functioning, able to work, socialize with others, and laugh. But beneath the surface he felt lonely, sad, and empty.

More men have died in the COVID-19 pandemic than women, leaving behind many widows. "It's very traumatic because of the unexpectedness of it," said one widow. "He made it back from two deployments [in Iraq]. He came home and this is what killed him."[2]

Younger widows in the COVID-19 pandemic are left with the daunting task of raising small children on their own. "This whole experience is so depleting and so draining," said the widowed mother of a 5-year-old daughter. "You have to lead your kid by example. You want them to be happy, and you're showing them how to behave."

Widowhood diminishes well-being and increases depression, but its effects are stronger among men than among women, in part, because men attend church less frequently than women and dislike household chores more intensely.[3]

Widowhood increases mortality from almost all causes, including cancers, infections, and cardiovascular diseases.[4] Yet widowers are more likely to die soon after the death of their spouses than widows, in part, because widows maintain social relationships and friendships outside of marriage, whereas widowers isolate themselves, losing these social relationships and support groups.

A woman responding to an article about widowhood[5] wrote: "My cousin and I, at 70, lost our husbands within the same year. Both of us are lifelong friends, and each has her own home—hers is in the city, mine in the country . . . we opened our homes and our routines, and friends to each other, becoming companions at events, trips, and in many evenings just hanging out."

Indeed, friendship can obviate the desire or need to remarry. "With friends aplenty, many widows choose singlehood," wrote journalist Anne Roark, describing Jane Austin, a retired schoolteacher who became a widow at age 69. She misses her husband, but has no desire to remarry.[6] "Most of the men I know who are widowed are not comfortable in their own homes alone," Austin said. "Either they seek replacement wives as housekeepers and social directors, or they end up in a chair watching CNN and the cooking channels . . . waiting for the end."

The likelihood of death of a widower is highest in the first month of widowhood. Among men that likelihood does not decline much until the sixth month of widowhood, and among women it does not decline much until the third month of widowhood.[7] The death of husbands often reduces widows to poverty, even when widows were not poor when married. A 1987 study by economists Michael Hurd and David Wise found that whereas only about 9% of couples are poor, approximately 35% of the subsequent widows are. A large proportion of the wealth of couples is lost when husbands die. Moreover, couples of subsequent poor widows earned and saved less than couples of subsequent nonpoor widows, more of their smaller accumulated wealth was lost at the death of the husband, and absence of survivorship benefits or life insurance leaves widows poor thereafter.[8]

More recent evidence indicates a general improvement in the financial situation of widows.[9] A 2018 study by economist Alicia Munnell and coauthors found that widows' poverty rate declined from 20% in

1994 to 13% in 2014. They also found that the decline in poverty rate is due mostly to increases in the education of women and greater labor force participation among them.[10]

Both widows and widowers lose much weight after the deaths of their spouses. They are more likely to eat meals alone, lose appetite, and find less enjoyment in meals than they once did. This is especially true among older widows and those with lower cognitive functioning scores.[11] "For many widows, the hardest part is mealtime," wrote journalist Amelia Nierenberg, describing Michele Zawadzki who lost her husband, Bill, after a 47-year marriage. Zawadzki was struck by her feelings when walking supermarket aisles, past the foods he loved. "There are triggers everywhere with food," she said. "You get home, you're still by yourself, and you're used to cooking a certain way. It's debilitating."[12] Economist Maja Adena and coauthors traced the evolution of well-being of women who become widowed by comparing them with their matched nonwidowed. They found a dramatic decrease in mental health and well-being after the loss of a partner, caused mostly by increased time spent alone.[13]

Yet both widows and widowers can be resilient.[14] Journalist Jane Brody quoted Stephen Goodman, a retired periodontist and widower. "It helps to be a positive, directed person." Joyce, Goodman's wife, used to write the monthly checks. But when she died, Goodman put them all on automatic pay and learned to do laundry and run the dishwasher. Brody herself, now a widow, learned to fold the sheets of the bed she shared for 43 years with a husband who had always helped. And when she goes to the movies alone, she now asks strangers to explain plot twists that baffle her.[15]

A woman responding to Brody's article described her resilience. She got her house in order with a new high-efficiency HVAC system, insulation, fencing, and paint. She traveled a lot on her own, including a wonderful trip to Italy. And she cuts her own grass. "I am not a religious person," she said. "My husband died; he didn't go to his eternal reward! But I know how he felt about most things and I regularly consult with him! I have been surprised at my own emotional resilience—it has carried me through. Life is still good."

Divorce

Honor Jones was contemplating a kitchen renovation in the house she shared with her husband when she slowly realized that what she really wanted was a divorce. Marriage satisfied Jones's material needs, fulfilling the expectations of the first marriage era, and also love, fulfilling the expectations of the second, but marriage did not fulfill her third era expectations of self-discovery and personal growth. "Everything I experienced—relationships, reality, my understanding of my own identity and desires—were filtered through him before I could access them," she said. "How much of my life—I mean the architecture of my life, but also its essence, my soul, my mind—had I built around my husband? Who could I be if I wasn't his wife?" Now, divorced, she felt raw, and liked it. "There was nothing between me and the world. It was as if I'd been wearing sunglasses and then taken them off, and suddenly everything looked different. Not better or worse, just clearer, harsher. Cold wind on my face."[16]

Divorced people suffer lower well-being than married ones, but divorce itself does not necessarily diminish well-being.[17] Indeed, as evident in the words of Honor Jones, divorce generally enhances well-being by dissolving unsatisfying marriages.[18,19]

Is divorce too easy now? Has the pendulum swing too far into the third era where divorce follows unfulfilled expectations of self-discovery and personal growth? Anglican priest Tish Harrison Warren thinks so. "We hear stories of people leaving a marriage as an act of self-love," she wrote, "to embark on a personal, spiritual, or sexual journey of self-discovery. There's even a new trend of divorce celebration parties." In contrast, she wrote, staying in a disappointing marriage for the children or because of a religious commitment or for some other mundane reason is seen as "inauthentic and uncreative, lacking in boldness and a zest for life."

Harrison Warren shared the lessons she had learned in her marriage. "I married the wrong person," she wrote, "and I'm so glad I did." She and her husband married young, and the 17 years since their wedding included long stretches of unhappiness, sometimes descending into yelling and contempt. But they are learning to love each other with each passing day. "There are nights when he sits quietly reading, and I look at his face and recall what a steep hill we've climbed and will keep climbing, and I am overwhelmed with gratitude that he has stuck with me, that we get to live this life together, with all the sorrow, betrayal, glory, loveliness, surprise, and mystery that entails."[20] Yet Harrison Warren is glad that divorce is available to people, usually women, in abusive marriages and relationships. Author Amy Butcher experienced such a relationship. She and her partner were on a road trip in their 20s when one evening he became enraged suddenly and uncontrollably, and she feared, ready to kill her.

Butcher was embarrassed to tell anyone that the person she loved was someone who could be so cruel to her. The photos she placed on social media gave no hint of his abuse. "No one would have believed how scared of him I was as I posted my cheerful images, and I wouldn't have really believed it, either, because we don't think these things happen to us until they do."[21]

"Shame permeates the experience of intimate partner violence," wrote law professor Rachel Camp. "People who perpetrate intimate partner violence commonly use tactics designed to cause shame in their partners, including denigrating their dignity, undermining their autonomy, or harming their reputation." Shame diminishes well-being as it devastates a person's sense of self-worth. Protection orders are the most common legal intervention for intimate partner violence, but survivors asking for them are forced to deprive themselves of their privacy and ability to control their self-image, experiences rooted in shame.[22]

The stay-at-home and social distancing policies of COVID-19 and its economic consequences were associated with an increase of intimate partner violence. The impact of economic consequences was double that of lockdown, and the increase of intimate partner violence was especially large where the relative position of the man worsened, especially where that position was already threatened.[23]

Violation of the social norms of a husband earning more than his wife or ranking higher in social status increase the likelihood of divorce. The probability of divorce doubles when wives are promoted to the top jobs of mayor, parliamentarian, or CEO. Divorces following such promotions are concentrated in gender-traditional couples, whereas rates of divorce in gender-equal marriages are unaffected.[24]

Disrespect can lead to divorce even in the absence of abuse. Author Jancee Dunn told the story of Matthew Fray, who failed to pick up after himself during his marriage.[25] "She divorced me because I left dishes by the sink," he said. Every time she walked into the kitchen to discover a drinking glass by the sink, inches from the dishwasher, she moved closer to ending their marriage. Of course, it wasn't about the glass. "It felt to her like I just said, 'Not taking four seconds to put my glass in the dishwasher is more important to me than you are.'" Now he coaches spouses about avoiding his mistakes.

Political disputes can be severe enough to break marriages. Journalist John Whitesides described 73-year-old Gayle McCormick, who separated from her husband of 22 years over attitudes toward Donald Trump. "It totally undid me that he could vote for Trump," she said. She, a Democrat leaning toward socialist, suffered through her marriage to a conservative Republican, but felt betrayed by his support for Trump.[26]

Differences in well-being between husband and wife can lead to separation and divorce even in the absence of disputes and disrespect. Economist Cahit Guven and coauthors noted that each spouse compares their well-being to that of the other, and both are averse to unequal well-being.

Moreover, Guven and coauthors found that the likelihood of separation and divorce is especially high when the well-being of a wife is lower than that of her husband, a finding reflected in the title of their article, "You can't be happier than your wife." Indeed, divorces are predominantly initiated by women, especially by women whose well-being is lower than that of their husbands.[27]

Divorces vary by amiability and expense. Journalist Deborah Copaken described her Do-It-Yourself divorce, inexpensive but less than amicable.[28] When she first made her painful decision to end her marriage, she was told that a divorce lawyer will ask for a $30,000 retainer just to get the process started. Copaken and her husband had two children, debt, but no assets and surely not $30,000, so they tried a mediator. "Big mistake," she wrote. "Though we both had a stated desire to keep things civil, the nature of our particular dysfunction was evident . . . torpedoing mediation as a viable alternative." It also left them with an additional $1,400 debt. Then she learned that she can represent herself at a divorce proceeding, obviating the need for a lawyer. The judge granted their divorce after they resolved a nerve-wracking disagreement about custody of their children.

Other divorces are expensive but amicable. These include the divorce by a private judge of Sergey Brin, Google cofounder, from Anne Wojcicki, founder of 23andMe, and also those of Bill and Melinda French Gates, and Jeff Bezos and MacKenzie Scott.

Yet other divorces are expensive and far from amicable. These include the divorce of Allison Huynh from Scott Hassan. Hassan rewrote the code of the slow web crawler by Larry Page and worked with Sergey Brin to build the search engine which eventually became Google. In 1998, Hassan bought 160,000 shares of Google for $800 that subsequently turned into many billions.[29] Huynh has accused Hassan of "divorce terrorism," claiming that he had told her that he planned to "bury her" and make sure that she "gets nothing." Hassan denied saying that, but noted that divorce is never easy, "and no one is at their best."

Divorce is unlikely to drive wealthy Scott Hassan and Allison Huynh into poverty, but it drives into poverty many couples with modest wealth, especially women with young children at home. Journalist Darlena Cunah quoted economist Stephen Jenkins: "The key differences are not between men and women, but between fathers and mothers." The poverty rate among separated women is 27%, almost three times that of separated men.[30] Cunah described a 38-year-old woman who had a well-paying job, perfect credit, substantial savings, and a seemingly happy marriage before her divorce. She and her husband decided that she would leave her job when their first daughter was born, and they abandoned the thought of her going back to work when their second daughter was born. Yet her husband filed for divorce seven years after they were married. "He said he was tired of my medical issues, and unwilling to work on things. . . . He kicked me out of my own house, with no job and no home, and then my only recourse was to lawyer up. I'm paying them on credit."

Divorce also drives into poverty some older women accounting for one in three U.S. divorces. Journalist Paula Span described Cynthia Palazzo, a 61-year-old woman who had spent most of her married years raising three sons. She was paid for her work in the manufacturing company she started with her husband, but never opened a retirement savings account. When she divorced after almost 30 years of marriage, Palazzo found a $17-an-hour job in medical billing, then lost it but found another. With spousal support, "I'm okay now," she said. She bought a condominium but feels stressed, knowing that she will be paying a mortgage until she is 80. "I basically started life over at 54."[31]

Children in divorce

Many children feel as if their worlds are falling apart when their parents divorce, and worries about the welfare of the children keep many parents in unhappy marriages. "My worst sense of well-being was the months and years leading up to [my divorce]," said Ruth, a 38-year-old

British woman interviewed by BlackRock. "I couldn't change a situation I desperately wanted to for fear of ruining my children's lives."[32]

Divorce came unexpectedly to Natalie Muñoz, an 8-year-old only child who grew up with two loving parents, reading books with her mother on weekdays and playing outside with her father on weekends. That happy life was suddenly interrupted when her parents came into the living room, switched off the TV, and "began to explain how their marriage wasn't working out, and how they were splitting up but remaining friends." Writing seven years later, at 15, Muñoz described fantasizing about her parents getting back together again before adjusting to her parents' divorce. She used to mourn the invisible person who linked her family together. "And I've since come to realize something—that person is me. I'm the link. I'm the biggest constant in our lives. I have been all along, and I'm glad I always will be."[33]

"Is divorce bad for children?" asked psychologists Hal Arkowitz and Scott Lilienfeld in an article by the same name. The breakup may be painful, but most kids adjust well over time," they answered.[34] Children of divorcing parents often feel as if their worlds are falling apart, and parents fear for the welfare of their children. Many children react to divorce with anxiety, anger, shock, and disbelief, but reactions typically subside by the end of the second year following the divorce.

Most children of divorce also do well in the years that follow. There are only small differences between children of divorced parents and those from intact families in academic achievements, emotional and behavior problems, delinquency, self-concept, and social relationships, suggesting that the vast majority of children adjust well.

Parental discord, rather than divorce, is associated with poor outcomes for children. Indeed, children of high-discord parents tend to adjust to divorce quickly because they anticipate it and perhaps welcome it as relief from their parents' discord. In contrast, children in low-discord families are surprised and perhaps terrified by their parents' divorce, retarding their adjustment.

Children of divorce fare better if parents limit children's exposure to it during the divorce process or minimize it. Also, children who live with at least one well-functioning parent do better than those whose primary parent is doing poorly. And parental behaviors, such as warmth and emotional support, can buffer the effects of divorce on children. So can post-divorce economic stability and social support from friends and teachers.[35]

Novelist Joyce Maynard described divorcing in 1989 when she and her husband were in their 30s, after 12 years of marriage. Their marriage began to crumble early on, as she wanted connection and her husband wanted space. They promised their 5-, 7-, and 11-year-old children that they will always love them and always care for each other. "I can still see their faces, not buying it," she wrote. The children turned out well, and now, more than 30 years later, she is offering the lessons she had learned. "As much as you need to forgive your partner, you need to forgive yourself as well," she wrote. No parent bears full responsibility for their children's future sorrows or pain. "To suppose that my divorce could set my children's future in stone was an exaggeration of my powers as a parent. In the end, each of us charts our own path."[36]

Many readers were not buying it. One wrote: "A divorce is not just the dissolution of a marriage; it is the destruction of a family. Once you have kids, it is not about you and your 'happiness' anymore . . . the kids are the only thing that matter."

Another recounted a question posed to his adult daughter by her good friend. Did she know what day it is? Their daughter did not know, and the friend said, "It is the anniversary of the day our parents told us they were getting divorced." That friend has a healthy relationship with her parents and has made a good marriage. So, on the surface, the divorce did not ultimately hurt her. Yet after almost 40 years, she remembers the day she learned of the split as clearly as she remembers birthdays and other happier occasions. "Divorce is usually not good for the children no matter how you frame it."

But another wrote: "If I hadn't divorced my first wife, I'd be dead from stress by now. My second wife is a wonderful woman, and I am keeping her. Sometimes it is best to just move on. . . ."

7

Parents and Children

"Isn't it bad enough that the beloved, with whom you have experienced genuine joy, will eventually be lost to you?" wrote novelist Zadie Smith, describing parenting as a strange mixture of terror, pain, and delight. "Why add to this nightmare the child, whose loss, if it ever happened, would mean nothing less than your total annihilation?"[1]

Total annihilation was the nightmare experienced by Choi Seon-mi, whose 19-year-old daughter Park Ga-young died in the 2022 Halloween crush in Seoul. "What to do about my child? What to do about my child?" cried Ms. Choi, her head and arms pressed against the wall of a community center where families were waiting to find out about their loved ones. She collapsed when her daughter's death was confirmed, overcome by grief. "She was a beautiful child," she said, holding a photo of her daughter before she broke down in tears.[2]

Sociologists Rachel Margolis and Mikko Myrskylä found that parents' well-being increases before first birth, likely reflecting the process of formation of partnership and the increase in its quality, but well-being soon decreases to its pre-birth levels.[3] Journalist Jason Stanford rejected these findings, based on his experience and that of his friends.[4]

"Of course, having young children is hard," admitted Stanford. "Having a newborn in the house feels like a permanent hangover without ever having fun in the first place." Yet he recalled a friend's counsel: "Don't worry, wait till he smiles at you."

"To this day," wrote Stanford, "there is nothing that makes me happier when my first son forgets he's a teenager and smiles, taking me all the way back to when his soft head fit into the palm of my hand and the rest of his body rested along my forearm. . . . When I fell, I fell hard."

Many parents share Stanford's experience, describing their increased well-being at the birth of their children. "I felt very comfortable and with a strong sense of well-being right after my daughter was born," said Bill, the previously mentioned 52-year-old American man. "For several weeks after her birth, I stayed home with her and my wife and I felt very comfortable."[5]

"When my first daughter was born, I felt happy and tired and strange all at the same time. It was a great and completely new experience in my life," said Adolfo, a 32-year-old Mexican man. And Xiaoying, the 33-year-old Chinese woman, said: "Having my daughter in my belly for nine months and getting to see her. It was a sense of anticipation and a feeling of responsibility towards her."

Others, however, echo the findings of Margolis and Myrskylä. Divya, the previously mentioned 33-year-old American woman, struggled with diminished well-being following the birth of her first child. She seldom had time for herself, she was never able to exercise, she didn't like her appearance, and most of all, she had a hard time with her daughter who was always getting sick. "It was a whole new world for me to bring this little human into the world and I was not prepared for it."

Yet others speak wistfully about life before children. Journalist Jessica Grose described her COVID-era fantasy, recalling a paddle boat ride on her honeymoon. "I have a visceral memory of raising my face to the sun, lazily paddling around while the sea breeze gently flowed around me. I recall that moment when I'm tossing and turning in these pandemic times; I felt so relaxed and free then . . . because I didn't have kids."[6]

Parents enhance the well-being of children by the utilitarian benefits of food and housing. Children reciprocate with utilitarian support as necessary when parents grow old, providing money and care in their parents' homes or their own. And parents and children enhance the well-being of one another by the expressive and emotional benefits of security, support, and love.

Economists John Ifcher and Chris Herbst found that the well-being of parents increased relative to nonparents during the last few decades.[7] They argued that the increase is due, in part, to the benefits of families as the last vestige of community life in an American society where people are "bowling alone," isolated from one another.

Journalist Tanya Basu quoted Herbst: "Parents are more likely to spend time with friends, get the news, be interested in politics, think people are honest, have faith in the economy, be trusting." Parents socializing in PTA meetings are one example of community life, and so are parents socializing over their children's playdates.[8] Moreover, children protect parents against social and economic forces that reduce well-being among nonparents.

Similarly, psychologist Katherine Nelson and coauthors found that parents evaluate their lives more positively than nonparents, feel relatively better day-to-day, and derive more positive feelings from caring for their children than from other daily activities.[9]

Yet parenting is expensive, imposing heavy utilitarian costs. The average total family expenditures on a child born in 2015 to a middle-class family with two children would be $310,605.[10] The burden of high costs of parenting is especially heavy on low-income parents because expenses on food, housing, and gas amount to large portions of their incomes.[11] The high costs of parenting lead many prospective parents to postpone having children or choose not to have them at all. A 2021 Pew Research Center survey found that 26% of Americans between the ages of 18 and 49 said it was "very likely" they will have children someday, a drop from 32% in 2018. The share of those who answered "not too likely" increased from 16% in 2018 to 21% in 2021, continuing a long-term trend.[12]

The expected well-being benefits and costs of parenthood are affected by culture. In the Netherlands, only 5% of people agreed with the statement "You cannot really be happy without having children"; in Belgium, 12%; and in Finland, 22%. In Cyprus, however, 68% agreed with this statement, and in Eastern European countries such as Hungary, Lithuania, Estonia, Czechoslovakia, and (East) Germany, 44–59% agreed.[13] Levels of agreement did not vary much between men and women, but there was much less agreement with the statement among the young and among the highly educated.

There was greater cross-cultural agreement with the statement "watching children grow up is life's greatest joy." Approximately 80–90%, and somewhat more women than men agree with this statement almost everywhere.[14]

Journalist Katherine Zoepf described her struggle to pay parenting costs when she became a single parent, posting her own bedroom on Airbnb and joining her children in their bunk beds.[15] "For about 15 months, the extra income this Airbnb arrangement generated was a lifeline for me and my children, a way to stave off financial catastrophe during a tricky transition in our lives." Zoepf carried her burden in secret, so as not to burden her children.

Many tech companies added benefits to employees in the time of COVID-19, including extra time off for parents caring for young children.[16] Some nonparent employees protested, complaining that companies place parents' needs ahead of theirs. A reader wrote: "Everyone seems to forget that being a parent is, for most people, a choice. . . . Should I not then demand extra privileges because I . . . make other choices that improve my life in other ways? Fairness does demand equal treatment."

But another wrote: "I am in awe of what parents are able to do while working from home. . . . To me, the fact that nonparents at these places are complaining about the 'extras' given to parents . . . speaks to a serious sickness in the corporate culture at these places."

The expressive and emotional costs of parenting increase when children grow into teenagers, navigating puberty which changes hormones, emotions, priorities, and desires. The dramatic changes in puberty creates volatility in teens' behaviors, attitudes, and moods as they prioritize fitting with peers over fitting with family.[17]

The teenage son of Tiffany Lee refused to wear a mask in the time of COVID-19. "He would see all of his classmates having pool parties and going bowling and he's angry at me because I won't let him go," said Lee. "He thinks I'm the bad parent because 'Mom is standing between me and my friends.'" To his mother's relief, the son chose to wear a mask when he returned to school, explaining that he was surprised to find that his friends didn't understand how vaccines work. "I think our relationship is stronger now," said Lee. "I'm not the evil mom he thought I was. And I'm gaining new respect for him."[18]

A reader offered a parallel in the conflict between Anne Frank and her mother. Leafing through her diary, Anne was sometimes taken aback by her own harsh judgments of her mother. In a rewritten version, Anne was kinder. "The period when I caused Mummy to shed tears is over, I have grown wiser and Mummy's nerves are not so much on edge. I usually keep my mouth shut if I get annoyed, and so does she, so we appear to get on much better together."

Another offered a bit of sarcasm, known to all teenagers' parents. "It's a horror show that eats your life and seems to have no end. Oh, and no one understands how awful it is and they all think they have useful advice. I wish this were not happening to you."

The costs of parenting persist when children grow into adults. Average transfers from American parents to adult children are large enough to be considered major spending items. Parents, at least one of whom was between the ages 50–64, transferred to children an annual average of

$8,350. The corresponding average was $4,787 when at least one parent was 85 or older.[19]

Parental support is also common outside the United States. More than 60% of British homebuyers younger than 35 received financial help from their parents, averaging $30,000 in 2019, up from $21,800 in 2016. Young Danes received from their parents an average net transfer of more than $100 per month, and 1 in 10 receives more than $1,000 per month.[20]

Parents are willing to sacrifice a lot for their children. Almost three quarters of parents place their adult children's needs ahead of their own.[21] Planning retirement and money for her children is important to Helen, a 51-year old British woman interviewed by BlackRock, and has an impact on her life. "I need my kitchen remodeled and I don't want to spend any savings as then I feel I may not have enough if anything happens or my children need it."[22]

"My son had a financial problem and was about to have his car repossessed," said Paul, a 70-year old American man. "I provided the funds to pay off his car and eliminate the problem. I was happy I had the ability to help him." Yang, a 51-year old Chinese man, said: "Give [my son] the money earned from rental during these few years to renovate his house, buy new appliances and furniture. . . ." And Jeronimo, the previously mentioned 65-year old Mexican man, said: "I am planning to start a new business that I can pass on to my daughter, given the characteristics of her professional development." Indeed, the well-being of parents is higher when the well-being of their adult children is higher.[23]

"I am retired now," said David, a 71-year-old American man. "I'm on a fixed income but get enough to pay bills and do whatever I want, within reason. I try to help my children as often as I can. You never stop being a parent." James, the previously mentioned 52-year old American man, reacted to David's words, "You never stop being a parent. No truer words have ever been said!" And David added, "You always worry about them. Well, not so much worry, but hope all is well."

Parents never stop being parents everywhere, but culture affects financial help offered by parents to their adult children. Sara Murphy's parents are Iranian-Americans, and Iranian culture continues to influence their support of their adult daughter. "This is my child," said Murphy's mother. "I have money. And then, as long as I am alive, I am responsible."[24]

Jason Rezaian, an Iranian-American writer, received financial support from his grandfather, and knows that his father, who owned a Persian rug business, would support him if necessary. "This idea that we're run out of the house when we're 18 is so opposite of how most Iranians are raised," he said. "We're entering an era already where some of these more traditional Iranian-type values probably make more sense."

Indeed, financial support from American parents to their adult children is increasing as Baby Boomers and other older Americans transfer record amounts to children. Approximately $61 trillion is estimated to be transferred to Millennials and Generation Xers between 2018 and 2042. Moreover, annual gifts from parents to children reported to the Internal Revenue Service amounted to $75 billion in 2016, a fraction to total gifts since most gifts are not reported.

Parental support enables 4-year-olds to delay gratification. In the famous marshmallow experiments, 4-year-olds who withstood the temptation of a marshmallow for 15 minutes received a second marshmallow and went on to do well in school and work. These findings have been interpreted as evidence that internally generated willpower pays great dividends, yet more recent findings indicate that parental support, not willpower, underlies delayed gratification. As sociologist Jessica McCrory Calarco noted, children in poor families may not wait for a second marshmallow because they have little guarantee of parental support. Their parents who wish to fulfill their promises might be forced to renege on them because the money is not there. In contrast, children in affluent families are willing to wait because money is always there to fulfill promises.[25]

Parental support enhances the well-being of children in expressive and emotional benefits beyond utilitarian ones. Adult children receiving support enjoy higher well-being than those who did not receive such support.[26]

Brianna Leavitt received approximately $93,000 after her father died, paying about $32,000 of student debt, $15,000 of credit-card debt, and an $8,000 car loan. The money provided Brianna expressive and emotional benefits in addition to the utilitarian ones. "My dad and I had a tumultuous relationship," she said. "It meant a lot to me knowing this was him taking care of me."[27]

Withdrawal of parental emotional support can reduce the well-being of both children and parents. This is evident when parents follow college leaders' lecture of "don't text or call, let your adult child reach out to you." A mother described the well-being costs of following that lecture. She was missing her son but sitting on her hands rather than texting, while her son thought that his mother no longer cared about him. "We re-established our relationship but it took work."[28]

Yet parents who perceive their adult children as needing too much support suffer lower well-being.[29] A woman wrote to an advice columnist about her 33-year-old son who graduated from college but is now working at minimum wage, and her 25-year-old daughter who works as a barista and spends eight hours each day railing against her parents. "We are thinking about retirement. . . . Should we help them financially? Buy them condos, pay for more schooling, get them cars? It seems like the majority of our friends have done this for their kids, and their relationships are better . . . any advice?[30]

And parental support for adult children often comes with strings that strain relationships, imposing expressive and emotional costs along with utilitarian benefits.[31] These are evident in the voice of Josh Maeir, a software-engineer out of a job, newly dependent on his mother and in-laws. "It feels strange to become dependent after all these years," he said. "My mother and my in-laws help out because they can, because they're generous, and because they really care about us. But there are some strings. . . . Once, when we hired an electrician to fix a ceiling fan, it turned into this big deal because my in-laws considered it to be an extravagance."[32]

Adult children's support to parents can also strain relationships, imposing expressive and emotional costs along with utilitarian benefits. Jean Ley, a 62-year-old woman, could not protect her financial independence when she lost her job, leaving her with little savings. She was grateful for the support of her son, Matt. "If my family weren't able to help me out at this point, I wouldn't have a home," she said. But Matt said, "I think money changes everything. . . . It's a cliché, but when you lend money to a friend, when you lend money to family, it changes things."[33]

Parents with ample financial means find it easier to enhance the well-being of their children and their own.[34,35] On an "everybody seems wealthy" forum an adult child of parents with relatively meager means wrote: "In my social circles . . . it was very common for parents to give their children down payments for houses . . . and sometimes they would also pay for cars, grad school, weddings, etc. . . . I'm seeing people who are regularly getting $28,000/year tax free from their parents as part of their estate planning. Ah, well, can't choose how rich your parents are!"[36]

Parents' wealth can bridge gaps between them and their children or widen them.[37] "Business acumen and bold timing, backed up by swarms of lawyers telling how far to the inch he could push, propelled Harold Simmons into the ranks of the nation's billionaires," wrote journalist Allen Myerson. "But early last year, with his entire fortune at stake, those attributes failed him in negotiations with his own daughters." Fearing a large tax bill, he demanded that his four daughters sign papers that would dissolve a trust for them. Two of his daughters sued, presenting themselves as victims of a tyrannical father.

Those who know the Simmons clan best see the case as evidence that you can, indeed, be far too rich. "I would say that everybody can learn a lesson—what money can do to a family," said Simmons's older brother.

Parents with ample means do not fear the costs of childcare, college tuition, a house, or even a trust fund, but some fear that their children will grow aimless, dependent on their trust funds, and resentful if their inheritance is too small.[38]

One heir, an intelligent man with an MBA from a top school, quit one job after another. "At some point, something would happen at each job that those who have to work for an income would learn to tolerate, and he'd just say, 'I don't want to deal with this.' Eventually he had to say, 'I don't have a career.'"[39]

Fathers derive greater well-being from parenthood than mothers, reporting higher well-being in interactions with their children than in other activities, whereas mothers report lower well-being.[40] This might be because fathers play with their children more than mothers, whereas mothers care for them more than fathers. "I have two wonderful daughters," said a father interviewed by Pew. "Both are very young and their innocence, joy, happiness, and absolute trust in me add such meaning and grant me a wonderful reprieve from more adult concerns. It's easy to forget what's wrong in the world when you are pretending to be a puppy with your daughter."[41]

The biological changes fathers undergo in the process of becoming fathers are not as obvious as those of mothers, but becoming a father is as biological as becoming a mother. Testosterone, the stereotypically male hormone, motivates men to find partners, but being successful fathers requires focusing on the family and resisting the urge to seek other partners. The birth of a child diminishes testosterone in men and elevates oxytocin and dopamine, the bonding hormones that bring rewards when men interact with their children.[42]

Indeed, childbirth is a turning point. Among women, criminal arrests drop markedly in the first months of pregnancy, stabilizing at half of pre-pregnancy levels three years after birth. Among men, there is a sustained 20% decline in crime that begins at pregnancy. These effects are concentrated among first-time parents, indicating a permanent change in preferences.[43]

Stories of children fathered by the mail carrier are exaggerated, but obsession with cuckolded men persists.[44] Until the 20th century, it was difficult to prove that a particular man was the biological father of a particular child, but DNA sequencing, ubiquitous since the 1990s, made it easy. It turns out that the cuckoldry rate is less than 1% everywhere, in Belgium, Spain, Italy, Germany, and agricultural villages in Mali.

Yet cuckoldry occurs. Revelations from a DNA test were devastating to Mike L., prompting him to divorce his wife, but he had not renounced their daughter, and continued to pay her child support.[45] But Mike found it unbearable supporting his daughter when he learned that his ex-wife was about to marry the man who is the girl's biological father. He asked the Pennsylvania courts to declare that he was no longer the father of his daughter.[46] Still, Mike loves his daughter. "Just because our relationship started because of someone else's lie," he said, "doesn't mean the bond that developed isn't real." This bond, however, became entangled with humiliation and outrage.

Parents' contributions to their children are regularly rewarded by the expressive benefits of high social status and the emotional benefits of pride. Jihong, a 55-year old Chinese woman interviewed by BlackRock, said: "My son told me he was going to be posted to Japan for work and I felt really happy. It felt as though my son had grown up, both in terms of career and in life. The sense of pride I feel is really different."[47]

Parents' pride is not always about major accomplishments of their children. A teacher asked parents to complete the sentence "I'm proud of my child because. . . ."[48] One parent wrote simply, "He is my son." Others wrote: "She has a lot of challenges and overcomes each one with a positive attitude"; "He is caring, respectful, and kind. He likes to help others, and he has compassion for those in need"; and "She is responsible, a hard worker, very helpful, very thoughtful of her sisters and brothers, and she makes her own car and insurance payments."

Children are often slow to comprehend their parents' pride in them. The mother of marketing scholar Lan Nguyen Chaplin fled Vietnam while pregnant with her. "She was so strong-willed that without speaking any English, she brought all of her children to America safely, located my dad five years later, and was a master lie detector who kept her 14 kids in line."

Nguyen Chaplin's mother expected her to follow a path to success rooted in 1950s' Vietnamese culture, but she chose a different path. During their last deep conversation, her mother took her by surprise. "It was the first instance she expressed pride in who I was. I was 32 years old."[49]

Parents seeking the expressive and emotional benefits of high social status and pride are sometimes tempted to brag about their children. Writer Jane Parent described a former friend who used to brag about her children's grades and athletic accomplishments. One day, exasperated, she bragged back about the test scores of her son, and soon regretted descending to the level of that friend . . . "it didn't feel so good later to know that I had not been my best self."

Deb, another former friend of the bragging mom, said "I love my kids, but to be honest, my son has a learning disability and sometimes, getting a C is for him a complete victory. When she brags about all of her kids' accomplishments, things my son will never achieve, I just can't take it."[50]

At times, however, parents suffer expressive and emotional costs in low social status and shame.[51] Therapist Harriet Lerner described a mother who began therapy soon after her 16-year-old son burned down a building. The event was front-page news in the small community where people had already been gossiping that this boy was descending from loser to low-life, and how his parents' acrimonious divorce damaged him. "I feel tainted," said the mother, describing the visceral sense of shame poured onto her from the outside. "It's like the shame of my son is oozing on to me."

The searing pain of shame drives some parents to choose death over life. A man awaiting extradition to the United States on murder charges committed suicide in his prison cell in France, where he fled. His parents committed suicide earlier, saying in a note that they could not bear the shame of what their son had done.[52]

Estrangement between parents and children can be based on accurate perception of reality or its misperception. Journalist Jane Brody noted that rifts can come from years of accumulated grievances that were never resolved, or from an old trauma that distorts perceptions of reality.[53]

A reader of Brody's article wrote. "My parents were (and my mother still is) seriously abusive, and so I cut them out of my life. . . . I did reconcile with them at one point, but then they turned around and hurt me terribly once again. No more. As a child, I had few choices. Now I can choose my family—and I have."[54]

Another wrote: "Out of the blue, during one of my (at least) weekly visits with my mother, she thought for a moment, took a deep breath, looked me directly in the eye and said "I don't like you. . . . I've just NEVER liked you. . . . Her words released me. . . . Sometimes estrangements are honest, and that honesty allows those involved to pivot to a more authentic life."[55]

Estrangements can also begin with conflicts about finances, religion, or politics. Leslie, a politically liberal 35-year-old woman, hoped that the riot at the U.S. Capitol on January 6, 2021, would serve as a wake-up call for her Trump-supporting parents. Instead, she found that her mother was among the rioters. Before, said Leslie, "there was a sense that perhaps there was some way to reconcile." Now, "it felt like a death, honestly."[56]

Racial prejudice was the cause of estrangement in journalist Robert Klemko's family. He described his father, a white man, whose mother rejected his marriage to a Black woman. When her son got married, the mother burned most of his childhood photos and sent him the rest, with a black marker scrawl on each, "Nigger Lover."[57]

Parenting children as hothouse plants or field plants, helicoptered or free-range

A man called the police, alarmed at the sight of a 14-month toddler in a stroller outside a Manhattan restaurant. The police arrested the parents who were dining inside, an actress from Copenhagen and her husband, and the city's Administration for Children's Services placed the toddler in foster care until ordered returned by a judge.[58]

Most parents interviewed in Manhattan said that the couple was negligent in leaving the child outside. Parents in Copenhagen, however, were astonished by the story. "Come on, we do this all the time," said a Copenhagen woman as she sat in a cafe while her 7-month-old son slept in his stroller outside. "We go in for a cup of coffee, sit so we can see the stroller, go out and check once in a while and that's it."

The practices of parenthood and their well-being benefits and costs vary by period, culture, and social class, highlighted by sociologist Viviana Zelizer. The arrival of a newborn in 18th-century America was welcomed for the utilitarian benefits of a child as a future worker and as security for parents in old age. By the mid-19th century, however, children of the urban elite ceased to provide utilitarian benefits as workers, but continued to provide expressive and emotional benefits in love, smiles, and success that made parents proud. Children, in Zelizer's language, became "sacralized," economically worthless but emotionally priceless.[59]

The process of sacralization was slower among the working-class and poor, as industry gained in the late 19th century, increasing the utilitarian benefits of children as workers. These utilitarian benefits are reflected in issuance of insurance policies on lives of children younger than 10. Some among the elite decried such insurance as profanation of children's lives as if parents derive nothing more than utilitarian benefits from their children, "ready to traffic in their offspring as if they were horses or goats."

This, however, was an excessively harsh judgment of working-class and poor parents. Parents always loved their children, and derived expressive and emotional benefits from their relationships with them. A judge presiding in a trial concerning the death of a young child noted the utilitarian benefits that children provide to their parents: "[A] father is entitled to the earnings of a minor child. . . . He has a pecuniary interest in the life of a minor child." Yet he also noted the expressive and emotional benefits that children provide. "Among the poorer classes, parents are very fond of their children"[60] By the early 20th century, working-class and poor parents joined elite parents in sacralizing their children.

Sacralization of children imposes responsibilities on today's parents not shouldered by their own parents or grandparents, including responsibility for "fat-proofing" their children. A study of two major parenting magazines in the United States and Canada during 1983–2014 shows that, in the early years, the magazines described children as responsible for their own fatness, whereas more recently the magazines described an "obesity epidemic" in increasingly frightening words, urging parents, especially mothers, to assume responsibility for reducing children's fatness by diligent intervention.[61]

Sacralization is reflected in the transition of American children from free-range, allowed to roam within limits, to being hovered over by parents and other adults. This transition is fairly recent, dating perhaps to 1979, when news reports dwelled on Etan Patz, a 6-year-old Manhattan boy who vanished on the way to his school's bus stop.

Psychologist Roger Hart found that in the early 1970s 4- and 5-year-old American children were allowed to roam their neighborhoods alone, and 10-year-olds were allowed to roam the entire town alone. Forty years later, although the crime rate has not increased, children are forbidden from roaming beyond their own backyards.[62]

Journalist Stephanie Murray told the story of writer Anna Rollins who went on a stroll with her 5-year-old son. "Always itching to do things himself, the boy announced that he wanted to walk alone." When Rollins refused, he offered a compromise. He would walk on one side of the row of the street, she would walk on the other, and they would meet at the far end. The distance was short and traffic was light, so Rollins agreed, thinking this is a good start to independence. But Rollin's son was not at the meeting place when she arrived. Panicked, she searched for her son. "Finally, she spotted him with an elderly couple across the road. "Is this your little boy?" the woman asked as Rollins hurried over. "He was out by himself." Rollins tried to explain—the boy's request, the plan, independence—to little avail. "Merry Christmas," the woman said icily as she handed the boy back.[63]

Disagreements about parenting practices cause friction. Journalist Michelle Buteau practices helicopter parenting, whereas her husband, born and raised in the Netherlands, practices free-range parenting that includes "dropping" children and letting them find their way home.[64]

"These differences in our backgrounds have created an interesting push-and-pull. And by 'interesting,' I mean 'annoying,'" wrote Buteau. "To my husband, I'm not just a helicopter mom. I'm a drone-on-top-of-a-snowplow mom. To me, my husband is too casual and relaxed. Toddler time is not a Jimmy Buffett concert!"[65]

An American reader noted that helicopter parenting in the United States is recent. "When I was a kid in the 1960s in a smallish town, we roamed all over the place with no adults in sight. Miles from home. . . . All my mother knew is that we were out playing. . . . The only real warning we followed was 'don't get in a car with a stranger.'"

Another, a Dutch woman, noted that Americans' notions of free-range Dutch children are exaggerated. "The 'dropping' of children is a very well-organized game for school-camps." Hidden all around the children are adults keeping the children safe preventing them from being lost. "We Dutch may be [more relaxed] about raising our kids, but we are not stupid! We teach them how to live in this world, and yes, they bike at an early age . . . next to mommy in the traffic."

Some elite American parents have moved somewhat away from helicopter parenting toward free-range parenting, but these moves come with a double standard, perceived as a corrective to helicopter parenting when practiced by the elite, but criticized as neglectful when practiced by the working-class and poor. [66]

Sociologist Annette Lareau describes the parenting style of the American elite as "concerted cultivation," and that of the American working-class and poor as "accomplishment of natural growth."[67] Sociologists Kathryn Edin and Maria Kefalas described *concerted cultivation* more vividly as tending to children as "hothouse plants," growing in soil is concertedly cultivated and fertilized by enriching playtime at children's early age, turning to extracurricular activities, such as music lessons, as they enter elementary school, and preparation for top universities as they enter high school. They described accomplishment of natural growth as tending to children as "field plants," expected to grow naturally.[68]

The transition from field parenting to hothouse parenting among elite parents is evident in a study of parenting magazines in four English-speaking industrialized countries from 1959 to 2000. It shows a transition from a focus on fun activities to an increasing focus on children's academic skills and cognitive development.[69]

Helicopter parenting is practiced by elite parents when children are young, and hothouse parenting is practiced by them when the children are a bit older. "I just felt that with the kids being in seventh grade and fourth grade, they were kind of getting to that age where . . . the babysitter does not cut it," said Denise Hortas, an elite woman in a demanding executive position to sociologists Pamela Stone and Meg Lovejoy. "When they're littler, they need people to be nice to them, and feed them, and take care of them, and smile at them. Little children ask 'When am I gonna have a cookie?' But as they get older, they ask you amazing questions and it's important how you answer that question—it has to do more with your values. . . ." Hortas left her executive position when her children were 9 and 12 to engage in hothouse parenting.[70,71,72]

Elite parents assess their success by their children's accomplishments. Asked whether she is a good mother, an elite woman is likely to say that she will know in 20 years, when she knows her children's SAT scores, the list of colleges that accepted them, and their career trajectories.[73] Elite parents challenge children to formulate questions for doctors, teach them to shake hands and look adults in the eye, broaden their vocabularies, and model how to demand action from social institutions.

Working-class and poor parents focus on providing children's basic needs while allowing them to develop their talents naturally. These children engage in fewer structured activities, more interaction with siblings, and clearer boundaries between adults and children. Whereas elite children learn to demand what they want, working-class and poor children learn to accept what is.

Working-class and poor parents expect their children to be silently obedient in the presence of adults, and emulate their parents' unease in their interactions with school officials and medical professionals. They assess their success by providing what is necessary for natural growth, shelter, food, and clothes, and basic knowledge of numbers and letters.

Sociologist Patrick Ishizuka found that working-class and poor parents increasingly say that they share the hothouse parenting norms of the elite, yet their parenting behaviors differ markedly from those of the elite.[74]

Ishizuka asked parents of all social classes to choose the best responses to vignettes. One response corresponds to hothouse parenting and the other to field parenting. For example, one vignette contrasts hothouse parenting of structured activities to field parenting of unstructured activities.

"Summer has ended, and the school year has just started again. Michael's daughter complains that she's been feeling bored after school." In hothouse parenting Michael says: "How about we look into different activities for you to do after school? What about signing up for a sports team or doing music lessons?" In field parenting Michael says: "How about you go outside and play with your friends? You can go play as long as you're being careful and are home before dinner."

Another vignette contrasts hothouse parenting of patient, well-articulated parental explanations of household rules and encouragement of reasoning and negotiation, to field parenting by directive. "It's late on a school night, and Angela repeatedly tells her daughter it's bedtime. Angela's daughter yells: 'I hate your rules! They're so unfair!'" In hothouse parenting, Angela says, "We can talk about why you think the rules are unfair, but first we need to have a conversation about your behavior." In field parenting, Angela says: "A rule is a rule whether you like it or not. We're not having a conversation about this."

Ishizuka found that working-class and poor parents, like elite parents, chose responses corresponding to the norms of hothouse parenting, yet working-class and poor parents do not practice hothouse parenting equally with elite parents because they lack the financial and social capital necessary for turning desired norms into practice.[75]

Lack of financial capital limits working-class and poor parents' abilities to pay for activities such as swimming or tennis lessons. It also inflicts stress, diminishing working-class and poor parents' energy, attention, and patience when interacting with their children. And lack of social capital limits access by working-class and poor parents to the informal conversations in which elite parents exchange information about hothouse parenting with other elite parents.

Journalist Claire Cain Miller illustrated the effects of lack of social capital in a description of Stacey Jones, a working-class mother whose son liked swimming, but only learned much later that he could have competed in swim team years before. "I didn't know because I don't live in a swim tennis community," she said. "I feel like a lot of kids who have working-class backgrounds don't benefit from the knowledge."[76]

Writer Kelly Corrigan described the transition from her mother's childhood in the time before sacralization, to her own childhood in the time of field parenting, and her daughter's childhood in the time of hothouse parenting. Children in her mother's generation joined their parents in farm work, seen but not heard, with no rights of their own. Children in her own generation were sent out to play after breakfast and called back at dinnertime. And parenting in her daughter's generation was turned into a verb, as parents cultivate their children and relish their relationships with them.[77]

Corrigan described the expressive and emotional benefits of hothouse parenting in her relationship with her daughter, highlighted as she was preparing to leave for college in the time of COVID-19. "I have watched her do her days. . . . At night, I leaned over her in bed and kissed her head. Her presence was a full-on 24/7 sensory experience. . . . But now it's time for her to go . . . it takes all of 43 minutes to set up her dorm room, and then the savage goodbye."

A reader described a similar experience as she was leaving for college. "My parents are immigrants from Asia and do not show much emotion, but as they were getting in their van to leave, my dad began to cry. I've never seen him cry. That was when I realized how much he loved me, his eldest daughter, and how proud he was. I will never forget that day."

Some elite parents now join their elementary school children for lunch at school, an unthinkable practice 20 years before, when writer Taylor Lorenz was in elementary school.[78] Then, parents dropped off their children at school in the morning, leaving them to play, learn, and grow until they were collected after school. Some parents said that lunch is the only uninterrupted quality time they get. But if school lunchtime becomes quality time for children and parents, then it ceases to be a time for children to learn how to interact with their peers.

Even elite parents find it impossible to be perfect parents. Attempts at perfection lead to chronic stress that can turn into burnout, an exhaustion that detaches parents from their children and diminishes parents' trust in their parenting abilities.[79] Burnout intensified in the time of COVID-19. Journalist Catherine Pearson noted that 66% of working parents meet the criteria for parental burnout, feeling they have nothing left to give because they are exhausted by the pressure of caring for their children.[80] "It's a state where you have been giving, and giving, and giving and giving—until you're totally empty," said Kate Kripke, a clinical social worker and the founder of the Postpartum Wellness Center in Boulder, Colorado.

The heavy schedules of extracurricular activities of hothouse parenting inflict stress and diminished mental health of elite members of Generation Z, those born after 1997, without improving their life prospects. "It is better for both parents and children to learn the value of unstructured time and greater civic participation," wrote author Shalini Shankar. She noted further that Generation Z children are keenly aware of the downside of heavy schedules, and some act to place well-being over professional accomplishments.[81]

A reader agreed, describing how her mother lifted the heavy load of activities from her shoulders and those of her brother, when they were seven and nine. She picked piano as the one activity she really liked, and her brother picked karate. "Thirty years later I am a successful surgeon and he is finally sober, helping take care of my aging parents and disabled brother." She remembers fondly playing with friends, and the friendships they continue to maintain. "I don't think our professional path would have turned out differently if we had been kept busy with all the lessons, but we would certainly be lacking lifelong friendships."

The heavy responsibilities of hothouse parenting move some to remain childless or have fewer children than they wish. Jessica Boer, a 26-year-old woman, is not sure that she can meet today's high standards and responsibilities of parenting: "I would have the responsibility to raise this person into a functional and productive citizen, and some days I'm not even responsible."[82]

Yet the burden of raising children falls heaviest on working-class and poor parents whose meager financial resources hamper energy, attention, and patience as they interact with their children.[83,84] They cope, in part, by tempering their expectations and those of their children.

Sociologist Marianne Cooper described Laura Delgado, who learned to temper her expectations and teaches her children to do the same.[85,86] Watching a TV program about the people who survived Hurricane Katrina in New Orleans, she said to her children, "See, they are just happy to be alive. At that point, all the stuff you have just doesn't matter because surviving and being with your family, that's all there is." Laura described lessons she learned from her grandmother, a widow who worked hard to raise her four children and lived with her daughter when she was old. She shared the small amounts of her Social Security benefits with her grandchildren, saying, "Here's a little bit of Gran to take with you."

Still, money, such as in paid time-off and childcare subsidies, eases the lives of parents and increases their well-being. Sociologist Jennifer Glass and coauthors found that the well-being of parents is lower in countries, such as the United States, where the government provides meager family support than in developed countries, where the government provides generous family support.[87]

Sociologists Kathryn Edin and Maria Kefalas noted the stark cultural differences by social class in the choice to have children, the ages at which to have them, and the practices of raising them. Elite women gain substantial economic rewards by refraining from having children until they have completed college and established themselves in careers, perhaps by their mid-30s. These economic rewards are likely to vanish if they have children in their teens.[88]

In contrast, poor young women who become pregnant, whether by accident or plan, often choose to have their children, despite obstacles that arise once their children are born. Children offer poor young women a source of meaning, social esteem, and personal satisfaction, when other sources, such as college, career, and marriage, seem vague and tenuous.

Edin and Kefalas quoted Sonia, a 23-year-old poor mother of a four-year-old son: "[My son is] my heart." When she has a hard time she always tells herself she wanted him. "Even if I get that rock on my finger, that white picket fence, and that deed that says the house is mine," she'll still have her son just in case anything goes sour. "I'll say to my husband, 'You leave! This boy is mine.'"[89]

Edin and Kefalas noted further that close relationships between mothers and children are especially valuable in poor communities, where trust is astonishingly low even among family members, and poverty marks relationships, not only finances, fostering a desire to give and receive love, and children are best at it. They quoted Pamela, a middle-aged woman with seven children. "I think [I got pregnant] mainly because I wanted to be loved. I went through my childhood without having it. Somehow, I knew that . . . I would grow up and have kids, and it was something that was mine. Nobody could take it away from me. It was something that would love me. I would be able to love it unconditionally."[90]

Moreover, many among the poor perceive abortion as shameful, judging those who choose it as immature, even immoral, unable to accept the consequences of their own choices. Young women change their perceptions of themselves and their responsibilities when becoming pregnant, striving to do what is right for the baby. Social expectations also change when pregnancy becomes visible, and pregnant women are judged unfavorably for having a drink at a neighborhood bar or spending a night hanging out with friends.

Parents and their disabled children

Parents have always sacrificed for their children, and the sacrifices of parents of disabled children are especially great. Children's disabilities can be physical, such as muscular dystrophy or multiple sclerosis; developmental, such as Down syndrome or autism; behavioral, such as attention deficit hyperactivity disorder (ADHD) and bipolar illness; or sensory, such as being blind or deaf.

Parents at their wit's end come to emergency rooms with children who have severe behavioral problems, but the visits offer little long-term benefit. "Their child's behavior may be a danger to themselves, but also to the parents, to the other children in the home," said Anna Cushing, a pediatric emergency room physician. "They really don't have anywhere else to go."[91]

"If you haven't seen a kid go from okay to dangerous in a matter of an hour," wrote one parent, "you might think the parents are doing a terrible job. They aren't. . . . Be kind to any parent dealing with a kid like this."

The son of Lillyth Quillan is afflicted by behavioral disorder, lacking empathy and skilled at manipulation.[92] She described the pain of parents shamed and shunned by the community, finding no comfort other than virtual hugs of fellow parents and rare meetings. "Just being physically present together with someone else who understood felt like a miracle."

The pain felt by such parents is exacerbated by the tendency to attribute all children's behavior to parents. "Too often, I heard, 'If it was my child, I would never let them get away with this,'" said Quillan. "Eventually I stopped trying to connect with other parents. They say it takes a village to raise a child, but what do you do when the village shuns you?"

Responding to an article about the relentlessness of modern parenting, a mother of two small children, one of whom is disabled, noted that all around she sees parents in tizzies about kindergarten, language lessons, and sports groups, being perfect for Instagram. But her disabled son gives her a reality check. "Who cares about Mandarin; just let his brain survive those seizures, just let him walk, just let him talk.[93]

Having a disabled child increases by 10 percentage points the likelihood that parents will separate in the following 12 to 18 months. And if parents continue to live together, it decreases by 6 percentage points the quality of their relationship.[94]

And parents of disabled children are three times more likely to make job sacrifices than other parents, and their earnings trajectories show a sharp break when a child becomes disabled. Both mothers and fathers make job sacrifices, but the sacrifices of mothers are usually greater because they are usually the primary caregivers.[95]

Livie, the daughter of James and Lindsay Sulzer, was almost four when a falling tree branch devastated her brain. James devoted his career to repairing damaged nervous systems, and Lindsay once worked on ways to treat traumatic brain injuries. They have access to all possible treatments, yet Livie cannot speak or walk unaided, and her cognitive disabilities are profound.

Lindsay assumed the immense tasks of arranging Livie's care, hiring nurses and personal attendants, getting equipment such as wheelchairs, and setting a cycle of feedings, medicine, and exercise. At lunch, a nurse put Livie in a stander and set up an iPad for her entertainment while a pouch of chickpea formula was placed into her feeding tube. Watching videos of Livie before the accident, James said, "Now it's like I have two daughters, in a way. One that passed away, and now this one."[96]

Political scientist Norman Ornstein described the toll of mental illness on himself, his wife, and especially, on their son Matthew, a "kind, brilliant, thoughtful young man, who experienced the sudden onset of mental illness at age 24." Ornstein and his wife flew to Florida, where Matthew lived, panicked by allegations about his behavior. But Matthew was gone by the time his parents arrived, transported to a mental health facility by police officers who handcuffed him as he emerged from the shower, not letting him dress, pick up his cellphone, or explain what was happening. The staff at the facility would not even confirm that Matthew was there, barred by privacy rules.

A reader of Ornstein's article wrote: "My daughter, too, has severe mental illness. . . . She is a kind person who wants to be 'normal' but cannot and maybe never will be able to control her impulsiveness and erratic moods." Another described facing the aftermath of a psychotic break of a child, more or less out of the blue. "The big problem: after your child is 18, you cannot make them get help . . . . So, you get to just watch, as the person you once birthed from your body, held in your arms, signed the perfect report cards of, clapped as they walked across the stage in cap and gown, twice, spirals into darkness and delusion."[97]

Mark Bertin, a physician, wrote about the extra burdens of parents of children with special needs in May 2020, the time of COVID-19. "Your child may have setbacks during the school shutdown. But remember, schools will open again at some point and help get things back on track."[98] The extra burdens shouldered by parents are clear in the words of a reader who faulted Bertin for glossing over significant disabilities that need constant daily care, single and working parents juggling jobs and teaching at home, and students who will have significant losses difficult to make up. "It's nice to give reassurance but to gloss over significant problems strikes me as cherry-picking the easier problems to talk about."

Several readers objected to the word *burden* in the title of Bertin's article, but others acknowledged that burden. One wrote: "I raised a son with special needs. . . . He is 28 and still at home with me, and it is just the two of us. I love him deeply and he is my greatest joy. I count myself lucky to be his mother every day. But *burden* is a word that applies." It is the burden of trying to get help for when resources are scarce, the burden of finding respite from the constant worry, the burden of realizing that the child may never be able to live independently, the burden of the unknown, of what will happen to him when his mother is no longer on this earth to look after him. "My son is not a burden, but the worry is. It is with me every single day."

Another wrote, "I, too, am a member of the 'club.'" He and his wife raised two children, now adults, one of whom is totally disabled by autism, requiring 24/7 care. Both have always lived with them. "If we are truly 'all in this together,' we will all act that way as a nation, now and forever more." He quoted from the book *Etz Hayim* (Tree of Life): "The decency of a society is measured by how it cares for its least powerful members."[99]

The ability to detect disabilities, such as Down syndrome, in the womb and get an abortion adds complexity and anguish to the lives of prospective parents. Down syndrome carries intellectual disability, low muscle tone, heart and gastrointestinal defects, immune disorders, arthritis, obesity, leukemia, and dementia.

Screening for Down syndrome has been common in Denmark since 2014, when the government offered it to every pregnant woman. Yet a gulf separates publicly expressed attitudes in Denmark, favoring giving birth to children with Down syndrome, and private decisions favoring abortion. Almost all expecting mothers choose to undergo the screen, and more than 95% who received a Down syndrome diagnosis choose to abort. Only 18 children with Down syndrome were born in Denmark in 2019, whereas approximately 6,000 children with Down syndrome are born in the United States each year.

A Danish couple announced a pregnancy to family and friends only after a screen detected no Down syndrome. "We wanted to wait because if it had Down syndrome, we would have had an abortion." Yet the screen failed to detect Down syndrome, and now they were afraid their family and friends would think they don't love their daughter, facing the moral judgments that accompany aborting or giving birth to a disabled child.[99]

Expressions of regret over having children are taboo, yet regret is especially common among parents of disabled children. Carrie, a British woman, regrets having her two disabled children, a 12-year-old and 10-year-old she shepherds to school and therapy appointments. She is reluctant to admit her taboo fantasies about visiting a friend in Hawaii and never coming back.[100]

A desperate mother broke a taboo, giving up custody of her 17-year-old mentally ill son after failing to get treatment for him. She made up her mind "sometime between the moment he lunged for the knife drawer and when she dialed 911 for the 14th time in less than a year." She still had a bruise on her right arm when she appeared before the judge, where her son had grabbed her weeks before, screaming expletives as she was driving him to school. "I'm not a monster," she told herself. . . . "I love him. I've tried everything."[101]

Some parents are straightforward not only about the burden of their disabled children, but also about their desire to offload that burden. A mother described the burden of caring for her 32-year-old disabled daughter, the only child of her and her husband. "One nurse told me I'd get my reward in heaven. It's so condescending. What annoys me the most is when people come up to you and say, 'God only gives these special children to people who can cope with them.' Well, he can take her back, then. Sorry. I'm going to be very straight about it: she's not special. She's damaged goods." She wanted the child who was going to have two children by now, and have finished university studies, and have a life for herself, in a home where her mother could visit and babysit her grandchildren. "I wanted to have that child."[102]

8

Elderly Parents, Grandparents, Siblings, and Pets

U.S. culture is described as individualistic, whereas China's is described as collectivistic. Psychologist Geert Hofstede defined *individualism* as "a preference for a loosely-knit social framework in which individuals are expected to take care of only themselves and their immediate families." He defined *collectivism*, its opposite, as "a preference for a tightly-knit framework in society in which individuals can expect their relatives or members of a particular in-group to look after them in exchange for unquestioning loyalty."[1] The United States ranks first in individualism among 88 countries, whereas China ranks 65th.

Reverence for elderly parents is indeed prominent in China. "When my parents see something that they like but couldn't bear to buy, I can see it in their eyes and when they put it down after picking it up," said Jihong, a 55-year old Chinese woman. "When I tell them that I would buy it for them, they will say that I'm wasting money." Jihong buys it secretly and when her parents see it, "that happiness on their faces makes me feel that no matter how much I spend, being able to grow old with them is truly happiness for me."

The collectivistic culture of China includes "filial loyalty," a cultural contract built on the premise that parents do everything to care for their children, and then end their lives in their children's care, enjoying utilitarian, expressive, and emotional benefits. Filial loyalty is illustrated in stories such as one in "The 24 Paragons of Filial Piety," about a son in the Jin dynasty, born to parents too poor to afford a mosquito net. The son took off his shirt and sat by his parents' bed, letting the mosquitoes bite him and spare his parents.[2]

Filial loyalty enhances the well-being of elderly parents, evident in lower rates of suicide during the Chinese Lunar New Year, when children commonly visit.[3] Yet filial loyalty is fraying in China as children leave parents' homes for work and life in cities. Elderly Chinese parents complain that they do not see their children often enough, and children explain that the stresses of work and life in cities make it hard to visit their parents. By 2016, only half of Chinese adult children living away from their parents returned home for the Chinese Lunar New Year. Children living in Beijing, Shanghai, and Tianjin were especially unlikely to return.[4]

The fraying of filial loyalty in China is illustrated in a recent story of a farmer who lived in poverty to pay for his son's college education. The son repaid his father by getting a new telephone number so his father could not contact him, when he found a job in a city far from his father's place. The father walked 10 miles every week to find a telephone to call his son at a disconnected number, unable to imagine that his son had abandoned him.[5] The Chinese social welfare system struggles to provide elderly parents utilitarian benefits no longer provided by their children, but no social welfare system can provide expressive and emotional benefits.

A 2013 Chinese law, "Protection of the Rights and Interests of Elderly People," aims to compel adult children to provide expressive and emotional benefits to their older parents, in addition to utilitarian benefits, by communicating with them, visiting them, and caring for them. Yet many doubt the effectiveness of replacing traditional filial loyalty with the law.[6] Other instruments and means have been developed as substitutes for filial loyalty. The Family Support Agreement (FSA) is a voluntary contract between elderly Chinese parents and their adult children about parental provisions. FSAs had been signed by more than 13 million rural families by the end of 2005, and are now making their way into cities. Violations of the FSA are subject to penalties by law, yet the effectiveness of FSAs is unclear.[7] Today's elderly Chinese parents receive more support from daughters than sons, despite the cultural expectation of filial loyalty from sons. This is especially true for the oldest-old aged 80 and older, and surprisingly more prevalent in rural areas, where preference for sons is more prevalent, than in urban areas.[8]

The individualistic culture of the United States is reflected in the words of Jeffrey, the previously mentioned 60-year-old American man. He and his wife are not expecting any inheritance from their parents, and their children know that they cannot expect much of an inheritance from their parents. "If they are working and still living with us, we expect some kind of rent to help out with expenses." Yet filial loyalty is practiced in the United States more than preached, evident is the prevalence of the "Sandwich Generation" of parents stressed financially and emotionally as they care for both young children and elderly parents.[9] Cash transfers from adult children to elderly parents in the United States understate the total support the young provide to the old because much of that support is in-kind, such as in caring for elderly parents in their own homes or in their children's homes.[10]

Tanya Brice, a 43-year-old single mother, cares for her medically fragile mother, her twin toddlers, one of whom suffers autism and intellectual disability, and a teenage son. Her budget, consisting of a social worker's salary, and her schedule are at a breaking point. Brice manages to pay for rent, utilities, and food, but cable, extracurricular activities, and everything else, is beyond her means. Indeed, sometimes even food is lacking.[11] A survey of American caregivers highlighted some of their sacrifices: 25% dipped into their retirement savings; 41% dipped into their personal savings; 25% spent 40 hours per week care-giving; and 45% of those who had outside jobs used some or all of their vacation time for care-giving. Caregivers have also sacrificed leisure activities and time with friends and family.[12]

The financial and career stress of caring for both children and parents can weigh heavily on relationships. Amanda Mayo, a 40-year-old mother of young children, cares for her in-laws, who live with her and her husband, and also makes frequent trips to Nebraska to care for her grandparents. "I'll be honest, it almost broke our marriage," she said. Readers added their stories. One wrote: "For only 10 months, I took care of my mother who had dementia. It was not like taking care of a baby. Often it was a question of getting my mother up to go to the bathroom, or maybe getting five hours of sleep and doing three extra hours of laundry the next morning because she wet the bed. . . ."

Yet caring for elderly parents can bring rewards. A man wrote: "Choosing to care for my mom for 25 years influenced every job I took and had a negative effect on my career." He spent very little on himself and all his extra earnings went toward his mother's living expenses and care. "I sacrificed my personal life and general happiness in order to do this. I would do it again, too. It was the right thing to do."[13]

Elderly people with kin are lucky to have people who care for them. Kinless ones are not as lucky.[14] Lynne Ingersoll, a 77-year-old retired librarian, never married or had children. When her sister died, she joined the group of older kinless Americans. She is not sure what she will do when she cannot manage on her own. A "solo" reader wrote that, at 73, she decided it is time to move to a life care community where she will have a support system in place in case she becomes disabled. "I know this is not for everyone, and many people don't have the finances to afford it, but it gives me peace of mind. I took care of my mother and my husband through the dying process and I know that being alone and sick would be a disaster." Another wrote: "My husband and I have chosen not to have children. The money that we would otherwise have invested in children has been saved and invested elsewhere. So, we will be financially fine in our post-retirement years, very able to employ a caregiver etc."

Help from adult children to elderly parents can bring them together, yet conflicts often accompany help. Elderly parents hope their adult children will help if needed, and they appreciate their children's concern, but they also want autonomy, and are annoyed by their children's over-protectiveness.[15] Elderly parents use a range of strategies to deal with their ambivalent feelings, including being stubborn, minimizing the help they receive, ignoring or resisting children's attempts to control, maintaining clear boundaries by withholding information from children, and seeking others as confidants.[16]

A sample of adult children completed a seven-day diary of their mood and how often they felt their elderly parents were stubborn. Thirty-one percent of adult children reported stubborn behavior by their elderly parents, and 17% reported risky behavior.[17] Such reports are associated with low well-being among parents and children alike, low quality of parent-child relationships, greater parent functional disabilities, higher neuroticism among adult children, and greater negative mood among them.[18] Gaps in knowledge of the problems of elderly parents among adult children can also lead to unmet needs among elderly parents.[19]

Responding to an article by journalist Paula Span about these findings, one wrote in exasperation. "If our parents want to be independent, they shouldn't expect us to come running when their independence has (totally predictable) awful consequences. But they do, and we will. Kind of like when we were growing up, just with roles reversed."[20] Another noted the role of distrust between elderly parents and their adult children. After years of trying to persuade her mother to move into a retirement community, she suddenly announced she had signed up for one because a volunteer from the American Cancer Society advised her to.

"Because it was a stranger, not someone trying to get rid of me, I decided to listen," said her mother. "We should have hired a stranger years ago," said the daughter's husband.

Author Claire Berman, an elderly parent herself, illustrated the ambivalence in the relationships between adult children and elderly parents, empathizing with the concerns of an adult son about his elderly father driving after dark, but also empathizing with his father's complaint about being badgered by his children about his driving. Another friend told Berman about the ambivalence in her relationship with her adult daughter who has moved to live closer to her. The mother is delighted to see her daughter more often but distressed that her daughter seems to use visits as inspections. "Does my home meet the clean test? Is the yogurt in my refrigerator long past its use-by date?" Conflicts arise because elderly parents, trying to maintain their independence, want to be cared about but fear being cared for.[21]

Older parents need transportation, but many are reluctant to use ride-hailing services such as Uber and Lyft. They are intimidated by the technology and concerned about scams and identity thefts, fearing that hackers might gain access to their bank accounts and empty them.[22] A reader offered an example of that reluctance in her experience as a caretaker of both her mother and grandmother, neither of which can drive. "I am burned out completely after two years of being their driver," she wrote. "They refuse to try a ride-hailing service though my mom is an avid iPhone user. Socially and emotionally, they would be better knowing they don't need to be housebound. I give up."

Another found a way to teach his stepfather how to use a ride-hailing service. His stepfather looked at him like he had grown a second head when he first suggested Uber. "But I took him to dinner a few times . . . and then downloaded the app on his phone. Next couple of times we went out, I had him order it up. Now he can order one when he wants or deems necessary." An experiment offered three free months of unlimited Lyft rides to elderly who suffer chronic diseases and report transportation problems. Almost all used the ride-hailing service, and almost all reported improved well-being.[23] Ride-hailing services are now collaborating with healthcare systems for nonemergency medical transportation, reducing patients' missed appointments, and improving their well-being.

Childcare is cheaper in multigenerational households, where grandparents care for grandchildren, obviating needs for paid childcare, and adult children care for elderly parents, obviating needs for nursing homes. And one house for a multigenerational household is cheaper to buy or rent than two or three for nuclear households. Indeed, rising house prices in China increased the prevalence of multigenerational households.

Yet multigenerational households are regularly riven by conflicts that diminish well-being, as disagreements arise about matters large and small, from privacy to children's education and adults' earnings and spending. Journalist Frankie Huang compared her lower well-being in China as a child in a multigenerational household to her subsequent higher well-being as a single woman and as a married woman ambivalent about having children. In China, wrote Huang, three or four generations commonly live together in one house. "At one point when I was a child, both my great-grandmother and grandmother resided with us. To say that I was over-parented is an understatement." She idealized dwelling alone and came around to the idea of cohabiting with a trusted partner and confidant. COVID-19 compelled Huang and her husband to move from China to the home of her in-laws in Connecticut, forming a multigenerational household.

We do not hear the voices of Frankie Huang's in-laws in her story but we hear the voices of parents and in-laws in a story about adult children in the time of COVID-19, moving back in with their parents, along with their spouses and children. Patricia Mitchell, a 74-year-old woman still grieving for her husband, was accommodating her daughter, son-in-law, their baby girl, and a four-year-old son. Mitchell recounted the upsides of living with her extended family, including the joy of helping raise her baby granddaughter and being helped by her son-in-law in chores and repairs. Yet she also noted the downsides. "The noise level. The house wakes up very early. The level of activity is a bit shocking to my system, if you want to know the truth."

Readers' reactions to the story are insightful and touching. One wrote: "Enjoy every moment with your parents, especially if they are elderly. I miss mine every day, every single day, even years after they have passed!" Another wrote about her 26-year-old son and his girlfriend who came for an extended holiday trip and were now stranded at her home by COVID-19. "Occasionally we slipped into parent-child roles but mostly, we share a home as equals. What a joy to see my child as a wonderful adult. I will relish getting my home back to myself and mourn their wonderful company."

Ample finances enable some families to enjoy the best of both nuclear and multigenerational households. Grandparents and parents enjoy well-being in their own homes, and they enjoy additional well-being when they visit one another. That well-being was evident in its disruption by COVID-19. "I miss my grandchildren," lamented science writer Robin Marantz Henig. Every Thursday she and her husband would take the subway ride from their apartment in Manhattan to their daughter's house in Brooklyn, picking up their grandchildren at daycare and pre-K. "We would walk them home, sometimes stopping at the playground to let them clamber and climb; we would read books to them, build with blocks together, cook up some mac and cheese; we would bathe them and snuggle them and put them to bed." The last time they did this was March 2020. "We haven't hugged our granddaughters—or, for that matter, our own adult daughters—since then, and my arms ache."

Childcare by mothers or mothers-in-law benefits families by facilitating employment among women with young children. Childcare consists not only of regularly scheduled childcare during work hours, but also irregular or unanticipated childcare. The likelihood of employment among married women with young children who live in close proximity to their mothers or their mothers-in-law is 4–10 percentage points higher than among those living further away. Journalist Jessica Grose testified to the benefits of childcare by her parents who live about 10 miles away. "If we hadn't lived with them during part of 2020 when child care was unavailable and we had two kids at home, my husband or I would have had to take a leave from work." Grose also testified to the extra benefits provided to her children by grandparents who join once a week for dinner, which everyone enjoys.

Family finances affect family cultures, and in turn, cultures affect finances. A Pew Research study noted that the proportion of Americans living in multigenerational households increased from 12% in 1980 to 20% in 2016. Pew attributed one part of the increase in multigenerational households to family finances. The relative incomes of young men have been declining since the 1970s, and they are more likely than young women to live at home. Meanwhile, home prices increased and their availability decreased.

The proportion of Americans living in multigenerational households increased sharply during the Great Recession of 2007–2009 and immediately after, as many young adults, especially those lacking college degrees, lived with their parents. A more recent increase in the proportion of multigenerational families was facilitated by more generous state allocations of Medicaid funds for long-term care services delivered in the home. A subsequent Pew Research Center study in the time of COVID-19 found that the share of young adults living with their parents is higher than at any time since the Great Depression. The youngest adults, ages 18 to 24, accounted for most of the growth, consistent with employment losses since the emergence of the virus.

Pew attributed another part of the increase to family culture. Asians and Hispanics, especially immigrants, are culturally inclined toward multigenerational households, and their proportions in the United States are increasing relative to the white population. Indeed, cohesion and quality of family ties is a key factor explaining the high well-being of people in Latin American families, relative to people in developed countries, despite their relatively low incomes.

Elderly people are targets of fraud by people who pretend to help them or enter into a romantic relationship with them. Adult children often warn their elderly parents about romantic scams, but elderly parents regularly dismiss such warnings, believing that they have found the love of their lives. This is the case of Desiree Boltos, the "Sweetheart Swindler" and her husband, who stole more than $3 million from elderly who believed they were in romantic relationships with her. James Olmstead, a retired Navy officer who was 75 at the time, was one of them. Boltos bumped into him at the checkout line at an Office Depot. He met her again by his car at the parking lot and they started to talk. She told him she was 32 and single, and her husband had died of cancer. Olmstead asked her out on a date, and over the following two years gave her almost all his life savings. "They come into your life," he said. "They trample over everything that is sacred in your life. . . . I got emotionally involved with her and emotions override common sense."[24] Sometimes, however, adult children abuse elderly parents rather than protect them. Examples include a son who uses his elderly mother's ATM card at casinos and liquor stores, and a daughter who steals jewelry from a mother who suffers from dementia. Elder abuse is pernicious because it often starts with good intentions. A son might begin caring for elderly parents with goodwill, but goodwill can turn into resentment and a choice to dip into his parents' account as payment for care-giving.[25]

Bequests from parents to children can be motivated by parents' altruism toward their children or by parents' self-interest in support from their children. A comparison of parents' motives in the United States,

India, China, and Japan shows that altruism is generally prevalent in the United States and India, whereas self-interest is generally prevalent in China and Japan.[26] Japanese adult children are more likely to live with or near their elderly parents and provide care and attention to them if they expect to receive bequests from them.[27] The magnitude of bequests from Chinese parents to their children is synchronized with the level of children's personal assistance. Both bequests and assistance are higher when parents' income is higher, and lower when children's income is higher.[28] Moreover, elderly Chinese parents use their houses as means for procuring care from adult children. Children tend to provide more financial and emotional support to their parents when the value of potential housing-bequest increases.[29]

Some elderly people have good experience in retirement communities, nursing homes, and long-term care policies, but they are expensive.[30] A woman wrote: "My mother's nursing home . . . costs a staggering $13,556 per month, [but] the care she receives is excellent." She pays half of it from her parents' savings and the other half from the long-term care policy her father purchased decades ago. "When I do, I always wish I could tell him how thankful I am for his prescience."

Government support for Americans is meager relative to the generous support in the United Kingdom and France. One noted that many in the United States cannot afford to buy long-term care insurance when paying off university debts, and when they want to buy insurance in middle age they find it too expensive and with too many exclusions. "Meanwhile my parents in the U.K. have home care, emergency on call, nurses who visit daily and take good care of them. Not a single dollar or worry from us because I know they're in good hands." Another wrote: "I live in France. . . . My aunt worked from a teenager until about 60, retired at home till 86, then a medicalized retirement home, suffering from dementia, she could no longer live at home." Her retirement home is government run, with attentive professional employees earning decent salaries, and the food is excellent. "I . . . Thank God every day to live in France."

Grandparents and grandchildren

Grandparents derive much well-being from their relationships with their grandchildren. Grandchildren can make grandparents feel younger, and they can enhance grandparents' well-being at a time when people of their age find less meaning in their lives.[31] Jonathan, a 67-year-old American man interviewed by BlackRock, described that well-being. They have two grandkids, aged 10 and 9, who are a huge part of their lives. They are setting up an education fund for their college expenses, and budgeting a summertime fund to pay for fun things for them to do. "We will also be setting up an inheritance fund for each of them." Other parents, however, are burdened by expectations of supporting children or grandchildren. Karen, the previously mentioned 60-year old British woman, noted that family members of her generation "who have kids have felt increased pressure to support their children or grandchildren through university and onto the housing ladder."

The evaluative well-being of parents with no grandchildren is equal to that of nonparents of the same age, but the evaluative well-being of grandparents to at least one grandchild is higher. This implies that there are long-term well-being benefits to having children even if they do not raise the well-being of their parents, if children go on to have children of their own.[32] Sanjeev Ranjan and Sadhana Prasad of India spent their savings to have their son trained as a pilot in the United States, and they paid for his lavish wedding back in India, along with a luxury car and an overseas honeymoon.[33] Six years later, they are suing their son and daughter-in-law for $650,000 in damages because they failed to have a child. A shopkeeper in their city said that residents had been discussing the case with great interest over tea outside his shop, and that older people tended to sympathize with the plaintiffs. "In old age, you want to play with your grandchild," he said. "What is the harm in giving them one?"

Moving to live closer to grandchildren is common among grandparents, and some retire to care for grandchildren.[34] The probability of moving is higher among grandparents reporting grandchild care.[35] In the early days of the pandemic, four of Marc and Cathy Joseph's grandchildren, along with their parents, came from Austin and Orlando to live with them, in Scottsdale, Arizona. Two other grandchildren living nearby were frequent visitors for meals and sleepovers with their cousins. "As you grow older, you grow wiser," said Marc. "I wish I was there more often for my kids". He was traveling much for his work when his children were young. "If I can spend more time with my grandkids, then maybe it's making up for what I didn't give my kids."[36]

A Japanese nursing home now has "baby workers," 32 children younger than four-years-old who spend time with its residents who are mostly in their 80s. Residents strike up conversations with the children, and the children offer the residents hugs. "I don't get to see my grandkids very often, so the baby workers are a great treat," said 85-years-old Kyoko Nakano. She drops everything to spend time with them when they arrive.[37] Yet caring for grandchildren can diminish the well-being of grandparents who set aside their own projects and interests and lose social connections. This is especially true when the burden of care becomes greater than expected or when one grandparent disagrees with a spouse about bearing that burden.[38]

Raising grandchildren in grandparents' homes can diminish grand-parents' well-being even more.[39] Barb, a 68-year-old woman, and Fran, her 69-year-old husband, are raising in their own home a granddaughter left by her son and his girlfriend. "No one expects to spend their retire-ment raising a child," said Barb, "It changes everything. Your life is turned upside down."[40] The toll on grandparents raising grandchildren includes depression, sleeplessness, and lack of privacy and time with their spouses, friends, and other family members. More than 40% of grand-parents raising grandchildren also suffer scarcity of economic or social-service support.

Estrangement of grandparents from their grandchildren is sadly com-mon, diminishing the well-being of all. It usually begins with estrange-ments of grandparents from their own children or their children's partners. These estrangements are especially sad because they are not initiated by grandchildren yet deprive them of opportunities to know their grandparents and be with them on holiday celebrations, birthdays and anniversaries, weddings, vacation trips, even funerals. Pat Hanson is a 75-year-old grandmother estranged from her granddaughter for 13 years since her granddaughter was four, when her daughter-in-law separated from her son. Hanson composes hundreds of letters, fantasizing about reconnection with her granddaughter and hoping that the letters would show her granddaughter how much her grandmother yearned to see her.[41]

A reader wrote: "It's a heartache that never goes away. . . . It's a loss like death but not quite the same because you grieve for someone that is still alive. . . . I pray to God that one day I will see [my granddaugh-ter] openly to touch, hug, kiss, and catch up on her life that was taken from me. I just hope I live that long." But another wrote: "I wish this article would have included discussion about grandparents who choose to alienate themselves from their adult children and grandchildren. . . .

When grandparents excommunicate their adult children, it's painful and often hard to reconcile—the feeling of being tossed aside like garbage by your parents. It cuts both ways."

Differences in norms of parenting between parents and grandparents are common. A survey revealed that 57% of parents disagree with grandparents about discipline, 44% about food, 36% about screen time, and 21% about bedtime.[42] Differences are usually resolved with goodwill or silence. Less than half of parents mentioned their concerns to grandparents. The agnostic parents of a three-year-old son were concerned at first, then baffled, and then amused, when he returned from his grandparents saying things like "God made us!" and "God watches us!" "It's been so precious to watch their bond with my children grow since they moved here," said the mother. The Jesus issue is just "one thing that causes some head scratching, and leads us to think harder about our own point of view and the way we're raising our kids."[43]

When concerns were mentioned by parents, almost half the grandparents who promised to do better, did. Yet about one-third of the grandparents who promised to do better did not, and almost a fifth refused to change their behavior.[44] This is where differences can escalate into conflicts and estrangements, especially when adult children disagree with the way they themselves were raised and strive to raise their own children in a better way. A reader responding to an article about estrangement between grandparents and grandchildren wrote: "Yes, parents are gatekeepers; that is their job. Many parents are abusive, neglectful, and toxic. . . . My partner and I have already agreed that [my mother-in-law] will not be informed when we have children. . . . We can't fix my partner's past, but we can make sure our kids never, ever have to go through what he did."[45]

A grandparent wrote to Carolyn Hax, an advice columnist, about estrangement caused when she gave a snack with nuts to a granddaughter suffering severe nut allergy. "It was completely accidental, but she had a minor reaction, and her parents were very upset." The grandmother apologized, paid the co-pay for the doctor visit, and purged her house of everything with nut traces, but she is no longer asked to babysit. "What else can I do to redeem myself from this minor mistake?" she asked.[46] A reader responded: "With a severe food allergy, there's no such thing as a 'minor mistake.'" Another wrote: "You could have killed your grandchild. Accidentally, and I'm sure you would feel horrendously guilty, but she would still be dead."

Siblings

Siblings fall into categories ranging from best friends, enhancing well-being, to bitter enemies, diminishing it. Siblings Harry and William, princes in the British royal family, fall close to the bitter-enemies category. Prince Harry described painful interactions with Prince William, ranging from a slight of having changed seats at his wedding reception to a physical altercation that left Prince Harry lying on the floor.[47] The friendship of 75-year-old Audrey Findlay and Barbara Rowe, her 63-year-old sister, is in the best-friends category. They start every weekday with an 8 a.m. phone call before leaving for Findlay Rowe, their gift shop. After dinner they join in a stroll and conversation. "Our dad was an orphan, and he felt very strongly about family," Ms. Rowe said to journalist Catherine Pearson. "We can have a knock-down, drag-out fight, and the next day it's like: 'Well, where are we going to dinner?'"[48]

Children spend more out-of-school time with their siblings than with anyone else, including parents and friends. The quality of their relationship affects well-being from childhood all the way to old age. Family life scholar Alexander Jensen and coauthors divided the components of siblings' relationship quality into closeness, marked by affection, warmth, intimacy, and care; conflict, marked by tension, fighting, arguments, insults, and bickering; and communication consisting of speaking on the phone, texting, emailing, interacting on social media, and spending time together in person.[49] Closeness tends to stay stable during adolescence or even increase, and many adolescent siblings communicate daily about media, academics, friends, family, and body image. Adolescents often continue to see siblings as role models and benefit as conflicts decline.

Many young adults enjoy increased closeness and diminished conflict when older siblings leave home or go away to college. Almost two-thirds of young adults communicate daily with their siblings, even when they no longer live together. Active communication such as by in-person and texting helps maintain a sense of closeness between siblings more than passive communication such as by emails and social media posts. Closeness with siblings is associated with high well-being. Siblings with intimate, connected, and warm relationships suffer lower loneliness and depression, and enjoy higher self-esteem and resilience. They have more positive attitudes toward school and greater school commitment, healthier attitudes and participation in exercise, and greater empathy toward others.

They are also less likely to be involved in delinquency, risky behaviors, or substance use.

Sibling support in young adulthood increases well-being by a sense of competence. Sibling support also serves as a buffer against negative experiences. Siblings' affection among adolescents reduces the tendency to internalize stressful life events, and siblings' warmth reduces suicide ideation. Close sibling relationships in childhood enhance well-being long into middle age. People who reported better relationships with siblings at age 18 or 19 had lower likelihood of major depression and use of mood-altering drugs by age 50.

Sibling relationships, however, are often fraught, beset by sibling rivalry. Much of that rivalry stems from competition for the affection and resources of parents. That rivalry is central in the story of Prince William, who is destined to be king, and Prince Harry, who will always be a "spare." And it is central in the biblical story of Joseph, his brothers, and Jacob, their father. Jacob favored Joseph over his brothers, tailoring for him a special garment of many colors. Joseph's favored position aroused his brothers' jealousy, and his arrogance added enmity as he told his brothers about dreams where the sun, representing his father, the moon, representing his mother, and the stars, representing his brothers, bowed to him. The brothers found an opportunity to exact retribution by selling Joseph into slavery.

Favoritism often comes when parents' resources are constrained. Constrained parents in Ethiopia reinforce educational inequality among siblings. Inherently healthy children are more likely to attend preschool, be enrolled in elementary school, and have more educational expenses paid. Still, parents allocate health expenditures to the children who need them most.[50] Rivalry among siblings for resources inclines parents to favor sons over daughters in societies where such favoring is the norm. This yields an advantage to sons who have more sisters than brothers. Children in Ghana with sisters but no brothers do 25–40% better on measured health indicators than if they had all brothers and no sisters.[51]

Sibling rivalry is a normal feature of family life, wrote physician Claire McCarthy.[52] Indeed, sibling rivalry may have an upside in long-term adaptation and coping. Sibling conflicts during childhood and adolescence provide a relatively safe place in which to face challenges and adversity, and increase adults' personal, social, and emotional competence. But too much rivalry can be hurtful, inflicting lasting damage. Sibling bullying diminishes well-being among young adults by lower sense of competence and self-esteem. And being bullied by a sibling doubled the risk of depression and self-harm. We may not think of fights and insults between siblings as bullying, but they can feel that way to a child. McCarthy advised parents to be aware of their biases, convey in words and actions that all children are loved and valued, and resist comparisons that make one child seem better than the other. She also advised parents to be aware of how life events affect siblings. A new baby can feel bad to a brother or sister. "Celebrate children's strengths without ranking them, encourage them to follow their own interests, and spend some individual time with each child regularly."

Siblings cooperation and rivalry are also common in the animal world.[53] The cattle egret species of heron are known to practice siblicide when the parents are away from the nest, hunting for insects and fish. Among elephants the older sister babysits her younger siblings while the mother is away. European shrews are so tiny that a litter of them can fit into a teaspoon. To keep from getting lost, they move in a caravan, with the mother leading and the children following along, grabbing onto the sibling in front of them with their teeth.

A greater number of siblings is associated with a greater amount of sibling conflict among humans and animals alike, often overlimited resources of food and parental care. Competition among domestic guinea pigs for their mothers' milk increases with the size of the litter and those from larger litters had higher cortisol levels and lower growth rates than those in two-pup litters. Inequalities between siblings in age and size add to conflict. Nestlings from bird broods with a senior male showed higher stress levels than nestlings from broods with a senior female.[54]

Journalist Jessica Grose described her 4- and 8-year-old daughters who are generally good friends but sometimes jockey over positions as rivals.[55] She told the story of rivalry as they were waiting to get flu shots. "The girls got into a brawl over who received the first shot. My older daughter 'won' that argument, but it was only as she was walking toward the pharmacist's door that she realized a shot was not actually a prize." Grose quoted psychologist Jeanine Vivona, "competition with siblings is just a fact of life. And we, as people with siblings and people with children, can just try to manage it as best we can." Rivalry helps children figure out what is unique about themselves and be special by differentiating themselves from their siblings, amplifying differences with siblings and minimizing similarities.

Vivona provided an example in the case of Mr. A, whose shock at being displaced as an only child at the birth of a younger brother reverberated into adulthood.[56] His father was largely absent during Mr. A's early years, and so it seemed to be just the two of them, mother and son. The birth of a brother when Mr. A was four years old threatened his position as his mother's favorite person in the world. Mr. A fought for his position by differentiating himself from his brother, becoming high-achieving, selfless, and self-controlled. "Indeed, the family story was that Mr. A was the mother's son, and his brother was the father's son, as though each parent had only one child and each child but one parent." Vivona provided another example in the case of Ms. C, the third of four children who differentiated herself by adopting the role of the rebel. "Squeezed between an adorable baby and an invincible prodigy, Ms. C believed she could not keep her mother's special love."

An 8-year-old Chinese girl coped with sibling rivalry by keeping a grudge diary, listing her conflicts with her 16-year-old sister.[57] "August 8, 2022: I helped my sister wash clothes, but she didn't recognize my efforts. I will tolerate it. . . . August 21, 2022: today, my sister didn't eat her dinner and was told off by mum. I laughed at her and was told off by her and cried. I will tolerate it. . . . August 30, 2022: the new term is coming. I helped my sister pack up her stuff, but accidentally broke her hair comb. She beat me up for it. I hope her school starts soon. I can't tolerate it anymore." Her 16-year-old sister said the diary contained some exaggerations, but admitted that she was not aware she hurt her little sister's feelings so much and promised to do better in the future. Many readers were touched by the interactions between the two sisters, reminded of their own interactions with siblings. "My sister and I always had small fights, too, but she also brought me snacks from school and I bought her stuff she wanted with my pocket money," wrote one.

Sibling rivalry can intensify in adulthood when one sibling is much more successful than the others, as when a company owned by an entrepreneurial brother goes public. "Once, you were more or less following the same road map," wrote journalist Ellyn Spragins. "Now he has gained entry to a territory that you don't have a prayer of seeing. If we share so much, you wonder, why have things turned out so differently for him?"[58] Spragins described the work of psychotherapist Eileen Gallo who studied people who became unexpectedly wealthy by initial public offerings of stocks or lottery winnings. Nearly all reported a negative effect on their relationships with siblings. Some siblings are beset by envy, and others by a sense of entitlement about a sibling's new wealth.

Yet having wealthy brothers can increase well-being in collectivistic countries where culture imposes financial obligations on wealthy ones. In China, brothers provide financial help to each other when needed.[59]

Sibling rivalry can turn hot when one believes that another receives more of parents' resources than another. A man wrote to Philip Galanes, an advice columnist, about his younger brother. For 15 years, his parents have paid for his brother to live "in an upscale apartment in the expensive city" where he went to college. "He doesn't work. He barely graduated from college, lost touch with his friends, then flunked out of graduate school . . . Now my parents are resigned to supporting him indefinitely." What can he do?[60] "If you'd expressed concern for your brother's emotional well-being or the roots of his seeming paralysis as an adult," responded Galanes "it would be easier to sympathize with you. But your question reads like a jealous tale of middle-age sibling rivalry: Mommy and Daddy give him too much!" Many readers noted that the man can help his younger brother by finding psychiatric care for him, and besides, the money his parents spend on him is theirs. One wrote: "Obviously the older son sees his inheritance withering away due to his younger sibling's failures," adding a bit of sarcasm. "Most likely the older sibling will die first due to the self-imposed stress of thinking about these types of things for over 30 years. Problem solved."

Some siblings find that care-giving to elderly parents brings them closer. Siblings Glenna Crooks and Jim Crooks drifted apart as adults. Each was in contact with their mother but not with each other. Lack of conversations between the siblings led to misunderstandings as their mother's dementia worsened, until a conversation revealed that their mother was pitting them against each other. The siblings grew close as they cared for their mother, talking about family dysfunction and difficult relationships with their parents. "If Mom had died before Jim and I figured this out a year ago, I would never have seen him again," said Glenna. "There will be a family going forward after she dies."[61]

Sibling rivalry can turn vicious in disputes over parents' bequests because they combine concerns about money with concerns about parents' love, opening old wounds. This is true even in collectivistic cultures such as China's. "My father-in-law passed away suddenly and his house was sold," said Jihong, the previously mentioned 55-year old Chinese woman. "Even though it was only 380 thousand yuan, four siblings were fighting for it and it really worsened our relationship within the family."

"Nasty family feud over mom's will lands two retired sisters in jail—and one may lose her home," wrote journalist Melissa Klein.[62] Frances Perrenod, who died in 2006, named two of her daughters, Jean Mamakos and Irene Savadian, as the executors of her estate, and all five of her children as beneficiaries. Anette Klingman, the oldest sibling, complained that her sisters were mismanaging the estate and taking money they were not entitled to. She was joined in her opposition by another sister and the brother. Savadian spent 21 days in jail over the dispute, and one of the disgruntled siblings started a proceeding to take Savadian's house.

An early will divided a bequest by James and Virginia Null equally among their three daughters, but in a later will, their father placed Amy, his middle daughter, above her two sisters. Almost all the father's estate went to Amy when he died, and the two other sisters received next to nothing. The two excluded sisters sued. "People do things to their families that they would never think about doing to a stranger," said Adam Gaslowitz, their lawyer. "You are fighting with your family, and it doesn't get any worse than that." A cartoon taped on his computer shows two men sitting on a cloud with angel's wings. One says "I love this. I have been up here for 11 years and my will is still in probate."[63]

Pets and their "parents"

"Pet parents tell us their biggest motivator for moving is more space," said a real-estate expert, surveying changes in the demand for houses in the time of COVID-19. "The cities with more homes that have pet-friendly features like fenced yards, dog doors, and close proximity to a dog park are going to be popular with pet parents right now."[64] Speaking about pet owners as pet parents might sound odd in the ears of those who neither own pets nor wish to own them. Yet pets are family members to many pet owners, enhancing the well-being of those who describe themselves as pet parents, as others describe themselves as children's parents.

Novelist Zadie Smith described the quandary of potential parents when choosing to have a child, knowing that they would be decimated if their child dies.[65] Columnist Michael Gerson described the same quandary when choosing to have a dog. "Why do we take new dogs into our lives, knowing we will be decimated by their deaths?" He described grieving hard for Latte, his beloved dog, yet choosing to have Jack, a puppy he picked up eight months later.[66] In their surveys, sociologists Nicole Owens and Liz Grauerholz found that pet owners who identified themselves as pet parents borrow heavily from the language of parenting. As one explained: "I don't want Max (her dog) to misbehave while we're doing this interview, and so I know I planned to have things in advance to distract him as if you're distracting a child."[67]

"The Power of Pets" is the title of an article by the National Institutes of Health, describing the health benefits of human-animal interactions.[68] "Interacting with animals has been shown to decrease levels of cortisol (a stress-related hormone) and lower blood pressure. Other studies have found that animals can reduce loneliness, increase feelings of social support, and boost your mood." Dogs can increase their owners' physical activity, as they compel them to walk their dogs several times a day. Therapy dogs are often brought into hospitals or nursing homes to reduce patients' stress and anxiety. Dogs can also help children who care for them.

Children with attention deficit hyperactivity disorder (ADHD) who read to therapy dogs once a week for 30 minutes showed better social skills and more sharing, cooperation, and volunteering than children who read to puppets that looked like dogs. And fish can reduce their owners' stress, as watching fish swim induces calmness, and they can help children who care for them. Children with type 1 diabetes who cared for fish by feeding them and replacing the water in their aquarium, checked their blood glucose more consistently than children who were not given fish to care for.[69] Another study found increased well-being following dog acquisition, reduced loneliness and distress, increased positive affect, and reduced negative affect. Dogs also increase human social interaction as dog owners engage in conversations with fellow dog owners.[70]

When a snake bit Rocky, the cat of journalism professor Fernanda Santos, she did not hesitate to clear out her bank accounts to save him. The bill for four doses of antivenin, several blood tests to check his clotting time, and three nights at the hospital amounted to $6,200. Santos described racing out the door, calling Rocky's name, her heart thumping, fearful of losing him. When Rocky rushed toward her, she saw puncture wounds behind his left digits. "I don't regret sacrificing the plenitude of our planned Christmas, canceling plans to replace our rumbling old freezer and reconfiguring my budget for, well, as long as it takes to pay the vet bills. All of that matters less than Rocky. He is part of our family."[71]

The war of Russia on Ukraine forced many Ukrainians to flee, becoming refugees. Some traveled to Mexico, hoping to cross over to the United States. Yet dog-owning Ukrainians faced a daunting hurdle at the U.S. Border: no dogs allowed. Federal health guidelines bar entry of pets from Ukraine and other countries with a high incidence of rabies. Journalist Miriam Jordan described Natasha Hrytsenko, a lifelong Ukrainian and now a refugee, who bought Eddie, a purebred mini-Maltese puppy, with her first two paychecks.[72] Now, at the Mexican-U.S. border, she said: "I can leave behind my best clothes, my favorite bags and even my cellphone. But I will never leave Eddie behind. I would rather go back to Europe."[73] A reader echoed Hrytsenko's sentiments. "There is no way I could or would leave my dogs behind. You might as well ask me to chop off my arms and leave them on the other side of the border. Not. Gonna. Happen. I would never be able to live with myself afterward; the guilt would be too much to bear."

"A Dog's Place Is at the White House," is the title of an article by writer Margaret Renkl.[74] "A home feels different when a dog lives there. Now 1600 Pennsylvania Avenue will be different, too." In the absence of a dog, a door is only the way into an empty house, "not the entrance to a party where everyone has been waiting for you far longer than they could bear." Renkl feels this emptiness acutely because she just had to say goodbye to her little rescue dog, Millie, whose epilepsy suddenly entered a catastrophic stage.

A reader described her husband who hated dogs until he experienced one at home. "Within 24 hours, my husband fell in love with the dog and finally understood dog lovers." But another dissented, describing being amazed by people's reaction when he walks away from their dog, or fails to appreciate that warm licking and wet nose rubbing on his hands or legs. "'What, don't you like my dog? It's so friendly' says the owner of a 100-pound beast reaching at my toddler in the stroller. Not really. Is that so difficult to understand?" Another observer counted pushing pets in baby strollers as something we will cringe at years from now, as others counted monarchy and Crocs as cringe-worthy.[75]

9

Friendship

"A group of friends and I do water aerobics several times a week, then breakfast afterwards," said a woman interviewed by Pew Research Center. "They have become close confidants and just fun to be with. I would be lost without them."[1] Spending time with friends and engaging in enjoyable activities, whether water aerobics, meals, or weddings, adds to well-being.[2] A man did not feel the urge to socialize after his wife's death, following 44 years of marriage. Yet Tony, his friend, kept inviting him to join a group of friends who gathered for dinner every Thursday. Finally, he said, "Okay, I'll go. Anything to keep you from calling me every week." Now, six years later, thanks to Tony, he has been going to dinner every week with the group they have dubbed ROMEO—Retired Old Men Eating Out.[3]

Friendships often interact with finances. Splitting a check for breakfast or a modest dinner among friends imposes relatively little financial burden. But some dinners are expensive, getting in the way of friendship when the finances of some are tighter than those of others.

A man described his dilemma to an advice columnist. He earns a good salary but also has a good amount of debt, and the high cost of living in New York City keeps him living paycheck to paycheck. His friends earn multiples of his salary and think nothing of spending $200 on a meal and $500 on a bottle of wine. "How do I tell them that their ideas of a casual hang are outside of my tax bracket without offending them or seeming like a cheapskate?" He is worried that he might alienate his friends by opting out of their expensive dates and losing them.[4]

Is it okay to RSVP "no" if you're broke, ask Gen Z and Millennials? "Weddings can be expensive," wrote advice columnist Michelle Singletary. "It's okay to decline an invitation."[5] Friendship carries the expectation of joining in special events, especially weddings, but typical wedding guests spent an average of $611 per wedding in 2023, including gifts, clothing and grooming, and travel and accommodations. A reader noted that after the third wedding, she told her friends that she could not afford to attend their weddings. "It cost me a lot to say that—but it would have cost more if I didn't."

Still, even casual check-ins with friends enhances well-being. Marketing scholar Peggy Liu found that "reaching out to check in on someone, just to say 'Hi,' that you are thinking of them, and to ask how they're doing, can be appreciated more than people think." Check-ins from those who had not been in contact recently are especially beneficial.[6]

"Loneliness often stems from unwanted solitude," wrote journalist Christina Caron. "But it is also driven by a discrepancy between how you perceive your relationships versus what you want or expect from them." This discrepancy underlies feelings of loneliness while surrounded by family. Kindness toward others is a cure to loneliness. Volunteering can ease feelings of loneliness and broaden our social networks.[7]

Caron told the story of Robyn Houston-Bean, a 52-year-old woman whose 20-year-old son died of an accidental overdose. Houston-Bean found it hard to share her grief with family and friends who have not experienced that kind of loss. She found comfort among new friends who shared her grief and joined them in distributing clothing, food, and other supplies to drug users living on the streets.

Forming friendships and maintaining them contribute to well-being by fulfilling a fundamental human need for social interaction. The link between friendship and well-being has been observed in children, adolescents, young and middle-aged adults, and the elderly. That link has also been observed across cultures.

Sages and Seekers is a program that fosters friendships between elderly people and high school students. The program connected 76-year-old Hannah Boulton, a retired nurse feeling isolated after two years of the COVID-19 pandemic, with Ally Brooks, a high school senior. The two bonded immediately over their love of travel. Boulton shared her adventures, living with her first husband in Okinawa during the Vietnam War, and with her second husband in Karlsruhe, Germany, where he worked. She encouraged Brooks to apply to colleges in England and Scotland, including the one that Boulton's late husband had attended. "I was so excited for her, and of course, I'll visit her" in college, she said. "I just feel like we're connected."

The establishment of "chumships," close relationships between children during pre-adolescence years, is crucial in acquiring social competencies.[8]

Relationships with chums forestall children's loneliness, promote their self-worth, and help them become sensitive to the problems and perspectives of others and the importance of mutuality in relations. Young Spanish schoolchildren mentioned being with their friends as their favorite activity. And young Finnish students mentioned happiness or hardship in relationships with friends as the experiences they considered most crucial.

Close friends are confidants in times of stress, lending sympathetic ears and providing practical help when needed most. Children, especially adolescents, are reluctant to discuss peer conflicts with their parents. They are more willing to discuss these conflicts with friends, and more likely to accept their advice. Absence of friends at school leads to disengagement and alienation, and precipitates dropout.

Children and adolescents read vignettes in which they or friends faced social problems.[9] One vignette described a best friend who does poorly in a presentation in front of the class, facing a couple of students whispering and laughing at her. What would you do when you see her at lunch? Strategies ranged from emotionally engaged such as "I'd tell my friend not to feel bad about the other students laughing at her because things like that happen to everyone" to avoidant or hostile such as "I'd tell my friend that the other students laughing at her was her own fault." Having more friends is associated with decreases in avoidant or hostile strategies, and having high-quality friendships is associated with increases in emotionally engaged strategies.

The COVID-19 pandemic shrunk our circles of friends, and some argue that we should keep it this way. "You don't need to rekindle your friendship with your kid's soccer teammate's father if you don't want to," suggested writer Kate Murphy.[10] Do you truly like the people in your pod? Are you willing to suffer through another Zoom happy hour? Is it really important that you travel to your former roommate's wedding?

Yet the pandemic offered opportunities to deepen friendships. Murphy described Rachel Ernst, who joined a pod of six single people at the start of the pandemic. Ernst knew little about her fellow pod members at the beginning of the pandemic, but she now sees them as her closest friends, following deep conversations about life, death, faith, and justice. Ernst described her social life before the pandemic as a mad dash from one social event to another. "I had a pretty broad group of friends in a lot of different places, but it wasn't always a deep or fulfilling connection.... Now I know I can just relax into deeper friendships."

Indeed, friendship is one part of life we should not optimize, wrote executive coach Brad Stulberg.[11] He described a conversation with a colleague about Zoom in the time of COVID-19, noting that the advantage of socializing with friends on video is the ability to leave conversations quickly, with no need for lingering or pleasantries. "Even better," laughed his colleague, "Stay on a free Zoom trial! This way, it kicks you off after 40 minutes, regardless of what is happening." Socializing over Zoom can be efficient, wrote Stulberg, but perhaps efficiency shouldn't be the goal when it comes to friendship. Friendship takes time to form and its well-being benefits are long term.

Support among friends

Perceived support from friends and relatives who act as friends is consistently linked to well-being, including evaluative well-being and experienced well-being.[12] People enjoying higher perceived support report lower levels of distress and disorder.[13] Indeed, answering "yes" to the question "If you were in trouble, do you have relatives or friends you can count on to help you whenever you need them?" is the single most important variable explaining differences in well-being.[14]

Fangfang, a 37-year-old Chinese woman interviewed by Black-Rock, described these well-being benefits: "When I encountered setbacks, my friends and family gave me words of encouragement, and it was really a bowl of warm chicken soup for the soul." And Jeffrey, a 60-year-old American man, said: "I didn't feel a loss of status [during my 14 months of unemployment] because of my financial situation. I saw friends A LOT, and had a lot of people pulling for me."[15]

Economist Lamis Saleh uncovered the well-being benefits of support from friends in a study of Syrian refugees in the Zaatari refugee camp in the Jordanian desert. More than half of them said that their life inside the camp is better than living outside. Support among friends in the camp is central in that well-being.[16]

People rely on information and advice from friends. Economist Michael Bailey and coauthors described a Los Angeles Facebook group of friends who exchanged information about houses, affecting their perceptions of future house prices and likelihoods of buying houses.[17] And people turn to friends for information and advice when taking out a mortgage. Economist Ben McCartney found that people are more likely to make mortgage choices similar to those of neighbors in the same block. "The most likely conclusion is that they were talking with their neighbors about their options," he said.[18,19]

People also rely on friends to manage spending when money is scarce. I'm a couponer," declared Becky Moore, a mother of four, to sociologists Jonathan Morduch and Rachel Schneider. Becky and a friend clipped, organized, and traded coupons, shopping at Walmart and a local supermarket, depending on which had the best discounts that week.[20]

Author Boris Fishman, a 43-year-old man, has an ability to form new friendships, rare among middle-aged men. His wife, a therapist, told him about one of her patients, a man his age, who couldn't think of a single male friend to ask to pick him up from a colonoscopy, a procedure that typically involves sedation.[21] Fishman used his wife's story as a yardstick for friendship. He asked each of his new male friends whether they would drive him home after a colonoscopy. Each said "yes."

The sharpest drop in heterosexual male friendships happens in the early days of a marriage or long-term relationship. The decline is steeper if that marriage or relationship involves children. Emotional overreliance by husbands annoys wives, who tend to maintain longtime friendships even during marriage. Men's interactions tend to be shoulder-to-shoulder, such as watching football games together or playing video games, whereas women's interactions are more likely to be face-to-face, such as sharing coffee and conversation.

One man's closest male friends were from the softball team he has played with for 14 years. Before the COVID-19 pandemic, it has never occurred to him to ask any of his friends to go for a walk and chat, as his wife has been doing with her female friends her entire adult life. In a recent month, however, he has gone on three walks and chats with male friends, and he plans to continue them. "It's totally logical," he said. "Why wouldn't we do this?"[22]

Journalist Billy Baker, a middle-aged man, described his amazement at his wife's ability to engage in long phone conversations with her sister and her friends. His own conversations with his friends tend to last about 45 seconds before one says "All right, I'll catch up with you later."[23] "Loneliness kills," he wrote, "And in the 21st century, by any reasonable measure, loneliness has become an epidemic." He cited a finding that the risk of premature death is 32% higher among lonely people, even those who simply lived alone.

Matt Ritter, a 43-year-old man, goes out to dinner with a group of seven men they befriended as second graders.[24] "I think men have been convinced that success in life does not necessarily include friendship—that if they're successful at work or they've started a family, they've won," Mr. Ritter said. "Our definition has always included having these thriving friendships."

Journalist Catherine Pearson noted a 2021 survey finding that less than half of adult American men said they were truly satisfied with the number of friends they had, and 15% said they had no close friends at all. Men were less likely than women to rely on their friends for emotional support or to share their personal feelings with them.

Pearson offered four strategies for enhancing male friendships. One calls for practicing vulnerability, even if uncomfortable. She told the story of Connor Beaton, a 39-year-old man who disclosed to an old friend his struggle with substance abuse. His friend surprised him by disclosing that he had recently struggled with suicidal ideation. "It really hit me at that moment that I simultaneously knew everything about this man right down to what kind of Scotch he liked to drink, and I had no idea he was struggling so intensely." A second strategy calls for rejecting the assumption that friendships happen organically. "Making friends as an adult requires initiative." Pearson offered the story of Quincy Winston, a 37-year-old man who, at the urging of his girlfriend, established a group for local, professional Black men. "I just wanted to get people in the same room to shed a light on the importance of being friends, and having a community and cultivating a group a brotherhood—of men." A third strategy suggests using activities that foster conversations, such as lunch together. And a fourth strategy calls for harnessing the power of casual check-ins. "People tend to think, oh, he's too busy or he's moved on with his life, he doesn't care." Yet that tendency creates unnecessary barriers to friendship. "Send the text—check in!"

A reader of the article, a gay man, noted that some straight men are afraid of growing too close to other straight men out of concern that the friendship might be labeled as gay. "Straight men don't seem to know what they're missing, namely, that male voice that says to them, 'You don't have to hurt alone. I'm here. And I'm not going to stand by and watch you be harmed—by anyone.'"

A woman wrote: "I'm friends with quite a few women whose husbands have no friends, including my own." Friendship requires a person to reach out to another person and none of these men are ready to do that. "Instead, they rely on us, the women in their lives, for all of their social interactions and emotional needs. If you are a man reading this and it describes you, your wife is tired. You need friends." But a man disagreed: "Women's friendships are based on talking to one another about their feelings. That is what makes them feel close. Men connect with one another through joint activities: playing or watching sports, hunting or fishing, building a deck, repairing a fence. . . . Let men have their way. Stop trying to turn them into women."

Self-disclosure comes easier when friends meet face-to-face, as at work. Work friendships have changed greatly with the advent of COVID-19, when remote work became the norm, and work friendships have changed with it, but remote work was increasing even before the pandemic. The title of a Gallup article in the time before the pandemic was "Why Friendships among Remote Workers Are Crucial."[25] In 2016, 43% of American employees worked remotely in some capacity, up from 39% in 2012, challenging managers and employees to develop better engagement, a critical element of performance. Remote workers feel distant, struggling to stay emotionally connected with the team. The pandemic made that challenge abundantly clear. As journalist Nichole Mo wrote: "Coworkers had little choice but to bond when they spent 40 hours a week together. But if widespread remote work sticks around, those relationships will never be the same."

Mo described two Bay Area tech marketers, a 27-year-old and a 23-year-old, who used to meet regularly at their office for tea and tarot readings "A lot of my work . . . is sending out emails, writing up docs, and there's nothing glamorous or particularly exciting about these individual tasks that make up my day," said the 27-year-old. "What makes it a lot more enjoyable is being able to hang out with people . . . as I'm firing off these emails."[26] Friendships that thrived on the convenience of shared offices now have to be configured into scheduled hangouts to video chats—the two keep their friendship but other relationships have become transactional, reduced to minimal communications about tasks. The 27-year-old said: "When the foundation of your relationship or your friendship with your co-workers is primarily work-based, it's hard to reach out, like 'Oh, let's hang out.'" He spends more time alone now, or with college and high-school friends.

Still, some workers find relief in remote work: "There's kind of an unspoken rule that when we're working remotely, we shouldn't waste time on relationships," said one. Two-hour lunches with work friends may be enjoyable, but leaving the workday a bit earlier might be more enjoyable.[27]

Social media are another place for friendship and self-disclosure, and Facebook is prominent among them, with 2.3 billion monthly active users worldwide, spending an average of 50 minutes per day on Facebook and its sister platforms Instagram and Messenger. Social media has the potential to improve well-being.

In an extensive study, economist Hunt Allcott and coauthors paid a sample of Facebook users who agreed to deactivate their Facebook accounts for four weeks ending just before the November 2018 elections. They found that Facebook provides large benefits for its users. Even after a four-week "detox," users spent much time on Facebook every day and needed to be paid large amounts of money to give up Facebook. Users' answers to follow up questions and interviews noted the many ways Facebook increases well-being as a crucial social connection to those isolated, source of entertainment, and a way to organize a charity or activist group.[28,29]

Readers' comments on an article describing the Allcott and coauthors' study illustrate the ways Facebook friendships enhance well-being or diminish it.[30] "I'm a 60-something who lives alone, works two jobs, and has few single friends," wrote a woman, "but I belong to Facebook private groups for family, for former classmates, and for friends who are like-minded politically. . . . Facebook is not the answer to my less-than-vibrant social life—nothing will ever replace the sound of the human voice—but it offers me an opportunity to connect with people, and for that I am grateful."

But a young man who decisively quit Facebook a couple of months before wrote that he has a clearer state of mind and ability to tolerate periods of time without needing distractions. "I have developed closer relationships to the people that matter because I am actually calling them and meeting them directly instead of being vaguely aware of their goings on. . . ."

Other readers noted diminished well-being among those unaware of the tendency of Facebook users to puff up the images they present, and the need to remember the maxim of "Never compare your insides to everyone else's outsides." A man wrote: "I took a break from Facebook over two years ago because it was too difficult to see how good everyone else's lives were compared to mine." And another wrote: "Life after Facebook is like life before Facebook, with its ups and downs, successes and tragedies, except without the unnecessary comparison, competition, and concern with people that you barely know."

Circles of friendship

Friendships vary in intensity, described by psychologist Robin Dunbar as "circles of friendship." On average, the innermost layer of the circle consists of one or two most intimate people, typically related to us by romantic relationships. The next layer consists of the five people who will drop everything to help us when we are in need. The next 15, including the previous ones, consist of our main social companions, those who join us in social activities and those we trust enough to care for our children when we are away. Next are the 50 who will join in a big-weekend-barbecue, followed by the 150 who will join in weddings and funerals. Sometimes friendships move closer to the innermost layer, as when friendship evolves into a romantic relationship. At other times, friendships move further away. Quality of friendship in strong ties matters most in well-being, but quantity of friendship in weak ties also matters. The layers of the circles of friendship reflect trade-offs between quality and quantity of friendship, as the time we have for friendships is limited. "Falling in love will cost you two friendships," said Dunbar. "If you meet a new person, fall in love, and get married, then you're investing a lot of time and mental energy in that relationship. And from our data, it seems that you essentially sacrifice two people."[31]

Yet "weak ties can offer strong rewards," wrote Journalist Allie Volpe. She tweeted to her weak-tie social network about being laid off in 2015, hoping that someone on the fringes of her social circle would point her to potential opportunities.[32] It worked. Soon after her tweet, a friend of a friend sent her a Facebook message about a position in her department. This friend of a friend is now her boss. "Think of the parents you see in the drop-off line at school. Your favorite bartender. The other dog owners at the park," she advised.

Indeed, there are great benefits in interacting with strangers, enhancing our well-being by making us mentally sharper, healthier, less lonely, and more trustful and optimistic.

Nic spent most of her childhood avoiding interactions with people. At 17, she visited Europe with her high-school classmates and was surprised to find that people started conversations with her. "If people in Europe randomly talked to me, then maybe I'm not so bad," she thought. "Maybe I'm not gonna die if I randomly talk to them." Speaking to strangers at restaurants, bus stops, and grocery stores became part of her life, enhancing her well-being.[33]

The lessons taught by interactions with strangers are worth learning, especially after the pandemic greatly shrank our social circles. Yet many of today's adults are less willing to interact with strangers. Writer David Sax compared the easy interaction between his five-year-old son and a younger boy at a playground to his own difficult interaction with the father of that child.[34] A few minutes into his son's "ninja training" regimen, that younger boy joined, edging closer and mimicking moves. Sax smiled at the child's father and tried some playground banter. But after a few reluctant answers, that father pointed to the AirPods in his ears.

Meanwhile, the two boys played together as if they were old friends. The other father seemed surprised at this instant friendship. "He walked over, knelt and asked his son who he was playing with. 'I don't know his name,' the boy said, as his tiny fingers clutched one of my son's Lego figures, 'but he's my friend.'"

Friendships over time and changing circumstances

Friendships change with age and circumstances. Childhood friends are mostly other children who are fun to play with. Adolescence friendship includes self-disclosure and support, and young adults seek friends who share their values.[35]

"Middle school is about lunch," noted writer Lydia Denworth. We have known for decades that abilities to form friendships and maintain them are crucial to children's well-being. Now we also know the biological and evolutionary reasons for these abilities. "The intensity of feelings generated by friendship in childhood and adolescence is by design." Middle-school children with friends gain well-being by acquiring new and more advanced social skills, whereas middle-school children without friends suffer low well-being in anxiety, depression, and low self-esteem, having no one to sit with them at lunch and no one to protect them when bullied.[36]

Friendship also improves educational attainment. A unique feature of the Tel Aviv school application process allows elementary school students to designate their preferred middle school and list up to eight friends with whom they wish to attend that school.

Economists Victor Lavy and Edith Sand used these lists to define three categories: reciprocal friends who listed one another; followers who listed fellow students as friends but were not listed as friends by these same fellow students; and nonreciprocal friends, who did not list fellow students as friends and were not listed by fellow students as friends. They found that the presence of reciprocal friends and followers in class was associated with significant improvements in test scores in English, math, and Hebrew. In contrast, the presence of nonreciprocal friends in class was associated with deterioration in test scores. Moreover, the presence of reciprocal friends and followers in class was associated with more time allocated for homework, less violent behavior, and enhanced well-being.[37]

An educational peer intervention paired previously high- and low-achieving students as desk mates in elementary schools in China, fostering friendship. That friendship boosted the mathematics scores of the low-achieving students. Moreover, it enhanced the extraversion and agreeableness of both high- and low-achieving students.[38]

Economist Raj Chetty and coauthors described "friending bias" as the tendency for people from working-class and poor families to befriend people of their class. Friending bias is shaped by the structure of the groups, such as high schools, in which people interact.

Some high schools have greater proportions of students from elite families than others, offering greater opportunities for students from working-class and poor families to form friendships with students from elite families. These friendships enhance upward social mobility among students from working-class and poor families.[39]

Friendships change in middle-age, as demands on time increase, with marriage, children, and work, leaving less time for friendships. Yet middle-aged people have typically accumulated many friends from different jobs, different cities, and different activities, classified into the categories of active friends, those we are in touch with regularly, dormant friends, those we are happy to hear from and visit if we are in their city, and commemorative friends, those we do not expect to hear from but are happy when we do.

Yet negativity in social ties is commonplace. Most people are likely to have in their network demanding relatives, noisy neighbors, competitive coworkers, bullying classmates, annoying friends, or offensive supervisors.

Sociologist Shira Offer noted that, with the exception of extreme cases, social relationships usually combine positive and negative interactions incorporating material, emotional, reputational elements, and different net balances of these two kinds of interactions. Negative ties are relationships in which negativity outweigh positivity, diminishing well-being rather than enhancing it.[40] "I'm less willing to tolerate toxic people and situations that sap my energy," said Helene, a 56-year-old American woman interviewed by BlackRock. "I feel it's crucial to conserve my resources for the people and activities I enjoy. Some friendships have deepened because of this, and others have run their course."[41]

The myth of the best-friends-forever is hard to live up to, wrote author Natalie Kon-yu. "In film and television, we often see female friendships portrayed in a highly romanticized and unrealistic manner; uncomplicated and lasting forever despite the differences of the women involved."[42]

Kon-yu told the story of her best friend of 20 years "and then, one day, nothing. She stopped returning my calls; she ignored my messages. . . . And I didn't know why." When she shared her experience with her women friends, she found that her experience is common, described in an anthology, *Just Between Us*, she edited. "It is rich with stories of failed friendships, both between girls and much older women that touch on themes such as envy, sexual jealousies, mental illness, betrayal of confidences, childhood disputes and resentments that have lasted for years."

Writer Pooja Makhijani described one such friendship that fell through the cracks, a friendship forged when she and L were pregnant.[43] They met often during their pregnancies, went to the same prenatal education classes on birthing, breastfeeding, and infant first aid, and exchanged information about yoga and baby clothes. Meetings dwindled after the babies were born, although Makhijani and L continued to text each other daily, bonding over baby stories, but also family and work troubles. Their stream of messages thinned in their second year of parenthood, and then ceased. "No single event marked our relationship's end," wrote Makhijani, "just our slow realization that, despite the intimacy of that first tumultuous year, beyond the traumas of infancy, we had little in common." Still, eight years later, she has come to appreciate and cherish her "seasonal" friendship.

Makhijani was fortunate in a friendship that faded away. Other new mothers suffer the pain of mom-shaming. Melanie Parker was grieving because she wasn't able to hold and nurse her baby immediately after her emergency C-section. She found solace in Instagram photos and posts of mothers sharing her experience. But her solace turned into dismay when she read a comment beneath the picture: "I can't even imagine not being able to hold and nurse my baby." "Mom-shaming isn't always overt," said

Parker, "It's often that side comment that feels like your truth but comes out as judgment." She deleted her Instagram account.[44]

Friendships among women tend to be more intense than among men, but that intensity makes breakups more painful. "It hurt more to lose her friendship than it did to lose my marriage," wrote a woman. A number of years ago she began socializing with a woman she met at work. They were both starting careers at the same university. They met after work to run together in the neighborhood park, and shared their goals, hopes, and frustrations. "And then . . . she stopped meeting me after work for our usual runs. We stopped attending conferences together. I tried to talk to her about the way things were changing between us, but she was not responsive. . . . In many ways there's something more intimate about a friendship with a woman. I trusted her implicitly. And when she just faded away, I felt horribly betrayed. It really hurt."[45]

Political views can establish friendships or demolish them. "Trump's presidency is over," wrote journalist Joe Pinsker, "so are many relationships." He told the story of the silences marking the end of a 30-year friendship between 74-year-old Mary Ann Luna and a close friend from her days at a federal-government job.

Luna and her friend did not speak much about politics before the 2016 election, when the friend started repeating things Trump said and making racist remarks. The end of their friendship neared when the friend sent Luna a prayer for Trump, knowing that Luna didn't like Trump. The end of their friendship came when Luna sent to her friend a message: "I am sorry that your guy lost, but let's leave politics out and just be friends." She never heard back. "I will miss the old person," said Luna, "not the new one."[46]

Friendships in communities

Friendship extends beyond the 150 we might invite to a wedding or funeral. It extends to communities, large and small. American colleges, especially community colleges, are communities to older Americans. They offer courses specifically for students age 50 and older, for fun, friendship, and career retooling. Moreover, some colleges include retirement communities on campus or close to it.

Charlie Klemick, an 84-year-old retired engineer and Ruth, his 82-year-old wife, live in an on-campus retirement community at Pennsylvania

State University and enrolled in The Art of Cinema course. "We get a great benefit out of associating with the young people, and they allow us to stand up and address the class and give our opinions," said Klemick, who noted one drawback. "Our class runs at night from 6:00 to 9:00 p.m. and that's a little long for old people to sit on hard chairs."[47]

Communities revolving around university courses for the elderly are also common in other countries. China offers them in "third-age" universities. "Many elderlies feel hollow after they retire, but I don't have such feelings," said 69-year-old retiree Liu Tian, who has been taking piano lessons.[48] People long for community. Karen, the previously mentioned 60-year old British woman, described that longing. She lives in a place lacking a sense of community or neighborliness. "I used to live in a seaside town with a 'proper' high street and a real sense of community and I miss that."[49]

People who volunteer in their communities enjoy higher well-being than those who do not.[50] "I have always been part of a nonprofit organization that helps homeless elderly," said Jesus, a 26-year old Mexican man. "People who could donate money to the organization used to do it and now that I have the possibility, I am doing it too and will continue doing it as long as I can."

Some are drawn to volunteering in their communities by personal experiences. Michelle, a 49-year old British woman, lost her daughter to mitochondrial disease, and the Lily Foundation helped her greatly. The charity is now part of her life. She donates monthly and does a lot of fundraising. "There is a real sense of self-worth in helping others and knowing that you are assisting in doing some good for someone. . . . It really will have a positive effect on your well-being."

Others are drawn to communities by religion. Mary, a 38-year old American woman grew up in a family that was not wealthy, but her parents never hesitated to help out a friend, family, or neighbor who needed help. "My parents never expected the money back because, as Christians, they knew it was more blessed to give than it was to receive. This was a way they gained a positive sense of well-being and lived up to a greater purpose rather than attempting to accumulate a great amount of wealth."

A Pew Research survey found that connections to friends and community members offer meaning in life to people all over the world.[51] A Greek woman said she finds meaning in life from her "personal life and social life with friends and people we are close to." And a German man said, "I find it remarkable how the COVID crisis affected our behaviors. I, for one, appreciate very much personal contact with those around me."

Australians are the most likely to say that connections to friends and community members offer meaning in life, as do a quarter of people in the Netherlands, New Zealand, Sweden, and the United Kingdom. East Asians, however, are least likely to mention friends or community members as offering meaning in life. No more than 1-in-10 bring up these relationships in these places.

Young adults, those between ages 18 to 29, bring up their friends and community members as offering meaning in life more frequently than older ones. The age difference is greatest in Greece, where 37% of young adults talk about their friends or other relationships outside of their family as offering meaning in life, compared with just 5% of those 65 and older.

Friends and community members are mentioned more frequently as offering meaning in life by those with more education. In the United States, 31% of those with a postsecondary education or more speak about their friends or community members when discussing what brings meaning to their lives, while only 13% of those with less than a postsecondary education say the same.

Those on the ideological left also tend to be more likely to mention friends or community members as offering meaning in life than those on the right. In Canada, 29% of left-leaning adults mention finding meaning in their friendships or community relationships, while just 11% of right-leaning ones say so.

Sharing conspiracy theories serves to form friendships in communities and expand them. People are ready to trade off accuracy for friendships when they share information.[52] Journalist Drew Harwell noted the analogy between members of the QAnon community and members of the WallStreetBets community. He described Jake, a member of the WallStreetBets community, working at an Amazon warehouse job he hated, buying shares of GameStop. "It was palpable, this energy: we were an internet forum taking on Wall Street." That same community power was on display on January 6, 2021, in the riot in the U.S. Capitol by Trump supporters and QAnon believers. "The online communities offered a sense of belonging and intimacy in a pandemic era of mind-numbing tedium, anxiety, and solitude. . . . Some said they were hungry for emotional connection. . . ."

Shared housing, cohousing, and village organizations, are ways to age-in-place in communities where they can maintain their independence yet avoid isolation, postponing institutional assisted living and nursing homes for as long as possible. Shared housing services match elderly people who need housing with others offering housing. These services can be limited to rent and companionship, or extended to lower rent in exchange for grocery shopping, dog walking, or driving, or other services.[53]

A reader described himself as an introvert who lived in shared housing from age 18 to age 41 and still misses it. "Should my spouse (who is a bit younger than I) agree, once we are both ready to move again, we will certainly be considering various forms of shared housing." Yet other readers noted obstacles to shared housing. "Now you are living with someone else's adult child, who has been raised in a different value system regarding housework, yardwork, home repairs, pet care, and so forth."

Elderly Chinese "huddle to stay warm" in communities where they depend on one another for social support, in part, because they cannot rely on the support of their only children or state care facilities. Deng Chao and Shen Exiang, men in their 60s, moved recently from the city of Wuhan, to the countryside. Chao was riding on his motorcycle to the home of Exiang, asking if he and his wife would join in hiking, now that the snow was melting around the village.[54]

Some homes in the Netherlands offer community.[55] A group of late-middle-aged people might renovate an old farmhouse in which to grow old together. Several young families might join in a rural setting to enjoy the peace and quiet and reduced expenses. And a shared home might be a place for refugees or L.G.B.T.Q. residents.

Overhoop is a community in the Netherlands with a core group of three families, including one of Iranian immigrants, and three residents who are single. There are also five guest rooms for visitors such as refugees or recently divorced people. A communal dinner is served once a week in a shared living room. The residents include Frank Mulder, a 42-year-old journalist and father of four. "With Overhoop, we never had a clear plan," he said. "But if you live, love, and pray together, and invite rich and poor to join, things will grow."

Black cultural centers are communities that benefit Black college students by connecting them to campus services that struggle to reach Black undergraduate students, coordinating resources and relationships to meet the needs of students, and collaborating with peer centers to streamline efforts.[56]

Hardships in the time of COVID-19 prompted some to create communities to help those in need, stocking refrigerators on sidewalks with free food.[57] All are invited to take food when they need and place food they don't need. The goals are simple," wrote journalist Amanda Rosa, "reduce food waste and feed the community."

A reader wrote "I just got back from Burlington, Vermont, where some friends tend a garden in a schoolyard . . . the vegetables are for the community. . . . People are beautiful. We need each other to remember what really matters. Together we can do anything."

Bicycle clubs are communities. Weekday Cyclists is a group of riders, mostly older people, that meets weekly at the Loeb Boathouse in Central Park.[58] One rider, an accountant from Ireland who is in New York temporarily, said these weekly rides had enhanced her social life. "It's super for expats," she said, "because it gives you an opportunity to meet real New Yorkers." Members of the group enhance their well-being by exercise and the camaraderie, gathering at a cafe following their rides for drinks, snacks, and chit-chat.

An anti-hate group is a community. The Facebook group #jagärhär (which means "I am here"), is a Swedish community of thousands responding en masse to hateful comments online. Researcher Catherine Buerger described how and why members of the #jagärhär community do what they do, how their joint work affects their willingness and ability to respond to hatred, and how their community takes advantage of Facebook's algorithms to influence ideas and conversation norms among the general public.[59]

Continuing Care Retirement Communities (CCRCs) offer another form of community. Typical CCRCs operate complexes or campuses where residents move from independent living to assisted living, and from there to memory-care units or nursing homes as their health and mobility decline.[60] Many are happy with the contributions of CCRCs to their well-being. One wrote: "I live in a lifecare community. It was a big decision, but not one I regret due to the sense of well-being and security I have that I will be taken care of for the rest of my life . . . it is expensive, but well worth it to me."

10

Health

"There is no life if there is no health," said Virginia, a 46-year old Mexican woman interviewed by BlackRock. "There are no dream; you become vulnerable. Health is human beings' most important wealth."[1] Indeed health, both physical and mental, is crucial in well-being.

Health enhances well-being by the utilitarian benefits of earnings from work unimpeded by illness or disability, and by savings on medical costs. "Five years ago, my husband had a health problem and could no longer support our family because he had no income," said Julia, a 42-year old Mexican woman, "We lost solvency to pay our bills."

Health also enhances well-being by expressive and emotional benefits, expressing ourselves as active rather than confined to a wheelchair or bed, and the emotional benefits of freedom from pain. "Nine years ago, I was pregnant when I suffered a deep thrombosis, and I almost lost my leg and my baby," said Virginia, the 46-year old Mexican woman. "It was a terrible moment, full of anxiety and despair, that made me value every second of my life and appreciate every single movement of your body." People who become disabled adapt, recovering some of their well-being, yet adaptation to severe disability is incomplete.[2]

Well-being promotes health by buffering stress and encouraging healthy behaviors.[3] High well-being is associated with more frequent exercise; healthier diets of fruits, vegetables, and whole grains; reduced cigarette smoking; higher sleep quality; and more preventive health-care visits.

"I try to balance work and life as much as possible," said Robert, the previously mentioned 35-year old American man. "Heading to the gym when I can after work. Walking to work to at least get some healthy perspective in my life."

The COVID-19 pandemic disrupted physical activity, sleep, time use, and mental health. Average daily steps walked declined from 9,400 to 4,600, sleep increased by about 25–30 minutes per night, time spent socializing declined by over half to less than 30 minutes, and screen time more than doubled to over five hours per day. The risk of depression doubled.[4] The pandemic also diminished people's well-being. A study of Chinese residents found that an extra 1% of cumulative death from COVID-19 was associated with a 0.54% decline in well-being. The decline in well-being was especially steep in regions with high COVID-19 risk and among females.[5] Yet people enjoying higher well-being reduced their COVID-19 risk by compliance with mitigation measures, including mask-wearing, physical distancing, and staying at home. Surveys of more than 119,000 adults in 35 countries showed that past and present well-being predicts compliance during lockdown.[6]

Links between physical and mental health

Physical and mental health are indeed inextricably linked. "The brain is intimately connected to the body and the body to the brain," said medical researcher David Spiegel. "The body tends to react to mental stress as if it was physical stress."[7] "Work is so stressful . . . I've come to realize I'm not in my 20s anymore and I need to look after myself and not just work myself to the bone," said Julian, a 36-year old British man. "I've also learned that mental health is just as important as physical health and that the two are inextricably linked." A diagnosis of a physical illness such as heart disease or cancer can inflict mental illness such as anxiety or depression. And mental illness can impose physical illness. Occasional sadness after a door closes leads us to pause, contemplate, and find open doors, perhaps leading to better destinations. Yet persistent sadness can descend into major depression, devastating well-being as people shut down.[8] Schizophrenia, another serious mental illness, leads to severe social functioning problems. People with schizophrenia are often ostracized, making it extremely hard to form close friendships.

Physical activity protects against depression.[9] "As I'm getting older, I'm finding that mental stress has a bigger impact on my physical health," said Helene, the previously mentioned 56-year old American. Stress creeps in slowly into her life and she has to make a conscious effort to identify and combat it. In turn, her store of physical energy affects her ability to handle stress. "I try to allow myself enough rest to face the challenges to my well-being."

Exercise, meditation, yoga, nature, and therapy alleviate stress and promote well-being. Julian, the previously mentioned 36-year old British man, spoke about their benefits. "I have support from a stress counsellor and am learning about (Cognitive Behavioral Therapy [CBT])." He tries to meditate every few days, and does his daily exercise to help his back. He hopes to get back into yoga as soon as he can find a suitable class nearby. He also tries to get up from his desk, take the dog for a walk, stretch, have a drink, and make sure he eats lunch. "Awareness is half the battle."

Michelle, the previously mentioned 49-year old British woman, spoke about the well-being benefits of yoga: "I first experienced a strong sense of well-being when I started to do yoga about three years ago." Yoga helped her focus on herself and be in the moment at a time when she was stressed and anxious. "The feelings and sensations were very positive, and I now try to focus on this philosophy of mindfulness in every aspect of my life." Ana Lía, a 46-year-old Mexican woman, spoke about the well-being benefits of meditation: "I felt well-being when I started taking meditation lessons," she said. "It makes me feel in peace; I feel my mind and my spirit are in perfect balance." And María Elena, a 52-year old Mexican woman, spoke about the well-being benefits of nature: "I went to the beach for a month and I was in contact with nature . . . . I realized how much I had forgotten to take care of myself."

Some illnesses and disabilities, such as a missing limb, are visible. Others, such as cancer or depression, are invisible. "I have depression and anxiety," wrote psychologist Andrew Solomon. "These conditions are well controlled most of the time, but when I have a significant dip, no one makes anything easier for me unless I explain it all to them, an unpleasant effort at the best of times. . . ."[10]

A reader of Solomon's article wrote: "Some of us with invisible disabilities can act 'normal' for a couple of hours every few days, but wearing my public face is exhausting. . . . Those of us with 'invisible' disabilities walk among you, even if you don't see us." Another wrote: "Autoimmune here. While I might look like a million bucks, I do indeed have days or weeks where I am not sure I will make it into the building. There are millions of us, and I can assure you that there is no way to gauge the level of discomfort just by glancing upon us."

Puberty brings changes in the hormones, emotions, priorities, and desires of teens. These changes often lead to brain fogginess, anxiety, low self-esteem, and mood swings. Estrogen, which greatly increases in girls during puberty is linked to depression.[11] The average age of puberty has been declining, and early puberty is associated with poor mental health outcomes. Girls and boys who develop early look different from other children, and therefore, feel self-conscious or isolated, unable to talk about it. They are more likely to suffer anxiety, depression, substance abuse, eating disorders, and increased risk of suicide.

Writer Matt Richtel provided an example of the turmoil of puberty in a story of a 13-year-old girl who ran into the woods, furious when her mother looked at her smartphone. The mother was alarmed by photos of blood on her daughter's ankles from intentional self-harm. Other photos showed the daughter's romantic obsession, the anime character Genocide Jack who kills classmates with scissors. The daughter was also struggling socially. A close friend got popular, while the daughter often came home from school and got into bed. "I felt like a plus one," she said. "I just wanted to be unconscious."[12]

High-speed internet diminished the mental health of teens, especially girls, and harmed the relationship between fathers and daughters most when that relationship was already frayed.[13] And the rollout of Facebook at colleges diminished students' mental health and impaired their academic performance as Facebook fostered unfavorable social comparisons.[14] High-speed internet increased addictive internet use and decreased time spent sleeping, doing homework, and socializing with family and friends.

The scars of poor mental health in early adulthood are long-lasting. People who were diagnosed with depression at ages 27–35 earned 10% lower hourly wages at age 50, and worked 120–180 fewer hours annually, together generating 24% lower annual incomes. Some of this income penalty occurs because depression is often a chronic condition, but more of it occurs because depression in early adulthood disrupts education and work experience, leading people into occupations with lower skill demands, offering lower income.[15]

Depression, schizophrenia, and bipolar illness also carry large earnings penalties in Denmark, ranging from 34% for depression to 38% for bipolar illness to 74% for schizophrenia. Access to treatment eliminates one-third of the earnings penalty associated with bipolar disorder and greatly reduces the risk to earnings.[16]

Treatments for mental illness exist, with recovery rates of 50% or more. In rich countries treatment is likely to have no net cost to taxpayers by savings on welfare benefits and lost taxes, and good outcomes can be had in poor countries at less than a $2 annual cost per person.[17]

Yet medicines for mental illness have drawbacks in side effects along with their benefits, leading many to refuse them. Writer Daniel Bergner described Caroline Mazel-Carlton, who began hearing voices when she was in daycare. Antipsychotic medicines quieted her voices but caused obesity, adding 50 pounds of her weight, and a loss of control of her fore-arms and neck. Her agitation, self-disgust, and terror drove her to yank her hair with her fingers. Classmates taunted her, calling her "fat-ass" and "crackhead." She chose to get off her medications.[18]

Some readers, however, described better experiences with medi-cations. One was diagnosed with bipolar disorder following a severely damaging mania episode. "Fast-forward 10 years, 2 divorces, 3 suicide attempts in and out of hospitals, the doctors finally got my medication right. . . . Since that time, I've gotten clean and sober, rekindled rela-tionships with my children . . . and live a happy and fulfilling life—not perfect but waaayyyy better than unmedicated!"

Another wrote: "There's more to psychosis than voices as my daugh-ter and I learned when she had a florid psychotic break in college. Until medication freed her, she simply sat in a chair, lay in a bed, or curled into a fetal position on the floor, sucking her thumb. . . . Yes, she's had a big weight gain and other challenging side effects. But she can think and reason, walk and talk, work and rest, and love."

Medicine often requires trade-offs. Opioids can relieve chronic pain, but they can also lead to addiction and death by suicide or accidental overdose. The opioid epidemic was not caused by economic distress, wrote economists Janet Currie and Hannes Schwandt. Instead, it was caused by widespread prescription of opioids to "opioid-naïve" patients who went on to become addicted. They recommended a solution in increased access to non-addictive pain treatments, expansion of the use of overdose-reversing drugs, and improved access to medication-assisted treatment.[19]

This solution, however, does not work for everyone. Writer Maia Szalavitz told the story of Anne Fuqua, a former nurse suffering an incurable genetic disorder that causes agonizing spasms and shaking. She is one of the estimated five to eight million Americans with chronic pain who can function only when they take opioids. But her doctor's license to prescribe controlled substances was suspended by the Drug Enforce-ment Administration, marking the second time she's been left to fend for herself to avoid pain and withdrawal symptoms.[20] "I am barely able to get by on my own," she said, noting that her entire body is shaking and jerking all the time as her condition went from well controlled to not controlled at all.

Inequality in health begins before school age. Indeed, it begins before birth, and large differences in health at birth matter greatly later in life. Prenatal exposure to mother's stress leads to higher likelihood of mental illness in children later on, increasing use of ADHD medications during childhood, and anti-anxiety and depression medications in adulthood.[21]

Pregnancy during Ramadan led to lower birth weight among women adhering to its fasting strictures. Muslims in Uganda and Iraq are 20% more likely to be disabled as adults if early pregnancy overlapped with Ramadan. The effects on mental and learning disabilities are especially large.[22]

The introduction of electronic toll collection (E-ZPass) greatly reduced traffic congestion and vehicle emissions near highway toll plazas. It also reduced prematurity and low birth weight among newborns of mothers living within two kilometers of a toll plaza, relative to mothers living 2–10 kilometers from a toll plaza.[23]

The Clean Air Act benefitted Black communities more than white ones, narrowing the gaps between their levels of health. Areas with larger Black populations saw greater Clean-Air-Act-related declines in particulate pollution. Indeed, the Clean Air Act accounts for more than 60% of the racial convergence in the particulate pollution exposure in the United States since 2000.[24] Increases in prenatal Medicaid eligibility in early life programs did more than improve the health of its direct beneficiaries. It also improved the health of their offspring.[25]

Higher education among mothers improves infant health, but there is great controversy about the best ways to improve educational attainment. Moreover, members of the elite are better at taking advantage of the benefits of higher education than members of the working class and the poor.[26]

Thin bodies and fat ones

A thin body was not a mark of high social status in the 16th century. As art historian Kenneth Clark wrote: "Rubens' nudes seem at first sight to have tumbled out of a cornucopia of abundance. . . . They have the sweetness of flowing water."[27] That sweetness has gone sour decades ago. Today, thin goes with rich, each marking high social status, as in "a woman can't be too rich or too thin," and bodies tumbled out of a cornucopia of abundance are now called obese.

Art historian Anne Hollander noted that for about 400 years, from the 16th century through the 19th, "physically substantial" bodies were considered not only beautiful, but also markers of stability and order.[28] European tastes changed in the 19th century as fascination with the smooth nudes of Greek and Roman statues replaced Rubens's fleshy nudes.

The desire for reform in the 19th century was reflected in an increasing preference for thin bodies and stark dress, along with revolutions, romantic fiction, scientific leaps, and religious ferment. Reforms attempted in the 19th century were implemented in the 20th century, adding to the preference for thin bodies. "Today," wrote Hollander, "people spend money, time and energy acquiring the skeletal look of galley slaves."

The preference for thin bodies is evident among people interviewed by BlackRock. "I felt the best around the age of 40—more than 10 years ago," said Anne, a 53-year old American woman interviewed. "I lost more than 50 lbs., felt confident and attractive!" "I feel proud at my slimming self, losing some 12 kilos since December," said Ashley, a 32-year-old British man, "and I am now comfy taking selfies with my yogic wife without worrying about how fat my silly face was!"

The benefits of mind-body practices such as yoga are usually attributed to ego-quieting, allowing practitioners to foster well-being by diminishing their sense of self-importance. Studies, however, suggest that the benefits of these practices arise from ego-boosting by the expressive and emotional benefits of high social status and pride in thin bodies.[29]

Hollander debunked the common notion that the passion for thinness is rooted in a quest for health. She noted that the preference for thinness was firmly established by the end of the First World War, long before wide knowledge of the medical dangers of obesity. "It seems as if the authority of science were now being invoked to give a very good practical reason for what has always been, and still is, a complex esthetic matter."

Indeed, preferences for body shapes vary across today's cultures. In the United States, obesity inflicts great well-being costs, and the well-being costs borne by obese white people are heavier than those borne by Black or Hispanic ones. The well-being costs of obesity are especially heavy among members of the elite in hig-status professions.[30]

Ginni Rometty eventually rose to become chair, president, and CEO of IBM, but her weight hampered her career progression. "Pat, you think I eat too much?" she asked her boss Pat O'Brien early in her career. O'Brien exhorted her to get in "good physical shape" if she wanted to become a high-level executive.[31]

Whereas obesity diminishes social status in rich countries, it enhances social status in poor ones. In Uganda, obesity is perceived as a reliable signal of wealth, but not of beauty or health. The obesity premium is equivalent to a 60% higher income, making it easier to get bank loans. That premium largely diminishes when more financial information is available, providing a more reliable signal of credit worthiness.[32]

Obesity is associated with high well-being in Russia, likely because it is a marker of prosperity.[33] And big and tall Chinese men in rural groups enjoy high well-being, likely because they are better at labor-intensive work. Also, obesity imposes no well-being penalty in urban groups, especially among men, perhaps because of the Chinese cultural practice of feasting while networking at banquets.[34]

The complex esthetic matter underlying the preference for thin bodies in the United States is evident in a study of thinness of *Playboy* centerfolds from 1978 through 1998. The average body mass index (BMI) of centerfolds was 18.1, lower than the 18.5 BMI indicating underweight. Medical researchers Peter Katzmarzyk and Caroline Davis, the authors of this study, wrote: "Given the perception of *Playboy* centerfolds as culturally 'ideal' women, the notion that 70% of them are underweight highlights the social pressures on women to be thin and helps to explain the high levels of body dissatisfaction and disordered eating among women."[35] A subsequent study of centerfolds during the 15 years from 2000 through 2014, found that they have become somewhat heavier on average, but still largely underweight. The highest BMI among them was 18.87.[36]

The MTV docusoaps were labeled as reality-based, yet the bodies of both women and men displayed in them were highly idealized. Communication scholar Mark Flynn and coauthors found that thinness was the most common body characteristic. The bodies of close to half of women were "curvaceously thin" and the bodies of more than half of men were "muscularly lean." The curvaceously thin ideal female body, combining thinness with large breasts, is highly unnatural. The muscularly lean V-shaped ideal male body, combining large muscular arms, chest and shoulders with narrow hips and waist, is also highly unnatural.

Women and men who strive to attain these bodies are susceptible to body dissatisfaction.[37]

Management scholars Christine Beckman and Melissa Mazmanian noted that the "ultimate body," curvaceously thin or muscularly lean, is a status marker among the elite. People who strive for ultimate bodies may perceive them as embodying health, energy, and longevity, yet ultimate bodies are unattainable and the desire for them is costly in money, health, and well-being.

Beckman and Mazmanian described Linda Waldo, who runs on the treadmill in the garage and drinks shakes that "taste disgusting, are pretty thick, and take a while to get down."[38] And they describe Roger Waldo, her husband, who worries about the fat he sees around his belly and posts photos on Facebook with captions such as "morning run with the boys" or "70 miles with this great group! Nice way to start the weekend!"[39]

The Waldos and their peers may understand that the bikini bodies of women in beer commercials and the sculpted chests of men in Equinox advertisements are photoshopped, yet the quest for the ultimate body is hard to resist because the quest for high social status is hard to resist.

A group of 1,148 U.K. adults completed a questionnaire about measures of body image, including body appreciation, and measures of well-being. Results showed that, once the effects of age and BMI had been accounted for, negative body appreciation was associated with low well-being. Women had more negative body appreciation than men, and high BMI was associated with negative body appreciation.[40]

The pressure to be thin is high, often leading to eating disorders. Audra Koopman, a college track and field athlete, was pressed by her coaches to reduce her body fat. "It's interesting how a lot of us have kind of been brainwashed into thinking that . . . it is good for you to lose your period and it is good for you to have that feeling of hunger in your stomach," said Koopman.[41]

Boys are also susceptible to eating disorders. Griffin Henry, whose life revolved around baseball, said, "I thought that slimming down would make me faster, so I started running a lot and watching what I ate," said Henry, "I put a lot of pressure on myself." Friends and relatives complimented him as he became thinner. "I was never big on how I looked and what people thought of me but I started seeing results in my body that I hadn't seen before, and I liked that." Half a year later he was hospitalized, diagnosed with anorexia nervosa. "I remember feeling really hungry, cold, and weak."[42]

Exercise at a gym was not a status marker in 1965 when Joe Gold, a crusty merchant marine, established Gold's Gym in California, where "muscle head" men exercised, and engaged in weightlifting and body-building.[43] Exercising at a gym turned into a status marker and more later. Activities at the Vertical Health Club, established in New York in the early 1980s, included exercise, but the Vertical was glamorous, quite different from Gold's Gym, catering to both men and women. "To be very blunt about it," said author Gay Talese, "it was kind of an elevated pickup joint of well-exercised people."[44]

SoulCycle, a New York gym with dozens of branches, attracts celeb-rities and ordinary people with trainers chanting motivational messages like "I want you to grow."[45] "Wellness, as any SoulCycle devotee will tell you, doesn't come cheap these days," wrote journalist Hayley Phelan. Trainers come at $500 per hour and facials at $750.[46] "It's like the only acceptable lifestyle brag," said Ana, a 26-year-old Manhattan spinning enthusiast. "You are a douche if you brag about your car or how much money you make, but bragging about how much you spin is normal. . . . The green juice, for example, is a display of wealth, discipline, and responsibility—all of which, taken together, reflect and express status."

"Think getting into college is hard?" asked journalist Danielle Braff. "Try applying for these gyms."[47] Cori Zigman, a 44-year-old real estate developer, filled out an application to join Heimat, a Los Angeles fitness club, answering questions about whom she knew at Heimat and what her social media handles were. She was accepted a month later, but some of her friends were not. "It was awkward," she said. "It felt like every-one wanted a membership, but they just weren't handing them out." Sebastian Schoepe, the president and chief executive of the company that owns Heimat, said he was very specific about the types of people who are accepted. Heimat welcomes "people who cultivate that ethos of mindfulness with their fellow members."

Walking groups have become popular in 2023, combining exercise with opportunities to form new friendships. "On a recent chilly Sunday in Manhattan," wrote journalist Chavie Lieber, "a mob of women clad in chunky sneakers and crossbody bags gathered at the corner of Central Park West and 72nd Street. By noon, there were more than 100 of them, all braving the cold for what has become a weekly ritual."[48]

Lieber quoted historian Natalia Mehlman Petrzela who believes that the popularity of walking groups is a response to expensive boutique gyms.

"There's a pushback against hard-core work-out culture, and a resurgence of going back to basics." Moreover, added Petrzela, camaraderie is top of mind for walkers. "There's only so much conversation that can happen during a spin class."

Few can attain the ultimate body, but many can dress the part, in "athleisure" clothing. Even people whose bodies are far from ultimate can signal their status with athleisure clothing in the gym and outside it, signaling that health and wellness matter to them. The Euromonitor noted that "The term *athleisure* includes all of the word leisure, but less than half of the word athletic!" The article quoted an athleisure brand whose website proclaims: "We believe that fitness does not have to be defined by performance."[49]

Healthy foods join exercise as markers of high social status. Brands are busy creating products with health-giving properties, including exotic vegetables, vitamins, and fiber. Mondelez International boasts that "We create snacks to bring people delicious moments of joy. To help consumers on their well-being journey."[50]

Erewhon, an upscale organic grocery store, is a prime Los Angeles place for the elite to see and be seen, wrote journalist Max Berlinger.[51] Health is intertwined with wealth in the lives of elite Angelinos, and the healthiest and wealthiest among them shop at Erewhon. Some readers offered satire. "Funny how many of these Erewhon shoppers look like they haven't actually eaten in years." Others offered good advice. "Just go to the farmer's market nearest you. Better produce, better food, and not an arm and a leg."

"New guidelines underscore how complicated childhood obesity is for patients and providers," wrote journalist Catherine Pearson.[52] She described new guidance by the American Academy of Pediatrics to understand childhood obesity as a complex disease rather than stigmatize it as the result of personal choices. The Academy urged pediatricians to examine and address their own attitudes, for example saying "a child with obesity" rather than an "obese child."

Indeed, a new class of diabetes and obesity drugs, such as Ozempic, show that losing weight is not a matter of willpower alone. Ozempic "shut off the intrusive constant thoughts about food," said Patricia McEwan to health journalist Julia Belluz. "Before Ozempic, Ms. McEwan thought her overeating was driven by her emotions and lack of willpower. After Ozempic, she understood that how she responded to food was the product of her physiology."[53]

Aging and end of life

Physicians regularly frame patients' stories and their degrees of tragedy by age, wrote physician Daniela Lamas. "Someone in her 30s should receive aggressive chemotherapy or a risky surgery or an organ transplant, but for someone in her 70s, those same interventions might do more harm than good."[54]

Lamas used to see human life span as an arc that ends naturally somewhere around the 80s or even 90s. But now, pregnant for the first time at age 41, she sees it differently, fascinated by the promise of longevity. She watches her father, a 70-year-old cardiologist and researcher, lifting his body on a set of pull-up bars, expecting to live long enough to see his first grandchild graduate from high school. Longevity researchers see aging as a disease they can understand and treat, considering cancer, heart disease, and dementia only as symptoms. Optimism leads some to believe that the first person to live until 150 has already been born.

Brian Hanley, 64-year-old a mathematical biologist is even more optimistic. He expects the gene therapies he is developing to extend to 150 his "health-span," the period of good physical and mental shape. He is not interested in life span without health-span.[55] What will he do if he lives that long, asked journalist Joe Pinsker. "Oh, I would like to see Mars—it would be really interesting to be part of that settlement and try to make that work."

Yet end-of-life comes to all, even to those who exercise regularly and eat the right foods, even to those who live to 150. End-of-life choices are agonizing to patients, their families, and the healthcare professionals who care for them. But choices must be made. "When very old patients suffer cardiac arrest," wrote journalist Paula Span, "doctors usually try to revive them—even if they were already near death."[56] A sample of clinicians—paramedics, emergency technicians, emergency physicians and nurses—was asked to recall their most recent patient over 80 who had undergone cardiopulmonary resuscitation (CPR). "Only 2% of these patients survived long enough to leave the hospital. Yet more than half the healthcare professionals thought CPR was appropriate in those cases. Only 18.5% thought it inappropriate."

An emergency room physician with 35 years of experience wrote: "We have gotten better at resuscitation, especially in younger patients. But I have to tell you, the times when I have felt multiple ribs break in [an older] patient I know will not likely survive makes me feel like a torturer. Period."

Some young people face end-of-life choices with touching grace. One of them was Francia Bolivar Henry, a pastry chef with a captivating smile in her 30s, cared for by physician Daniela Lamas. She suffered an inflammatory disease that damaged her lungs, and her only hope to stay alive long enough for a transplant was a machine that would take the place of her damaged lungs. When hope for transplant was gone, her boyfriend proposed to her, and a wedding followed. Ms. Henry wore a wig with a veil that covered her catheters, and her wedding dress hid the chest tubes. "There was a wedding playlist. A first dance. She beamed. . . . Perfect and so messed up at the same time." When Ms. Henry was ready, she was dosed with medications for pain and anxiety. "Her oxygen levels dropped. Her eyes closed. . . . And just as the sun set that evening, Ms. Henry died."[57]

Some make peace with dementia or Alzheimer's, as the late Supreme Court Justice Sandra Day O'Connor did when announcing her diagnosis at age 88.[58] Others choose euthanasia or suicide. Novelist Amy Bloom wrote about her marriage, her husband's Alzheimer's diagnosis, and his decision to end his life.[59] Her husband, Brian Ameche, a 66-year-old accomplished architect and former football player, said, "I'd rather die on my feet than live on my knees." The couple considered suicide by carbon monoxide, firearms, or drowning, but each has risks and legal ramifications. Bloom located Dignitas in Zurich, Switzerland, offering "accompanied suicide," following examination of medical records and a $10,000 fee.

John Griffith, a 99-year-old man, made clear to his three sons that he would end his life rather than prolong his misery by unwanted treatment in assisted living.[60] Ben, his 67-year-old son, knew his father would have chosen assisted suicide, but it was not legal in Missouri. John chose to stop eating and drinking, a dying process that takes between seven and 15 days. Ben stayed with his father. As death was at hand, Ben "laid his hand on his father's shoulder and leaned over him so that his lips nearly brushed his father's ear. "It's okay," he said. "Let your body go. We love you." And within a few minutes, John Griffith was gone.

"Suicide is not an act of cowardice," wrote attorney Ken White. People do not commit suicide because death seems suddenly appealing. A person who commits suicide is like the trapped person who jumps from the window of a burning high-rise. "You'd have to have personally been trapped and felt flames to really understand a terror way beyond falling.[61]

Responding to an article about suicide among the elderly, one wrote: "My father did not commit suicide. He took his own life." Her father was 84 years old, having suffered two major heart operations, a significant cognitive loss from much time under anesthesia, and a diminished world he found unacceptable. He called her one night, told her he loved her, and several hours later, jumped off the roof of his condominium. "He was not, in his life, a brave man. Far from it, but he came to that moment when death became his friend. I never had more respect for him than for his decision to take control of his life, and his death."[62]

Health and finances

The domain of health is closely linked to the domain of finances. "If we are healthy, our working ability and earning capacity are improved," said Greg, the previously mentioned 63-year old British man. "Conversely, if we are financially healthy, we can afford better and more healthcare services and products as well as better quality foods. . . ."

Concerns about the cost of healthcare and medical insurance are prominent among Americans. Meredith, the previously mentioned 31-year old American woman, posted a photo of a notice at her physician's office: "Your Insurance Company Requires that We Collect Your Copay at the Time of Service." Meredith added, "If you're lucky enough to be able to afford insurance, or are provided insurance through your employer, you still have to pay copays and find in-network healthcare."

Concerns about the cost of healthcare and health insurance are especially prominent among retired Americans and those nearing retirement who worry that healthcare expenses, especially nursing home expenses, will leave them destitute. "I think our biggest financial worry is that the cost of our healthcare grows beyond our budget," said Bill, the previously mentioned 52-year old American man. "I have talked to my [financial] adviser about healthcare issues. He did not have a solution for healthcare other than to include the projections for increased costs into our long-term plan."

Absence of medical insurance can result in substantial medical debt.[63] Unpaid medical bills were the largest source of debt that Americans owe collections agencies between 2009 and 2020. People in the states that have declined to expand Medicaid had more medical debt before the Affordable Care Act was enacted, and the difference between their medical debt and that of people in states that had expanded Medicaid had grown wider. Moreover, debt has risen among older people, and those who carry more debt are also more likely to have multiple illnesses, including hypertension, diabetes, cancer, heart and lung disease, and heart attacks and strokes.

Denise Revel, a 62-year-old woman, lacks medical insurance. She was compelled to go to the emergency room when a blood clot in her leg grew painfully swollen and hot to the touch. Ms. Revel recovered from the clot, but could not pay the medical bill. "It's like a dark cloud over your head," she said. "You get people calling you, being demanding; some can be very rude. You don't even want to answer your phone."[64]

A woman reacting to Revel's story noted that the burden of debt carried by the elderly poor is often passed on to their adult children who deplete their own savings or health if they become caregivers. "Lack of decent medical care for all has the potential to produce multigenerational harm."

Disclosure of dementia or Alzheimer's by public figures eases stigma, but it does little to ease financial burdens. A reader wrote about the financial burdens of caring for her father following his Alzheimer's diagnosis. "Whether it's a famous person who comes out to acknowledge her journey with this terrible disease or someone like my Dad, an ordinary man to most but a great man in my eyes, the best resources should be available to all who are diagnosed with this terrible disease." But these resources are not available.[65]

Another reader noted the additional financial burdens imposed by providers of health insurance. She will not disclose to her physician that her father has dementia for fear that her opportunity to buy long-term care insurance would be diminished and its cost would rise. "I don't necessarily care about people knowing in general, but I don't want to be victimized by an insurance company."

The benefits of medical insurance are evident in the long-run effects of childhood Medicaid eligibility on adult health and economic outcomes. Early childhood Medicaid eligibility reduced mortality and disability, increased employment, and reduced disability payments up to 50 years later. Medicaid has saved the American government more than its original cost and saved more than 10 million quality-adjusted life years.[66]

The benefits of medical insurance are also evident in the consequences of the health insurance mandate in Massachusetts and its coverage expansion. Massachusetts residents experienced significant improvements in well-being relative to residents of Connecticut and other New England states.[67]

And the benefits of medical insurance are evident in the consequences of health insurance in Oregon whereby some low-income and uninsured adults were chosen by lottery to enroll in the Medicaid program. Medicaid coverage increased outpatient visits, hospitalizations, prescription medications, and emergency department visits. Coverage greatly reduced medical debt, and virtually eliminated catastrophic medical expenses. Coverage also greatly reduced the prevalence of depression, but had no significant effects on physical health, measured by blood pressure, cholesterol, or cardiovascular risk.[68]

The American medical safety net is relatively weak. The British safety net is stronger, but not strong enough for everyone. "When I had lymphoma, I was receiving full pay, etc.," said Helen, the previously mentioned 51-year old British woman, "but if it had happened to my husband and he couldn't work then we may have had a problem as he was self-employed at the time." Moreover, worries abound about the future of the British National Health Service. "If the current and future governments continue to underfund the system it will collapse," said Julian, a 36-year old British man.

The Finnish medical safety net is strong. "I live with bipolar disorder and severe PTSD," wrote a reader of an article about Americans living with disabilities.[69] "Thank heaven I live in a country where we all pay taxes for healthcare. I have all the medical and social assistance I need. . . . I don't know how Americans with mental illness disabilities go about their lives healthfully. I suppose they don't."

11

Work

"No words can actually describe the absolute amazing feeling it takes to deliver a new life into this world," said Barbara, the previously mentioned 28-year-old British midwife in a National Health Service (NHS) medical unit She enjoys great satisfaction in ensuring that all medical issues or worries of her patients are quickly dissolved before major health issues occur, "and just the gratefulness of my patients towards me does a lot to my spirit and the nature of my personality."

Work is prominent among the domains of life well-being, in part, because it accounts for large portions of our waking hours, often dictating where we live, how we spend our days and nights, and what we do in our leisure time. We derive utilitarian benefits from our work in earnings, and also expressive and emotional benefits, in identity, meaning, community, dignity, and pride. We celebrate work events at our workplaces, whether promotions or retirements, and also life events whether births or birthdays.[1]

Attitudes about work illustrate differences between experienced well-being and evaluative and meaning well-being. Nobel Laureate psychologist Daniel Kahneman and economist Alan Krueger assessed net affect, a measure of experienced well-being, of activities such as work, socializing after work, watching TV, and commuting, by the average of three positive adjectives: happy, warm/friendly, and enjoying myself, minus the average of six negative adjectives: frustrated/annoyed, depressed/blue, hassled/pushed around, angry/hostile, worried/anxious, and criticized/put down.[2] They found that intimate relations ranked first in net affect, followed by socializing after work. Work ranked next to last, lower than evening commute and higher only than morning commute.

Yet economists Jan-Emmanuel De Neve and George Ward found that employed people enjoy higher evaluative life well-being than the unemployed, standing on a Cantril ladder step that is higher on average than the step of the unemployed.[3] And economist Andrew Bryce found that most people derive high meaning well-being from their jobs, considering work more meaningful than consumer purchases, socializing, relaxing, or leisure.[4]

Workers report the same evaluative well-being on workdays and weekends, but they report greater experienced well-being on weekends and public holidays, including more happiness, enjoyment, and laughter, and less worry, sadness, and anger. Social context, both at work and at home, matters in experienced well-being. Weekend effects are twice as large among full-time paid workers as among the rest of the population, but they are much smaller among workers who consider their work supervisors as partners rather than bosses, and whose work environments are trusting and open.[5]

John, the previously mentioned 30-year-old British man, illustrated the difference between meaning well-being and experienced well-being as he described the high meaning well-being he derives from his job, and the low experienced well-being he suffers in commuting to and from that job. He loves working with clients, helping them purchase properties that are right for them. What he dislikes is the commute to Manchester, "it can be draining at times."

Links between work and well-being run in both directions. Work enhances well-being and well-being enhances work prospects and outcomes. Men who work longer live longer, evident in the outcomes of a Dutch program that reduced taxes on those working past age 60. Men who worked longer saw the mortality rate in their 60s fall from about 8% to 6%.[6] And high employee well-being leads to high employee productivity, high customer loyalty, low employee turnover, and ultimately, tangible benefits to employers in increased profitability.[7]

Company leaders increasingly understand that employee well-being benefits companies, not only employees. "For Chief Financial Officers, well-being can offer healthy returns," wrote Jen Fisher, chief well-being officer at Deloitte, a consulting and accounting company, and her colleague Anh Phillips.[8]

They noted that chronic overwork inflicts health problems that diminish employee productivity, such as depression, diabetes, heart disease, and sleep disorders, and cited a survey showing that 80% of organizations identify employee well-being as important or very important in their organization's success. They added that well-being is promoted by a holistic approach, providing employees with the tools they need to enhance well-being.

Yet employee wellness programs are still struggling to prove their benefits.[9] Health policy researchers Zirui Song and Katherine Baicker followed thousands of BJ's Wholesale Club employees for a year to monitor the effects of its wellness program. Workers who enrolled in the program reported that they exercised more and watched their weight, but Song and Baicker found no significant differences in outcomes like lower blood pressure or sugar levels and other health measures. And they found no significant reduction in workers' healthcare costs.

"These findings may temper expectations about the financial return on investment that wellness programs can deliver in the short term," concluded Song and Baicker, but they added that the BJ's Wholesale Club program should be seen as a necessary first step rather than the final verdict on workplace wellness programs.

Utilitarian, expressive, and emotional

A man interviewed by Pew Research Center illustrated the utilitarian, expressive, and emotional benefits of work: "I restore old homes and LOVE doing that because I am a bit of an artist and love to design these old beauties back to their former glory. . . . I couldn't care less about being rich." This man expresses himself as an artist, restoring 'old beauties,' and enjoys the emotional benefits of 'love' for his work. He 'couldn't care less about being rich,' but he cares about the utilitarian benefits of earnings from work necessary for even modest living.

Flaviana Decker, a 44-year-old woman, did not expect to be rich before she lost her 14-year job as a Disney World waitress, a victim of COVID-19. Decker's loss of the utilitarian benefits of her work was compounded by the expressive and emotional costs of being addressed as "Dear Cast Member" in the layoff letter she received. A fellow laid-off worker texted "They could have at least used our name," and another added "That's all we are, just a number."[10]

Work offers expressive and emotional benefits in dignity. An Italian man interviewed by Pew said: "Without a job it is difficult to have dignity." And work offers expressive and emotional benefits in a sense of accomplishment and personal growth. A Japanese man said: "I got the job that I wanted. . . . I'll have left my mark when I look back on my life.[11]

Job security enhances well-being and job insecurity diminishes workers mental health as much as unemployment does. "I have job security in what might otherwise be unstable economic times," said a man interviewed by Pew. "I have enough to pay my bills plus a little more." Sadly, job security was always absent in the life of Flaviana Decker, diminishing her well-being even before she was laid-off.

H1-B visas allow foreign workers, mostly Indian nationals, to work in the United States. Many assumed that their tech skills provide job security but that security was illusory and vanished in massive layoffs in the tech sector in 2023. They would be compelled to leave the United States within 60 days unless they found a new job.

"It's upsetting because things were going good and soon my wife will be delivering a baby," said 36-year-old Indu Bhushan. Bhushan has been searching for a new job, but competition for tech jobs is fierce. "Returning to India just because my H1-B is not being supported is the worst way to leave a country, which is known as the opportunity place."[12]

The contributions of the expressive and emotional benefits of work to well-being are evident in a study of refugees in Bangladesh camps. Some were assigned to a group that worked and received cash for their work, and others were assigned to a group that received the same amount of cash with no work. Work increased well-being substantially more than cash alone, and 66% of refugees assigned to the group that worked were willing to continue working for free. The high value refugees assigned to the expressive and emotional benefits of work is especially remarkable given poverty that made urgent its utilitarian benefits.[13]

Mere satisfaction with work provides fewer expressive and emotional benefits than being engaged in work. Gallup defines *engaged workers* as those who are involved in, enthusiastic about, and committed to their work and workplace. It defines *actively disengaged workers* as those with miserable work experiences, and *not engaged workers* as generally satisfied but not cognitively and emotionally connected to their work and their workplace—they show up to work and do the minimum required, but are likely to leave their company for a slightly better offer. In 2018, 34% of American workers were engaged, 13% were actively disengaged, and the remaining 53% were not engaged.[14]

Divya, the previously mentioned 33-year-old American woman, works at an IT firm, but is not engaged in that work, or perhaps, actively disengaged from it: "My life goal is to start a food truck business. I love cooking and I'm tired of working in tight schedules and completing projects in my work environment."[15]

Highly paid workers are not necessarily engaged in their work. Indeed, some are actively disengaged from it, seeing their jobs as no more than means to an end. Sociologist Marianne Cooper quoted Brooke Mah speaking about her husband Paul. "I always think he's not a happy person because I don't think he enjoys work. He just knows that he has to do it." It's not always fun, he tells his children, but you have to do it. "So, I kind of feel bad for him." Paul admits he doesn't like the work he does: "Do I like it? Not particularly. I do it because it pays the bills. But the nature of what I do day to day, am I competent at it? Yes. Do I love doing it? No."[16]

Cooper also quoted Bret Colson who was promoted at work, taking on an additional layer of responsibility, in part, because of higher financial rewards. "I frankly don't like the job I'm doing now as much as what I was doing before." Indeed, promotions provide higher financial rewards and greater privileges, but they do not always enhance well-being because they are accompanied by increased responsibility, accountability, and work hours. Promotions improve work satisfaction in the short term, but mental health is significantly lower two years after receiving a promotion.[17]

"Not engaged" turned into "Quiet quitters" in the time of COVID-19, describing workers who do no more than meet their job descriptions.[18] As a Gallup survey noted, this is a problem because most jobs today require some level of extra effort to collaborate with coworkers and meet customer needs. The increase in quiet quitters in the time of COVID-19 was largely due to unclear expectations, absence of opportunities to learn and grow, feeling uncared about, and lack of connection to the organization's mission or purpose. The decline in engagement was especially pronounced among Gen Z and younger Millennials working remotely.

The time of COVID-19 was also the time of the Great Resignation, as workers reflected on their well-being and some chose to quit their jobs. A study in Oregon during COVID-19 found that 27% of people changed employment status, 11% of workers lost their job, 5% quit, and a little more than 2% retired.

Yet Oregon workers who quit their jobs did not necessarily hate working. Indeed, 26% of workers indicated they were considering quitting their job despite 75% indicating they were very or somewhat satisfied with their current job.[19]

Journalist Sydney Ember described Justin Hoffman, a 28-year-old marketing director at an orthopedic practice, who probably would have quit his job eventually because he was not engaged in his work, and perhaps, actively disengaged from it, but the pandemic hastened his decision. "For Mr. Hoffman, the decision to leave his job was the culmination of months of perceived injustices, which he said he was able to evaluate more clearly because of the pandemic."[20]

Indeed, "resignations are rising because people are seeing more job listings, not because they're feeling more Marxist," wrote journalist Derek Thompson.[21] "We probably shouldn't even call it the Great Resignation. It's more like the Great Job Switcheroo."

Some quit jobs for self-employment, as Melody and Ian Karle did.[22] Ian was sick of his job as a quality manager at a company in the oil and gas industry in Texas. Melody was working as an academic librarian. They moved to Montana, where Melody took a job as a remote library system administrator, and Ian started his own artisanal chocolate company. "You don't even know how much stress is on you until it's gone," said Melody.

Self-employment frees workers from stress inflicted by bosses. Indeed, the well-being of self-employed workers is higher than that of employees, regardless of income gained or hours worked.[23] Yet the self-employed tend to be overoptimistic, predicting higher well-being five years in the future than their actual well-being five years later. This might be because they underestimate their working hours and overestimate their leisure satisfaction.[24]

Jobs, careers, and vocations

Jobs become careers when they follow a professional ladder, such as from Second Lieutenant in the army to First Lieutenant, Captain, Major, and on to General. Jobs and careers become vocations or callings when they are closely linked to their identity, the answer to the question "Who am I?"[25]

Energy healing is a vocation to a man interviewed by Pew. He loves his work, helping people to overcome limitations, improve their health and expand their consciousness. "Personal human connections with friends, clients, students and other people in my life help me contribute to creating a better world."[26]

Work that offers personal autonomy, opportunities to help others, and a sense of positive social impact, is most likely to serve as a vocation, including the work of therapists, physicians, nurses, teachers, and social workers.[27]

Luis, a 34-year-old Mexican man interviewed by BlackRock, described the well-being he derives from his vocation, helping people and the planet. He felt a strong sense of well-being when he built a renewable energy company. "I feel satisfaction and I am proud of being able to help the planet in these times in which so many people are trying to destroy it."[28]

High well-being among workers who help others is consistent with the observation that doing so enhances the well-being of both helpers and helped. Positive social impact is even more important in enhancing well-being than desire to help.[29] Yet approximately 8% of workers perceive their work as socially useless, and another 17% doubt the usefulness of their work, diminishing their well-being.[30]

Workers in one study were asked to label tumor cells. Some workers were told the purpose of their task was to identify tumor cells while other workers were not told anything about the purpose of their work. Workers were more likely to participate when told their task is to identify tumor cells, and when participating, labeled more images.[31]

Another study manipulated the usefulness of a task—assembling a Lego structure—by varying whether the assembled structures were dismantled immediately after completion or kept intact. People asked for a 40% higher wage to do the assembly task when the structures were dismantled immediately, compared to when the structures were kept intact.[32]

Senator Diane Feinstein was 90 years old when she passed away, and in obvious failing health when she declined to resign. "It is not just the perks, like free, reserved parking spots at D.C. airports, that make it appealing to hang on," wrote journalist Annie Karni. "Ms. Feinstein, after all, is wealthy, and has flown on private planes for the majority of her career." Feinstein referred to her work as her calling. "I continue to work and get results for California," she said.[33]

The end of the life of George Eastman, founder of Eastman-Kodak photography company, is an extreme illustration of work as vocation and identity. Journalist Kaitlyn Tiffany told the story of her fifth-grade class field trip to the George Eastman Museum in Rochester, New York. At the end of the tour they read the words Eastman wrote before shooting himself in the heart. "My work is done. Why wait?" "Telling this story to a bunch of 10-year-olds was not meant to be morbid, it was meant to be edifying: To work is to live."[34]

Leaving work that serves as identity diminishes well-being. Sociologist Pamela Stone described Wendy Friedman, a book editor, contemplating leaving her work. "How could I do this?" she thought. Yes, she was a mother and a wife, but "my whole identity was work."

Maeve Turner was a district attorney before she left work. "You know, the first question they always ask you is, "Well, what do you do? Where do you work?" And I say, 'Well, I'm not working now. I'm staying home with my children.' And it was like this wall of invisibility."[35]

Leaving work that is not a vocation can enhance well-being. Dorothy Lennon, a 43-year-old woman, switched from a focus on her work as a senior banking executive to a focus on her family. She described it as a switch from "doing" to "being." And a woman interviewed by Pew described her good fortune, being able to withdraw from the labor force to stay home and raise her children: "I knew from a young age that I wanted to stay home and raise children. I was incredibly fortunate and married a man who felt that was important for a family too."[36]

But another woman interviewed by Pew described her frustration at being a stay-at-home mom, devoid of hobbies, career, and even friends: "Currently, I don't feel very satisfied with my life. I'm a stay-at-home mom, and my life is endless monotony and chaos."

Work among the working class and the elite

Work enhances well-being but not all work enhances it equally. Moreover, no work fits everybody. Averages of well-being by particular work can mask differences in fitness of particular work to particular workers. People enjoy high well-being when they do work that fits their interests and personalities.[37]

Still, blue-collar work yields lower well-being on average than white-collar work in labor-intensive industries such as construction, mining, manufacturing, transport, farming, fishing, and forestry. Managers, executives, officials, and professional workers place themselves on average higher than the sixth step of Cantril's well-being ladder, whereas people working in farming, fishing, or forestry place themselves on average lower than the fifth step.[38]

Blue-collar work requires physical strength and agility that diminish rapidly as workers age, whereas white collar work requires mental strength and agility that diminish more slowly. We see the difference between blue-collar and white-collar workers in Social Security sign-up ages. Half of blue-collar workers sign up for Social Security as soon as they are eligible—at age 62. In contrast, a large majority of white-collar workers work beyond age 62.[39]

Lorraine Porto retired from her white-collar job, but her family is filled with craftsmen, carpenters, electricians, farmers, and truckers who worked until they were worn out. People in white-collar jobs are not always aware "just how tough and demanding it is to climb poles every day, descend into manholes, build skyscrapers, or bring in hay in 90-degree heat and sub-zero temperatures," she said.[40]

Delaying sign-up for Social Security was impossible for Mark Roberts, a 67-year-old former electrician. He had to apply for disability benefits because his foot injury got worse over time. He was not able to work long enough or earn enough to save for retirement and struggles to live on his Social Security checks. "I have to survive for a month on what I used to make every week." [41]

Yet blue-collar workers take pride in their technical expertise and derive well-being from it. Law professor Joan Williams described a pipe fitter criticizing white-collar "shirt and ties types" for "too much politicking." "They are jockeying for jobs and worrying about whether they are making the right moves and stuff. I feel that I don't have to get involved in that." More generally, working-class men often see elite professionals as phony. A man who had left Wall Street to be a firefighter said: "In big business, there's a lot of false stuff going on." And an auto mechanic said: "You know what I hate? Two-face. I can't stand that. You're a fake, you're a fake. Why be a fake?"

Dignity and esteem among members of the elite comes from work in professions.[42] Dignity and esteem is also available to some in the working class, firefighters, police officers, or soldiers. For most members of the working class, however, dignity and esteem do not come from work. "What do you do?" is a common ice-breaker question among the elite, yet members of the working class see it as displays of class privilege.

Williams described attending her husband's high school reunion when he posed the "What do you do?" question to a working-class classmate. The classmate's face got very red as he came right up into her husband's face and hissed, "I sell toilets." [43]

Philosopher Michael Sandel noted that the high esteem bestowed on members of the elite diminishes the esteem granted to members of the working class. It tells them that the work they do is not only less valuable in utilitarian earnings but also in expressive and emotional benefits of dignity and honor. "At the heart of the populist resentments that roil American politics are grievances about work."[44]

Sandel quoted Martin Luther King Jr.'s words to striking sanitation workers in 1968. "The person who picks up our garbage is, in the final analysis, as significant as the physician," King said, "for if he doesn't do his job, diseases are rampant. All labor has dignity."

Williams noted further that the jobs of working-class people tend to be rigid, highly supervised, and often boring and repetitive. Men's jobs, such as in factories, construction, and long-haul truck driving, are hard, physically and emotionally. Women's jobs, such as in nursing, customer service, and managing small stores can be emotionally draining, even when not as physically hard as those of men. People in the working class value responsibility and obedience because their conditions of work and life combine with few financial resources to make it hard to protect themselves against adversities.

Members of the elite value independence rather than obedience. Whereas disruption can get working-class workers fired, disruption among the elite means founding a successful start-up. Economist Daron Acemoglu described the effect of the difference in values in the way parents prepare their children for the work world. Working-class parents convey values of obedience to their children to help them fit in a work world where they will be taking orders, whereas elite parents convey values of independence to their children to help them fit in a work world where they will be giving orders. Values of independence prepare elite children to work as professionals or entrepreneurs, promoting social mobility, whereas values of obedience retard social mobility.[45]

The increased work-from-home practice in the time of COVID-19 widened the well-being gap between members of the elite and those of the working class. Many among the working class were designated as "essential workers," such as supermarket cashiers, which brought little pay increases but much exposure to COVID-19. In contrast, work-from-home was prevalent among members of the elite, common in industries with better educated and better paid workers.[46]

Work-life balance

Work and life, especially family life, can be mutually incompatible, diminishing well-being. Heavy workload, long hours, and stressful work situations can increase work-family conflicts, whereas family stressors and demands such as childcare responsibilities or marital discord can increase work-family conflicts.[47]

Sociologist Marianne Cooper quoted a teenage boy, "My dad is at work a lot. I don't talk to him a whole lot." He likes to hang out with his father, he says, "but I'm not really close with my dad as much as I am with my mom."[48]

James, the previously mentioned 52-year-old American man, described poor work-life balance.[49] He built a psychological outreach program with his fiancé and it was a great business and things were going very well. He felt financially and personally gratified because he was providing a tremendous service to the public. Yet the stress of the company growth took a toll on their relationship and he was ousted from the company. "For several years after, I felt lost and it was a very trying time for me emotionally."

Hannah, a 30-year-old research scientist in Scotland, described good work-life balance. Her research work can consume life with pressures to create outputs. Yet her organization encourages work-life balance. "When I started, I was told that hour-long lunch breaks were the norm and actually taken, with many people going for walks, exercising, socializing, running or even sailing in that break. . . . I am more productive in work time: I know I have a lot to do and a limited time, so I achieve it."[50]

A four-day work week is an attempt to increase work-life balance and enhance well-being without diminishing productivity. A study of a four-day work week in the United Kingdom found that most employees maintained their productivity. Moreover, almost 4-in-10 employees experienced less stress, half experienced improvement in mental health, and almost 4-in-10 also experienced improvement in physical health.[51]

Work can diminish well-being when it conflicts with family, but work can also enhance well-being of families in income that sustains them, and in friendships, skills, and a sense of competence. This bi-directional enhancement of work and family is evident in a study of employees of a retail organization asked to state their work satisfaction by levels of agreement with statements such as "I am generally satisfied with the kind of work I do in my job," family satisfaction by levels of agreement with statements such as "I am happy with the progress toward the goals I have for my family," work-to-family family enrichment by levels of agreement with statements such as "Helps me understand different viewpoints and helps me be a better family member," and family-to-work enrichment by levels of agreement with statements such "Helps me acquire skills and this helps me be a better worker." The study found that work-to-family enrichment promotes job satisfaction, and family-to-work enrichment promotes family satisfaction.[52]

Time and money

We convert time into money by income from work, balancing work and life and enhancing our well-being by the utilitarian benefits of what money can buy. And we convert money into time, balancing work and life and enhancing our well-being by the expressive and emotional benefits of what free time can provide. We combine time and money, and substitute one for the other to reach our best work-life balance.

Retirement reduces available money but increases available time. Retired people convert time into money by shifting their purchases into products that cost less money but require more time to turn into consumption experiences.[53]

The typical American home of 1900 had no electricity, wrote journalist Derek Thompson, and only the rich had indoor plumbing. The decades that followed brought time-saving refrigerators, stoves, washers and dryers, and vacuum cleaners.[54]

People could have converted their newfound time into the expressive and emotional benefits of leisure, but most chose to convert it into the expressive and emotional benefits of laundered clothes and clean homes. "Because we housewives of today have the tools to reach it," said a woman in the 1920s, "we dig every day after the dust that grandmother left to a spring cataclysm."

Few people have all the time and money they want. Money squeeze is common, and so is time squeeze. But these two squeezes take different forms among the working class and the elite.

A Brookings Institution report described Kevin, a working-class father working in his financially strained family business. He cares about his children and would like to provide them with all the money and all the time they need, but he feels squeezed, compelling him to choose money over time. "Right now, all my time is on making money, any which way possible. . . . I try to give the kids stuff . . . just all the stuff I didn't have."[55]

Trevor, a working-class father working in pest control, faced the choice between time and money when his son asked to take him to the Renaissance festival. Trevor, like Kevin, chose money over time. "I've got to make this money," he told his son. When Trevor's wife said that his son was upset, he said, "Yeah, but you got to understand."

Working-class mothers are pressed into choices between time and money as much as fathers, if not more. More working-class mothers now work full-time while continuing to do most of the household work and childcare. Single-parent families are now more common, especially among mothers at the lower end of the working class, adding to the pressure to provide both time and money. Working-class mothers typically feel they never have enough time, are unable to catch up, and suffer the nagging sense that their work is never done.

The Brookings report described Wendy, a married mother of four who is homeschooling her children and picks up "Uber deliveries, Instacart, and all that kind of stuff" on top of running her household. "I never have enough time," she explained. "That's the one thing I always say I'm short on . . . time. I feel like there needs to be three of me . . . because I just don't have time to do everything."

Wendy chooses to take on additional work, sacrificing time for money, to improve her children's experiences in both time and money. "I'm trying to get ahead or make money, so I can spend more quality time with them and go more places and do more things."

Many among the working class, especially women, lack advanced scheduling in their work, diminishing their well-being by squeezing both time and money. When her employer calls Maria, a woman working in retail, "It doesn't matter if that day someone passed away or someone had a birthday," she must go to work.

Sociologist Sarah Halpern-Meekin and coauthors described Rose Alvarez, a single mother with two teens, working as a home health-care aide and trying to work 40 hours a week: "Sometimes I work only five hours a day, so that's no good. But the reason is because when the people get more sick, they get put in a nursing home. Some of them, they go and pass away. . . ."[56]

Instability and unpredictability of work schedules greatly diminish well-being. Indeed, friendly scheduling enhances well-being as much as large increases in wages.[57] A study at the Gap clothing stores found that employee-friendly scheduling increased sales, decreased labor costs, and increased store productivity.[58]

Some members of the elite prioritize work over family because of financial needs familiar to members of the working class. Economists Peter Kuhn and Fernando Lozano concluded that members of the American elite work longer hours because doing so provides greater utilitarian benefits. These utilitarian benefits are not necessarily immediate, as the salaries elite workers earn rarely include overtime pay, but the longer hours increase their likelihood of future raises, bonuses, or promotions at their current companies or future ones. And as job security has declined among elite workers, long work hours may enhance their likelihood of keeping their jobs in layoffs.[59]

Yet sometimes members of the elite also prioritize work over family also because their work is their vocation and identity. "I am a lawyer, a law professor, and a writer," wrote Lara Bazelon. "I am also a divorced mother of two young children. I'm often asked some version of: 'How do you excel at work and be the best mother you can be?' This question presupposes that a work–life balance is achievable; it's not."[60] Bazelon prioritizes her work over her children because she is the sole breadwinner in a single-parent family, but also because her work is her vocation and identity. "I prioritize my work because I'm ambitious and because I believe it's important. If I didn't write and teach and litigate, a part of me would feel empty." Bazelon described her work as trial lawyer on a case to free an innocent man. At the time her son was four and her daughter was two. "Why are you gone so much?" asked her son. She explained what was at stake.

One reader wrote: "As a professional writer and the mother of three children, six grandchildren, and three great-grandchildren, I found this article to be among the most chilling feminist arguments I have ever read. I hope that her children are forgiving."

But another wrote that her daughter just turned 12 and recently read *To Kill a Mockingbird*. She showed her daughter the Bazelon article to explain why her mother was spending so much time on her work, and asked what she thought. "She's doing what Atticus did for his client," said the daughter, "You can always celebrate a birthday on another day, but you can't always help an innocent man." "My work is done," concluded the mother.

Journalist Derek Thompson described the belief that work is the centerpiece of one's identity and life's purpose as "workism."[61] "The best-educated and highest-earning Americans, who can have whatever they want, have chosen the office for the same reason that devout Christians attend church on Sundays: It's where they feel most themselves."

Management scholars Christine Beckman and Melissa Mazmanian found that members of the elite strive to be ideal workers, perfect parents, and diligent stewards of their health. "We expected people to be like, 'Ugh, I want to do less,'" Mazmanian said. But what they heard was, "I want to do it all *better*. . . . The idea of doing less is just not coded into high-achieving people's sense of self."[62]

Many American elite workers also derive expressive and emotional benefits from long hours of work in high social status. Status symbols vary by culture and time. Leisurely lifestyles signal high status in some cultures and times, whereas overworked lifestyles signal high status in others.

Marketing scholar Silvia Bellezza and coauthors placed side by side a quote from Thorstein Veblen's 1899 book, *The Theory of the Leisure Class*, and one from a 2014 Cadillac Super Bowl commercial.

Veblen wrote: "Conspicuous abstention from labor . . . becomes the conventional mark of superior pecuniary achievement." In contrast, the Cadillac commercial said: "In other countries, they work, they stroll home, they stop by the café, they take August off—off! Why aren't you like that? Why aren't we like that? Because we are crazy-driven hard-working believers, that's why!"

Bellezza and coauthors found that in the United States, busyness and lack of leisure time connote high social status, driven by the perceptions that a busy person is competent, ambitious, and in demand in the job market. In Europe, however, leisure still connotes high social status, as in Veblen's time.[63] When members of the American elite are asked, "How are you?" The correct answer is "So busy," indicating that they are in great demand.[64]

Work as family and coworkers as family members

We often hear approving comments about workplaces that feel like home and coworkers who feel like family members. Indeed, coworkers who act as helpful siblings and bosses who act as caring parents enhance well-being.[65]

Jean, the previously mentioned 31-year-old American woman, was fortunate to have a boss who acted like a helpful older sibling. "She was five or six years older than me so was a bit of a mentor in the sense that we were close enough in age to feel like she knew what was going to come next for me."[66]

Alexia Rowe, a 25-years-old woman, was fortunate to have a boss who acted like a caring parent. Rowe, who works at a box office, called ticket holders to say that a show has been rescheduled. One began screaming at her. The next morning, she felt a surge of anxiety, and her boss allowed her to take a break from making calls. "If I leave this position," said Rowe, "I'm not going to find a manager that's like her."[67]

Yet, as journalist Joe Pinsker noted, workplaces as home and coworkers as family can also be unhealthy, manipulative, and toxic. "When I hear something like 'we're like family here', I silently complete the analogy: 'We'll foist obligations upon you, expect your unconditional devotion, disrespect your boundaries, and be bitter if you prioritize something above us.'"[68]

Coworkers as toxic families brought tragedy to nine workers killed by a coworker at a transit agency in Silicon Valley.[69] The gunman kept a notebook expressing his anger toward his coworkers. "He was very deliberate, and very fast," a spokesperson of the agency said. "He knew where employees would be."

Coworkers as toxic families diminish well-being by damaging mental and physical health even when they do not lead to tragedy. Surgeon General Vivek Murthy told Americans that "disrespectful or cutthroat workplaces could be hazardous to their health." Chronic stress interferes with sleep, magnifies vulnerability to infection, and is associated with health problems ranging from heart disease to depression.[70]

Indeed, disrespect at work diminishes well-being more than respect enhances it. A Black teacher described by sociologist Michele Lamont noted the daily wear and tear of disrespect, as coworkers fail to greet her when she enters the teachers' room, while they greet a white teacher who enters the room with her.[71]

Not all workers are fortunate to have coworkers who act as helping siblings and bosses who act as caring parents. April, a 31-year-old American woman interviewed by BlackRock, described frustration that drove her to change jobs. "A manager I trusted told my boss I was interviewing with another team, and the environment became very hostile." She felt stressed, betrayed, and uncertain of how things would pan out. Luckily, within a few weeks she found a new role and left. And Zihan, a 34-year-old Chinese man, said: "I was pulling a lot of late nights, but in the end,

I did not receive the recognition from my boss despite all the hard work. It was quite demoralizing."[72]

Trust in management was low at the workplace of John, the previously mentioned 30-year-old British man, diminishing his well-being. His boss "had a negative vibe and seemed stressed all the time," and his "stupid demands, angry, bullying," made John feel bad, stressed, and anxious about his health. "I started to show rashes on my head and wasn't in a great place."

Corporate acquisitions resemble blended families, diminishing well-being by increasing stress, anxiety, depression, psychiatric medication usage, and even suicide. These effects are prevalent among workers from both acquired companies and acquiring ones, in struggling companies and profitable ones. Workers most affected by acquisitions are those whose careers are stunted, blue-collar workers, and workers with lower cognitive and noncognitive skills.[73]

Burnout

Roy Coops, interviewed by *Business Insider*, described his burnout at a stressful workplace and the damage it inflicted on his well-being. "A few years back I worked for a large fitness company which provided me with a good salary, a company car, laptop, and mobile phone. All I had to do was work 7 days a week, 10 hours a day." Coops performance was measured by the number of new members he recruited to the fitness club, but that meant that existing members did not get the attention they needed, and left. Coops preferred to care for existing members rather than suffer the stress of recruiting new ones. So, he was kicked out of the company in a very bad way.[74]

The burnout experienced by Coops is all too common, and so is its negative effect on both workers' well-being and the financial success of their companies. "At its core," wrote journalist Olga Khazan, "burnout is a work problem . . . and changes to the workplace are the best way to fix it."[75]

Burnout can come from workload that is too heavy; cutthroat, bottom-line, or results-oriented culture; inadequate control or autonomy; lack of recognition or reward for work; absence of community; and a sense of unfairness. Workplace features that guard against burnout include treating colleagues as friends, and inspiring one another with respect, gratitude, trust, and integrity.[76]

Management scholars Emma Seppälä and Kim Cameron noted that too many companies act as if stressful workplace cultures yield financial success. Yet stressful workplaces not only diminish the well-being of workers, but also diminish companies' financial success.[77]

Companies find it difficult to change culture that leads to burnout, evident in the effects of banks' "protected-weekend" policy for junior bankers, aimed at preventing burnout by guaranteed free time during weekends, specifically on Saturdays. The policy did induce bankers to stay home on Saturdays, but it also induced them to work longer on other days.[78]

The difficulty of changing culture was also evident at Pacific Investment Management Co. (PIMCO), a giant bond money manager.[79] Some workers liked its dog-eat-dog culture of cutthroat competition. One said, "I went there not because I wanted a cushy place. . . . You got there and made money. . . . Everything else was, like, details." Yet younger PIMCO workers are no longer willing to accept jobs as endurance tests, or that engage in unfair treatment or lack of diversity. And large investors such as pension systems press money managers to change their dog-eat-dog cutthroat cultures.[80]

Naomi Osaka, the world's second-ranked women's tennis player at the time, resisted burnout as she prioritized her well-being over an opportunity to play in the prestigious French Open tennis tournament. She withdrew from the tournament after tennis officials fined her $15,000 and threatened to oust her from the tournament for opting out of its mandatory news conferences. Speaking to the international media takes a heavy toll on her mental health, said Osaka, compounding the anxiety inherent in prestigious tournaments. As writer Kelli María Korducki noted, the problem is not a sudden bout of laziness. The problem is work. "Osaka has given a public face to a growing, and long overdue, revolt."[81]

Unemployment

Loss of a job can devastate well-being. Unemployment deprives workers of income and its utilitarian benefits and also the expressive and emotional benefits of time structure and a sense of belonging, purpose, and competence necessary for well-being.[82] The longer people are unemployed, the more likely they are to suffer depression.[83]

Gabriel, a 46-year-old British man interviewed by BlackRock, was stripped of time structure and a sense of belonging and purpose when he lost his job: "I was feeling depressed, not worthy, and had a sense of lack of belonging." He did not know what to do with his time, so for 8–10 hours of the day he "went around in circles."[84]

Unemployment remains a scar on well-being long after regaining employment.[85] Moreover, unemployment spills over on everyone, even those employed, who fear that they might be next on the unemployment line.[86] Indeed, the expressive and emotional costs of unemployment and their effects on well-being are not mitigated when many in the community are unemployed. And the strongly harmful impact of being unemployed on well-being does not wear off over time, nor do repeated episodes of unemployment make it any better.[87] And whereas there is well-being adaptation over time to divorce, widowhood, and birth of first child, there is little adaptation to unemployment for men.[88]

Anthropologist Katherine Newman told the story of David Patterson, a member of the elite, who was laid off from his position in a computer industry on Long Island in the late 1980s, when the entire industry was in a slump. He tried to find a new job, with no success. "People don't understand that you can send out 150 letters to headhunters and get 10 replies. Maybe one or two will turn into something, but there are a hundred qualified people going after each job."

He and his wife exhausted their savings and were forced to sell their house. Friendship in Patterson's circle revolved around outings to fancy restaurants, dances at the country club, and the occasional Broadway show or concert in New York City, so he stopped calling his friends because he had no good news to share. He blamed himself for his predicament and wondered if his wife blamed him.[89]

Sociologist Victor Tan Chen told the story of John Hope, a member of the working class, who lost his job in 2009. For 14 years he had worked at a car plant near Detroit, lifting heavy truck bumpers in a machine that polishes away the blemishes of the rough steel, readying them for immersion in a chemical bath that coats each bumper with a thin layer of bright chrome.[90]

Hope took pride in the strength required to hold the bumpers without tipping over, and the skill to buff each piece precisely so all abrasion disappears. As his job disappeared by automation, so did his pay, status, and pride. All his good friends worked at the plant. "When you work 14 years, them are all the friends you got." He blames himself for not working harder, and his union, and his employer.[91]

Indeed, economist Daron Acemoglu found that at least half the widening gap in wages among American workers in the last 40 years comes from the automation of tasks once done by people.[92] Globalization and the weakening of unions have played roles. "But the most important factor is automation." Still, unions enhance the well-being of members of the working class by improving their financial situation, personal health, and workplace quality, including on-the-job safety, work-life balance, interpersonal trust, and workers' autonomy.[93]

The negative effects of unemployment on well-being can be somewhat mitigated by stress-reducing activities such as art participation, socializing, going on trips, and visiting a church. These also increase the probability of finding new employment.[94]

The negative effects of unemployment on well-being can also be somewhat mitigated by social norms. At age 50, the well-being of unemployed people is much lower than that of employed ones. But the well-being of the unemployed rises after age 50 as employed people increasingly retire.[95]

Part-time employment

Part-time employment, unlike unemployment, does not necessarily diminish well-being. Much depends on whether one actually wants to work any more hours. Indeed, part-time employees who do not seek full-time employment enjoy higher well-being than full-time employees, and suffer lower stress and worry.[96]

A man interviewed by Pew said, "I am fortunate to have a profession (psychiatry) that allows me to work part time even though I am older, and provides me with a good income. I come from a lower middle-class family and do not need a lot of money."[97]

The relation between employment and well-being varies by gender.[98] Men, more than women, perceive themselves as the family providers, and therefore, consider work essential. Jonathan, the previously mentioned 67-year-old American man interviewed by BlackRock, was desperate when his job was eliminated. "Where do I go from here? How will I support my family?"[99]

A study of medical students points to differences between the work preferences of men and women. Women prefer occupations characterized by lower expected earnings and time requirements, less competition, and a higher social contribution. And women are more likely than men to choose residency positions in places where they are going to live.[100]

Variation by gender is evident in Australia. Mothers with part-time jobs enjoy higher well-being than mothers who work full-time, especially when their children are younger than four-years-old.[101] That variation is also evident in the United Kingdom. Men enjoy the highest well-being if they work full-time without overtime, whereas women prefer part-time jobs.[102]

Men of working age who are out of the labor force, such as stay-at-home fathers, disabled, or retired, suffer greater reductions in well-being than women. Moreover, such men experience higher negative and lower positive affect, whereas there is not much difference between the affect, positive or negative, of women who are out of the labor force and those who are full-time employees.[103]

Disability caused a man interviewed by Pew to withdraw from the labor force, and diminished his well-being: "As I look back on my life, I miss the work that I can no longer do. I find satisfaction that I was able to be a police officer and detective in my youth and was able to help many people." He was highly decorated for exceptional work until he was shot in the face as he came to the aid of a person being beaten on the street, and was forced to retire.[104]

Conflicts between work and motherhood, heightened by COVID-19, drove some white-collar women to quit their jobs or switch to part-time work. Journalist Olga Khazan described the frustration of Molly Quigley, a woman unable to "lean in" and "have it all."[105] Quigley was working seven days a week from home as the communications director for a restaurant. Meanwhile, her three children were around her, doing Zoom school. "I was just, like, yelling at everybody all day long," Quigley said. "And my six-year-old wasn't staying on his Zoom class. And I finally realized, I just can't do it all."

Khazan noted that the women she interviewed are fortunate, working in fields where part-time work is possible, with husbands who bring in money. Some were laid off, and others quit, as Karen Craigo did, tired of working for a boss who would ask for her suggestions, only to immediately reject all of them. She quit to do freelance writing, and now gets more positive reinforcement from clients.

Part-time work is more common among women outside the United States. A quarter of American women work part-time, compared with about 12% of men. But the majority of Dutch women work part-time, spending the work week "playing sports, planting gardens, doing art projects, hanging out with their children, volunteering, and meeting their family friends."[106] Still, there are disadvantages to part-time work. Dutch women are less likely than American women to be managers. And part-time workers are paid less and garner less prestige.

Retirement

Some find the transition from work to retirement easy, enhancing their well-being. "Husband and I have made a huge effort in downsizing our life," said a woman interviewed by Pew. "No daily harrowing drives to work, no immediate manager/supervisor who is stressed and passing along stress. . . ."[107]

Yet changeover from work to retirement can be choppy because it stops paychecks and their utilitarian benefits. Moreover, retirement also halts the expressive and emotional benefits of identity, structure, and meaning, leaving old relationships and forming new ones.[108] How will we fill our days? And how will we figure this out?[109]

Indeed, early retirement can increase the likelihood of early death. Swiss men retiring two years before the statutory retirement age increase their risk of death before the age of 83 by 41 percentage points. The effect is driven by loss of structure provided by work and corresponding unhealthy lifestyles, including increased alcohol consumption and smoking. It is most pronounced among unmarried men and men living in the German-speaking part of Switzerland who adhere to a social norm favoring work than men living in the Latin-speaking part.[110]

Also, complete retirement leads to a 5–16% increase in difficulties associated with mobility and daily activities in an average post-retirement period of six years, a 5–6% increase in illness conditions, and a 6–9% decline in mental health. The effects stem from lifestyle changes, including declines in physical activity and social interactions. The adverse health effects are lower among married people, those with social support, those who continue to engage in physical activity, and those who continue to work part-time.[111]

The effects of retirement on mental health and well-being vary by gender and marital status. Retirement of partnered men enhances the mental health and well-being of both themselves and their partners. But retirement diminishes the mental health and well-being of single men, in part, because of loneliness.[112]

Retirement is especially difficult for those whose work was also their vocation and identity. They enjoyed their highest well-being during their working years, and retirement greatly diminishes their well-being.[113] Some declare themselves "failed retirees," choosing to resume work.[114] Indeed, having too little time is associated with low well-being and so does having too much time.[115]

Responding to an article about failed retirees, a reader wrote:[116] "Yep, I'm one of those returnees. . . . I joke that I thought I was burned out but it turns out that I was just singed." Another wrote: "Some of us who have long professional careers do find it difficult to 'pull the trigger' and retire [because we] tie our professions so closely to our identities. . . . It has much less to do with finances than it does with our identity."

Direct "cold turkey" transition from full-time work to full retirement is still most common, but many prefer gradual retirement with bridge work. Among older Americans with adequate financial resources, 38% are engaged in bridge work and another 7% are looking for bridge work. Those doing bridge work tend to work fewer hours, have flexible schedules, and receive lower compensation.[117] The well-being effects of cold turkey retirement are similar to those of gradual retirement, but the well-being effects of retirement perceived as chosen are more positive than those of retirements perceived as forced.[118]

A reader described himself as an attorney doing bridge work after retiring at age 69 after 40 years of private law practice. "I was bored to death in retirement and was fortunate enough to switch my talents to the public sector . . . at greatly reduced compensation. As finances clearly are not the issue, I am working because I love what I do, not because I have to."

Many, however, were compelled to retire early in the time of COVID-19, unable to switch to another full-time work or find bridge work. Journalists Nelson Schwartz and Coral Murphy Marcos described Dee Dee Patten, a 57-year-old woman, and Dana, her husband, who were compelled to retire when business dried up at their mechanical repair shop. Most of their revenues came from inspecting school buses, which stopped in March 2020 when schools shifted to remote learning.[119]

The Pattens feel unnerved by the sudden shift into retirement after 22 years of nonstop work, but they are looking at the upside. "We both know that, at our age, it was probably the best thing for us," Mrs. Patten said. "We will get used to all of this time on our hands. Our plan is to volunteer, travel, and look for a new place to live after 30 years on the old homestead."[120]

Age discrimination makes the situation worse among those compelled to retire. As a reader noted: "Many older workers are shut out of jobs they are qualified for merely because of their age and the sense by hiring managers that they won't "fit" with the younger cohorts in the business." Another wrote: "My wife and I, both 66, are part of the exodus. In my case, I certainly did not want to leave my job but I was asked to, and regardless of my qualifications, finding a new role as a marketing executive at my age is impossible, so I call myself reluctantly retired." Indeed, age discrimination is rampant. One experiment constructed job ads for administrative assistant, retail, and security guard jobs, using language from real job ads, varying by age-related stereotypes. Job ad language related to ageist stereotypes deterred older workers from applying.[121]

Transitions in retirement can be fraught even when retirement is voluntary and finances are plentiful. Men make bigger changes after retiring than women. Sociologists Michal Engelman and Won-tak Joo found that men become more dependent on family, whereas women already had a larger network and had always worked on maintaining relationships.[122]

"Looking back over the last 12 months," asked Engelman and Joo, "who are the people with whom you most often discussed things that are important to you?" Each person listed up to five people in their networks, the nature of the relationships, and how often they are in contact.

Retired men are more likely to give money to offspring or other family members. The choice to give money is often made jointly by husband and wife, but the actual money transfers are done by men. This might be because men in these older generations have traditionally been the primary source of financial support for the family, or because men are the only ones who need to enhance their ties to family, and money facilitates that enhancement.

Journalist Peter Finch described the journey of 78-year-old John Strumsky, and Dawn, his wife, to a retirement community.[123] Dawn badly wanted to move into a retirement community, free of cooking, cleaning or yardwork, but John detested that idea. Eventually, John acquiesced to Dawn's wishes and they moved to a retirement community. Now both love it.

John's reluctance to move into a retirement community, wrote Finch, is common. People often fear forfeiting their independence, reluctant to leave their home, and apprehensive about confronting their own mortality. Now John sees his journey as that of a high school student going to college: "You can't just hand them a brochure and say, 'This is where you're going.' It's a journey."

Volunteer work

Sandy Drisk, a 72-year-old woman, and John, her husband, were running low on groceries in the early days of the COVID-19. Going out for groceries was perilous because Sandy had bronchitis and John was fighting Parkinson's disease.

A friend told Sandy about a note from Greg Dailey, the man who delivered her morning paper, volunteering to deliver groceries. "I understand during these trying times it is difficult for some to get out of their house to get everyday necessities. I would like to offer my services free of charge to anyone who needs groceries, household products, etc." Greg delivered groceries to Sandy, free of delivery cost. "What a godsend this man has been," said Sandy.[124]

"I have always been an avid creative writer, both professionally and for fun," wrote Victoria H. So, she jumped on an opportunity to volunteer, engaging low-income children in creative writing. "The creative energy bursting from these kids at 6 p.m., after a full day of school and after-school activities, was unbelievably inspiring. . . . There will be some serious novelists coming out of that group, that's for sure!"[125]

The work of volunteers does not provide the utilitarian benefits of income, but it enhances their well-being by expressive and emotional benefits. Volunteering increases the well-being of volunteers by the equivalent of more than £911 ($1,156.27) per year.[126] The relation between volunteering and well-being goes both ways. People enjoying high well-being volunteer more hours, and volunteering increases their well-being. Volunteer work increased volunteers' well-being in greater happiness, life satisfaction, self-esteem, sense of control over life, and improved physical and mental health.[127]

Britain's National Health Service (NHS) set a Volunteer Responders program in response to the COVID-19 pandemic. Active volunteers benefitted in higher life satisfaction, feelings of worthwhileness, social connectedness, and belonging to their local communities. The benefits of the program were at least 140 times greater than its costs.[128]

Solicitation of volunteer work and money donations are central to the success of nonprofit organizations. Nonprofits prefer money donations, but donors prefer to donate volunteer work, even when doing so is less effective for the cause. This is because volunteers feel more personal control over volunteer work than over money donations, leading to greater interest in volunteering.[129] Regular volunteer work is especially effective, increasing well-being over time if regular volunteering is sustained, especially among those with low initial well-being.[130] Volunteering can also provide utilitarian benefits, helping volunteers reach career goals. It expands networks, meeting professionals who can be good mentors or sponsors, especially for young professionals. And volunteering says good things about volunteers' values, showing care and generosity that would make them good team members. Employers offering pay for work expect candidates to possess skills and experience, but nonprofits looking for volunteers are ready to let candidates try new skills and acquire experience. The skills and experience volunteers acquire can serve them later in paying jobs.

Kellogg, a food products company, has developed a skills-based volunteering program with United Way. Kellogg employees in the program are matched with nonprofits that could use the skills they wish to volunteer. Matt Reid, a Kellogg employee and a self-described introvert who volunteered to help a local diaper bank develop job profiles and an evaluation process. As he taught the team how to plan for growth and identify the skills employees needed as the organization grew, he also achieved some of his professional development goals and acquired skills he will need to eventually lead a team at Kellogg.[131]

Hobbies and activities

Hobbies, like volunteering, provide no utilitarian benefits of earnings but, like volunteering, enhance well-being by expressive and emotional benefits. Flora, an older woman, described the benefit of quilting and its contribution to her well-being. "I think [learning new techniques] keeps your brain active. You feel that you are still valuable and I think after having had a family . . . you do miss that . . . once they are away, they don't need you anymore . . . that was part of my wellbeing to do something creative. . . ."[132]

Americans interviewed by Pew listed hobbies and activities as part of what makes lives feel meaningful, fulfilling, or satisfying. Work and hobbies merge for the fortunate few whose hobbies are also their vocations, reflecting their identity. A man interviewed by Pew said: "They say if you love your work, you'll never work a day in your life. It's true." That man is close to fortunate, even if not fully so. "I wanted to make a living in music, and I have. Not as a rock star, but by repairing musical instruments. I still get to be a rock star every weekend with my band."[133]

Indeed, music is a hobby for many and work for few because it is hard to make a living playing music. Matthew, a 28-year-old British man interviewed by BlackRock, works as a freelance musician. He loves his job, but it provides no steady income. "Stressing about my financial situation, and worrying that I won't have enough to put down for a house, etc."[134]

Reading is also prominent among hobbies. A woman interviewed by Pew said: "I love reading because it's like a nice little vacation from everything I have going on in my own life." For others, arts and crafts are prominent, whether quilting, knitting, or woodwork.

Many hobbies and activities yield "flow experiences." Psychologist Mihaly Csikszentmihalyi illustrated flow experiences with the example of a skier going down the slope: "[Y]our full attention is focused on the movements of your body, the position of your skis, the air whistling past your face, and the snow-shrouded trees running by. . . . The run is so perfect that all you want is for it to last forever, to immerse yourself completely in the experience."[135] Flow comes when challenge meets skill. Skiers with intermediate skills lose themselves in intermediate-level ski slopes because their skills match their challenges. Beginner-level slopes cannot hold their attention because they are too slow and boring, whereas advanced-level slopes are too fast and scary, demanding skills they do not have.

John, the previously mentioned 30-year-old British man, enjoyed peak well-being in the flow of music at a festival. He arrived with his band at noon and enjoyed socializing before playing at 3 p.m. To an audience of almost 2,000 people who enjoyed the music, singing along and dancing. "I felt fantastic within the build-up of us playing and then actually playing it felt euphoric." Playing with his mates made it great, and the brilliant weather and vibe in the area just felt amazing.[136]

Perri Klass, a physician, describes her experience of flow in knitting: "Knitting puts me in the moment. . . . My hands move, I am aware of their movement. The yarn moves through my fingers, around my fingers, and I am aware of the tension. . . ."[137]

Well-being comes with flow in activities that promote growth over a lifetime, open new opportunities for action, and stimulate the development of new skills. Well-being is enhanced when flow comes from active physical, mental, or emotional involvement—from work, sports, hobbies, meditation, and interpersonal relationships.[138] This kind of involvement can come at work, church, or volunteer activities. A woman interviewed by Pew found well-being in her volunteer work at a wildlife rehabilitation hospital, and leading bird tours: "The people and experiences I have there are like nothing else, I learn something new every week."

Hobbies and activities are especially important in retirement, after regular work ends. Jeanne Stellman's interest in activities in retirement arose when she was doing a health study of shipyard workers in Chester, Pennsylvania. She is now a retired health-policy professor and past president of EPIC, Emeritus Professors in Columbia. "There was a man in his 60s who was retiring. On his last day at the job, he left in a state of shock. After 40 years at a shipyard there should be bells and whistles, but there was nothing: he just walked out with his stuff."

Stellman vowed to avoid such sad stories for herself and fellow retired professors and staff by connecting them to university life. "Once you no longer have the structure of work, you have to figure out what to do with your time," she said. "EPIC is a way of continuing intellectual involvement and socializing here at Columbia." EPIC is "the kind of place where you'll have a neuroscientist talking to a Russian scholar about the Big Bang," said EPIC vice president Lou Cleveland who retired from the microbiology department. Interactions at EPIC offer spectacular benefits because loneliness is a bigger source of anxiety for older academics than decreased mobility or hearing loss. "Intellectual companionship in retirement," he said, "is very hard to find." EPIC is also aware of the benefits of exercise to cognitive function. Ginny Papaioannou, a retired professor of genetics and development, conducts two EPIC yoga classes each week. "Many older people become very inactive physically," she said. "That's partly because the exercise culture—running, aerobics—is designed for young people. As you age you have to make accommodations. Yoga was a way for me to do that. And I felt it was something I could offer to EPIC."[139]

12

Education

The diminishing utilitarian benefits of school, specifically at the college level, were evident during the COVID-19 pandemic. "My college students are not okay," wrote college instructor Jonathan Malesic.[1] One-third of his students were missing nearly all of his online classes, and those who were there were less engaged, burying their faces in their laptop screens, and some openly sleeping. That was true at both the diverse public university and the wealthy private one where he taught. Colleagues at other universities told him similar stories. Malesic tried to help by creating looser course structures, flexible deadline policies, and lenient grading, but these did not help much.

The utilitarian benefits of school are also evident in their decline in elementary, middle, and high school during the pandemic. Journalist Frank Bures noted that the lessons of his two middle-school daughters continued online when their school closed in March 2020, but their quality fell, and his daughters tired of staring at a screen.[2] Their math skills dwindled, their Spanish vocabulary narrowed, their knowledge of science diminished, and now they were months behind on their curriculum.

The utilitarian benefits of school are regularly seen as their only benefits, yet expressive and emotional benefits matter greatly in enhancing well-being, also highlighted in their decline during the pandemic. In-person education at schools, face-to-face with classmates and teachers, enhances well-being by more than online education at home because it provides expressive and emotional benefits in addition to utilitarian ones.

"I never thought that I would miss school, but I do," wrote a high-school student. "It's been hard not to see my classmates and teachers. I didn't realize that all of the random conversations in class and catching up with my friends at lunch were such a big part of my life."[3]

Another high-school student described these benefits in a poem.

> "I miss school because when I am there, I can see all
> my teachers and friends,
>
> At school, the love never ends...
>
> I miss doing my everyday math,
>
> it always leads me to the right path...
>
> I really miss doing art,
>
> it makes me feel like I am smart."[4]

The time of the pandemic also revealed the utilitarian, expressive, and emotional benefits of education outside the classroom.[5] The two middle-school-aged daughters of Bures learned that the world is fragile and can change in an instant, that fear can cause some to lash out and others to be brave and kind, that going to the store for groceries is a privilege, and that life goes on even when the world is fragile.

The well-being of students is enhanced by satisfaction of three basic psychological needs, autonomy, relatedness, and competence. These combine to promote personal growth and development, and motivate engagement in discovery activities. The need for autonomy refers to students' experience of choice and feelings of control. Students enjoy high autonomy when they feel free to choose topics for class presentations and when they feel free to express their ideas.

The need for relatedness refers to feeling connected and belonging in significant relationships. Teachers promote relatedness by treating students with empathy and demonstrating a desire to enhance their well-being, and school principals promote it by showing genuine interest in students' family difficulties.

The need for competence refers to feelings of effectiveness and mastery of the environment. Students experience competence when they understand difficult materials taught in class. And they are more inclined to move toward growth activities if they feel they can succeed at them.[6]

Teachers join parents in guiding students and demonstrating optimism and resilience. Teachers' support ranges from utilitarian assistance with academics to expressive and emotional expressions of respect and protection from bullying. These benefits are especially important among children and adolescents who bring personal problems to school.

The well-being benefits of school are also evident in its role as a refuge from stress and abuse at home. A survey of high school students in the time of the pandemic found that more than two-in-five suffered persistent sadness or hopelessness, more than half suffered emotional abuse from a parent or another adult in their house, and more than 1-in-10 suffered physical abuse. By comparison, a survey preceding the pandemic found that less than 2-in-5 suffered emotional abuse, and only 1-in-20 suffered physical abuse.

Journalist Ellen Barry quoted Dr. Moira Szilagyi, the president of the American Academy of Pediatrics and a specialist in abuse cases, saying that teenagers benefit from the large network of adults at school. "There is a sea of people there, and among them—your teacher, your coach, the school administration—there are caring adults that youth can seek out, and who identify when a youth isn't doing well."[7]

Psychologist Francisco Juan García Bacete and coauthors noted that well-being tends to decline during adolescent years, as children undergo physical, social, and psychological transformations that are crucial but difficult.[8] A survey of Hong Kong children from the fourth to the eleventh grade and their parents reveals that the decline in well-being as children grow into their teens is related to declines in the four components of love, insight, fortitude, and engagement. In turn, the declines in these four components are associated with increasing pressures on children as they grow up. Pressures from extracurricular activities have a much greater negative effect on children's well-being than pressures from schoolwork. The decline in children's well-being as children grow older may reflect the decline in their free time as extracurricular activities occupy increasing portions of that time.[9]

Satisfaction at school eases transformations as children grow into teenagers, and enhances well-being. An ethnographic study of students in two Canadian high schools uncovered extensive communications among students, increasing well-being by the expressive and emotional benefits of friendship and social acceptance.

The importance of teachers in promoting the well-being of students declines as students move on from elementary to high school. This is especially true among students with little intrinsic motivation to learn. In elementary school years, children typically have extended contacts with one or a small number of teachers, forming close personal relations. In high school, however, children may not be able to establish such close personal relations with their teachers.

Well-being in education among the elite

Competition among the elite for seats at prestigious schools begins early as parents want to do right by their children. This is what journalist George Packer and his wife did, bringing their two-year-old son to his first school interview at a private school where annual tuition amounts to $30,000. The admissions officer gave the child a sheet of paper and crayons and he drew the moon, a yellow circle over a green squiggle, as Packer and his wife answered questions. The rejection letter came soon afterward.[10]

"The pressure of meritocracy made us apply to private schools when our son was two," wrote Packer, "not because we wanted him to attend private preschool, but because, in New York City, where we live, getting him into a good public kindergarten later on would be even harder. . . ."

The pressures on today's young children in elite families, such as Packer's, include transformation of kindergarten into first grade. Kindergarten children are now guided to finish their "work" before they can play, and the walls of classrooms are now a "word wall" covered with instructional posters, schedules, and motivational platitudes, far beyond the ability of four-year-olds to "decode" today's word for reading.[11]

Competition among the elite continues in "redshirting," whereby parents delay enrollment of their children into kindergarten or first grade to give them developmental advantages, helping average children reach the top of their class. Sociologists Pamela Stone and Meg Lovejoy quoted a mother who complained about the practice, but admitted that it exerts pressure on her and other parents to do the same.[12] "I think it's important for my son to understand that being competitive is not going to just apply in playing soccer," said a parent, "it's going to apply for the rest of his life, in competing for school admissions, jobs, and everything else in life."

Some elite parents have turned to web-based project management tools, such as Trello, to organize their children's schedules of school and extracurricular activities. Tonya Parker set her four kids, ages 9 to 18, on Trello.[13] "I use it every day to keep track of what schoolwork I need to do, or places I need to be, things to buy," said Hannah, her 15-year-old daughter. Now the mother can ask, "How are you doing on your checklist?"

The pressure on children in elite families is evident in a 10-year-old who exclaimed "I want to run a start-up," when asked what he would like to do when he grows up. He does not know what a start-up is, wrote psychologist Madeline Levine, but he knows the straight-line track he needs to stay on if he wants to run one. He will apply to the most competitive high school in his city, and will proceed to a prestigious college.[14]

Levine noted that the elite parents of this child and similar ones encourage staying on straight-line tracks to success. Yet such insistence tends to diminish the likelihood of success. Only 1-in-10 of people who consider themselves successful describe their track to success as a straight line. The others describe tracks of serendipitous zigzags, taking risks, failing, recovering, often failing again, before finding success. Levine added that children encouraged to keep on a straight-line track tend to be cautious and competitive, when they would do better by being curious, willing to take risks, and good at collaboration.[15]

Competition reached an extreme when Raffaela Spone created deepfake videos to improve her daughter's standing on the cheerleading squad of her high school by harassing rivals. Spone posted photos she edited to make it look like members of the cheerleading squad had posed nude or were smoking and drinking.[16]

Law professor Daniel Markovits noted that elite parents feel they have little choice, even if they fear the detrimental effects of the pressure on their children because their greater fear is seeing their children drop behind the competition. Parents observe their middle and high-school children do three to five hours of homework each night and sign them up to an education dominated by whatever is necessary for admission to prestigious colleges and securing elite jobs in finance, management, law, or medicine.[17]

The fears of elite parents that their children will lag in the competition are not without reason. Journalist Kaitlin Flanagan described a Princeton graduate, a top student at his public high school, who found that he could not catch up to classmates from private high schools. Less than 2% of American students attend private high schools, but 25% of Princeton's class of 2024 graduated from private high schools, 24% of Yale's, and 29% of Brown's. Two-thirds of Princeton's Rhodes Scholars came from private high schools. So did more than half of the winners of Princeton's prestigious Sachs Scholarship, and almost half of the winners of "class legacy prizes," another top award. "This is why wealthy parents think it's life-and-death to get their kids into the right prep school," wrote Flanagan, "because they know that the winners keep winning."[18]

Flanagan taught at a private high school for seven years and described her frustration with demanding students and their parents, intent on creating transcripts that assure seats at prestigious colleges. She told the story of giving an *A*– on an assignment to a student who was bright but also aggressive and mean. Soon after, his angry mother called to dispute the grade. Yet Flanagan could see the benefits of private high schools and was determined to get that kind of education for her own children, whatever the cost.

Elite parents expect their children to graduate from prestigious colleges and continue into white-collar careers. They possess the cultural, social, and financial capital necessary to guide their children to prestigious colleges and support them throughout their college years, whether prestigious, as they hope, or less prestigious, if they must. They bear the utilitarian costs of college expenses, but their well-being is enhanced by the expressive and emotional benefits of high social status and pride as they watch their children graduate from colleges and proceed into white-collar careers.

Ditra and Paavan Chopra, described by sociologist Marianne Cooper, are typical of these elite parents. Ditra has an M.B.A. and Paavan has a Ph.D. in engineering, and their high income allows them to accumulate substantial savings and dedicate much of them to support their children throughout college and even graduate school. Lila, their 13-year-old daughter, adopted her parents' expectations. She already chose the classes she will take in her coming high school freshman year. "If you want to get into a highly distinguished [college], these are the classes you need to take each year. . . . I like getting straight *A*s. Like, if I am given an option, I will do more instead of less. . . ."[19]

Elite parents, whether managers, engineers, physicians, or lawyers, set their sights on prestigious colleges for their children because they perceive their own prosperity as fragile and fear that the prosperity of their children will be even more fragile. Unlike prosperous owners of family businesses who can leave them to their children, they cannot leave their Ph.D., M.B.A., M.D., or J.D. degrees to their children.[20]

These elite professionals see people as standing on an economic ladder with a single bottom rung, a single top rung, and no rungs in between. They press their children to do what is necessary to secure seats at prestigious colleges because they fear that graduation from lower-ranked colleges would doom them to the bottom rung. This makes competition for seats at prestigious schools all the way down to preschools so stressful for elite parents and their children.

An elite professional said to sociologist Marianne Cooper: "I think the rich are getting richer and I think the poor are getting poorer, and the middle is getting squeezed. . . ."[21] Another spoke about the challenges of global competition and the need to meet them by graduating from prestigious colleges. Jobs were plentiful for his generation, he said, but he worries that jobs would not be plentiful for his children because more and more of work is done in China and India.

An American child, said that father, will have to compete with a child in China "who's just as smart, who's willing to do everything that an employer is asking for one-tenth the price. I don't know that [American children] know what they're in for. . . ." He worries that his children will not be aggressive enough for the global competition they will face. "They've always been a little more on the passive side, and I worry about whether they will be able to compete as things move forward."[22]

The fears of elite American parents that their children are doomed to stand on the bottom rung of the economic ladder unless they graduate from a prestigious college are exaggerated. In truth, the economic ladder has many intermediate rungs between the bottom and top ones, and many who graduate from less prestigious colleges and even many who do not graduate from college stand on them. Responding to the article about the burden of college costs, a father noted that a state university is neither as flashy as an expensive and prestigious private university, nor has the same cachet among friends, but it provided his daughter with solid educational opportunities, including qualification for a state graduate school and a successful career.[23]

Moreover, global competition threatens the economic positions of members of the working class and poor more than those of the elite. Yet many members of the elite seem more worried about the threats of global competition than members of the working class and poor, and fight more fiercely for admission to prestigious colleges.

Wants for the utilitarian benefits of high income are one motivator of the fierceness of the competition among elite families for places at prestigious universities. Yet in an early study, economists Stacy Berg Dale and Alan Krueger found that, on average, students who graduated from prestigious colleges, other than students from poor families, earned subsequently little beyond what they would have earned if they had graduated from a lower-ranked college.[24] Krueger described his findings in an interview with writer Malcolm Gladwell, placing the University of Pennsylvania, an Ivy college, side by side with the Pennsylvania State University (Penn State).

Consider two students who were accepted at both schools, yet one chose Penn and the other chose Penn State. Dale and Krueger found that the two students are likely to earn similar incomes in the years following graduation. Students who are likely to earn higher income by graduating from an Ivy League college are those from poor families.[25]

Interpreting these findings, writer Derek Thompson noted that parents in elite families provide their children contacts helpful in obtaining desired internships and high-paying entry-level jobs. Children from poor families obtain similar benefits from contacts with students from elite families at prestigious colleges.[26]

The findings of a more recent study, by economist Sandra Black and coauthors, are consistent with those of Berg Dale and Krueger. The Texas Top-Ten-Percent rule grants the top 10% of students in each Texas high school access to the prestigious University of Texas. The rule displaces students ranked below the top 10% at relatively advantaged high schools with students ranked in the top 10% at relatively disadvantaged high schools. College enrollment and graduation increased among highly ranked students at relatively disadvantaged high schools. Students ranked below the top 10% at advantaged high schools shifted toward less-selective colleges, but did not suffer declines in college enrollment, graduation, or earnings.[27]

Still, graduating from a prestigious college followed by a prestigious graduate school, especially law school, does provide substantial utilitarian benefits. Responding to an article about colleges, one reader wrote:[28] "I have a friend who is a lawyer at a top law firm who, when asked, admitted that they rarely consider someone for employment whose undergrad degree is from a second-tier school, even if their law degree is from an Ivy."

Yet another reader disagreed: "Harvard law grad here. The opposite is true; firms want both competent grads and diversity. In my experience, an undergrad Ivy is a black mark, not an asset. A top-tier law degree is, however, essential."

Evidence is more consistent with the view of the first reader than the second. The findings of a study by law professor Joni Hersch contradict the perception that a prestigious graduate degree in business, law, medicine, and doctoral can scrub a less prestigious undergraduate degree.

Few graduates of less prestigious colleges earn graduate degrees from prestigious universities, and even when they do, the lower prestige of their undergraduate university continues to hurt their earnings. The earnings advantage to having both an undergraduate and a graduate degree from prestigious universities greatly exceeds any likely cost advantage from attending a less prestigious undergraduate university.[29]

A recent study by economist Raj Chetty and coauthors added fresh findings about the utilitarian benefits of graduating from prestigious universities. The earnings of top students who graduated from Ivy-like colleges placed them at the 81st percentile when ranked by income. The earnings of top students who graduated from other colleges placed them only marginally lower, at the 79th percentile.

Yet 19% of students who graduated from Ivy-like schools ascended into the richest 1% of the income distribution, whereas only 12% of top students who graduated from other colleges ascended into the richest 1%.

"Do you want to become a highly paid professional at a very good company? For those kinds of outcomes, the school you go to matters a little but not a ton," said Chetty. "Where it matters enormously is reaching the upper tail, the path to becoming a CEO, leading scientist at a top graduate school, political leader . . . these upper-tail outcomes that are rare in percentage terms but incredibly important in society."[30]

Much of the earnings advantage of graduates of prestigious universities at top investment banks, management consulting firms, and law firms comes from their hiring processes. These firms recruit only at Core and Target Universities, wrote sociologist Lauren Rivera. Core universities are the three to five prestigious universities from which firms draw most of their new hires. Target schools include an additional 5 to 5 universities from which the firms accept applications and interview candidates on a smaller scale.

Evaluators place the greatest weight on experiences that favor students from elite families, and consider admission at prestigious universities as a sign of intellectual power and roundness. As one law-firm evaluator put it, "Number one people go to number one schools."[31] Another evaluator noted that clients can search law-firm websites to find how many lawyers are graduates of Harvard, Yale, and other prestigious universities. Clients might say, "Great, we're paying an exorbitant amount in legal fees for these people; they better have the educational background to back it up."[32]

Still, the benefits to lawyers graduating from prestigious colleges followed by graduating from prestigious law schools may turn out to be smaller than anticipated because law firms ruthlessly separate even their partners into rungs based on their contributions to their firms' profits, and differences in compensation among partner rungs can reach 20-to-1.[33]

Moreover, as veteran lawyer John Goodell noted, positions at top law firms tend to engender extreme competitiveness and jealousy because law students nearly always possess competitive personalities and because competition within law firms is a zero-sum game. Many lawyers soon abandon law-firm life, exhausted by long hours and high-pressure unfulfilling work, moving into less stressful careers of lower income and higher well-being.

Goodell noticed that few of his peers who began in law firms as associates became partners. Most left to become in-house counsel at corporations, law professors, government attorneys, and judges.[34]

Wants for the utilitarian benefits of high income are one motivation for the fierceness of the competition for admission to prestigious universities, but wants for the expressive and emotional benefits of high social status and pride might be a greater motivation. Any parent with money can buy a Mercedes automobile or pay for a family safari, but not every parent with money can buy their children admission letters from prestigious universities.

Still, some parents do buy their children admission to prestigious universities by contributions of many millions and others try to buy such admission by bribes in the hundreds of thousands. The utilitarian benefits of education at a prestigious college were not likely on the mind of Douglas Hodge, a former executive at a large investment company, when he paid $850,000 in bribes—$325,000 to have his eldest daughter and son accepted at Georgetown University, and $525,000 to have another daughter and son accepted at the University of Southern California.[35] Instead, Mr. Hodge and other elite parents were likely motivated by wants for the expressive and emotional benefits of high social status and pride.

Utilitarian benefits were also not likely in the mind of Blair Riley, a former lawyer at a top firm and Ivy college graduate, anxious about getting her daughter into an Ivy college. "I was a little neurotic about the subject," she said to sociologists Pamela Stone and Meg Lovejoy. Her daughter was talented and creative in arts, but her grades were mediocre and her career focus was weak. The counselor at the prestigious boarding school she was attending advised her to apply to a group of colleges whose names Riley had never heard of.[36]

Riley was far from ready to surrender. She and her husband, also an Ivy graduate and son of an Ivy professor, coached their daughter on the college admission process. "I have to confess," said Riley, "I went over and over her essays with her. Nothing went in that I hadn't seen and that her father hadn't seen, and we called upon all the academics we knew too." The daughter was admitted to her parents' Ivy and another Ivy she chose to attend. [37]

Other elite families hire educational consultants to support their children in the college admission race. Drawing on interviews with parents who work with consultants, sociologists Ken Chih-Yan Sun and Jill Smith reported that elite American parents use consultants to establish bridges between their own social world and the academic world that appears beyond their control. Elite parents rely on the expertise and status of these consultants to cope with their and their children's vulnerability in the college admission race, while preparing their children for the unknown future.[38]

The expressive and emotional benefits of admission and the costs of rejection are evident in teens' choices to share or withhold college admissions and rejections.[39] Gael Aitor, a high-school senior who cohosts the Teenager Therapy podcast, asked his fellow hosts if they were willing to open their college notification letters on-air for an episode on the admissions process. They declined, preferring to open their notifications in private. "We are aware that some people didn't get in to where they wanted, and we didn't want to rub it in their faces," said Aitor. "It feels a little cringeworthy to make a big deal out of your college acceptance."

Kelsey Moore did open her college notification online. Moore set her heart on the University of Georgia. Both of her parents graduated from that school and her boyfriend had received an early admission to the school. But instead of fireworks, Moore saw the dreaded words, "We regret to inform you. . . ."

Moore decided to post her emotional video to TikTok anyway, where it went viral, garnering more than a million views. "Most people only post the good things that happen in their life and I wanted people to realize it's not always good news." The comments she received were encouraging, testifying to the pressure to be admitted to a desired college. Viewers thanked her for her honesty and shared their own college rejections.

The expressive and emotional benefits of admission into prestigious colleges are also evident in reader responses to the suggestion by David Kirp, a professor of education, that Stanford, Harvard, Yale, and other prestigious universities clone themselves. How about Harvard-San Diego and Yale-Houston? "If Yale can open a campus in Singapore, why can't it start one in Houston?"[40]

One reader responded to Kirp by noting that both Houston and San Diego "are home to world-class institutions (Rice University and University of California San Diego) that attract brilliant and motivated students from around the world." Another reader, a Harvard graduate, hit the nail closer to its head. "Hogwash!. . . . Here's a radical notion. Maybe we don't need more luxury-branded schools. . . . And maybe de-emphasizing name brands and looking at the actual experience of getting an education would solve this 'problem' overnight."

We observe the fierceness of the race for admission into prestigious colleges in the experience of 18-year-old Kaitlyn Younger, a perfectionist and academic star since third grade. She took 11 advanced placement courses, scored high on the SAT, and maintained a close-to-perfect grade-point average. She also founded the school's accounting club, performed in and directed about 30 plays, sang in the school choir, helped run a summer camp, and held down a part-time job.[41]

Younger was pained by rejections from prestigious colleges, including Stanford, Harvard, Yale, Brown, Cornell, University of Pennsylvania, University of Southern California, University of California, Berkeley, and Northwestern. "I expected a bunch wouldn't accept me," she said. "I didn't expect it to be this bad."

The pain of rejection from prestigious colleges is reflected in a letter by a high-school senior to "Dear Therapist" Lori Gottlieb.[42] "I recently applied to colleges and among the rejections I received, one was from my dream school: Brown University. The moment I read, 'I regret to inform you. . . .' the tears streamed down my face, and everything I had planned for, an Ivy League education, was gone. I feel like my identity was rooted in receiving an Ivy League education, and suddenly I feel lost and discombobulated."

Journalist Pamela Paul advocated after-school jobs while in high school, instead of common extracurricular activities. "Personally," she wrote, "I learned more working outside school—starting with three afternoons a week when I was 14 and ending with three jobs juggled, seven days a week, my senior year of high school—than I did in the classroom." Paul's weekly work schedule left her little time for extracurricular activities, yet she applied early to a good college and got in.

A reader of Paul's article found in a quick internet search that Paul is now in her early 50s and the "good college," as she modestly called it, is Brown University, an Ivy college. "You got into Brown with no extracurriculars," she exclaimed, "Try that today!"[43]

Some students at prestigious colleges strive to gain additional expressive and emotional benefits by perceiving their own colleges as superior to other prestigious colleges. Drawing on interviews, sociologists Amy Binder and Andrea Abel found that Harvard and Stanford students perceive their universities as more prestigious than other prestigious universities because they offer "well-rounded" liberal arts education, whereas other prestigious universities are too intellectual, too connected to the old-world status system, overly associated with partying and athletics, or having a student body too concerned about career preparation. Binder and Abel concluded that by defining these distinctions, students justify their higher social status and contribute to the ongoing status distinctions among elites.[44]

A degree from a private college may add greater expressive and emotional benefits in social status and pride than one from a public college, but it does not necessarily enhance well-being by more.[45] A Gallup-Purdue University survey of 30,000 college graduates found that graduates of public colleges are just as engaged in their work and committed to it as graduates of private colleges, and they thrive equally in all areas of their life. The engaged attitude of students during college spills over to the workplace years later, when students are adjusting to life after college.

Well-being and job satisfaction are closely tied to whether a graduate had a mentor in college or a professor who fostered learning, whether college prepared them well for life after school, and whether they were emotionally attached to their college.[46]

Debt accumulated during college detracts from well-being. Graduates with no debt are more likely to thrive than graduates with student debt. As the survey says, "the higher the loan amount, the worse the well-being."

The message of the survey to parents stressing over their children's college prospects is that well-being depends little on the kind of college attended, private or public, prestigious or less so.

Still, it is often parents who make the biggest deal out of college admission and who are most distressed by college rejections. A mother wrote to Gottlieb: "My son is in the middle of the college-application process. He has very good grades and very good SAT and ACT scores; he is an Eagle Scout and a captain of the cross-country team. . . . According to all of the statistics and reports, he should be accepted at Ivy League schools, but he has not been." The mother suspects that her son is being rejected by Ivy schools because he is "also white, male, and upper-middle-class."[47]

Elite parents find it hard to quit the race for prestigious colleges because much of their own social status depends on it. Those who quit the college race pay a price in expressive costs, unable to express themselves as parents of children admitted to prestigious colleges.

Responding to an article about the guilt some parents feel if they cannot pay the college expenses of their children without sacrificing their own financial security,[48] a reader described her smart and personable son who loved cars and building with Lego, but never liked school. She felt inadequate when her friends were stressed by worries that their children will not gain admission to prestigious colleges and worries about paying these colleges' tuition and other expenses if their children gain admission.

Her son is now in his second year as a diesel mechanic, maintaining snow plows and dump trucks, learning hydraulics, and getting his commercial driver's license in the time of COVID-19, while college students sit in front of computer screens. "I never imagined I would be so relieved to have a kid who didn't go to college. And the financials? This is a full-time union job with benefits and a pension. The swing between what he makes, and what a lot of parents are spending to send their kid to college, is a good $100,000." But another reader responded snidely, noting the expressive costs of quitting the college race. "It's great that you've really made strides accepting your fate. I wonder how much your parenting factored into his choices. One always wonders."

Setting aside snide comments, choosing a trade instead of college can impose utilitarian costs in addition to expressive and emotional ones. Responding to an article about men who fall behind in college enrollment,[49] one noted that working in trades, such as HVAC, is looked down on by many. Yet a good union job assures a full pension, good healthcare, a truck, uniforms, and no student debt. "You also get to be outdoors some of the time instead of getting stuck in an office at a computer all day." But another noted that union jobs are disappearing fast, and the pay is not great. HVAC union members make an average $53,000 per year. "These jobs are also extremely hard on the body—no coincidence that American workers in trades have higher levels of addiction than other workers."

We gain insight into prestigious American universities as emblems of high social status, yielding expressive and emotional benefits, as we compare the university landscapes in the United States and Canada. Sociologists Scott Davies and Floyd Hammack noted that the two countries are similar in that more than 60% of high school graduates proceed to postsecondary education. Both have decentralized governance university systems, and both experienced increased university enrollment. Yet whereas the Canadian university system consists of a fairly flat prestige pyramid, the U.S. university system is distinguished by a steep prestige pyramid, leading to distinctive forms of competition. As Davies and Hammack wrote: "Where one studies is seen as more important in the U.S., while what one studies dominates in Canada."[50]

Sociologist Janice Aurini and coauthors explored the attitudes of elite parents in Toronto, Canada, about their children's activities and postsecondary educational choices.[51] They found that elite Canadians enroll their children in multiple activities and cultivate their skills. Yet their parenting logic, unlike that of their American counterparts, is not guided by desire for seats at prestigious universities. Instead, it is guided by interests of their children, proximity to their homes, and contributions to their children's health.

A Canadian mother said: "We let them choose what they want to choose. We didn't want to force them into things. Our dream is about their dream." Another mother described the distressing experience of her six-year-old daughter in a music class, before she quit. The teacher was yelling, "B-sharp! B-sharp! B-sharp!" The daughter said "Mommy, the only sharp I know is when I sharpen my pencil."

Compare this story to the one of elite American parents, described by sociologist Marianne Cooper, preparing to send a recording of a violin performance by Alec, their son, as they compete for a seat at a private junior high school. Listening to her son play the mother exclaimed "What is he doing? . . . . Alec has to be perfect . . . perfect."[52]

Elite Canadian parents expect their children to acquire postsecondary education, and many see such education as a must. But they expressed little concern about the kind of postsecondary education, "university, or a college, or an apprenticeship to get them on the path that they want to take."

A Canadian mother whose son wanted to attend medical school noted that having a medical degree is more important than the particular medical school. "For a doctor, I don't know anybody who goes to the doctor's office and looks at what school they graduated from and what marks they got, right?"

Moreover, Canadian parents prefer postsecondary education close to home, in part, because living at home is less costly. One parent said: "I would have liked them both to go to [University of] Toronto . . . because I can help them out more that way." Callum, their older son, went to that university and was able to live at home for the first three years, with little expense and little debt. Their younger son is going to Concordia University because it is one of few places offering degrees in creative writing. "So, that's going to be . . . a big challenge financially." The fact that the University of Toronto ranks much higher overall than Concordia University mattered little. What mattered was the preference for a particular program, "substance over name brand."

The highly steeped prestige pyramid of American universities can be traced to the origins of the most prestigious American universities as finishing schools for the American elites, where academic qualifications mattered relatively little. A switch of emphasis to academic qualifications in 1905 got Harvard in trouble as it detracted from its role as a finishing school.

As Malcolm Gladwell noted,[53] citing sociologist Jerome Karabel, by 1922 Jews made up more than a fifth of Harvard's freshman class.[54] Harvard's solution was to focus on applicants'"character.""Starting in the fall of 1922, applicants were required to answer questions on 'Race and Color,' 'Religious Preference,' 'Maiden Name of Mother,' 'Birthplace of Father,' and 'What change, if any, has been made since birth in your own name or that of your father? (Explain fully).'" By the end of 1933, the percentage of Jews at Harvard was back down to 15%. "Harvard, Yale, and Princeton didn't abandon the elevation of character once the Jewish crisis passed. They institutionalized it." Athletic ability rose in significance as a selection criterion, reflected in the fact that even now athletes are accepted into prestigious universities at double the rate of other students, despite significantly lower SAT scores.

The gap in rates of admission between the most prestigious universities and the less prestigious ones is wider now than ever. Only the top 10% of colleges, including members of the Ivy League, Stanford, Duke, and the like, are substantially more selective now than they were in 1962. Less prestigious universities have become less selective. Economist Caroline Hoxby pinned the widening gaps on a transformation of the university market from regional to national, facilitated by declining costs of travel and communication.[55]

The 1983 introduction of the *U.S. News & World Report* rankings widened the gap further. Economists James Monks and Ronald

Ehrenberg found that lower ranks in the report prompt universities to accept higher percentages of applicants, and accept applicants with lower average SAT scores.[56]

The surge in the number of college-bound students since the mid-1990s widened the gap even more, into what economists Garey Ramey and Valerie Ramey called the "Rug-Rat Race." They noted that the resulting "cohort crowding" has led parents to compete more fiercely for seats at prestigious colleges by spending increasing amounts of time and money on college preparation of their children.[57]

Some of that surge is likely due to the influx of highly educated immigrants from Asia, especially from China and India, following the 1965 American immigration law that gave preference to highly educated immigrants, replacing the earlier preference by country of origin that limited immigration from Asia.

Sociologist Natasha Warikoo described competition for admission to prestigious colleges at the Woodcrest public high school. Woodcrest, Warikoo's name for a wealthy East Coast suburb, has always been home to elite white families, but is now also home to an increasing number of elite Asian-American families. Competition between children of white families and Asian-American families strains the relationships between children, and especially the relationships between parents. Elite white-American families have always been at the top of the status pyramid with the best chances of placing their children at prestigious colleges, but now they encounter great competition from elite Asian-American families.

Warikoo asked Shannon, a white mother, how the increasing number of Asian-American children in Woodcrest's public high school had affected her children. Shannon started with the positive. "They had great friends who cared about education," before turning to the negative. "My kids, and especially my older daughter, who was very bright and very motivated, felt like an average student because there were so many geniuses and superstars and kids that are just off the charts."[58]

Rory, another white mother, blamed parenting in Asian-American families for her son's diminished status and his inability to gain a seat in the honors math track she thought he deserved. Still, Rory's eldest daughter was attending an Ivy college, indicating that her family still did well in the competition for spots at prestigious colleges.[59]

"The irony of Rory's child attending an elite and expensive college was not lost on me," wrote Warikoo. Like Asian-American families she critiqued, Rory pulled out all the stops when it came to her children's college application process. "The only difference was the strategies they engaged in."

Rory did support her son in math, in an elementary school math team, but not in the Russian School of Math favored by elite Asian-American families. And her daughter benefited from a boost as a "legacy" in admission to Rory's college. Asian-Americans families are less likely to enjoy that legacy boost because most Asian-American parents got undergraduate degrees in Asia.

Some elite white American families respond to educational competition by Asian-American students by moving away. White student enrollment declines in higher-income suburbs as Asian students arrive, a pattern that cannot be fully explained by racial animus, housing prices, or correlations with Black or Hispanic arrivals. Parental fears of academic competition likely explain this pattern.[60]

The claim that the Asian-American academic advantage over whites comes from greater academic effort rather than better cognitive abilities is validated in a study by sociologists Amy Hsin and Yu Xie.[61] In particular, they found that the advantage comes from stronger beliefs among Asian-Americans in the connection between effort and achievement, and from the immigration status of many Asian-Americans.

The academic pressures felt by elite children, white and Asian-American alike, diminish well-being and harm the emotional health of some students, inducing depression and anxiety. Yet these pressures seem to diminish well-being among Asian-American children more than among white children.

Hsin and Xie suggested two possible mechanisms underlying Asian-Americans' lower well-being. One is the immensely high educational expectations of Asian-American parents, children, and society. These high expectations make those who fail to meet them feel like failures. Moreover, those who reach great academic achievements may consider them as assumed, or believe that they are expected to achieve even more.

The other mechanism underlying Asian-Americans' lower well-being is the complicated position of Asian-Americans in the racially stratified American society. Asian-Americans are recognized for their work ethic and intelligence yet marginalized by an outsider status that prevents their full integration into American society.[62]

The desire of white parents to reduce academic pressure on students at the Woodcrest public high school and similar ones, such as by reduced homework, might well be motivated by the desire to mitigate emotional health problems. Yet Warikoo noted that many white Woodcrest parents who expressed great concern about emotional health also supported their children in competitive sports teams, honors and AP classes, and more. She suggested that the drive to reduce academic competition and schoolwork is also motivated by the desire of white-Americans to preserve their status by handicapping Asian-Americans in the race to prestigious colleges.[63]

"Fencing can be six-figure expensive, but it wins in college admissions," was the title of an article by journalist Stephanie Saul. She described the Manhattan Fencing Center, where hanging from the ceiling are flags from Duke, Harvard, N.Y.U., Johns Hopkins, Notre Dame, Princeton, and Columbia—colleges and universities with fencing teams. Fencing, along with crew, golf, sailing, skiing, and squash are called "country club sports," played mostly in white suburbs.

"Parents realize that fencing is one of the best sports to put your child in a good university," said Yury Gelman, founder of the Center. Recruited athletes had an acceptance rate of 83% at Harvard, compared to 16% of other students with similar scores.

A few readers agreed with the message of Saul's article. One wrote: "Hard to complain about elitism when the whole point of attending an Ivy is to become the elite. This is the dirty little secret. . . . The point is to meet the kids of senators, movie stars, and CEOs—people who fly on private jets and determine monetary policy at Davos." Brand is what Ivies sell, she added, and "if they became pure academic meritocracies, they'd lose a lot of what makes students want to attend in the first place."

Yet most readers reacting to the article disagreed, many vehemently. One wrote: "What percentage of University of Michigan football players and Duke basketball players would be admitted if they weren't elite athletes? Likely close to zero. But, of course, as that doesn't further the social justice narrative, it is simply ignored."[64]

Some parents respond to the fierce competition at elite public high schools by transferring their children to private high schools with good records of placing graduates at prestigious universities. Sophie Callcott, a junior at Stanford University who grew up in Silicon Valley, described the advantages conferred by private high schools. "Every American high schooler knows the supposed secret to a lifetime of success: admission to an elite university. Competition for coveted spots is so fierce that while an admission victory can't be guaranteed, it can be gamed, if you know how to play." Callcott played the game and won. Counselors at elite private high schools have behind-the-scenes access to admission officers. When Callcott was deferred from a school she applied to for early admission, the counselor called the admission officer and was told that Callcott should keep her *A* in honors calculus, implying that if she did, she would get in during regular admission decisions.[65]

Other parents move their families away, as from Silicon Valley to New Hampshire. A woman described a very successful friend who decided to move to New Hampshire, where he grew up. "Because, you know what he says? In New Hampshire you can have average kids and they can feel like they're successful. Here, if you have an average kid, it makes them feel like a failure."[66]

The lives of parents and children in elite American families are stressful, but the lives of parents and children in elite Chinese families and those aspiring to join them are even more stressful, ruled by "chicken parenting" of "chicken babies."[67] Researcher Han Chang noted that only a few schools in Chinese urban areas are considered prestigious, and getting into them requires an early start. "Many people don't realize that if you don't go to a good middle or high school, you have basically said goodbye to [prestigious] Tsinghua and Peking University," said a mother whose son is enrolled in a prestigious high school.

Chicken parents send their children to cram schools where they are tutored in English, math, Chinese, and other subjects. "The sad part is that once you start chickening your children, it's hardly possible to stop," explained a high school teacher, noting that extracurricular activities of children no longer serve to cultivate hobbies or fun. "Today, chicken babies play chess to improve cognitive skills, participate in Math Olympiads for logical reasoning, sports to prevent myopia. . . . Everything has to serve one purpose: to be good at school."

"Extracurricular activities are just the norm," said a mother. Her daughter, a fourth grader, was voted class president, plays in the school orchestra, and takes piano, martial arts, Chinese, and math classes on the side. "How many extracurriculars children have, and how much time and money parents are willing to spend on it . . . that is what makes the real difference here."

The Chinese government attempts to reduce academic competition, motivated by the desire to encourage parents to have more children. Yet these curbs also serve elite Chinese families in their efforts to preserve their status by handicapping those who strive to join them.[68] Scott Yang, a father who strives to see his child join the elite, worries that banning after-school classes will give a further edge to elite families that can afford private tutors.

The emotional costs of the race to prestigious colleges leads some young Chinese to see hyper-competition in education and work as a pointless hamster wheel, noted writer Jianan Qian. "The term 'tangping,' or 'lying flat,' went viral on Chinese social media. It was China's version of the Great Resignation that began in the United States around the same time."[69]

A mother is California was "gutted by the recent tragedy" of a student at a competitive high school who died by suicide. She wrote on Next Door, an online communication hub, about a support group for parents who want emotionally healthy families and children. "To be quite honest, I expect this to be a gathering of many East/South Asian American parents, but all parents are welcome." The mother remembers the heart-breaking moment when she asked her first-born daughter why she felt so much pressure in high school. "She said this . . . 'Both you and dad went to Stanford. I feel like I have to make you proud.' I don't recall expressing that I wanted her to apply to Stanford . . . but then again, I admit I have blind spots as a parent."

The emotional costs of the race to prestigious colleges led Kaitlyn Younger to change her perspectives. Younger, the previously mentioned perfectionist who was rejected by all the prestigious colleges she applied to, said: "I used to be the kind of person who, if I got a low *A*, anything lower than a 95, I would be upset with myself because I thought that was the standard for the types of institutions I wanted to attend," she said. "All that stress was not worth it. I want to do the best I can, but in a way that does not deteriorate my mental health if I struggle."[70]

A reader of Younger's story wrote: "In the end, what matters is that one finishes college, no matter what school you go to. What matters is that the process leaves you more rather than less capable, and with enough of a social structure built to enter adulthood engaged rather than alienated." Another wrote: "After your first job, no one cares where you went to school. After 40, no one cares if you even went to college. As an experienced engineer I can assure every aspiring engineer it doesn't matter where you studied if you didn't learn the material and how to solve problems."

Education among the working class and poor

The elite notion that preschool is best for children when it is centered on academics is now pressed down into the children of the working class and poor. Early childhood educator Erika Christakis noted a cultural shift, starting in the early 2000s, from "protected" childhood to a "prepared" one, pushing parents' preferences ever further in the direction of preparation for academic goals.[71] Yet preschool programs built on that notion do not help working-class and poor children any more than they help elite ones. They diminish the skills acquired by young children, including academic skills, rather than enhance them.

Tennessee's pre-kindergarten program is centered on academics, whereby large passive groups of children learn language, math, and executive functioning from teachers. A study of the program revealed that it diminishes children's initiative and shrinks educational outcomes. Indeed, children who attended the program did worse subsequently on academic and behavioral outcomes than those who did not attend the program.[72]

Young children learn best when their learning is playful, active, engaging, meaningful, iterative, socially interactive, and joyful, centered on reading, telling stories, solving puzzles, and playing with blocks, facilitating the development of attention, social development, working memory, and persistence.[73]

Preschool programs centered on play provide substantial lifelong well-being benefits, especially to children of poor families. A study by economist Martha Bailey and coauthors of children of poor families in Head Start preschool found that, compared with children who were six-years-old, and therefore, beyond the age of eligibility for Head Start preschool, three- to five-year-old children in Head Start preschool gained substantial benefits. This is especially true among children who attended Head Start preschool for more years and benefited from its gradual improvement. [74]

Students in three years of a fully implemented Head Start preschool were 3% more likely to finish high school, 8.5% more likely to attend college, and 39% more likely to complete college. Moreover, Head Start preschool students were more likely to work at professional jobs, female students were 32% less likely to live in poverty as adults, and male students were 42% less likely to receive public assistance.

Studies of the effectiveness of other preschool programs reveal similar high effectiveness. David Kirp, professor of education, described the Perry Preschool program that started half a century ago, enrolling three- and four-year-old children from poor families. The program yielded substantial lifelong benefits to children, including greater academic accomplishments, higher earnings, and better health.[75]

Moreover, a study of the Perry Preschool program by economist Jorge Luis Garcia and coauthors found that its beneficial effects extend to future generations. The benefits of the Perry Preschool program to the first-generation of students include a better family environment for a second generation. Second-generation Perry Preschool children have higher levels of education and employment, lower levels of criminal activity, and better health than other children.[76]

Another study, by economist John List and coauthors, revealed similar great benefits in an intensive program directed at poor parents and their young children. The program, combining home visits and feedback and enriched interactions between parents and children, improved children's vocabulary, math, and social-emotional skills.[77]

The benefits of Head Start and other publicly supported preschools are greater when parents are involved in school events. A study in six Chicago preschools offered parents a $25 incentive per event and text message reminders. This increased the likelihood of attending events by 28%. Moreover, the habit of attending school events persisted when the incentive was no longer offered.[78] The benefits of extra education extend to ninth- and tenth-grade adolescents in public schools who fall behind. Intensive individualized in-school tutoring increased substantially their grades in math and nonmath courses, and these effects persisted into their future.[79]

Many working-class and poor parents care as much about the education of their children as elite parents, and they may have the cultural capital to do so. Yet they often struggle to accumulate the necessary social and especially financial capital.

SNAP, also known as food stamps, is a nutritional assistance program providing monthly benefits to eligible poor. SNAP money diminishes during the month as it is spent, and hunger increases. Students taking high-stakes exams during the last two weeks of SNAP benefit cycles earn lower test scores and have lower likelihood of attending a four-year college.[80]

Parents in working-class and poor families often save money for their children's education and help them study, hoping for college scholarships, and if necessary, willing to bear debt. Carly, a 55-year-old British woman interviewed by BlackRock, said: "At the moment I am concentrating on my daughter's A-levels. . . . I sometimes feel that it is me taking them."[81] A-levels, shorthand for Advanced Level Exams, are recognized by many universities in England, Wales, and Northern Ireland as the standard for assessing the suitability of applicants for admission.

Bill, the previously mentioned 52-year-old American man, is saving for his children's college education. "Right now, we are focused on being able to pay for our kids' college education," he said. "My daughter is a junior in high school and is looking into schools. We have a 529 [education saving] plan that we have been saving for college and I think we should be on track for this goal." Bill is balancing the benefits of education at a private college against their costs. His most meaningful money conversation with his daughter was about college. "I told her that we have saved enough money for her and her brother to go to any state school in [their home state]. However, she was very interested in going to a private school in the Northeast."

Bill noted that most of the private colleges that his daughter is interested in do not offer any scholarships for merit, and his family does not qualify for need-based aid. "This was a difficult discussion that made us think about what it would take for us to go beyond our plan and how much my daughter is willing to go into debt for the education that she wants."

Elite parents and their children usually prefer four-year colleges offering bachelor degrees, but working-class and poor children often begin at community colleges, whether with an associate's degree as their final destination, or as a way-station to a four-year college and a bachelor's degree. Community colleges enroll 45% of all U.S. undergraduate students, and 80% of them strive to transfer to four-year colleges and obtain a bachelor's degree.[82]

The utilitarian benefits of college education are enormous. Community college students who complete one- or two-years' worth of credits earn 25% more than high school graduates, even if they have not obtained an associate's degree. Yet, whereas a community college adds to the earnings of students who would have otherwise not gone to college, it detracts from the potential earnings of students diverted from attending a four-year college.[83] College students who earn a four-year bachelor's degree earn 21.7% beyond that of graduates of community college.[84]

There are many stories of enhanced well-being among those who graduated from community colleges and those who transferred to four-year colleges. One student wrote that he hated high school and barely graduated. He worked crappy jobs until he was 25 and realized that he will continue to work crappy jobs unless he acquired further education. He enrolled at a community college, transferred to a four-year college and graduated with a degree in chemistry. He worked as a chemist for many years, then returned to school for a graduate degree and a career in teaching. "Not bad for a guy that hated school. I tell my students this story often. You are never too old to learn. And without an education, your choices are limited."[85]

Another wrote that she will always be grateful for what community college did for her. "However much older you think you'll be than other students, you won't be. However hard you think it'll be; your lecturers will be a great resource." She noted further that many community colleges have great relations with four-year colleges, so transfers are possible and transfer students face no stigma.[86]

Yet few succeed at graduating from community colleges. Writer Ann Hulbert noted that the national graduation rate after three years is only 16%, and fewer than one-third graduate after six years.[87] The strengths of community colleges in easy access, flexibility, and expansive menu of programs and majors, are also their weaknesses. Community college students whose life disadvantages call for clear guidance and strong structure, receive little of either, whereas students at prestigious four-year colleges who have been provided guidance and structure by parents and teachers since preschool are provided more of it.

First-year students at Harvard are supervised by a freshman adviser, a resident dean of freshmen, a proctor, and a peer-advising fellow. Residential house tutors and faculty advisers lend support later. In contrast, students at the nearby Bunker Hill Community College are largely on their own, with student-adviser ratios that can reach 1,500-to-1, choosing from more than 70 associate's-degree or certificate programs, in more than 60 majors, then figuring out the optimal course load, and how to best mix online and in-person classes.[88] It is little wonder that most fail.

Moreover, graduating from a four-year college or even a community college seems distant to people with little money, whereas money earned today, even at minimum wage, seems urgent. Indeed, uncertainty about the future benefits of four-year degrees combined with the necessity of earning money today deter many high-achieving but poor students from applying to four-year colleges. Economist Susan Dynarski and coauthors examined the effects of an early commitment of financial aid at a flagship university, guaranteed before application, equal to what students would qualify if admitted. The commitment reduced uncertainty facing students, increasing applications and rates of enrollment.[89]

More typical, however, is Angie, described by sociologist Ranita Ray. Angie enrolled in classes at the Port City Rivers Community College, pursuing her dream of a college degree.[90] But by the time she enrolled, she had already missed a few weeks of classes, and she heard about job opportunities from friends who worked at the mall, local bakeries, and hair salons. She decided to withdraw for the semester and take on three jobs.

The following semester, Angie re-enrolled at the community college right on time, but dropped out to complete an eight-hour driving course. Angie's third semester in the community college looked promising, but halfway through the semester her car broke down, and asking for rides or using public transportation to her three jobs and college was exhausting. She chose to keep the jobs.

College and no-college groups among the working class and poor

We can divide working-class and poor parents into two groups, the college group and the no-college group. Parents in the college group, many of whom are immigrants, possess the cultural capital necessary for college admission and are willing to sacrifice much to acquire the necessary social and especially financial capital. They, like elite parents, gain high well-being in expressive and emotional benefits in high social status and pride as they watch their children graduate from college, even if not a prestigious one, and proceed into white-collar careers.

Hasiba Haq and her parents are in the college group. Her parents immigrated from Bangladesh and her father worked as a taxi driver. "I became aware of internalized shame at not being white and wealthy," Haq said.[91]

By the time Haq turned 11, her parents heard about examinations by which students are selected into specialized public schools, and enrolled her in a rigorous tutoring center. The sticker price was $4,000 and her parents paid a substantial portion of it, even after a discount. "It was every weekend and classes over the summer," said Haq. "Everyone in the community knew it was your turn to take the test." The local Bengali newspaper printed the names and photographs of Bengali teenagers who were admitted to specialized high schools. "Family honor is tied to it," she said. "It's kind of embarrassing." She graduated from Brooklyn Tech, a specialized public high school.

Working-class and poor parents in the college group struggle to help their children into college and white-collar careers, hoping that their children would not have to struggle as hard. Tom Sit is one of those parents, the owner of a Chinese restaurant where he cooked seven days a week, 12 hours a day, in a kitchen where he worked as a young immigrant from China. Sit is now 76 years old, and working 80 hours a week is hard. His grown daughters have college degrees and well-paying white-collar careers. They do not intend to take over the restaurant.[92]

Readers shared similar stories. One wrote: "I am the first in my family to go to college, and am now a professor at an Ivy League institution. My parents are so proud that their journey and hardship paid off, but often I am proud they had the courage to leave everything behind and take a chance in a new country."

Another, also the child of immigrants who owned Chinese restaurants, wrote that he and his siblings went on to earn five college degrees, an M.S., three Ph.D.s, and a J.D. degree. "This story of first-generation immigrants working hard in whatever jobs that would improve the lot of their offspring, however, is the story of the American Dream. . . ."

Many working-class and poor Indian parents and their children see admission to elite colleges as the only way to move up in life. "In Kota, students from across the country pay steep fees to be tutored for elite-college admissions exams, which most of them will fail," wrote journalist Mansi Choksi.[93] "All told, roughly 150,000 students arrive every year, some of them children of fruit vendors, farmhands, welders, freight-truck drivers, construction workers, sweepers and rickshaw-pullers from the poorest corners of the country, hoping to improve their chances on the nation's highly competitive college entrance exams."

Working-class and poor members of the college group who rise into the elite enjoy extra expressive and emotional benefits, knowing that they rose by their own merit, not by membership in the elite, and surely not by status as "legacy," accepted at college by their parents' college attendance.

Sociologist Rachel Sherman quoted Warren, a private equity entrepreneur from what he called a "middle-class-slash-working-class" background, who felt different at his Ivy college. But "the difference was empowering" because it was clear that he was there because of his intelligence, not his family history or connections. "The people who were around me . . . recognized that the fact that I didn't go to Andover makes me a little special. 'Cause it wasn't kind of like, quote-unquote 'handed to me' . . . "The fact that his father didn't go to college was a badge of honor, or talent. "It's like, 'Oh, I'm no legacy . . . I didn't go to private school. I'm just, you know, I'm actually smart.'"[94]

Working-class and poor patents in the no-college group are content to see their children rise into the working-class or remain there, or see no way to ascend into the elite. They do not prepare their children for college, in part, because they lack the necessary cultural, social, or financial capital, and in part, because they do not gain much expressive and emotional benefits from seeing their children graduate from college.

Economist George Bulman and coauthors[95] examined the trajectory of children whose parents won lottery prizes. They found that the effects of prizes on college attendance were significant among the elite, promoting college attendance, but not among the working-class and poor. Bulman and coauthors noted that working-class and poor parents may have more pressing demands for the lottery prizes, such as paying off high interest loans, buying a car or house, quitting their jobs, or helping their extended families. Or perhaps, these working-class and poor parents and children place less value on college education relative to other options.

Other working-class and poor parents lack the social capital available to elite parents in informal conversations where they exchange school information with parents like them. Yet other working-class people in the no-college group reject the cultural and social capital of the elite, much of it founded on a college degree. As law professor Joan Williams noted, they regard college-educated managers as kids "who don't know shit about how to do anything, but are full of ideas about how I have to do my job." But they suffer affronts every day from members of the elite, the doctor who unthinkingly patronizes the medical technician, the harried office worker who treats the security guard as invisible, the overbooked business traveler who snaps at the TSA agent.[96]

Some low-income white people are skeptical of higher education, in part because it was not necessary to obtain stable blue-collar jobs and lifestyles in the past. In contrast, many low-income Black people continue to believe in higher education as a path to stable jobs and better lifestyles. Economist Carol Graham found that young adolescents in low-income minority neighborhoods who graduate high school are more likely to continue on to college than their white counterparts.[97]

The mills of Bethlehem Steel have long been shuttered, and sociologist Andrew Cherlin examined the paths of children of Bethlehem Steel workers in Baltimore. Black workers lived in segregated housing, and suffered discrimination in the workplace. Yet most of their children attended college and moved on to better neighborhoods. In contrast, most children of the white workers did not attend college, remained in their parents' neighborhoods, and work in the gig economy.[98]

Many among the working-class no-college group admire the wealthy, especially those who keep the cultural and social capital of the working class, despite owning financial capital that can place them high among the elite. Williams quoted a machine operator who said "The main thing is to be independent and give your own orders and not have to take them from anybody else."[99]

Indeed, college and subsequent white-collar careers are not the sole route to wealth or even the main route to it. A possibly better route to wealth is ownership of a flourishing business. Sociologist Michele Lamont describes Larry Relles, a police officer who strives for substantial financial capital by buying homes and renting them out. "I own three homes. I'll be living in a $300,000 house. . . . I'm only 34 years old . . . I got a boat, a jet ski, a motorcycle. I can pretty much do what I want to do. . . ."[100]

Moreover, some members of the working class place themselves higher in social status than the elite by placing morality higher than income and education as its markers. Lamont noted that white members of the working class identify morality as "disciplined self," their ability to accept discipline and conduct themselves responsibly, placing them above the elite they perceive as lacking morality. And Black members of the working class identify morality as "caring self," reflected in their solidarity and warmth, placing themselves above white people.

Some of the wealthy in the no-college group are "millionaires next door" such as a 35-year-old millionaire Texan, the owner of a flourishing business that rebuilds large diesel engines. He refers to college-educated professionals, such as trust officers in the bank that serves him, as "Big Hat, No Cattle."

The man maintained his working-class cultural and social capital, driving a 10-year-old car, wearing jeans and buckskin shirts, and living in a working-class area, next to neighbors who are postal clerks, fire fighters, and mechanics. "[My] business does not look pretty," he said. When his British partners first met him, they thought he was one of the truck drivers. "They looked all over my office, looked at everyone but me. Then the senior guy of the group said, 'Oh, we forgot we were in Texas!' I don't own big hats, but I have a lot of cattle."[101]

This millionaire next door is a member of what author Patrick Wyman called the American Gentry. They are owners of agricultural companies growing apples, peaches, hops, and wine grapes, McDonald's franchises, beef-processing plants, construction companies, or car dealerships. They either have no college education or do not define themselves by it. Most are born into the gentry, inheriting businesses, and successful at maintaining them.[102]

Wyman lived in Yakima, Washington, home to some agricultural gentry, but he left for college and never returned to live there. The same is true for many of his high-school classmates, working now in elite jobs in corporate or management consulting, nonprofits, media, and finance—jobs that are rare in Yakima.

Still, many among the millionaires-next-door and gentry suffer expressive and emotional costs, aggrieved by a sense that less-wealthy college-graduate white-collar elites look down on them. And lower-earning working-class people are aggrieved not only by the increasing gap between their incomes and social status and those of the elite, but also by the diminishing gap between their incomes and social status and those of the poor.

13

Religion

Answering a Pew Research survey question about what makes life meaningful, fulfilling, or satisfying, one wrote, "Most important is my relationship by faith with God through Jesus Christ." Another wrote, "A fulfilling life is a life with Allah. Where you're reading the Bible, Quran, and praying."[1]

Religious values and practices are effective at enhancing well-being.[2] Religions set moral values, ethical principles, and practices such as the "golden rule," enhancing well-being by fostering connections to others. They guide adherents to place virtue ahead of wealth. Islam teaches that true riches come from the soul, not from wealth, Christianity lists money as the root of all evil, and Buddhists are warned against using wealth for harmful ends.

Religions encourage contentment with what we have, by comparing ourselves to those who have less than to those who have more, and by encouraging expressions of gratitude. The Buddha encouraged adherents to express gratitude, and the Quran notes that gratitude benefits the soul. Indeed, feeling gratitude and expressing it enhance well-being.

And religions enhance well-being by urging forgiveness of wrongdoings. Belonging to a religious group increases the likelihood of forgiving, and people who forgive enjoy higher well-being in higher self-esteem and lower grief, anger, anxiety, and depression.

Suffering is not an illness with a cure, wrote author Michael Ignatieff in *On Consolation*. The essence of Psalms, he wrote, is not in the conviction that the Messiah will come, but in the depiction of suffering as a common human experience, alleviated by the balm of consolation.[3]

Economic transitions, such as in Eastern Europe and Russia, lowered well-being among most residents, but religious involvement alleviated some of the negative effects of the transition on well-being.[4,5] In developed countries, Germans who became more religious gained well-being, whereas those who became less religious lost well-being.[6]

Religious rituals enhance well-being. In Christian traditions, adherents gather for worship at churches, listening to sermons of pastors or priests. Songs are sung and passages of Scripture are read aloud. Muslims gather in mosques, Jews in synagogues, and Hindus and Buddhists in temples. A gathering for worship provides a sense of unity, enhancing well-being by binding people together.

Moreover, religious gatherings, prayer, sermons, and reading religious texts trigger positive emotions, including awe, gratitude, love, peace, and optimism that enhance well-being. Religions also teach adherents to assess their emotions, enhancing their well-being by making them better at regulating them.[7]

Social support is a buffer against adverse life events, and religions enhance well-being by social support. Indeed, strong social support is one of the most important predictors of well-being. Religiosity measured by frequency of attendance at religious gatherings enhances well-being by more than religiosity measures by private religious acts and beliefs, such as prayer. When tragedy strikes, such as the sudden death of an infant, parents who attend religious gatherings receive great social support from fellow attendees, and that support restores well-being.

Sociologists Christopher Ellison and Gabriel Acevedo found that the risk of death is approximately 20% lower among people who attend religious services more than once per week than among those who do not attend services at all. On average, frequent religious attendees can be expected to live approximately seven years longer than non-attendees, and the increase in life expectancy among Blacks is double that. Ellison and Acevedo noted that health benefits are associated with public religious practice rather than private religiosity, suggesting that the link between religion and health is associated with the collective nature of public worship rather than its religious elements.[8]

Religious communities also protect members against losses of food and other life necessities when income drops, and against losses of well-being.[9] Sociologist Marianne Cooper illustrated that protection by the story of a woman in her early 30s, a member of the Mormon church. "The woman's voice shakes and her hands tremble, but the emotions she wants to convey come through clearly" as she talks about her difficult transition from living with her parents in Utah to getting married, moving to California, and starting a family. Her anxieties were eased by the warm welcome from people of the Mormon ward. They helped her and her husband in many ways, babysitting their children, teaching them about parenting, having them over for dinner and mentoring her husband in his professional studies.[10]

The Mormon religion, the religion of the woman described by Cooper, is a strict religion, like Orthodox Judaism and Jehovah Witness. Strict religions provide much to adherents, such as help when in need, but they also expect much from their adherents, such as tithing and helping fellow adherents. Lenient denominations include Reform Judaism, Episcopalian, Unitarian, and Presbyterian. They ask little from their adherents, but also provide little other than a social network favored by well-educated adherents.[11]

Strict religions place their members in a bind when they ask for more than members are willing to provide. This bind is illustrated in Cooper's story about Peter Faleau, who expressed interest in going on a mission when he was in his late teens. Young Mormons on a mission spend two years away from their families, spreading the gospel and engaging in community work, often in a foreign country.[12]

Faleau received a scholarship from the Mormon church for his undergraduate studies by Eric, the Mormon elder in charge of coordinating scholarships and missions in Faleau's ward. At first, Faleau was not asked to go on a mission because he was not an American citizen. A few years later, Congress passed a bill making it legal for noncitizens to go on missions within the United States. Yet Faleau declined to go on a mission, and Eric terminated his scholarship. "It's church money that did the scholarship for him," said Eric. He wanted to make sure that Faleau understood that he ought to honor that help.

Strict religions also place their members in a bind when they ask for more than members can provide. That bind is illustrated by sociologists Jonathan Morduch and Rachel Schneider in the story of Janice Evans, a 55-year-old casino employee. Janice works the night shift at the Pearl River Resort, dealing cards. Her low earnings vary greatly by the tips contributed by customers at her table, higher in the summer when customers are drawn in by the casino's air conditioning, and lower in the fall. Church is a constant in Janice's life, along with work and family, and contributing to the church is important to her. Yet, like the rest of her finances, her ability to tithe—give 10% of her income to the church—depends on how many people come to the casino and how much they leave in tips. Janice's father, the preacher at the church she attends, senses Janice's stress in months when her paycheck is slim. "He knows I'm on my own without a husband. He came to me and said, 'It's good you pay your tithe. But you are not supposed to lose things because you pay your tithe. Pay your car note first.'"[13]

The difference between strict and lenient churches also provides the solution to a puzzle about the link between religious attendance and education. Religious attendance rises with education across individuals, but declines with education across religious denominations. The puzzle is solved if education increases the benefits of a larger social network and also reduces religious beliefs. The positive effect of education on sociability explains the positive association between education and religion. The negative effect of education on religious beliefs leads more educated people to shun strict religions in favor of lenient ones.[14]

Different groups of Americans find different meanings in religion, and they find different meanings of well-being. The Pew survey found that Evangelical Protestants are more likely than other Christians to say that they find a great deal of meaning in religion. Conservatives are more likely than liberals to bring up faith as adding meaning to their lives. And Black Americans find more meaning in religion than do whites and Hispanics. Three-in-ten Black Americans mention spirituality and faith as giving meaning to their lives, higher than the 1-in-5 of whites and the 1-in-7 of Hispanics.

Younger Americans are less likely to mention religion than older Americans. Only 1-in-10 American adults under age 30 mentioned spirituality, faith, or God when describing what makes their life meaningful, lower than the 3-in-10 adults ages 65 and older who mention them.[15] Moreover, the religious landscape continues to change at a fast pace. A 2022 Gallup survey found that 81% of Americans expressed belief when asked "Do you believe in God?", much lower than the 98% in the 1950s and 1960s.[16] A 2019 Pew survey found that the share of Americans who identified as Christians was 65%, down 12% during the preceding decade, whereas the share of Americans who identified as atheist, agnostic or nothing-in-particular, was 26%, up 9% during that decade.[17]

Church attendance is also declining. "Aside from weddings and funerals, how often do you attend religious services?" The share of Americans who attend religious services at least once or twice a month dropped by 7% during the decade ending in 2019, whereas the share of those who attend religious services less often, if at all, has risen by the same degree.

These changes in the American religious landscape are evident across many demographic groups: white, Black, and Hispanic; men and women; in all regions of the country; and among college graduates and those with lower levels of education. Religious "nones" now account for one-third of Democrats, although they account for a smaller share of Republicans.

Meanwhile, the share of Americans who identify with non-Christian faiths has increased slightly, from 5% in 2009 to 7% in 2019. This includes 2% who are Jewish; 1% each who are Muslim, Buddhist, or Hindu; and 3% who adhere to their own personal religious beliefs or describe themselves as spiritual.

Still, another Pew Research survey in 17 advanced economies found that higher proportions of Americans find meaning in religions than people in other developed countries.[18] Among Americans, 15% find meaning in religion. New Zealanders come second, at 5%. And no more than 1% in France, Sweden, Belgium, South Korea, or Japan.

Religion as unifier and divider

Religion can unify people, enhancing their well-being by helping them live in large groups and cooperate by enforcing ethical and cultural norms. Joseph Henrich, a scholar of human evolutionary biology, noted that small hunter-gatherer societies used dance and moving in synch to unite people. Larger communities do the same with shared beliefs in powerful gods and rituals like Sunday services. United communities are able to outcompete their neighbors and enhance well-being by sharing resources, attracting converts, and fielding larger armies, further evidence of their gods' powers.[19] The role of religion as a unifier, wrote Henrich, is now gradually taken over by secular institutions, and the task of enforcing ethical behavior is now in the domain of the justice system, where crimes are punished with prison sentences in this world instead of damnation in the afterworld.

Yet whereas religion can unify people, enhancing well-being, it can also divide them, diminishing well-being. Political scientist Alan Wolfe noted that it has been a long time since religion served as a unifying force, perhaps since the 14th or 15th century when Catholicism could claim something like a universal status. "Whatever unifying potential Catholicism once possessed, the rise of Protestantism was synonymous with the rise of sectarianism."[20]

Wolfe noted that the conflict between religion and nonreligion in the United States may be more divisive than any conflict among religions.

"Conservatives Catholics, Protestants, and Jews are more likely to find a common enemy in secular humanism than they are to struggle with each other over the fine points of theology."

The idea that the United States has always been a bastion of religious freedom is reassuring, noted writer Kenneth Davis, but it has always been a myth. In that myth, the Pilgrims and Puritans came to America in search of religious freedom, and ever since, millions came to a welcoming America where everyone is free to practice their own faith. In truth, religion in the United States has often been a cudgel, "used to discriminate, suppress and even kill the foreign, the "heretic" and the "unbeliever"—including the "heathen" natives already here."[21]

The myth of India as a bastion of religious freedom may well be deeper than the American one. A Pew Research report found that Indians see religious tolerance as a central part of their nation, and see respecting other religions as central in being members of their own religious community. Yet Indians display consistent preferences for keeping their religious communities in segregated spheres.[22]

Most members of India's major religious communities see little in common with one another. Most Hindus see themselves as very different from Muslims, and most Muslims say they are very different from Hindus. Marriages across religious lines are exceedingly rare, and so are religious conversions. And Indians' circles of friends tend to be limited to people of their own religion. This is true even among Sikhs and Jains, who each form a small portion of the national population.

Journalist Jessica Grose started writing a series about religion because she felt that the rise of "nones" is misunderstood, discussed mostly among atheists who cheer it and religious observants who decry it. She noted that somewhere between 6,000 and 10,000 churches close down every year, either to be converted into apartments, laundries, laser-tag arenas, or skate parks, or to be demolished. Her own apartment was once the rectory of a church, built in the 1800s and transformed, a couple of decades ago, into "condos for yuppies who want dramatic windows and a hint of ecclesiastical flavor."[23] Grose noted her own ambivalence about religion. She is Jewish, with a strong cultural identity, but not observant. She has no desire to return to a synagogue, yet wishes to pass down Jewish rituals to her children. She asked readers for their experiences and 7,000 responded.

"Community," wrote Grose, was mentioned by more than 2,300 who responded. One, a 50-year-old woman, wrote: "I was raised Pentecostal and went to church three or more times a week, so I desperately miss the community. It was where my friendships came from. I have very few friends now." She is no longer part of a church because she hasn't found one that affirms gay people or supports separation of church and state. She has joined groups that are fighting for these things, like Christians Against Christian Nationalism, but they don't provide the kind of community provided by a church.

Religious prejudice diminishes well-being. Indeed, prejudice diminishes well-being even when people do not experience it directly. Seeing prejudice toward other people, or simply knowing about prejudice, can be enough to raise anxiety and lead people to avoid situations where prejudice is likely.[24]

American Muslims and Jews perceive more religious threats than Christians. More than half of Muslims surveyed said that it was "somewhat true" to "very true" that they felt targeted because of their religion. Jews reported the second-highest level of religious threats. Religious threats diminish well-being by lower mental and physical health, and lower motivation and success.

Very religious people suffer higher levels of religious threats. Indeed, highly religious American Protestants reported levels of threats as high as those reported by religious minorities. This finding may reflect a sense that Christianity is under attack in the United States.[25]

People who perceive more religious threats often cope by hiding their religion from others at work or school. But hiding this important part of identity is stressful, preventing people from forming trusting relationships with others outside their group.

"As religious faith has declined," noted writer Shadi Hamid, "ideological intensity has risen." American faith is as fervent as ever, as religious beliefs have turned into political beliefs.

Conservatives believe that they uphold the American idea and that liberals have abandoned it, and liberals believe that they are faithful to the American idea and that conservatives are betraying it. The left repurposes religious notions such as original sin, atonement, ritual, and excommunication for secular ends. And the far right finds comfort in conspiracies, such as QAnon, that tell religious stories of earthly corruption redeemed by godlike forces.[26]

The struggle between religion and nonreligion was evident in Israel in the time of COVID-19. Law professor Shai Stern noted that the pandemic intensified existing tensions in Israel between the liberal state and illiberal religious communities. These communities resisted complying with COVID-19 public health regulations issued by state authorities, and therefore, suffered high rates of morbidity and mortality.

Stern argued that the resistance of the Israeli religious communities to COVID-19 regulations stemmed from their unique characteristics and deeply held norms. These include hierarchical decision-making, whereby decisions are made by religious leaders, social and spatial characteristics of communities living in segregated communities, the struggle of religious communities to control and limit information available to their members, the clash between social distancing and communal norms of close contact, such as in synagogues, and the effects of existing tensions and distrust between the state and these communities.[27]

Yet divisions by religion can be narrowed. A manufacturing plant in West Bengal assigned workers to religiously mixed or homogeneous teams. Some production tasks were high-dependency, requiring much coordination among workers, and other tasks were low-dependency. At first, mixed teams were less productive than homogeneous ones in high-dependency tasks, but the lower productivity disappeared completely after four months. Mixing improved attitudes of Hindu workers toward Muslim ones. The improvements in production and attitudes in high-dependency tasks were created mostly by Muslim workers who initiated and carried the burden of integration.[28]

Divisions by religion in Lebanon are as wide as in India. But they too can be narrowed. A Lebanese university assigns first-year students to peer groups, mixing graduates of Christian, Islamic, and secular high schools. Exposure to peers from different religious backgrounds decreased the enrollment of graduates of Islamic high schools in courses taught by instructors with distinctively Muslim names, indicating that contact narrowed divisions and enhanced trust among Christians and Muslims.[29]

14

Society

The 2022 World Happiness Report ranked Finland first in well-being among 146 nations, followed by Denmark and Iceland. New Zealand ranked 10th; the United States, 16th; and the United Kingdom, 17th. At the other end, Afghanistan ranked at the very bottom, preceded by Lebanon and Zimbabwe.[1]

The World Happiness Report and much of the growing interest in national well-being comes from Bhutan, which popularized the notion of Gross National Happiness, augmenting or replacing Gross National Product. Bhutan sponsored a resolution, adopted by the United Nations in 2011, encouraging national governments to "give more importance to happiness and well-being in determining how to achieve and measure social and economic development."[2]

National well-being is the goal of New Zealand's government, described in its 2019 Budget Policy Statement. Enhancing New Zealand citizen's well-being entails transitioning to a sustainable and low-emissions economy, supporting a thriving nation in the digital age, lifting Māori and Pacific citizens' incomes, skills and opportunities, reducing child poverty and improving child well-being, and supporting mental well-being for all New Zealanders.[3]

Societies vary in well-being and governments vary in enhancing it. The goal of increasing Gross National Happiness underlies New Zealand government's decision to impose one of the world's strictest lockdowns in the time of COVID-19, prioritizing citizens' health and well-being over Gross National Product.[4] Governments can do much to enhance well-being by investing in healthcare and education, and by subsidies and services such as electricity, running water, and sewage systems.[5] A comparison of well-being in countries where government services improved by most to the 10 countries where they deteriorated by most shows a 0.4-point difference on the 0 to 10 Cantril's ladder evaluative well-being scale.[6] Yet government actions involve well-being trade-offs among citizens.

Some trade-offs center on utilitarian benefits and costs reflecting self-interest. Taxes diminish the well-being of wealthy citizens fretting about paying more taxes than they receive in government services. But subsidies enhance the well-being of poor citizens who receive more than the taxes they pay.

Other trade-offs center on expressive and emotional benefits and costs reflecting social values, such as those differentiating the political right from the left. On the right, millions of members of the American white working class have shifted their focus away from the utilitarian benefits of income redistribution that favor them, traditionally promoted by Democrats, to the expressive and emotional benefits of adhering to conservative social values, traditionally promoted by Republicans.

On the left, millions of members of the white American elite shifted their focus away from the utilitarian benefits of low taxes that favor them, traditionally promoted by Republicans, to the expressive and emotional benefits of adhering to liberal social values, traditionally promoted by Democrats.[7] Members of each group, left and right, elite and working class, Democrats and Republicans, are affected by life circumstances and struggle over social values and government actions, enjoying high well-being when circumstances favor them and values and actions go their way, and suffering low well-being when circumstances disfavor them, and values and actions go in the opposite direction.

Circumstances changed in recent decades, favoring members of the elite and disfavoring members of the white working class, affecting well-being along with social values and preferences for government actions. These changes drove many of the white working class toward nativist politics, increasing their vulnerability to fake news, populist messages, and skepticism about science.[8]

Partisanship

Do liberals enjoy higher well-being than conservatives? And what values underlie well-being differences?[9] Psychologists Jaime Napier and John Jost concluded that conservatives enjoy higher well-being than liberals because their values justify income and wealth inequality. Indeed, they found that increased inequality over the years increased the gap between the well-being of conservatives and liberals.[10]

Psychologist Barry Schlenker and coauthors agreed that conservatives enjoy higher well-being than liberals, but disagreed about the values underlying it.[11] They concluded, instead, that conservatives enjoy higher well-being because they maintain good self-control and adhere to the Protestant work ethic, centering on the importance of work and a strong belief that achievements come from effort, promoting effort and achievements.

The effects of partisanship on well-being are especially evident in periods surrounding presidential elections. Surveys preceding the 2020 presidential election revealed that Democrats were confident that Joe Biden would win, and Republicans were equally confident that Donald Trump would win. Both Democrats and Republicans expected benefits in a strong economy if their candidate won and costs in a weak economy if their candidate lost.[12]

In the weeks following Trump's loss in the 2020 election, Democrats and Republicans traded places in their views of the economy's direction.[13] An environmental attorney and Democrat who called the economy weak before Biden won, now expected a strong economy: "The outlook with the Biden administration coming in to replace the Trump administration is what will improve things." And a Republican married to an oil field worker worried about the effects of Biden's likely energy regulations on their income: "I'm 100% sure if Biden ends up in the White House, it won't be good for my family."

Partisanship persisted into 2022, evident in attitudes toward American actions in the Russia-Ukraine war. Whereas 61% of Republicans favored the early alerts about Russia's war plans when framed as alerts by the United States, only 28% favored them when framed as initiated by the Biden administration. And whereas 58% of Republicans favored mobilizing NATO support when framed as initiated by the United States, only 38% favored it when framed as initiated by the Biden administration.[14]

Partisanship affects well-being by expressive and emotional benefits and costs beyond utilitarian ones. Donald Trump's supporters enjoyed expressive and emotional benefits and higher well-being following his 2016 win, whereas Hillary Clinton supporters suffered expressive and emotional costs and lower well-being. The well-being of Trump supporters returned to pre-election levels six months after the election, but the well-being of Clinton supporters remained below pre-election levels.[15]

Partisan losers suffered substantial declines in well-being following Barack Obama's 2012 election. The effect of the loss on experienced well-being dissipated quickly, but its effects on evaluative well-being persisted.

The election loss diminished the evaluative well-being of partisan losers by more than the Newtown shootings diminished the well-being of parents and by more than the Boston Marathon bombings diminished the well-being of Boston residents.[16]

The decline in well-being among those who identified with the losing party in 2016 was triple the decline in 2012. In contrast, outcomes of local and congressional elections had little effect on well-being. In both elections, experienced well-being gaps across party affiliations dissipated within two weeks, but evaluative well-being gaps persisted following the 2016 election.[17]

Partisanship plays a role in people's finances, affecting the resolution of complaints about financial services companies filed with the Consumer Financial Protection Bureau (CFPB). Under the Trump administration, complaints by consumers residing in zip codes where low-income and Black people predominate were 30% less likely to be resolved in their favor than complaints of consumers residing in other zip codes. That gap in financial restitution was scarcely present under the Obama administration. The difference in financial restitution between the Obama and Trump administrations is likely due to a more industry-friendly CFPB in the Trump administration.[18]

Partisanship affects rates of evasion of personal income taxes, as presidential elections move voters in partisan counties into and out of alignment with the party of the president. In the absence of alignment, taxpayers report less income that is easily evaded, suspect claims for Earned Income Tax Credit (EITC) claims increase, and so do audits resulting in additional tax.[19]

And partisanship affects biases in CEOs' forecasts of earnings. Companies with CEOs whose partisanship aligns with that of the U.S. President issue more optimistically biased earnings forecasts than other CEOs. This is true even where CEOs have strong incentives to provide accurate forecasts.[20] Corporate executives have become increasingly partisan during the 2008–2020 period. The share of Republicans among executives increased and so has homogeneity by political affiliation. Executives whose political affiliations differ depart the company, and departures reduce the value of companies for shareholders.[21]

Partisanship shapes the flows of international capital. Partisanship alignment affects capital allocations by American institutional investors in syndicated corporate loans to foreign entities and investment in stock mutual funds.[22]

Partisanship affects the portfolio choices of ordinary investors. Republicans increased the proportion of stocks in their portfolios following the 2016 presidential election, whereas Democrats reduced theirs. The behavior of both Republicans and Democrats was driven by partisan attitudes rather than by hedging needs, preferences, or local economic exposures.[23]

It also affects employment. Employees do well to hide political views that conflict with those of their bosses, and job seekers do well to highlight political views that accord with those of their prospective bosses.[24] Owners of small- and medium-sized businesses are much more likely to hire employees who share their political affiliation. Employees who do not share their bosses' political affiliation receive lower pay, get fewer promotions, and have shorter tenures at their companies.

Partisanship can drive the choice of products, such as coffee, by expressive and emotional benefits and costs. Black Rifle Coffee sells weapons-themed coffees such as the AK-47 Espresso Blend that will "conquer your taste buds," and extra-dark Murdered Out roast that "will fuel your midnight ops or your morning commute."[25] Evan Hafer, the company's founder and chief executive, said: "I know who my customer is. I know who I'm trying to serve coffee to. I know who my customer isn't. I don't need to be everything to all people." Justin Cheung, a conservative Black Rifle Coffee customer said, "I do feel better about my purchase knowing that they stand for things I believe in."

The partisanship of Black Rifle Coffee and its customers is far from unusual. Indeed, commercial brands are commonly associated with political values. Brand polarization increased since 2016, when Donald Trump became president.[26] The top brands among Trump's supporters are the golf brands of Titleist, Masters Tournament, and Callaway Golf; the alcohol brands of Miller Lite, Coors Light, and Maker's Mark; and the financial services brands SmartyPig and PIMCO. Liberals also have a diverse brand universe, including the entertainment brands of Hulu, Showtime, and Syfy; the tech brand of Lyft; and the retail brands of Barnes & Noble and Pier 1 Imports.

Conservatives are more likely to associate themselves with the National Rifle Association, veteran organizations such as Disabled American Veterans and Wounded Warrior Project, Christian nonprofit organization, Billy Graham Evangelistic Association, and the habitat conservation and hunting organization Ducks Unlimited. Liberals are more likely to associate themselves with causes related to reproductive healthcare such as Planned Parenthood, immigration and civil rights organizations such as American Civil Liberties Union, and environmental organizations such as the Environmental Defense Fund and the Sierra Club.[27]

Feelings about gender roles are associated with partisanship. Conservative politics tend to align with traditional or stereotypical roles of women and men. Whereas democratic politics tend to align with more egalitarian roles.[28] Gender inequality is associated with low well-being among men and especially women in liberal countries, but not in conservative countries.[29]

The mishap of IKEA in Saudi Arabia illustrates the difficulty of catering to groups of customers who adhere to different views of gender. IKEA is a Swedish company of furniture and home goods that expanded globally, but adheres to the values of the Swedish society in furniture design, lifestyle, and even food. Its logo, in yellow and blue, is reminiscent of the Swedish national flag. For many decades, IKEA has overtly advertised liberal values such as gender equality, racial diversity, and same-sex families. In 2013, however, a Swedish newspaper reported two versions of the IKEA catalog, one for Sweden and the other for Saudi Arabia. A promotional picture in the Swedish catalog presented a pajama-wearing woman and child in their bathroom, surrounded by IKEA's furniture and goods. But the woman has been excised in the Saudi Arabian catalog. IKEA suffered a backlash when information about the two versions of the catalog spread in Europe and North America.[30]

People intuit a sense of belonging in neighborhoods and communities by cues, some obvious such as demographic characteristics, and some subtle such as indicated by the proportion of electric cars to gasoline powered sport-utility vehicles. People tend to migrate to communities where they intuit a greater sense of belonging.[31] Republicans and Democrats live now in two different worlds, almost literally.[32,33] Democrats are politically segregated in large cities and Republicans are equally politically segregated in rural areas. Life in politically fitting communities enhances well-being by social capital, social integration, and within-group cooperation. Yet it diminishes well-being by hostile interactions between groups living in different political communities.

Partisanship affects attitudes about marriage partners. A 2020 survey asked Democrats and Republicans how they would feel if their child married a person of the other party.[34] Among Republicans, 13%

would be very upset if their child married a Democrat, and another one-quarter would be somewhat upset. Among Democrats, 16% would be very upset if their child married a Republican, and another 22% would be somewhat upset.

A reader of an article about the increased reluctance to see a child marry a person of the other party, wrote: "Our political alignment reflects perhaps more than anything else on our basic philosophy of life or even our character. Religious differences are small potatoes compared to political differences."[35] Another wrote: "Until last year I was open to dating a Republican. No more! I'm dating for marriage. . . . I can't imagine binding myself to someone who doesn't value decency, dignity, fidelity, truth, and kindness. . . . The first thing I used to want to know about a man was his religious affiliation, now I just want to know if he voted for Trump."

Partisanship even affects decisions about having children. Fertility increased in Republican-leaning counties, relative to Democratic counties, following the 2016 election of Donald Trump.[36]

Income and wealth distribution

Should income and wealth be distributed more equally or is existing income and wealth inequality fair even if large? Analysis of World Values Survey data shows that well-being is high in countries where the distribution of income and wealth is perceived as fair, and demand for redistribution is pronounced in countries where it is perceived as unfair.[37]

Both liberals and conservatives care about fairness in income and wealth distribution, but their values are different, reflected in their different definitions of *fairness*. Liberals tend to define *fairness* in terms of equality, advocating government help to those in need and favoring policies that redistribute income and wealth from the wealthy to the poor, such as by greater healthcare benefits and student loan forgiveness. Conservatives however tend to define *fairness* in terms of equity, entitling people to income and wealth proportional to their contributions, and prefer that individuals and private organizations help those in need.

Psychologist Job Krijnen and coauthors described three perceptions of fairness in the distribution of income and wealth. Inequality is fair by the "rewarding" perception that it is due to factors within people's control such as hard work and conscientious saving. Inequality is unfair by the "rigged" perception that it is due to factors outside people's control such as favoritism and discrimination, and by the "random" perception that it is due to family wealth or luck.

Conservatives perceive inequality as rewarding whereas liberals perceive it as rigged or random. Consistent with their perceptions of fairness, liberals support social welfare policies that redistribute income and wealth, whereas conservatives oppose them.[38]

Inequality is generally perceived as fair in countries with high intergenerational mobility, enhancing well-being as people can reasonably hope to move upward in income and wealth. But inequality is perceived as unfair in countries with low social mobility, diminishing well-being as people are disappointed in their inability to move upward.[39] Liberals and conservatives differ in their perception of intergenerational mobility. Liberals are more pessimistic about mobility than conservatives, and they support greater redistribution. Conservatives oppose redistribution not only because they define *fairness* in terms of equity but also because they are more optimistic about mobility and see the government as a problem, not a solution.[40]

Inequality is greatest in in Latin America, where the very wealthy possess persistent advantage and the poor see little opportunity to move upward. Inequality adds to the well-being of those in the highest quintile by income and subtracts from the well-being of those in the bottom quintile.[41] Moreover, poverty is a public bad, diminishing the well-being of poor and wealthy alike. Average well-being is lower in countries where the proportion of the poor is higher.[42]

Working with Gallup, economist Bertil Tungodden and coauthors surveyed 65,000 people in 60 countries about the fairness of differences in income and wealth between the wealthy and poor.[43] Globally, 69% of the surveyed said that the differences in their country are unfair. Even more, 79%, said that their government should work to reduce these differences.

American liberals perceive the fairness in differences between the wealthy and poor similarly to the global average. But the fairness perceptions of American conservatives differ not only from those of American liberals, but also from those of conservatives in other countries. Only 26% of American conservatives said that differences between the wealthy and poor are unfair, and only 26% of them said that the government should work to reduce these differences. In contrast, most supporters of conservative governments in countries such as Israel, India, and Britain said that differences between the wealthy and poor are unfair.

American conservatives resent claims that their income and wealth come from a rigged or random system. This resentment reveals the interplay between utilitarian, expressive, and emotional benefits and costs, and their effects on well-being. The well-being of the wealthy is enhanced by the utilitarian benefits of their income and wealth, but diminished by the expressive and emotional costs of others' claims that they do not deserve it.

Sociologist Rachel Sherman described that interplay and its well-being effects in an interview with Paul, an executive in his mid-40s earning $500,000 annually, with two young children and a stay-at-home wife. Asked if he feels that he deserves his income and wealth, Paul responded without hesitation. "Absolutely. Damn right I fucking deserve it. . . . Where I am today, I've earned every dime on my own. No one's done it—I mean, my in-laws have helped, but I've done it." Asked if people who have less deserve less, Paul said: "Occupy Wall Street [a movement protesting income and wealth inequality] what have they done? They sat in a park doing nothing. You know?" He insists that his children have paying jobs when they are in high school to make sure they know that income and wealth come from hard work.[44]

Paul's insistence that he deserves his income and wealth, however large, because he earned them on his own is common among the wealthy, and so is minimization of help they receive, as from Paul's in-laws. These are also evident in the 2009 resignation letter sent to the *New York Times* by Jake DeSantis, an executive vice president of the American International Group's (A.I.G) financial products unit.

"After 12 months of hard work," he wrote, "during which A.I.G. reassured us many times we would be rewarded in March 2009, we . . . have been betrayed by A.I.G. and are being unfairly persecuted by elected officials."[45] He was promised a $742,000 after-tax payment, but that payment had been blocked by the government because of A.I.G's role in the financial crisis.

Like Paul, DeSantis attributed his income and wealth to his hard work and minimized the help he received. "My hard work earned me acceptance to M.I.T., and the institute's generous financial aid enabled me to attend." Yet he seems blind to the fact that M.I.T.'s "generous financial aid" must have come from somewhere, perhaps private donors or perhaps taxpayers' money channeled to M.I.T. through government grants.

The reactions of readers to DeSantis's letter reveal the perspectives of the less wealthy. One wrote: "I'm very sorry for Mr. DeSantis' loss. As sorry as a single mother with a less than $50K salary who filed bankruptcy three months ago can be. . . ." Another wrote: "OK, Jake, I'm going to say it again: NOBODY deserves to be paid $700,000 for a year's work. It's an obscenely huge amount of money that can have no relationship to the work actually done." And yet another argued that the system is rigged in favor of DeSantis and his ilk who are smart enough to elect their henchmen to political office, "while hoodwinking a gullible public into believing they too would profit by the game."

Some differences in attitudes about redistribution stem from experiences that become embedded in culture. European immigrants to the United States bring with them preferences for redistribution, common in their countries of origin, and these preferences affect not only on their own preferences, but also on those of their American-born children.[46]

Other differences stem from differences in the compositions of populations. Economist Alberto Alesina and coauthors pinned much of the difference between attitudes in the United States and Europe on racial heterogeneity in the United States. Racial animosity in the United States makes redistribution of income and wealth to the poor, who are disproportionately Black, disagreeable to many white voters. Also, American political institutions inhibit the growth of a socialist party and constrain the political power of the poor.[47]

Psychologist Jennifer Richeson found that white Americans respond with negative attitudes toward other racial groups when they see projections that whites are about to become a minority. These projections increase support for politically conservative candidates and policies, including those who oppose diversity.

At the heart of the paradox of diversity, said Richeson, is status threat, a sense that an increase in the social status of an outgroup, such as Black Americans, diminishes the social status of the white American ingroup. There is also a sense among many white Americans that greater diversity erodes "Whiteness" as what it means to be an American.[48]

Indeed, concern for social status is evident in surveys that found that Trump supporters were more likely than Clinton voters to feel that high-status groups, like men, Christians, and whites, are discriminated against.[49]

Immigration

Immigrants add utilitarian benefits to citizens in Europe and North America as they make up for low fertility rates.[50] The utilitarian benefits of immigration are evident in a reform that granted European workers free access to the Swiss labor market, increasing the number of foreign workers especially in places close to the border. Many foreign workers were highly educated, yet wages of highly educated natives increased. The reform increased the size, productivity, and innovation of skill-intensive Swiss companies and attracted new companies, creating opportunities for natives to pursue managerial jobs.[51]

Yet, for some, the expressive and emotional costs of immigration, peaking in "white extinction anxiety," diminish well-being by more than the utilitarian benefits enhance it.[52] A Pew Research Center survey in the second year of Donald Trump's presidency asked people to assess their well-being.[53] Trump's presidency enhanced the well-being of those who welcomed his anti-immigration policies.[54] One wrote: "What was happening to our country was a downward spiral of idiotic politically correct stupidity. Taxpayers getting stiffed with paying for medical insurance and education for illegals!! . . . Our President Trump is straightening this out. . . . It's happening—thanks to our President."[55]

The well-being of this person is enhanced by expressive and emotional benefits now that government immigration policies are aligned with his preferences, now that he knows that many citizens share his preferences, and now that he can speak about "illegals," no longer afraid of censure or stigma for not calling them "undocumented immigrants."

Some of today's immigration preferences resemble those of a century ago. Increased European immigration into American cities following World War I added to citizens' utilitarian benefits by higher employment and greater industrial production, and did not lower earnings even among citizens working in sectors greatly exposed to immigration. Yet immigration diminished the well-being of some citizens by the expressive and emotional costs of cultural adjustment more than enhanced their well-being by utilitarian benefits. That diminished well-being was evident in hostile political reactions to immigration, including election of more conservative legislators and increased support for anti-immigration legislation.[56]

Immigration changes attitudes toward income redistribution. A study in 28 European countries found that native workers lower their support for redistribution if the share of immigrants in their country is higher. This effect is larger among native workers who hold negative views about immigration, but is smaller when immigrants are culturally closer to natives and come from richer-origin countries.[57]

Circumstances, such as terrorist attacks, affect attitudes toward immigrants and immigration. A July 7, 2005, bombings in London killed 52 people and injured 770.[58] Participants in a survey following the bombing rated their agreement with statements about attitudes toward Muslims, such as "Britain would lose its identity if more Muslims came to live in Britain," and immigrants, such as "Government spends too much money assisting immigrants." Attitudes toward Muslims and immigrants turned more negative following the attacks, but only among liberals. Conservatives' negative attitudes stayed relatively constant.

Public concern about immigration affects customer complaints against minority financial advisers. Minority advisers are more likely to receive complaints in periods of high public concern about immigration than in other periods, relative to their white colleagues at the same time in the same office. This is true for both complaints with merit and dismissed complaints, and is more pronounced in counties where people hold stronger anti-immigration views.[59]

Preferences about immigration are swayed by misperceptions about the number of immigrants and their characteristics. Surveys and experiments in six countries show that people greatly overestimate the number of immigrants, exaggerate their cultural and religious differences, and believe that immigrants are less educated, more unemployed, and more reliant on government transfers than they actually are. Indeed, simply making people think about immigration reduced their support for income redistribution.

Yet information about the true number of immigrants and their true characteristics did not increase support for income redistribution. An anecdote about a "hard-working" immigrant increased support for redistribution somewhat, but not enough to counteract the decrease in support caused by making people think about immigration. Evidently, narratives shape people's views on immigration more deeply than facts.[60]

Globalization enhances well-being by making everyone everywhere more peaceful, driven to satisfy the common desire to settle down rather than fanatical ideologies and hunger for conquest.[61] Indeed, globalization provides utilitarian benefits by increasing trade, supplying Americans and others with inexpensive goods made in China, and facilitating relocation of workers within the European Union. Yet globalization continues to be countered by anti-globalization sentiments, including those that drove Britons to exit the European Union and Americans to elect Donald Trump as president.

Brexit and Trump's election made obvious that well-being calls for more than inexpensive Chinese goods and other utilitarian benefits; it also calls for expressive and emotional benefits in satisfaction of desires to be seen and respected. Globalization enhanced well-being among the elite, but not among the working class who turned to populist leaders to regain the well-being they had lost.

People are susceptible to hatred if it provides expressive and emotional benefits, such as explaining their own past failure. The demand for hatred diminishes and well-being is enhanced when people of different groups interact.[62] A field experiment randomly assigned Dutch high-school students from the ethnic majority group to perform cooperative tasks in ethnically homogeneous or mixed teams. Participation in the mixed-team reduced discrimination among students from the ethnic majority group who had no peers from a minority group in their regular classes.[63] And Dutch citizens living near refugee facilities developed a more positive attitude toward ethnic minorities and became less inclined to support anti-immigration parties.[64]

Ride-hailing services such as Uber connect people from different groups into each ride, offering chances for intergroup interaction. These interactions yield better mutual understanding, diminish prejudice and hate crimes, and enhance well-being.[65]

Greater long-term exposure to Arab-Muslims in the United States resulted in decreased explicit and implicit prejudice against Arab-Muslims, decreased support for policies hostile to Arab-Muslims, and increased knowledge of Arab-Muslims and Islam in general.[66]

Sometimes actions, such as helping Afghan evacuees following the American withdrawal, align people across partisanship, even if motivated by different values. A pastor in an Evangelical church said: "Even the most right-leaning isolationists are coming forward to help those fleeing Afghanistan."[67] Parishioners in his church disagreed about mask mandates, the validity of the presidential election, and what to do about migrants on the border. But they agreed on the need to welcome Afghan evacuees, and they were collecting contributions to help them.

One parishioner said she had tried over the past year to persuade the church's leaders to care for immigrants, with no success. "With Afghanistan, something completely shifted," she said. Another parishioner said "This is an issue where vaxxers and anti-vaxxers meet."

Vaccination and anti-vaccination

Values underlie attitudes toward vaccinations, evident even before the COVID-19 pandemic, and they affect well-being. A 2018 study noted that many programs countering anti-vaccination attitudes are based on the faulty assumption that vaccination skeptics lack knowledge of the scientific evidence urging vaccination. Yet programs countering anti-vaccination attitudes by scientific evidence proved to be unproductive, if not counterproductive.

The 2018 study found that anti-vaccination attitudes are prominent among people who believe in conspiracy theories, are averse to impingements on personal freedom, and are prone to disgust when considering blood and needles.[68]

Similarly, a 2017 study found that vaccine skeptics adhere to the purity and liberty foundations of values, but not to the harm and fairness foundations. Parents hesitating to vaccinate their children are more likely to emphasize purity, disapproving of things they consider disgusting, whether by religion, such as non-halal or non-kosher foods, or secular, such as toxins in foods or the environment. Moreover, these parents adhere to liberty, guarding their right to choose and exhibiting less deference to those in power.[69]

Kasheem Delesbore, a warehouse worker and vaccine skeptic, illustrated the findings of these studies in the time of COVID-19. Illustrating the findings of the second study, Delesbore values purity, influenced by online information that the COVID-19 vaccine is bad for his body. And he values liberty, insisting on his right to choose whether to get vaccinated or not. "I have that choice to decide whether I put something in my own body," he said. Illustrating the findings of the first study, Delesbore expressed conspiratorial thinking. "There's a whole world of secrets and stuff that we don't see in our everyday lives," he said. "Everything is a facade."

Adherence to purity and liberty is bolstered by the deepening political polarization. Branden Mirro, a Republican, has been skeptical of all claims about the pandemic. He does not plan to get vaccinated and believes that mask requirements impinge on his liberty. "This whole thing was a sham," he said. "They planned it to cause mass panic and get Trump out of office."[70] Authoritarianism and libertarianism, two values prevalent among right-wingers, are associated with dismissal of COVID-19 and resistance to government measures mitigating it.[71]

The values and attitudes of people in former East Germany tilt toward pro-state and pro-collectivism more than those of people in the former West Germany, and less toward liberty. Former East Germans benefited from their values and attitudes in the time of COVID-19 as they complied more easily with measures that mitigated infections.[72]

Social norms are also part of values, evident in study of the effectiveness of signs asking hotel guests to participate in an environmental conservation program. Signs noting norms, such as "the majority of guests reuse their towels" turned out to be more persuasive than general appeals to environmental conservation. Moreover, appeals to norms were most effective when describing group behavior in settings that match people's immediate circumstances, such as "the majority of guests in this room reuse their towels."[73]

The effects of norms were evident in the time of COVID-19, as the nature of the pandemic and its magnitude made it impossible to force people to comply with measures mitigating infections, such as social distancing, wearing masks, and staying at home. Norms, reflected in what others practice and approve of, were effective in persuading people to comply with these measures.[74]

The effects of norms in the time of COVID-19 were evident in the choices of Japanese to wear masks. Expectations of risk reduction did not affect mask use, but conformity to social norms in wearing masks did. Mask wearers felt relief from anxiety when wearing masks.[75]

Partisanship plays a particularly important role in periods of crisis when politicians manipulate information, such as by insisting on "alternative facts." Mask use in the United States is strongly associated with partisanship, much more prevalent among Democrats than among Republicans, and partisanship is the single most important predictor of local mask use, not COVID-19 severity or local policies.[76] A 10% increase in Fox News cable viewership led to a 1.3% reduction in the propensity to stay at home during the COVID-19 crisis time.[77]

Taxes and subsidies

Governments can increase the well-being of their citizens by taxes and subsidies. Their effects on well-being depend on people's preferences for utilitarian, expressive, and emotional benefits and costs, and the balance among them, preferences that vary from person to person.

Different preferences for tax and subsidy policies can come from different perceptions of their effects on behavior and economic efficiency, reflected in the answer to the question: "Will people stop working if taxes and subsidies are higher?", from perceptions of their effects on the distribution of income and wealth: "Who benefits if taxes are cut and subsidies increase?", and from perceptions of their fairness: "How fair is it that children born in wealthy families inherit more?"

Different preferences for tax and subsidy policies can also come from perceptions of the trustworthiness and efficiency of government: "Will the government waste a lot of the tax revenue?", how tax revenue will be spent: "Will revenues finance investments in infrastructure or defense, or an increase in subsidies to the poor?", or from perceptions and misperceptions of the current tax system.

Economist Stefanie Stantcheva found differences between Democrats and Republicans in reasoning about taxes beyond differences in preferences for tax policies. Democrats tend to think actual taxes are lower and less progressive than Republicans. Both Democrats and Republicans tend to think that high-income people are more responsive to taxes than middle-class ones, and that the main forms of the response of high-income people are increased tax evasion, increased likelihood of moving to a different state, and diminished entrepreneurship and willingness to work. But Republicans believe that taxes exert large effects on behavior, especially in reduced entrepreneurship and willingness to work, whereas Democrats think that taxes exert little effect.[78]

Both Democrats and Republicans believe that the wealthy are very responsive to estate taxes. Yet Republicans perceive greater effects of estate taxes on taxpayers' behavior and especially on their overall effects on the economy. Democrats and Republicans sharply disagree on whether cuts in top income and estate tax trickle down to benefit everyone, and whether cuts in top income and estate taxes increase tax revenues by inducing entrepreneurship and willingness to work.

Moreover, Democrats and Republicans differ greatly in the perception of fairness, whether income inequality is fair, whether people earning high incomes are entitled to keep a large share of them, or whether it is fair that wealthy parents can pass on their wealth to their children. Democrats also have more positive views than Republicans about the trustworthiness of government and its scope.

Perceptions of the fairness of taxes and subsidies are more important in people's judgments than perceptions of the effect of taxes and subsidies on the economy. People who think that inequality in income and wealth is a major problem support more progressive tax policies, and so do people who trust the government, even if they think that more progressive tax policies would have negative effects on the economy.

A prominent view in discussions about taxes stresses the role of self-interest in preferences. According to this view, people's preferences depend on whether they are directly affected by these policies. This view, however, is inconsistent with the evidence. Self-interest has some effect on people's preferences for tax policies, but not much. Informing people of whether they are directly affected by a cut in the top federal income tax rate has little effect on their preferences.

Instead, preferences for tax policies are shaped mostly by notions of fairness. Providing people with information about the level of inherited wealth among the rich induces them to believe that tax policies are unfair, and reduces their support for cutting top income tax rates.[79]

The important role of fairness in preferences for tax policies is evident in the propensity of Americans to file appeals to reduce their property taxes. People are more likely to file appeals if they perceive their taxes as unfair or believe they overpay relative to others. When people are shown that the average tax rate is higher than they originally thought, they perceive their own taxes as fair and are less likely to file appeals.[80]

The well-being effects of subsidies are even greater than those of taxes. Subsidies form a large part of the safety net.[81] They include Social Security, unemployment insurance, Supplemental Security Income (SSI), Women, Infants, and Children (WIC) nutritional program, Medicaid, Earned-Income Tax Credit (EITC), food stamps (SNAP), housing assistance, home energy assistance, free or discounted school lunches, and cash assistance.

Child poverty in the United States declined by 59% between 1993 and 2019. It declined in every state, equally among white, Black, Hispanic, and Asian children; among children living with one parent or two; and in native or immigrant households. In 1993, almost 28% of children were poor, lacking income for basic needs. By 2019, child poverty dropped to about 11%.

Many forces reduced child poverty, including lower unemployment, increased labor force participation among single mothers, and increased minimum wages. But a dominant force was increased government aid, as the decline in child poverty coincided with major changes to the safety net. Stringent welfare laws in the 1990s diminished cash assistance to parents without jobs. But other subsidies increased, especially for working families, and total federal spending on low-income children roughly doubled.

The set of programs that diminished child poverty was shaped by conflict and compromise between Republicans who want less spending, more local control, and more work rules, and Democrats who want greater benefits for more people and broader income guarantees.

Stacy Tallman, a mother of three, was working as a waitress when Jakob, her teenage son, suffered serious injuries in a car accident. Both Ms. Tallman and her partner missed work to care for Jakob, and their income fell by about a quarter to $36,000.

But the safety net delivered more than $16,000, including $8,000 in Earned Income Tax Credits and $6,500 from food stamps. Medicaid paid for Jakob's care and saved the family from bankrupting medical bills "I don't know where I'd be right now if I didn't have that help," Ms. Tallman said. The safety net provided emotional benefits in addition to utilitarian benefits, easing Ms. Tallman's anxiety. A year after the accident, Jakob became the first in the family to earn a high school degree.

An anti-poverty program in Colombia, Familias en Accion Urbano, improved not only financial well-being but also life well-being. Three years into the program, beneficiaries reported well-being enhanced by higher income, greater consumption, and increased participation in formal employment. Government subsidies in the program were more than offset by increased government tax revenues, generating substantial benefits to poor families at reduced costs to taxpayers.[82] Similarly, a noncontributory pension program in Paraguay, Pensiones Alimentarias, increased older adults' well-being by increasing consumption by almost one-half.[83] And higher child benefits in Canada improves both child and maternal mental health and well-being. Benefits had stronger effects on the educational outcomes and physical health of boys, and the mental health of girls.[84]

Nothing demonstrates the well-being benefits of the safety net than the outcomes of the expansion of the Earned-Income Tax Credit in the 1990s. These credits are often augmented by extra tax withholding into substantial tax refunds.

These refunds enable working-class people to buy new refrigerators, washers or dryers, or repair used cars. A woman described the well-being benefits of the refunds to sociologist Halpern-Meekin and coauthors, noting that spending during the year is too tempting if money is paid out a little at a time. "I love the lump sum because something always happens. You always need your tax return."[85]

Tax refunds enhance well-being by their expressive and emotional benefits in addition to their utilitarian benefits. Women receiving these refunds experience lower depression and greater self-efficacy.[86] Moreover, filing tax returns at commercial tax preparation companies like H&R Block add expressive and emotional benefits and well-being by respect accorded to filers there, respect absent when standing in line at government offices.

At H&R Block, Cassandra Jackson, a 23-year-old Black single mother, is greeted by a smiling receptionist who addresses her by name and gives her a worksheet to complete before she meets Joe, the tax specialist, a middle-aged Black man dressed in a blue button-down shirt, striped tie, and khakis. Joe calls Cassandra's name, shakes her hand, and asks her how she is doing. He guides her through a series of prompts on his computer screen, gathering information, and finally announces the grand total of her refund: $5,900![87]

Yet subsidies such as food stamps that enhance well-being by utilitarian benefits often diminish it by expressive and emotional costs, described by writer Bobbi Dempsey. "You get dirty glances for looking poor, but are also judged if you look "too rich," by wearing something an observer deems too nice for someone on public assistance."[88]

A reader of Dempsey's article described her experience at a grocery store that had food stamps equipment at only a few registers, so she got to experience the cashier flipping on their flashing light for a manager who would then take her to another register to run her food stamps card for the amount covered by that program. Then she would go back to the first register to pay cash for the nonfood items, like toilet paper, not covered by food stamps. "Nothing like having cashiers hollering your info at each other across multiple lanes while you are holding up your line."

Nudges, bans, and mandates

Nudges by the government, both informational or architectural, can enhance well-being. Calorie information on menus can enhance the well-being of overweight people by decreasing the calories they consume. Calorie information on Starbucks' menus decreased average calories per meal by 6%.[89] Yet calorie information can diminish well-being by the emotional costs of refraining from eating large amounts of appetizing foods.

Moreover, nudges toward small amounts of healthy food are not always successful. Indeed, such attempts often backfire. Information portraying food items as healthy leads people to infer they are not tasty.[90] People are more likely to underestimate the caloric content of main dishes and choose higher-calorie side dishes, drinks, or desserts when fast-food restaurants claim to serve healthy food than when they make no such claim.[91]

The consumption of meat from intensive farming diminishes animal welfare. People nudged by information on animals' living conditions in intensive farming reduce their propensity to consume meat by about 12% in the laboratory and 6–9% in university canteens. Approximately one-third of people, however, avoid such information, and those who avoid that information are the ones particularly responsive to it.[92]

Automatic enrollment into defined-contribution retirement saving plans has proven to be an effective architectural nudge, increasing the proportion of employees who enroll. Other architectural nudges, such as inducing the poor into greater savings, are less effective because the poor have little available for saving, and little time and energy for saving goals. Telephone calls encouraging saving "could be overwhelming when you are busy, almost like a bill collector;" said one. They were like telemarketing calls, said another, "I knew I had to save, so I just hung up on the calls."[93]

Governments go beyond nudges to establish mandates and bans that affect well-being. Examples of mandates include taxes, driving licenses to those who drive, and in some states, disclosure by homeowners of defects in houses they sell. Examples of bans include sale of cigarettes and alcohol to minors, and possession of particular drugs, such as heroin, to everyone.

Some mandates and bans are premised on the goal of enhancing well-being by protecting people from themselves. Sale of cigarettes to minors is banned because smoking is damaging to health and addictive, and addiction established in early age might be difficult to overcome in adulthood. Other mandates and bans are premised on the goals of protecting people from others, such as protecting people from injuries or death by unlicensed drivers, or benefiting others, such as taxes that pay for national defense or local schools.

The COVID-19 pandemic has led to supply shortages and price increases that have renewed the debate about regulating "price gouging."

Laissez-faire economics is at one end, advocating price increases as a means of allocating scarce goods. Perceived norms of fairness are at the other end, advocating limits to price increases amid shortages.

Price gouging laws vary among states. Nine states and the District of Columbia ban price gouging of all goods. Other states ban it for goods that are vital for health, safety, and welfare.[94] People's attitudes toward price gouging and its ban are displayed in readers' reactions to the story about brothers Matt and Noah Colvin. In the three days following March 1, 2020, when the first coronavirus death in the United States was announced, they amassed 17,700 bottles of hand sanitizer and thousands of packs of anti-bacterial wipes, bought in a 1,300 miles road trip around Chattanooga, Tennessee, mostly from "little hole-in-the-wall dollar stores in the backwoods."[95] They immediately sold 300 bottles of hand sanitizer on Amazon at prices between $8 and $70 each, many times what they paid for them. To the brothers, this was a laissez-faire "retail arbitrage." Indeed, they perceived their actions as public service, sending supplies to where they are needed most.

To many others, it was unfair price gouging. Mikeala Kozlowski, a nurse who has been searching for hand sanitizer since before she gave birth to her first child on March 5 described sellers as selfish, hoarding resources for their own gain. The next day, Amazon deleted thousands of listings for sanitizer, wipes and face masks, suspended their sellers and warned potential ones. The brothers were compelled to donate their huge cache.

Some readers were on the side of laissez-faire. One wrote: "I honestly don't see the problem. If folks are willing to pay that amount, who cares? If I really wanted something, I'd prefer to have the option of buying it rather than be denied that opportunity." Others, however, were on the side of fairness norms against price gouging. One wrote: "I have one friend in heart failure unable to get hand sanitizer and face masks . . . and this guy, the new poster child for the banality of evil, stripped all the store shelves from there to the border."

Freedom, democracy, and corruption

Analysis of 86 countries indicates that citizens of countries with high economic freedom, including legal security and property rights, enjoy high well-being. The well-being benefits of economic freedom are especially pronounced in developing countries.[96] Economic freedom also enhances well-being by increasing the likelihood of legal recognition of same-sex marriages and tolerance toward gay people.[97] And economic freedom is enhanced most in tolerant societies with positive attitudes toward a market economy.[98]

Democracy also enhances well-being. A study of 28 countries found that well-being is higher in democracies.[99] Democracy even enhances well-being by making men taller. Experiencing democracy in early childhood increases average men's stature by .52 to .95 inches (1.33 to 2.4 cm). Yet no such effect is evident among women.[100]

Education and democracy are highly correlated. Schools teach people to interact with others and raise the benefits of civic participation, including organizing and voting.

Democracy, however, is fragile. Democracy has a wide potential base of defenders, but it offers them only weak incentives in the battle against dictatorship, which provides stronger incentives to a narrower base. As education raises the benefits of civic participation, it raises support for more democratic regimes relative to dictatorships. This increases the likelihood of democratic revolutions against dictatorships, and reduces that of successful anti-democratic coups.[101]

Corruption involves government officials or business representatives demanding bribes, gifts, or favors for services that people are entitled to receive for free. It diminishes the well-being of both corruption's victims and recipients.[102] The level of corruption in a country is usually measured by answers to the questions: "Is corruption widespread throughout the government in this country or not?" and "Is corruption widespread within businesses in this country or not?"

Denmark, Finland, and New Zealand ranked first in freedom from corruption among 180 countries in the 2021 survey of Transparency International.[103] The United States ranked 27th; China, 66th; Ukraine, 122nd; and Afghanistan, 174th.

Corruption can be transparent or disguised. A disguised form of corruption in China was uncovered in a study of credit card lines extended by banks. Government officials received 15% higher credit lines than others with similar income and demographics, yet the delinquency rate among government officials was higher than among others, and the likelihood that banks will forgive government officials' debt and write it off was also higher. These patterns of corruption were especially prevalent among government officials with greater power, working in regions known to be more corrupt.

Bank branches providing higher credit lines to government officials receive more deposits from local governments, indicating a quid-pro-quo arrangement. Moreover, in regions where government officials receive higher credit lines, others receive lower credit lines.

A crackdown on corruption in China eliminated banks' preferential treatment of government officials. New credit lines extended to government officials ceased to be higher than those extended to others, and rates of delinquency and debt forgiveness and write-offs among government officials ceased being higher than among others.[104]

Attitudes of citizens to corruption depend on their perception of their power to mobilize against corruption and the willingness of the government to fight corruption. The Chinese government campaign against corruption must have encouraged those not involved in corruption and enhanced their well-being, knowing that the government is fighting corruption on their behalf.

Yet this encouragement and enhanced well-being were absent in Afghanistan, evident in Afghans' reaction to corruption revealed in the 2010 Kabul Bank crisis. The crisis increased Afghans' perception that government officials are corrupt, but did not mobilize them to fight corruption because they perceived corruption as endemic and perceived themselves as lacking power to counter it.[105]

The story of corruption in Ukraine echoes that in Afghanistan. Social scientist Sofiya Lutsiv described corruption in Ukraine as a "cancer" of the government system.[106] Surveying Ukrainians, Lutsiv found that almost three-quarters of those surveyed experienced corruption in their own lives, and even more believe that corruption is endemic, part of everyday life. And whereas 9-in-10 believe that fighting corruption is a duty of citizens, few believe that they have power to do so. Concern about corruption in Ukraine was heightened by the high cost of supporting it in the war with Russia. Alexandra Gillies, director of the global anti-corruption consortium at Brookings Institution and coauthors argued that supporting Ukraine and rebuilding it offer opportunities to build anti-corruption mechanisms, beyond helping the country recover from a devastating war.[107]

Rooting out corruption takes effort and time since corruption culture changes slowly, but it can be done. First-generation immigrants from high-corruption countries have lower tax morale in their destination countries. But the effect of corruption culture diminishes among second-generation immigrants as they integrate into the local culture.[108]

Trust

Governments have much control over services, enhancing the well-being of citizens by improving them, but they have less control over the cultural features of its society, such as trust.

Trust is a glue that holds societies together, enhancing our well-being even as it makes us vulnerable. When we trust people, groups, or institutions, we make ourselves vulnerable, presuming that those we trust will act in ways that enhance our well-being. As we trust, we accept the risk that those we trust will betray our trust and diminish our well-being.

A Finn reacted to Finland's top ranking by well-being by noting the well-being benefits of trust, common in Finland, including trust in government. "I trust in our government on a larger scale. . . . Trust comes down to smaller details, too. It is indeed natural for kids aged seven and up to walk to school, hobbies, and parks on their own. I have told them that if they ever need help, they can turn to any adult and will receive it."[109]

Think of your answer to the standard trust question of the World Values Survey: "Generally speaking, would you say that most people can be trusted or that you need to be very careful in dealing with people?"[110] People vary in their answers. At one end, in countries such as Norway, Sweden, and Finland, more than 60% of people say that most people can be trusted. At the other end, in countries such as Colombia, Brazil, and Peru, less than 10% do.

In one experiment, wallets containing approximately $50 in local currency, together with photographs, names, and phone numbers, were "dropped" in the streets of various countries. The proportion of wallets returned in each country was highly correlated with their level of trust.[111]

There is much evidence that trust enhances well-being. Indeed, living in a high-trust society enhances well-being as much as doubling family income. Resilience induced by trust diminishes the negative effect of adversities on well-being, whether discrimination, ill-health, unemployment, or disasters.[112] That resilience was evident in the 2011 Great East Japan Earthquake, as trust buffered the effects of the disaster on well-being.[113] Resilience induced by trust is especially effective in enhancing the well-being of people at the lower end of the societal distribution of well-being.[114]

Trust enhances well-being. In turn, well-being enhances trust. People enjoying high well-being trust others more, and help create more social capital. They are more likely to vote, extend help to others, perform volunteer work, and participate in public activities. They are also likely to be more attached to their neighborhoods, and be members of associations.[115]

Trust is rooted in culture and changes with it. The effects of culture on trust are evident in the lower trust among residents of Quebec than among fellow Canadians. Sociologists Cary Wu and Andrew Dawson attributed the lower trust among Quebecers to the province's Catholic cultural heritage, and they attributed the increase in trust among Quebecers to the abrupt modernization in the province. Younger cohorts socialized following modernization are much more trusting, most evident among Catholics.[116]

"Generally speaking, would you agree that most people can be trusted" is a question about generalized trust. Categorical trust is about trust in particular categories, such as family, coworkers, races, nationalities, religions, or science.[117]

Categorical trust is the most realistic middle ground in everyday trust decisions, where trust is neither customized to each specific instance nor generalized across all possible situations.[118] Categorical trust, like generalized trust, can enhance well-being.

The well-being benefits of categorical trust are evident in choices of wholesalers to extend trade credit to retailers within their particular community. Formal market institutions, such as financial reporting systems, auditing, and courts, function poorly or are nonexistent in places such as the northeastern part of India. Wholesalers there extend trade credit and impose moderate credit terms on retailers within their community. They experience few defaults among retailers, and they are lenient when retailers default.[119]

Trust in financial institutions is another kind of categorical trust. Debit cards provide not only easier access to savings, but also a mechanism to build trust in financial institutions. Debit cards were handed to beneficiaries of a Mexican cash transfer program whose benefits were deposited into a savings account. Beneficiaries saved little in these accounts before receiving their debit cards, but they increased their savings substantially afterward.

During this initial period, beneficiaries used their cards frequently to check their balances, but they reduced that frequency over time as their trust in the bank increased. After 1 to 2 years, debit cards led to increases in savings rate by 3–5% of income.[120]

A study of 10 emerging market economies in Central, Eastern, and Southeastern Europe found that trust in financial institutions increases the probability of holding formal savings and diversification among types of formal savings. Trust in the safety of deposits has the largest positive effect on bank savings.[121]

The well-being costs of categorical mistrust in both science and government were evident in the time of COVID-19 as they affected willingness to accept vaccines. In his many years of practice, pediatrician Robert Froehlke had seen parents reject vaccines because they prefer natural lifestyles or ask that vaccines be administered on different schedules, but before COVID-19, he had rarely seen parents of vaccinated children refuse additional vaccines. Froehlke quoted a mother's response when he suggested that it was time to vaccinate her four children, including with the COVID-19 vaccine. "I'm not going to kill my children," she said, shaking and weeping.

Froehlke suspects the rejection of vaccines is due to misinformation about the COVID-19 vaccine, magnified by erosion of categorical trust in physicians and in science more generally, and by mistrust in government, associated with political affiliation.[122] People who do not trust science or government to guide them right might trust other messengers, such as local religious leaders, celebrities, or athletes, based on the characteristics of populations and communities.[123]

Sometimes trust is misplaced, leading to losses from fraud and financial scams. Trust increases the rate of adoption of cryptocurrencies, but issuers of cryptocurrencies exploit that trust, identifying naïve investors and misrepresenting their offerings to them. Misrepresented cryptocurrency offerings have high scam risk.[124,125]

Ponzi schemes are more likely to occur in United States where the citizenry is more trusting. Most SEC-prosecuted Ponzi schemes involve sums much lower than the famous ones perpetrated by Bernard Madoff and Allen Stanford. The mean average per-investor investment of around $431,700 and a median of $87,800. The success of a Ponzi scheme, measured by duration, total amount invested, and the percentage cut to perpetrators tends to be greater when an affinity link is present, indicating high trust.[126]

People's trust in financial institutions declines following revelation of fraud. Also, stock prices decline following revelations of corporate fraud and so does stock market participation, as people reduce their holdings of stocks of both fraudulent and nonfraudulent companies. Moreover, people with greater lifetime experience of corporate fraud hold smaller proportions of their portfolios in stocks.[127]

Mass shootings in the United States devastate victims and their families. They indicate low trust, and diminish trust further. Mass shootings are associated with a 27% decline in the likelihood of excellent community well-being, and a 13% decline in the likelihood of excellent emotional health. The effects are stronger and longer lasting among individuals exposed to deadlier mass shootings. And the reductions in well-being are greater for parents with children below age 18.[128]

Generosity

Generosity, like trust, is a feature of society, enhancing well-being. Generosity is about giving good things to others freely and abundantly, placing the needs of others ahead of our own, in charitable donations, volunteering, or helping strangers. Generosity enhances the well-being of givers by expressive and emotional benefits exceeding their utilitarian costs, it enhances the well-being of receivers by utilitarian, expressive, and emotional benefits, and it enhances the well-being of all who observe them by expressive and emotional benefits.

Generosity by charitable donations is exemplified by Genevieve Via Cava, a teacher who left a $1-million gift for scholarships to special needs students. "She was a rough-exterior type of a person. But she could light up a room," said a friend.[129]

Generosity by volunteering is exemplified by a man describing his life in San Francisco; a fantasyland for foodies at one end and a place of hungry people at the other. He volunteered at a local shelter, helping prepare food, serving meals, and cleaning the kitchen and dining room afterward. "Simply serving a meal felt minuscule compared to how much needed to be done," he said. "If we could make just one person's night brighter, then we were working toward something better."[130]

Generosity is exemplified by a young girl on an Alaska Airlines flight who spoke to a blind and deaf passenger in American Sign Language, signing letters into his hands. A fellow passenger described the girl kneeling in front of the man and spelling out "How are you? Are you O.K.?" The girl told the man about her school and her grandmother, and the man told her about his childhood and his sister. "It seems like such a lonely life to be deaf and blind," said the girl, "to not be able to see and hear." The generosity of the girl toward the man enhanced not only the well-being of the two of them, but also that of all the passengers around them. "All of us in the immediate rows were laughing and smiling and enjoying his obvious delight in having someone to talk to."[131]

Surveys in 136 countries show that generosity is not only associated with high well-being but causes it. Experiments within two very different countries, Canada and Uganda, show that increases in well-being increase spending money on others. This suggests that well-being by helping others is deeply ingrained in human nature, evident in diverse cultural and economic settings.[132] Acts of generosity stimulate greater generosity. Asking people to donate time to a charity also increases the amount of money they ultimately donate to the charity.[133]

Hardship prompted parents to establish a charitable foundation in the name of Jonathan Rizzo, their murdered son. The foundation helps ill people with rent and food, and helps children with warm clothing in winter and food in summer. The foundation helped a mother of two children and her 45-year-old husband, ill with cancer, who fell behind on bills and rent during more than a year of surgeries, chemotherapy, and radiation. "The landlord has been pretty patient up until now, but they called and gave me till Monday to come up with some money. I really don't know what to do, so I am reaching out to your foundation for help." The foundation provided two months' rent and added gift certificates for food and other necessities.[134]

Generosity also flowed in $13 million donated to the families of the Uvalde children and teachers killed at the Robb Elementary School.[135] Mickey Gerdes, a Robb graduate who heads the charitable fund, said: "Almost immediately after the event, wonderfully kind-hearted people all over the world started pouring money into the community." A youth group in Pittsburgh held a car wash, an Oregon resident has been selling T-shirts, and a Florida film festival donated its proceeds.

People are more generous toward people like themselves. Journalist Eduardo Porter noted that Americans' resistance to government spending on social programs is largely rooted in the nation's racial and ethnic diversity. Americans are not selfish. Indeed, they contribute to charity much more than Europeans, but they tend to contribute to people like them, reflecting racial and ethnic divisions.[136]

Not all giving, however, is motivated by generosity. Some giving is motivated instead by social pressure, likely reducing well-being by utilitarian costs without increasing it by expressive and emotional benefits. In a door-to-door fund-raising experiment, some people were informed about the exact time of solicitation by a flier placed on their door-knobs, leaving them free to seek or avoid the fund-raiser. The flier reduced the share of people opening the door by 10–25%, and if the flier allowed checking a "Do Not Disturb" box, reduced giving by 30%.[137]

15

Conclusion

"What about your life do you currently find meaningful, fulfilling or satisfying?" asked a Pew Research survey. "What keeps you going and why?"[1]

"I want to get to a point in my life, not where I'm rich," said one, "but I can go to the grocery store, the gas station, the movies, or go on vacation, and not worry about the amount of money in my bank account. I want it to be an afterthought." Another said: "It is very satisfying to see my children be independent and responsible. I personally feel that raising two people to become decent, hard-working, responsible citizens is very important."

Financial well-being comes when we can meet current and future financial obligations, absorb financial setbacks, and keep driving toward financial goals. Financial well-being comes when finances are "an afterthought." Life well-being comes when we enjoy well-being in the domain of finances, but also in the domains of family, friends, health, work, education, religion and society. Life well-being comes when we are satisfied to see children grow to "be independent and responsible." Life well-being is at the center of this book.

The domain of finances is only one of the domains of life well-being, yet it has a special place in it because it underlies life well-being in all other domains. We need finances to support ourselves and our families, paying for food and shelter. We need finances to maintain our own health and that of our families, paying for the services of physicians and hospitals. We need finances to pay for education that would qualify us for well-paying and satisfying jobs, careers, and vocations.

A woman interviewed by Pew highlighted the place of finances in underlying life well-being in the domain of family. "To me, the only thing good and amazing about my life is my kids and my husband. Every day is a struggle just to make a paycheck. Money comes, money goes, but it's not ever enough to live on." A man highlighted its place in underlying life well-being in the domain of health. "Resulting from extended medical costs for my wife, our largest single expenditure each month is not mortgage payments, or car loan payments, it is medical bills." And another highlighted its place in underlying life well-being in the domain of work. "I am a teacher. We are not paid enough and the resources for our students are limited. But I do enjoy helping them learn and there is some satisfaction in helping them succeed."

This book assigns to the domain of finances the special place it deserves among the domains of life well-being, but it does not overlook the other domains.

Well-being perceptions, constraints, injuries, and medicines

People vary in their perceptions of life well-being and the relative importance of its domains. Religion is an important life well-being domain for some people, whereas others are atheists. Work is a prominent well-being domain for some people, whereas others count the days till retirement. Some sacrifice well-being in the domain of finances for well-being in the domain of family, choosing flexible work schedules that accommodate family. Others choose the opposite, sacrificing well-being in the domain of family for well-being in the domain of finances, working long hours that keep them away from family.

Life well-being is constrained by circumstances, whether poverty, illness, a disabled child, or an early death. Journalist Sarah Wildman described the pain of losing Orli, her first-born daughter. "I have struggled, since writing a eulogy for my 14-year-old, to use the past tense," she wrote. "How can I apply the past tense to someone so fully present? So fully herself, so fully formed, so insistently alive?" She described the loss of her daughter as a phantom limb that wakes her in the night, or sometimes, lies dormant with her for hours.[2]

Yet she knows that she must find life well-being as she lives with her pain. Hana, Orli's 9-year-old sister, "still needs us to run with her to the park, to continue to experience the world anew. We cannot sink. We must all float together."

Few are fortunate enough to enjoy well-being in all its domains. Life well-being calls for applying well-being medicines from one part of a domain to heal well-being injuries in another. This is what Wildman does, applying well-being medicine from one part of her family domain, promoting the life of Hana to heal the well-being injury of the passing of Orli. Yet an injury to well-being in one part of a domain can easily injure another part rather than heal it, multiplying injury and diminishing well-being. The well-being injury of a child's early death can easily injure a marriage, as one parent blames the other.

Life well-being also calls for healing well-being injuries in one domain with well-being medicine from another. Well-being medicine from an ample finances' domain can heal well-being injuries of a disabled child in the family domain. And volunteer contributions in the domain of work, helping families with disabled children, can heal well-being injuries further.

Aspirations and situations among the young and old

High aspirations, such as for high-income in satisfying careers, motivate us to aim for high future life well-being at the cost of low present life well-being. Well-being increases when situations improve to equal aspirations, or when aspirations diminish to equal situations.

Gaps between aspirations and situations underlie the U-curve of well-being by age, declining from young adulthood until middle-age, and increasing afterwards into old age.[3] High aspirations relative to situations when young reduce life well-being but motivate to push up future situations and life well-being, such as by acquiring education, switching jobs, initiating enterprise, or migrating within a country or to another country.

Gaps between aspirations and situations widen in middle age, as people find that they have not advanced in their professions as much as they had aspired, that their business plans did not succeed, or that their paintings fit over sofas better than on walls of museums.

Aging brings frailty, declining independence, loss of loved ones, and approaching death. Indeed, people tend to predict high life well-being in young age and low in old. Yet people press down their aspirations following middle age, as they become increasingly aware of their narrowing time horizon. They gravitate toward activities that are more pleasing than self-improving, and they gradually accept themselves for who they are, rather than who they were supposed to be.[4]

"That aging can make us better than ever may be the biggest dirty little secret of all time," wrote consultant and essayist Bob Brody. He noted that 8 out of every 10 deaths from COVID-19 in the United States have happened to adults 65 and older, but at age 68, much to his surprise, he finds his life to be decidedly wonderful.

He is now old enough to know that human lives, like all of nature itself, go in cycles. When he has a bad day, he knows what he never recognized as a young man, that tomorrow is likely to be better. And the older he gets, the more comfortable he feels in his own skin, accepting himself as he is. The many uncertainties that afflicted him while young, about his identity, role in the community, and philosophy of life have largely evaporated.[5]

Financial advisers and their clients, and finance professors and their students

The third generation of behavioral finance is also at the center of this book, and its implications extend especially to financial advisers and their clients and to finance professors and their students. The third generation broadens its lens beyond standard finance and the first and second generations of behavioral finance to see people as whole persons and show them in life well-being domains beyond finances.

Financial advisers working within the third generation of behavioral finance are well-being advisers. They enhance their clients' well-being, and in the process, enhance their own. A financial adviser told me about a 93-year-old client, a woman living in a superb assisted-living home. She was adamant about spending only dividends and interest from her $2.5 million portfolio and income from a rental property. Speaking with his client, the adviser found that she was refraining from visiting friends because she was concerned about taxi fares, neglecting her love of the arts because she was concerned about museum entrance fees, and shunning the idea of a new winter coat. The adviser finally persuaded her to spend additional money from her portfolio. The woman said that she might just get herself a manicure, something she had not done since her 30s. That adviser increased his client's life well-being, enhancing her lifestyle and diminishing her fear, while increasing his own life well-being, knowing that he had served his client as a well-being adviser.

Advisers feel regularly compelled to engage in trade-offs between their need for the utilitarian benefits of income derived from serving clients and their desire to avoid the expressive and emotional costs of serving clients they find distasteful, diminishing well-being. Elliot Dole is an adviser who is now able to turn away potential clients he finds distasteful. It was many years before he felt secure enough, professionally and financially, to do so. "It's really hard to walk away from those shiny objects and those high-dollar engagements," he said.[6]

Moreover, financial advisers must evolve into well-being advisers if they are to compete for today's clients and future ones because many of the traditional services of financial advisers are now generic. Financial advisers provide portfolio asset allocation, but so do robo-advisers at a lower cost. Financial advisers rebalance portfolios, but so do robo-advisers at a lower cost. Yet robo-advisers cannot serve as well-being advisers.

Few of today's professors of finance work within the framework of the third generation of behavioral finance, where all investors are "normal." Indeed, almost all finance professors still work within the framework of standard finance, where investors are "rational," or within the first generation of behavioral finance where investors are "irrational." Finance professors can enhance their scholarship and add to their contributions to their students by working within the third generation of behavioral finance. Moreover, by doing so they are likely to enhance the well-being of their students and their own.

People often ask me: "What is on the frontier of finance?" Is neuro-finance on the frontier, is ESG, is AI? I say that we should think of finance as an expanding circle rather than search for its single frontier. Neuro-finance is in that circle, and so are ESG and AI. Standard finance is in that circle, with its option pricing formulas; the first generation of behavioral finance is there, with its emphasis on overconfidence, excessive fear, and other cognitive and emotional errors; and the second generation of behavioral finance is there, with its distinctions among utilitarian, expressive, and emotional benefits. Yet the third generation of behavioral finance is also there, with its lessons about turning financial well-being into life well-being. That circle of finance is sure to expand further.

Life well-being

Not all are content to find well-being in graceful aging, as 68-year-old Bob Brody does, knowing that human lives, like all of nature itself, go in cycles. Bryan Johnson, a 46-year-old millionaire, reaches for immortality. He believes death is optional.

Johnson knows that his quest for immortality comes at the cost of all that makes us human, the joy of watching our toddlers play, the sadness of losing our parents. That quest also sets obstacles to marriage and its well-being benefits, including dinner before noon, bed before 9, no small talk, and always sleeping alone. Yet Johnson is willing to sacrifice everything for immortality, "all philosophy, all ethics, all morals, all happiness."[7] Johnson's quest for immortality evokes King Gilgamesh of Mesopotamia's quest, four-millennia before, and his reflections on well-being in a long life and a good life:

> Humans are born, they live, then they die,
>
> this is the order that the gods have decreed.
>
> But until the end comes, enjoy your life,
>
> spend it in happiness, not despair.
>
> . . . Love the child who holds you by the hand,
>
> and give your wife pleasure in your embrace.
>
> That is the best way for a man to live.[8]

Notes

Introduction

1. Steptoe, A., Deaton, A., and Stone, A. A. (2015). Subjective well-being, health, and aging. *Lancet* 385: 640–648. doi:10.1016/S0140-6736(13)61489-0
2. Gross, J., and Lemola, J. (2021, April 20). Finland is again the world's happiest country, report finds. *New York Times*. https://www.nytimes.com/2021/04/20/world/europe/world-happiness-report-ranking.html.
3. Lemola, J. (2022, August 18). Party videos of Sanna Marin, Finland's prime minister, draw criticism. *New York Times*. https://www.nytimes.com/2022/08/18/world/europe/finland-prime-minister-sanna-marin-parties.html.
4. Colston, P., and Michaels, J. (2023, April 9). Why is Finland the happiest country on Earth? The answer is complicated. *New York Times*. https://www.nytimes.com/2023/04/01/world/europe/finland-happiness-optimism.html.
5. Loewenstein, G. (1999). Because it is there: The challenge of mountaineering for utility theory. *Kyklos* 52: 315–344, 332.
6. Lamont, M. (1992). *Money, morals, and manners: The culture of French and American upper-middle class.* Chicago: Chicago University Press, pp. 62–63.
7. Leland, J. (2018). *Happiness is a choice you make: Lessons from a year among the oldest old.* New York: Farrar, Straus and Giroux, pp. 29–30.
8. Bartholomew, J. (2021, February 1). After the Covid vaccine, people find joy in little things. *Wall Street Journal.* https://www.wsj.com/articles/after-the-covid-vaccine-people-find-joy-in-little-things-11612198522?mod=article_inline

9. Lynam, D. (2020, November). The love of money. *Greenmoney*. https://greenmoney.com/the-love-of-money/

10. Statman, Meir. (2020, Winter). Well-being advisers. *The Journal of Wealth Management* 23(Supplement 1), 2–44: 2. doi: https://doi.org/10.3905/jwm.23.s1.002

11. Richard A. Easterlin & Onnicha Sawangfa, 2009. "Happiness and domain satisfaction: New directions for the economics of happiness". Chapters, in: Amitava. Krishna Dutt & Benjamin Radcliff, (ed.), Happiness, Economics, and Politics, chapter 4, Edward Elgar Publishing.

12. Ditlev-Simonsen, Caroline Dale. (2020, October 30). What is happiness to Norwegians—And how happy are they? (October 30, 2020). Working Paper 1/2020—BI Forum for Stiftelser (Forum for Foundations). Available at SSRN: https://ssrn.com/abstract=3721884 or http://dx.doi.org/10.2139/ssrn.3721884

13. Kapteyn, A., Smith, J. P., and Van Soest, A. (2012). Are Americans really less happy with their incomes? *Review of Income and Wealth* 58: 1475–1499.

14. Statman, Meir. (2020, Winter). Well-being advisers. *The Journal of Wealth Management* 23 (Supplement 1): 2–44, p. 2. doi: https://doi.org/10.3905/jwm.23.s1.002

15. Netemeyer, Richard G., Warmath, Dee, Fernandes, Daniel, and Lynch, John Jr. (2018, June). How am I doing? Perceived financial well-being, its potential antecedents, and its relation to overall well-being. *Journal of Consumer Research* 45(1): 68–89. https://doi.org/10.1093/jcr/ucx109

Chapter 1: Financial, social, cultural, and personal capital

1. Williams, Joan C. *White working class*, with a new foreword by Mark Cuban and a new preface by the author. Harvard Business Review Press. Kindle Edition, p. 9.

2. Cohen, P. (2015). Middle class, but felling economically insecure. The New York Times (April 11). https://www.nytimes.com/2015/04/11/business/economy/middle-class-but--feeling-economically-insecure.html.

3. Twenge, Jean M., and Cooper, A. Bell. (2022). The expanding class divide in happiness in the United States, 1972–2016. Affiliations expand. PMID: 32567878. doi:10.1037/emo0000774

4. Sawhill, I., and Reeves, R. (2023, June 17). A new contract with the middle class—Introduction | Brookings. https://www.brookings .edu/essay/a-new-contract-with-the-middle-class-introduction/

5. Van Kessel, P., Hughes, A., and Walker, K. (2023, November 20). The meaning of life: 100 quotes from Americans on what keeps them going. Pew Research Center. https://www.pewresearch.org/religion/ interactives/what-keeps-us-going/ https://www.pewforum.org/ interactives/what-keeps-us-going/

6. Land, Stephanie. (2019). *Maid: Hard work, low pay, and a mother's will to survive*. New York: Hachette Books, p. xii in Barbara Ehrenreich' Foreword.

7. Bradford, H. (2014, February 5). Billionaire defends fellow billionaire: "The 1 percent work harder." *HuffPost*. https://www.huffpost.com/ entry/sam-zell-1 percent_n_4733196

8. Anderson, Cameron, Kraus, Michael W., Galinsky, Adam D., and Keltner, Dacher. (2012). The local-ladder effect: Social status and subjective well-being. *Psychological Science* 23(7): 764–771. https:// greatergood.berkeley.edu/article/item/happiness_is_about_respect_ not_riches

9. Ehrenreich, Barbara. *Fear of falling: The inner life of the middle class*. (1989). New York: Harper/Collins, p. 137.

10. Statman, Meir. (2020, Winter). Well-being advisers, *The Journal of Wealth Management Winter* 23 (Supplement 1): 2–44, p. 2. doi: https:// doi.org/10.3905/jwm.23.s1.002

11. Killingsworth, Matthew A. (2021, January). Experienced well-being rises with income, even above \$75,000 per year. Proceedings of the National Academy of Sciences 18(4): e2016976118. doi:10.1073/ pnas.2016976118

12. Kahneman, Daniel, and Angus Deaton. (2010). High income improves evaluation of life but not emotional well-being. *PNAS* 107: 16489–16493.

13. Castriota, Stefano, Rondinella, Sandro, and Tonin, Mirco. (2022, May 19). Does social capital matter? A study of hit-and-run in U.S. counties. IZA Discussion Paper No. 15212. Available at SSRN: https://ssrn. com/abstract=4114787 or http://dx.doi.org/10.2139/ssrn.4114787

14. Singer, N. (2022, September 24). LinkedIn ran social experiments on 20 million users over five years. *New York Times*. https://www.nytimes .com/2022/09/24/business/linkedin-social-experiments.html

15. Morduch, J., and Schneider, R. (2017). *The financial diaries: How American families cope in a world of uncertainty*. Princeton, NJ: Princeton University Press, pp. 133–134.

16. Keltner, D. (2011, August 8). Social class as culture. *Association for Psychological Science*. https://www.psychologicalscience.org/news/releases/social-class-as-culture.html

17. McCaulley, E. (2023, August 11). A hidden currency of incalculable worth. *New York Times*. https://www.nytimes.com/2023/08/11/opinion/time-poverty-money.html

18. Lareau, A. (2011). *Unequal childhoods: Class, race, and family life*. Berkeley and Los Angeles: University of California Press, p. 204.

19. Ibid., p. 57.

20. Lamont, M. (1992) *Money, morals, and manners: The culture of French and American upper-middle class*. Chicago: Chicago University Press, p. 10.

21. Pinsker, J. (2019, February 26). The "hidden mechanisms" that help those born rich to excel in elite jobs. *The Atlantic*. https://www.theatlantic.com/entertainment/archive/2019/02/class-ceiling-laurison-friedman-elite-jobs/582175/

22. Wang, Jinhua. (2022, March 8). Survival of the fittest? Managerial Cultural Fit and Tenure. Available at SSRN: https://ssrn.com/abstract=4001438 or http://dx.doi.org/10.2139/ssrn.4001438

23. Currid-Halkett, E. (2017). *The sum of small things: A theory of the aspirational class*. Princeton, NJ: Princeton University Press, p. 79.

24. Hitt, R. (2020, February 20). The case against breastfeeding. The Consciously Parenting Project. https://consciouslyparenting.com/blog/the-case-against-breastfeeding/

25. Currid-Halkett, E. (2017). *The sum of small things: A theory of the aspirational class*. Princeton, NJ: Princeton University Press, p. 91.

26. Zhai, Shengying, Chen, Qihui, and Zhao, Qiran. (2020). Beauty and popularity in friendship networks—Evidence from migrant schools in China. Available at SSRN: https://ssrn.com/abstract=4015048 or http://dx.doi.org/10.2139/ssrn.4015048

27. Palmer, Carl. L., and Peterson, R. D. (2021). Physical attractiveness, halo effects, and social joining. *Social Science Quarterly* 102(1): 552–566. https://doi.org/10.1111/ssqu.12892

28. Ravina, Enrichetta. (2019, February 15). Love & loans: The effect of beauty and personal characteristics in credit markets. Available at

SSRN: https://ssrn.com/abstract=1101647 or http://dx.doi.org/10.2139/ssrn.1101647

29. Bai, Chengyu, and Tian, Shiwen. (2023, January 11). What beauty brings? Managers' attractiveness and fund performance. Available at SSRN: https://ssrn.com/abstract=4322134 or http://dx.doi.org/10.2139/ssrn.4322134

30. Deaton, Angus, and Arora, Raksha. (2009, June). Life at the top: The benefits of height. NBER Working Paper No. w15090. Available at SSRN: https://ssrn.com/abstract=1422968

31. David, Susan. *Oxford Handbook of Happiness*. Oxford Library of Psychology. OUP Oxford. Kindle Edition, p. 177.

32. Ryff CD. Psychological well-being revisited: advances in the science of practice of eudaimonia. Psychother Psychosom. 2014;83(1):10-28. doi: 10.1159/000353263. Epub 2013 Nov 19. PMID: 24281296; PMCID: PMC4241300.

33. Statman, Meir. (2020, Winter). Well-being advisers, *The Journal of Wealth Management Winter* 23 (Supplement 1): 2–44, p. 2. doi: https://doi.org/10.3905/jwm.23.s1.002

34. Association for Psychological Science (2019). Cheer up! Optimists live longer. https://www.psychologicalscience.org/news/cheer-up-optimists-live-longer.html (accessed 15 October 2023).

35. Costello, N. L., Bragdon, E. E., Light, K. C., Sigurdsson, A., Bunting, S., Grewen, K., and Maixner, W. (2002). Temporomandibular disorder and optimism: Relationships to ischemic pain sensitivity and interleukin-6. *Pain,* 100: 99–110.

36. Diener, Ed, and Ryan, Katherine. Subjective well-being: A general overview. *South African Journal of Psychology* 39(4): 391–406. https://doi.org/10.1177/008124630903900402

37. Li, C., Zuckerman, M., and Diener, E. (2021). Culture moderates the relation between gender inequality and well-being. *Psychological Science* 32(6): 823–835. https://doi.org/10.1177/0956797620972492

38. Kirchick, J. (2022, November 10). Norah Vincent's gender Trouble. *Tablet.* https://www.tabletmag.com/sections/news/articles/norah-vincent-gender-trouble-jamie-kirchick

39. NeJaime, Douglas. (2012, May 1). Marriage inequality: Same-sex relationships, religious exemptions, and the production of sexual orientation discrimination. *100 California Law Review* 1169. Loyola-LA Legal Studies Paper No. 2011-46. Available at SSRN: https://ssrn.com/abstract=1969560

40. Langowski, Jamie, Berman, William, Holloway, Regina, and McGinn, Cameron. (2017). Transcending prejudice: Gender identity and

expression-based discrimination in the metro Boston rental housing market. *Yale Journal of Law and Feminism* 29: 321. Suffolk University Law School Research Paper No. 17-9. Available at SSRN: https://ssrn.com/abstract=2941810

41. Tweedy, Ann E., and Yescavage, Karen. (2013, July 24). Employment discrimination against bisexuals: An empirical study. *William & Mary Journal of Women and the Law* 21: 699. Available at SSRN: https://ssrn.com/abstract=2297924 or http://dx.doi.org/10.2139/ssrn.2297924

42. Furth-Matzkin, M. (2022, February 14). Meirav Furth-Matzkin: Racial bias in retail stores is real. *Chicago Tribune*. https://www.chicagotribune.com/opinion/commentary/ct-opinion-discrimination-racial-shopping-while-black-20220214-xuja2qx4dbgxheyot3ytgciacq-story.html

43. Regev, Tali, and Kricheli Katz, Tamar. (2020). Biased reputations: Using cross-listed properties to identify the negative effects of race on users' reputations on Airbnb. Available at SSRN: https://ssrn.com/abstract=4278441 or http://dx.doi.org/10.2139/ssrn.4278441

44. Luca, Michael, Pronkina, Elizaveta, and Rossi, Michelangelo. (2023, March 4). Scapegoating and discrimination in times of crisis: Evidence from Airbnb. Harvard Business School NOM Unit Working Paper No. 23-012, Université Paris-Dauphine Research Paper No. 4187181. Available at SSRN: https://ssrn.com/abstract=4187181 or http://dx.doi.org/10.2139/ssrn.4187181

45. Van Kessel, P., Hughes, A., and Walker, K. (2018, November 20). The meaning of life: 100 quotes from Americans on what keeps them going. *Pew Research Center's Religion & Public Life Project*. https://www.pewresearch.org/religion/interactives/what-keeps-us-going/

46. Harpaz, Y. (2021). Conspicuous mobility: The status dimensions of the global passport hierarchy. *Annals of the American Academy of Political and Social Science* 697(1): 32–48. https://doi.org/10.1177/00027162211052859

47. Toft, M., and Friedman, S. (2021). Family wealth and the class ceiling: The propulsive power of the bank of Mum and Dad. *Sociology* 55(1): 90–109. https://doi.org/10.1177/0038038520922537

48. Freeland, Chrystia. (2012, October 8), Super-rich irony: Why do billionaires feel victimized by Obama?" *The New Yorker*. https://www.newyorker.com/magazine/2012/10/08/super-rich-irony

49. Cohen, Patricia. (2015, April 10). A shifting middle class, but feeling economically insecure. *New York Times*. https://www.nytimes

.com/2015/04/11/business/economy/middle-class-but-feeling-economically-insecure.html

50. Le Van, G. (2011, April). Wealth: Its joys and its discontents—The Boston College Survey. Upchurch Watson White and Max. https://www.uww-adr.com/blog/wealth-its-joys-and-its-discontents-the-boston-college-survey

51. Ibid.

Chapter 2: Financial capital

1. Halpern-Meekin, S., Edin, K., Tach, L., et al. (2015). *It's not like I'm poor: How working families make ends meet in a post-welfare world.* Berkeley and Los Angeles: University of California Press, p. 48.

2. Giovanis, Eleftherios, and Ozdamar, Oznur. (2020, August 1). Income losses and subjective well-being: Gender and ethnic inequalities during the COVID lockdown period in the UK. Available at SSRN: https://ssrn.com/abstract=3752239 or http://dx.doi.org/10.2139/ssrn.3752239

3. Disney, A. (2021, June 17). I was taught from a young age to protect my dynastic wealth. *The Atlantic.* https://www.theatlantic.com/ideas/archive/2021/06/abigail-disney-rich-protect-dynastic-wealth-propublica-tax/619212/

4. Cattaneo, Matias D., Galiani, Sebastian, Gertler, Paul J., Martinez, Sebastian, and Titiunik, Rocio. (2009, February). Housing, health, and happiness. *American Economic Journal: Economic Policy* 1(1): 75–105, February 2009.

5. Agarwal, Sumit, Chia, Liu Ee, and Sing, Tien Foo. (2020, September 8). Straw purchase or safe haven? The hidden perils of illicit wealth in property markets. Available at SSRN: https://ssrn.com/abstract=3688752 or http://dx.doi.org/10.2139/ssrn.3688752

6. Barcelona, William, Converse, Nathan, and Wong, Anna. (2021, November). U.S. housing as a global safe asset: Evidence from China shocks. Available at SSRN: https://ssrn.com/abstract=3965183 or http://dx.doi.org/10.17016/IFDP.2021.1332

7. Goodell, J. (2022, February 18). Saving their souls. *HumbleDollar.* https://humbledollar.com/2022/02/saving-their-souls/

8. Odermatt, Reto, and Stutzer, Alois. (2020). Does the dream of home ownership rest upon biased beliefs? A test based on predicted and

realized life satisfaction. IZA Discussion Paper No. 13510. Available at SSRN: https://ssrn.com/abstract=3660256

9. Bucchianeri, Grace Wong. (2011, April 1). The American dream or the American delusion? The private and external benefits of homeownership for women. Available at SSRN: https://ssrn.com/abstract=1877163 or http://dx.doi.org/10.2139/ssrn.1877163

10. Bhattacharya, Utpal, Huang, Daisy J., and Nielsen, Kasper Meisner. (2020, August 24). Spillovers in prices: The curious case of haunted houses. Review of Finance. Available at SSRN: https://ssrn.com/abstract=3679828 or http://dx.doi.org/10.2139/ssrn.3679828

11. He, Jia, Liu, Haoming, Sin, Tien Foo, Song, Changcheng, Wong, Wei-Kang. (2019). Superstition, conspicuous spending, and housing market: Evidence from Singapore. *Management Science* 66(2): 783–804. https://doi.org/10.1287/mnsc.2018.3198 or http://dx.doi.org/10.2139/ssrn.2769207

12. Lucia van der Post. (1999, August 30). Little time for the second-rate. *Financial Times*, 6.

13. Danny Hakim. (2002, November 21). BMW design chief sees art on wheels; some just see ugly. *New York Times*, A1. https://www.nytimes.com/2002/11/21/business/bmw-design-chief-sees-art-on-wheels-some-just-see-ugly.html

14. Di, Wenhua, and Su, Yichen. (2021, May 31). Conspicuous consumption: Vehicle purchases by non-prime consumers. Available at SSRN: https://ssrn.com/abstract=3857387

15. Kurysheva, Anna, and Vernikov, Andrei V. (2021, June 1). Veblen was right: Conspicuous consumption and car loans in Russia. Available at SSRN: https://ssrn.com/abstract=3857764

16. Currid-Halkett, E. (2017). *The sum of small things: A theory of the aspirational class*. Princeton, NJ: Princeton University Press, p. 95.

17. Berger, Jonah, and Ward, Morgan. (2010, December 4). Subtle signals of inconspicuous consumption. *Journal of Consumer Research* 37(4): 555–569. https://doi.org/10.1086/655445

18. Goor, Dafna, Ordabayeva, Nailya, Keinan, Anat, and Crener, Sandrine. (2020, April 6). The impostor syndrome from luxury consumption. *Journal of Consumer Research* 46(6): 1031–1051. https://doi.org/10.1093/jcr/ucz044

19. Easterlin, Richard A. (1973). Does money buy happiness? *The Public Interest* 30: 3–10.

20. Tugend, A. (2019, November 6). Wait a minute. How can they afford that when I can't? *New York Times.* https://www.nytimes.com/2019/11/06/your-money/financial-security-envy.html

21. Luttmer, Enzo F. P. (2005, August 3). Neighbors as negatives: Relative earnings and well-being. *Quarterly Journal of Economics* 120(3): 963–1002.

22. Leites, Martin, Paleo, Camila, Ramos, Xavier, and Salas, Gonzalo. (2022) Choosing or inheriting the Joneses: The origins of reference groups. IZA Discussion Paper No. 15584, Available at SSRN: https://ssrn.com/abstract=4232713 or http://dx.doi.org/10.2139/ssrn.4232713

23. Goerke, Laszlo, and Pannenberg, Markus. (2015, October 13). Direct evidence for income comparisons and subjective well-being across reference groups. CESifo Working Paper Series No. 5546. Available at SSRN: https://ssrn.com/abstract=2686491

24. Andersson, Matthew A. (2022). Modern social hierarchies and the spaces between: How are subjective status inconsistencies linked to mental well-being? *Social Psychology Quarterly* 81: 48–70. 81(1https://doi.org/10.1177/0190272517753687

25. Banuri, Sheheryar, and Nguyen, Ha. (2020, September 30). Borrowing to keep up (with the Joneses): Inequality, debt, and conspicuous consumption. Available at SSRN: https://ssrn.com/abstract=3721084 or http://dx.doi.org/10.2139/ssrn.3721084

26. Chen, Xiaofen, and Zhang, Lin. (2017, June 1). Will high household saving in China persist? An application of the conspicuous consumption theory. *International Journal of Economic Behavior* 7(1): 3–24, Available at SSRN: https://ssrn.com/abstract=2995004

27. Agarwal, Sumit, Mikhed, Vyacheslav, and Scholnick, Barry. (2020, January). Peers' income and financial distress: Evidence from lottery winners and neighboring bankruptcies. *The Review of Financial Studies* 33(1): 433–472. https://doi.org/10.1093/rfs/hhz047

28. Agarwal, Sumit, Qian, Wenlan, and Zou, Xin. (2021, May). Thy neighbor's misfortune: Peer effect on consumption. *American Economic Journal: Economic Policy* 13(2): 1–25.

29. Killingsworth, Matthew A. (2021, January). Experienced well-being rises with income, even above $75,000 per year. Proceedings of the National Academy of Sciences 118(4): e2016976118. doi:10.1073/pnas.2016976118

30. Frey, Bruno S., and Stutzer, Alois. (2004, December). Economic consequences of mispredicting utility. IEW Working Paper No. 218. Available at SSRN: https://ssrn.com/abstract=639025 or http://dx.doi.org/10.2139/ssrn.639025

31. Kasser, Tim. (2018). Materialism and living well. In: E. Diener, S. Oishi, and L. Tay (eds.), *Handbook of well-being*. Salt Lake City, UT: DEF Publishers.doi: nobascholar.com

32. Hsee, Christopher K., Yang, Yang, Li, Naihe, and Shen, Luxi. (2009, October 30). Wealth, warmth and wellbeing: Whether happiness is relative or absolute depends on whether it is about money acquisition or consumption. *Journal of Marketing Research*. Available at SSRN: https://ssrn.com/abstract=1292175 or http://dx.doi.org/10.2139/ssrn.1292175

33. Parker, J. (2021, February 15). An ode to low expectations. *The Atlantic*. https://www.theatlantic.com/magazine/archive/2021/03/an-ode-to-low-expectations/617801/

34. Perez-Truglia, Ricardo. (2020, April 4). The effects of income transparency on well-being: Evidence from a natural experiment. *American Economic Review* 110(4): 1019–1054.

35. Card, David, Alexandre Mas, Enrico Moretti, and Emmanuel Saez. (2012). Inequality at work: The effect of peer salaries on job satisfaction. *American Economic Review* 102(6): 2981–3003.

36. Narula, S. (2021, May 3). How much money do Millennials make? It's no longer a taboo question. *Wall Street Journal*. https://www.wsj.com/articles/how-money-much-do-millennials-make-theyre-more-than-happy-to-tell-you-11620061103

37. Baker, Michael, Halberstam, Yosh, Kroft, Kory, Mas, Alexandre, and Messacar, Derek. (2023). Pay transparency and the gender gap. *American Economic Journal: Applied Economics* 15(2): 157–183.

38. Chen, Xinghui, Talukdar, Debabrata, and Goswami, Indranil. (2022, May 31). To be or not to be like the Joneses: Effects of "income transparency" on consumption attitude and behavior among low–income consumers. Available at SSRN: https://ssrn.com/abstract=4131802 or http://dx.doi.org/10.2139/ssrn.4131802

39. Harrington, B. (2022, March 5). The Russian elite can't stand the sanctions. *The Atlantic*. https://www.theatlantic.com/ideas/archive/2022/03/russian-sanctions-oligarchs-offshore-wealth/623886/

40. Wood, G. (2011, February 24). Secret fears of the super-rich. *The Atlantic*. https://www.theatlantic.com/magazine/archive/2011/04/secret-fears-of-the-super-rich/308419/

41. Frank, R. (2013, November 15). China has a word for its crass new rich. Consumer News and Business Channel. CNBC. https://www.cnbc.com/2013/11/15/china-has-a-word-for-its-crass-new-rich.html

42. Bellafante, G. (2018, April 13). Facebook, generator of envy and dread. *New York Times.* https://www.nytimes.com/2018/04/13/nyregion/facebook-generator-of-envy-and-dread.html

43. Mujcic, Redzo, and Oswald, Andrew J. (2018, February). Is envy harmful to a society's psychological health and wellbeing? A longitudinal study of 18,000 adults. *Social Science & Medicine* 2018 198: 103-111. doi:10.1016/j.socscimed.2017.12.030. Epub 2017 Dec 27. PMID: 29316510.

44. Givi, Julian, and Galak, Jeff. (2019, April 29). Keeping the Joneses from getting ahead in the first place: Envy's influence on gift giving behavior. Available at SSRN: https://ssrn.com/abstract=3379405 or http://dx.doi.org/10.2139/ssrn.3379405

45. Hornik, Jacob, Rachamim, Matti, and Grossman, Ori. (2021). Ripples of contempt: Aversive responses to others (mis)fortunes. *Motivation and Emotion* 45. 10.1007/s11031-021-09905-2.

46. Bonior, A. (2023, October 17). Ask Dr. Andrea: I think I'm a good person, but I'm so jealous of others. *What Can I Do? The Lily.* https://www.thelily.com/ask-dr-andrea-i-think-im-a-good-person-but-im-so-jealous-of-others-what-can-i-do/

47. Hornik, Jacob, Rachamim, Matti, and Grossman, Ori. (2021). Ripples of contempt aversive responses to others (mis)fortunes. *Motivation and Emotion* 45. 10.1007/s11031-021-09905-2. http://dx.doi.org/10.2139/ssrn.4000371

48. Smith, Tiffany Watt. (2018). *Schadenfreude: The Joy of Another's Misfortune.* Welcome Publisher.

49. Fraga, J. (2022, November 25). The opposite of *Schadenfreude* is *Freudenfreude.* Here's how to cultivate it. *New York Times.* https://www.nytimes.com/2022/11/25/well/mind/schadenfreude-freudenfreude.html

50. Parker, Paul, Albuquerque, Paulo, and Bart, Yakov. (2020, June 25). Impact of lottery play decisions on consumer and retailer earnings. Available at SSRN: https://ssrn.com/abstract=3660130 or http://dx.doi.org/10.2139/ssrn.3660130

51. Maryland Lottery (2022). Baltimore man plays mother's birth date, wins $50,000 Pick 5 Prize. https://www.mdlottery.com/baltimore-man-plays-mothers-birth-date-wins-50000-pick-5-prize/ (accessed 16 October 2023).

52. Eligon, J., and Silva, J. (2021, July 4). A diamond rush in South Africa, born of desperation and distrust. *New York Times*. https://www.nytimes.com/2021/07/04/world/africa/south-africa-diamond-rush.html

53. Berger, Lawrence M., Collins, J. Michael, and Cuesta, Laura. (2013, January 15). Household debt and adult depressive symptoms. Available at SSRN: https://ssrn.com/abstract=2200927 or http://dx.doi.org/10.2139/ssrn.2200927

54. Carpenter, J. (2021, January 30). Some GameStop investors got in with one goal—to pay off debt. *Wall Street Journal*. https://www.wsj.com/articles/some-gamestop-investors-got-in-with-one-goalto-pay-off-debt-11612008000

55. Cooper, M. (2014). *Cut adrift: Families in insecure times*. Berkeley and Los Angeles: University of California Press, p. 123.

56. Wood, G. (2011, February 24). Secret fears of the super-rich. *The Atlantic*. https://www.theatlantic.com/magazine/archive/2011/04/secret-fears-of-the-super-rich/308419/

57. Sherman, R. (2017). *Uneasy street: The anxieties of affluence*. Princeton, NJ: Princeton University Press, p. 33.

58. van Landeghem, Bert, and Vandeplas, Anneleen. (2017). The relationship between status and happiness: Evidence from the caste system in rural India, IZA Discussion Papers 11099, Institute of Labor Economics (IZA).

59. Guvenen, Fatih, Kaplan, Greg, Song, Jae, and Weidner, Justin. (2021, May 25). Lifetime earnings in the United States over six decades. University of Chicago, Becker Friedman Institute for Economics Working Paper No. 2021-60, Available at SSRN: https://ssrn.com/abstract=3853355 or http://dx.doi.org/10.2139/ssrn.3853355

60. Cohen, Patricia. (2015, April 10). Middle class, but feeling economically insecure. *New York Times*. https://www.nytimes.com/2015/04/11/business/economy/middle-class-but-feeling-economically-insecure.html

61. Brockmann, Hilke, Delhey, Jan, Welzel, Christian, and Yuan, Hao. (2008, February 6). The China puzzle: Falling happiness in a rising economy. *Journal of Happiness Studies* 10: 387–405. Available at SSRN: https://ssrn.com/abstract=2391703

62. Zhang, Xinyu, and Pak, Tae-Young. (2022, January 23). Keeping up with the Wangs: Relative deprivation and conspicuous consumption among Chinese consumers. Available at SSRN: https://ssrn.com/abstract=4015833 or http://dx.doi.org/10.2139/ssrn.4015833

63. Galiani, Sebastian, Gertler, Paul J., and Undurraga, Raimundo. (2016, February 28). The half-life of happiness: Hedonic adaptation in the subjective well-being of poor slum dwellers to the satisfaction of basic housing needs. Available at SSRN: https://ssrn.com/abstract= 2592256 or http://dx.doi.org/10.2139/ssrn.2592256

64. Di Tella, Rafael, Haisken-DeNew, John P., and MacCulloch, Robert. (2004). Happiness adaptation to income and to status in an individual panel. Available at SSRN: https://ssrn.com/abstract=760368 or http://dx.doi.org/10.2139/ssrn.76036

Chapter 3: Saving and spending

1. Guven, Cahit. (2009, August). Reversing the question: Does happiness affect consumption and savings behavior? SOEP paper No. 219. Available at SSRN: https://ssrn.com/abstract=1476886 or http://dx.doi.org/10.2139/ssrn.1476886

2. Sharma, Eesha, Wang, Xiang, and Tully, Stephanie. (2002, September 1). Scarcity and intertemporal choice. FRB of Philadelphia Working Paper No. 22-27. Available at SSRN: https://ssrn.com/abstract=4207232 or http://dx.doi.org/10.21799/frbp.wp.2022.27

3. Mullainathan, Sendhil, and Shafir, Eldar. (2013, September 3). *Scarcity: Why having too little means so much*. New York Times Books.

4. Dahan, Momi, and Nisan, Udi. (2020). Late payments, liquidity constraints and the mismatch between due dates and paydays. CESifo Working Paper No. 8733. Available at SSRN: https://ssrn.com/abstract=3744596

5. Collinson, Robert, Humphries, John Eric, Mader, Nicholas, Reed, Davin, Tannenbaum, Daniel I., and van Dijk, Winnie. (2022, August). Eviction and poverty in American cities. NBER Working Paper No. w30382. Available at SSRN: https://ssrn.com/abstract=4196326

6. Lee, Jacob C., Hall, Deborah L., and Wood, Wendy. (2018, July 1). Experiential or material purchases? Social class determines purchase happiness. *Psychological Science* 29(7): 1031–1039.

7. Sherman, R. (2017). Uneasy street: The anxieties of affluence. Princeton, NJ: Princeton University Press, p. 33.

8. Stanley, Thomas J., and Danko, William D. (1996). *The millionaire next door: The surprising secrets of America's wealthy*. Atlanta: Longstreet Press.

9. Kreiner, Claus Thustrup, Leth-Petersen, Søren, Louise Charlotte Willerslev-Olsen, Louise charlotte. (2020, January). Financial trouble

across generations: Evidence from the universe of personal loans in Denmark. *The Economic Journal* 130(6): 233–262. https://doi.org/10.1093/ej/uez046

10. McCartney, W. Ben, and Shah, Avni. (2021, April 1). Household mortgage refinancing decisions are neighbor influenced. FRB of Philadelphia Working Paper No. 21-16, Available at SSRN: https://ssrn.com/abstract=3843821 or http://dx.doi.org/10.21799/frbp.wp.2021.16

11. Loibl, Cäzilia, Letkiewicz Jodi, McNair, Simon, Summers, Barbara, and Bruine de Bruin, Wändi. (2021, September). On the association of debt attitudes with socioeconomic characteristics and financial behaviors. *Journal of Consumer Affairs* 55(3): 939–966.

12. Almenberg, Johan, Lusardi, Annamaria, Säve-Söderbergh, Jenny, and Vestman, Roine. (2020, May). Attitudes toward debt and debt behavior. CEPR Discussion Paper No. DP14801. Available at SSRN: https://ssrn.com/abstract=3612870

13. Xiao, Jing Jian, Zhang, Shu, and Li, Feng. (2019, September 15). Debt holding and subjective wellbeing: Borrowing source and income as moderators. Available at SSRN: https://ssrn.com/abstract=3454133 or http://dx.doi.org/10.2139/ssrn.3454133

14. Cookson, J. Anthony, Gilje, Erik, and Heimer, Rawley. (2020, August 26). Shale shocked: Cash windfalls and household debt repayment. Available at SSRN: https://ssrn.com/abstract=3682223 or http://dx.doi.org/10.2139/ssrn.3682223

15. Herskowitz, Sylvan Rene, Kleemans, Marieke, and Pulido, Cristhian. (2021, December 31). Kin transfers as safety nets in response to idiosyncratic and correlated shocks. IFPRI Discussion Paper 2097. Available at SSRN: https://ssrn.com/abstract=4017833

16. Pugliese, M., Le Bourdais, C., and Clark, S. (2021). Credit card debt and the provision of financial support to kin in the US. *Journal of Family and Economic Issues* 42(4): 616–632. https://doi.org/10.1007/s10834-020-09731-7

17. Bahrami-Rad, Duman, Beauchamp, Jonathan, Henrich, Joseph, and Schulz, Jonathan. (2022, August 25). Kin-based institutions and economic development. GMU Working Paper in Economics No. 22-41. Available at SSRN: https://ssrn.com/abstract=4200629 or http://dx.doi.org/10.2139/ssrn.4200629

18. Carranza, Eliana, Donald, Aletheia Amalia, Grosset, Florian, Kaur, Supreet. (2022, September). The social tax: Redistributive pressure and labor supply. NBER Working Paper No. w30438. Available at SSRN: https://ssrn.com/abstract=4216224

19. Rolf Engelbrecht. (2005). *The hernia—amusing anecdotes and cultural insights from missionary life in Guinea, West Africa*, self-published.

20. McCarthy, Yvonne. (2011, February 14). Behavioural characteristics and financial distress. ECB Working Paper No. 1303. Available at SSRN: http://ssrn.com/abstract=1761570

21. Morduch, J., and Schneider, R. (2017). The *financial diaries:* How *American families cope in a world of uncertainty.* Princeton, NJ: Princeton University Press, pp. 5–6.

22. Ibid., p. 66.

23. Halpern-Meekin, S., Edin, K., Tach, L. et al. (2015). *It's not like I'm Poor: How working families make ends meet in a post-welfare world.* Berkeley and Los Angeles: University of California Press, p. 30.

24. Wang, Hongchang, and Overby, Eric M. (2021). How does online lending influence bankruptcy filings? 68(5): 3309–3329. https://doi.org/10.1287/mnsc.2021.4045

25. deHaan, Ed, Kim, Jungbae, Lourie, Ben, and Zhu, Chenqi. (2022, September 27). Buy now pay (pain?) later. Available at SSRN: https://ssrn.com/abstract=4230633 or http://dx.doi.org/10.2139/ssrn.4230633

26. Morduch, J., and Schneider, R. (2017). *The financial diaries: How American families cope in a world of uncertainty.* Princeton, NJ: Princeton University Press, p. 25.

27. Ibid., p. 82.

28. Bernstein, Asaf, and Koudijs, Peter. (2020, July). Mortgage amortization and wealth accumulation. Stanford University Graduate School of Business Research Paper No. 3569252. Available at SSRN: https://ssrn.com/abstract=3569252 or http://dx.doi.org/10.2139/ssrn.3569252

29. Morduch, J., and Schneider, R. (2017). *The financial diaries: How American families cope in a world of uncertainty.* Princeton, NJ: Princeton University Press, p. 103.

30. https://www.nytimes.com/2019/10/04/your-money/weekly-allowance-average.html?smid=nytcore-ios-share

31. Beshears, J., Choi, J., Laibson, D., Madrian, B. C., and Skimmyhorn, W. L. (2022). Borrowing to save? The impact of automatic enrollment on debt. *Journal of Finance* 77(1): 403–447.

32. Cuffe, Harold E., and Gibbs, Christopher G. (2015, August 26). The effect of payday lending restrictions on liquor sales. Available at SSRN: http://ssrn.com/abstract=2652018 or http://dx.doi.org/10.2139/ssrn.2652018

33. Ben-David, Itzhak, and Bos, Marieke. (2017, March). Impulsive consumption and financial wellbeing: Evidence from an increase in the availability of alcohol. NBER Working Paper No. w23211. Available at SSRN: https://ssrn.com/abstract=2938755

34. Banerjee, Abhijit, Hanna, Rema, Olken, Benjamin A., Satriawan, Elan, and Sumarto, Sudarno. (2023, February). Electronic food vouchers: Evidence from an at-scale experiment in Idnonesia. *American Economic Review* 113(2): 514–547.

35. Halpern-Meekin, Sarah. *It's not like I'm poor.* University of California Press. Kindle Edition, pp. 193–194.

36. Sherman, R. (2017). *Uneasy street: The anxieties of affluence.* Princeton, NJ: Princeton University Press, p. 61.

37. Giuliano, Paola, and Paola Sapienza. (2020). The cost of being too patient. AEA Papers and Proceedings, 110: 314–318.

38. Sherman, R. (2017). *Uneasy street: The anxieties of affluence.* Princeton, NJ: Princeton University Press p. 123.

39. Sela, Aner, Berger, Jonah, and Kim, Joshua. (2017). How self-control shapes the meaning of choice. *Journal of Consumer Research* 44(4): 724–737. doi:10.1093/jcr/ucx069

40. Sussman, Abigail B., and Rourke L. O'Brien. (2015). Knowing when to spend: Unintended financial consequences of earmarking to encourage savings. *Journal of Marketing Research.*

41. Statman, Meir. (2020, Winter). Well-being advisers. *The Journal of Wealth Management* Winter 23 (Supplement 1): 2–44, p. 2. doi: https://doi.org/10.3905/jwm.23.s1.002

42. Malmendier, Ulrike, and Shen, Leslie Sheng. Scarred consumption. *American Economic Journal: Macroeconomics* (Forthcoming).

43. Span, P. (2021, October 2). Tallying the cost of growing older. *New York Times.* https://www.nytimes.com/2021/10/02/health/elderly-health-care-finances.html

44. Andriotis, A. (2020, September 20). No job, loads of debt: Covid upends middle-class family finances. *Wall Street Journal.* https://www.wsj.com/articles/covid-unemployment-debt-middle-class-family-finances-11600122791

45. De Nardi, Mariacristina, French, Eric, Bailey Jones, John, and McGee, Rory. (2021, May). Why do couples and singles save during retirement? NBER Working Paper No. 28828.

46. Vettese, Fred M. (2016, June 16). How spending declines with age, and the implications for workplace pension plans. C.D. Howe Institute e-brief 238. Available at SSRN: http://ssrn.com/abstract=2799376

47. Baek, Ingul, and Noh, Sanha. (2021, March 11). Does home equity liquidation reduce the poverty rate of older adults? Evidence from South Korea. Available at SSRN: https://ssrn.com/abstract=3802230 or http://dx.doi.org/10.2139/ssrn.3802230

48. Moulton, Stephanie, Haurin, Donald, and Loibl, Caezilia. Project of Center for Financial Security WI20-11: Housing Wealth and Economic Security in Retirement.

49. Blanton, K. (2022, April 14). Her home purchase builds children's wealth—Center for Retirement Research. Center for Retirement Research at Boston College. https://crr.bc.edu/her-home-purchase-builds-childrens-wealth/

50. Berger, C. (2023, June 25). A couple who retired early with $4.3 Million says the FIRE lifestyle is wearing thin: "We don't want to just keep throwing money on the pile and keep being cheap." Yahoo Finance. https://finance.yahoo.com/news/couple-retired-early-4-3-130000806.html

51. Keinan, A., and Kivetz, R. (2008). Remedying hyperopia: The effects of self-control regret on consumer behavior. *Journal of Marketing Research* 45(6): 676–689. https://doi.org/10.1509/jmkr.45.6.676

52. Cowles, C. (2021, July 14). The pandemic forged new FIRE followers, with a difference. *New York Times.* https://www.nytimes.com/2021/07/14/business/financial-independence-retire-early-fire-retirement-savings.html

53. Statman, M. (2017, October 19). How financially literate are you really? Let's find out. *Wall Street Journal.* https://www.wsj.com/articles/how-financially-literate-are-you-really-lets-find-out-1508421702

54. Simonetti, I. (2023, January 20). In their 20s, struggling to save and tired of being lectured about it. *New York Times.* https://www.nytimes.com/2023/01/20/business/saving-money-inflation-economy.html

Chapter 4: Investing

1. Das, Sreyoshi, Kuhnen, Camelia M., and Nagel, Stefan. (2020, January). Socioeconomic status and macroeconomic expectations, *The Review of Financial Studies* 33(1): 395–432. https://doi.org/10.1093/rfs/hhz041

2. Galil, Koresh, Spivak, Avia, and Tur-Sinai, Aviad. (2022). Lemons for the poor, lemonade for the rich: Individual investors' behavior in

response to a financial crisis. Available at SSRN: https://ssrn.com/abstract=4257305

3. Statman, M. (2020, August 8). 5 myths about stock diversification. *Wall Street Journal*. https://www.wsj.com/articles/5-myths-about-stock-diversification-11596896778

4. Ibid.

5. Sui, Pengfei, and Wang, Baolian. (2022, April 12). Social transmission bias: Evidence from an online investor platform. Available at SSRN: https://ssrn.com/abstract=4081644 or http://dx.doi.org/10.2139/ssrn.4081644

6. Goetzmann, William, and Peles, Nadav. (1997). Cognitive dissonance and mutual fund investors. *Journal of Financial Research* 20: 145–158.

7. Liu, Chang, and Fan, Maoyong. (2022). Stock market declines and the psychological health of investors. Available at SSRN: https://ssrn.com/abstract=4101078 or http://dx.doi.org/10.2139/ssrn.4101078

8. Statman, M. (2017, April 24). The mental mistakes we make with retirement spending. *Wall Street Journal*. https://www.wsj.com/articles/the-mental-mistakes-we-make-with-retirement-spending-1492999921

9. Hoffmann, Arvid O. I. (2007). Individual investors' needs and the investment professional: Lessons from marketing. *The Journal of Investment Consulting* 8(2): 80–91.

10. Dorn, Daniel, and Snegmueller, Paul. (2009). Trading as entertainment? *Management Science* 55(4): 591–603.

11. Dhar, Ravi, and Goetzmann, William N. (2005). Bubble investors: What were they thinking? Yale ICF Working Paper No. 06-22.

12. Lee, Steven, Cummings, Benjamin F., and Martin, Jason. (2019, January 31). Victim characteristics of investment fraud. 2019 Academic Research Colloquium for Financial Planning and Related Disciplines. Available at SSRN: https://ssrn.com/abstract=3258084 or http://dx.doi.org/10.2139/ssrn.3258084

13. Phillips, M. (2021, March 18). Penny stocks are booming, which is good news for swindlers. *New York Times*. https://www.nytimes.com/2021/03/18/business/penny-stocks-trading.html

14. Agarwal S., Driscoll, J. C., Gabaix, X., and Laibson, D. (2009). The age of reason: Financial decisions over the life-cycle with implications for regulation. *Brookings Papers on Economic Activity* (2): 51–117.

15. Smith, R. (2021, June 6). Baby Boomers' biggest financial risk: Cognitive decline. *Wall Street Journal*. https://www.wsj.com/

articles/baby-boomers-biggest-financial-risk-cognitive-decline-11622942343

16. Livni, E. (2022, September 1). Abortion rights loom larger in investment decisions. *New York Times.* https://www.nytimes.com/2022/09/01/business/abortion-rights-investing.html

17. Statman, Meir. (2008, February). Quiet conversations: The expressive nature of socially responsible investors. *Journal of Financial Planning* 21(2): 40–46.

18. Hirst, Scott, Kastiel, Kobi, and Kricheli Katz, Tamar. (2021, August 9). How much do investors care about social responsibility? Available at SSRN: https://ssrn.com/abstract=4115854 or http://dx.doi.org/10.2139/ssrn.4115854

19. Meir Statman, Socially Responsible Investors and Their Advisors Journal of Investment Consulting, Vol.9, No.1, pp.15-26, Fall 2008.

Chapter 5: Dating and marriage

1. Cosaert, Sam, Theloudis, Alexandros, and Verheyden, Bertrand. (2023). Togetherness in the household. *American Economic Journal: Microeconomics* 15(1): 529–579.

2. Stutzer, Eloise, and Frey, Bruno. (2006). Does marriage make people happy, or do happy people get married? *The Journal of Socio-Economics* 35: 326–347; Grover, Shawn, and Helliwell, John F. (2019). How's life at home? New evidence on marriage and the set point for happiness. *Journal of Happiness Studies* 20: 373–390. https://link.springer.com/article/10.1007/s10902-017-9941-3

3. Harker, L., and Keltner, D. (2001). Expressions of positive emotion in women's college yearbook pictures and their relationship to personality and life outcomes across adulthood. *Journal of Personality and Social Psychology* 80: 112–124. doi:10.1037/0022-3514.80.1.112

4. Stutzer, Eloise, and Frey, Bruno. (2006). Does marriage make people happy, or do happy people get married? *The Journal of Socio-Economics* 35: 326–347; Grover, Shawn, and Helliwell, John F. (2019). How's life at home? New evidence on marriage and the set point for happiness. *Journal of Happiness Studies* 20: 373–390. https://link.springer.com/article/10.1007/s10902-017-9941-3

5. Wilson, Chris M., and Oswald, Andrew J. (2005, June). How does marriage affect physical and psychological health? A survey of the

longitudinal evidence. IZA Discussion Paper No. 1619. Available at SSRN: https://ssrn.com/abstract=735205

6. Williams, K. (2003). Has the future of marriage arrived? A contemporary examination of gender, marriage, and psychological well-being. *Journal of Health and Social Behavior* 44: 470–487. doi:10.2307/1519794

7. Powdthavee, Nattavudh. (2009, August 14). I can't smile without you: Spousal correlation in life satisfaction. *Journal of Economic Psychology* 30(4): 675–689. Available at SSRN: https://ssrn.com/abstract=1452651

8. Uğur, Erol. (2016). Marital attitudes as a mediator on the relationship between respect toward partner and subjective happiness. *Journal of Family Counseling and Education* 1: 25–30.

9. Barnes, Z. (2015, October 15). Under 30 and divorced: 5 women share what it's like. *Women's Health*. https://www.womenshealthmag.com/relationships/a19918885/under-30-divorced/

10. Chen, Shuai, and van Ours, Jan. (2017, September 21). Subjective well-being and partnership dynamics: Are same-sex relationships different? Center Discussion Paper Series No. 2017-041. Available at SSRN: https://ssrn.com/abstract=3040596 or http://dx.doi.org/10.2139/ssrn.3040596

11. Grillo, E. (2022, July 1). Falling fast, then fiancés for seven years. *New York Times*. https://www.nytimes.com/2022/07/01/style/luke-kalat-justin-conner-wedding.html

12. Carmel, J. (2022, July 1). On their first date, plunging into a relationship. *New York Times*. https://www.nytimes.com/2022/07/01/style/stephanie-schulter-halle-bauer-wedding.html

13. Haring-Hidore, M., Stock, W. A., Okun, M. A., and Witter, R. A. (1985). Marital status and subjective well-being: A research synthesis. *Journal of Marriage and the Family* 47, 947–953.

14. Coombs, R. H. (1991). Marital status and personal well-being: A literature review. *Family Relations* 40: 97–102. doi:10.2307/585665

15. Antonucci, T. C., and Akiyama, H. (1987). An examination of sex differences in social support among older men and women. *Sex Roles* 17: 737–749. doi:10.1007/BF00287685

16. Gurung, R. A. R., Taylor, S. E., and Seeman, T. E. (2003). Accounting for changes in social support among married older adults: Insights from the MacArthur Studies of Successful Aging. *Psychology and Aging* 18: 487–496. doi:10.1037/0882-7974.18.3.487

17. Proulx, C. M., Helms, H. M., and Buehler, C. (2007). Marital quality and personal well-being: A metaanalysis. *Journal of Marriage and Family* 69: 576–593. doi:10.1111/j.1741-3737.2007.00393.x

18. Jung, H. (2023, January 27). Opinion | Women in South Korea are on strike against being "baby-making machines." *New York Times.* https://www.nytimes.com/2023/01/27/opinion/south-korea-fertility-rate-feminism.html

19. Nelson-Coffey, S. K. (2018). Married . . . with children: The science of well-being in marriage and family life. In: E. Diener, S. Oishi, and L. Tay (eds.), *Handbook of well-being.* Salt Lake City, UT: DEF Publishers. doi: nobascholar.com

20. Stravrova, Olga. (2019). Having a happy spouse is associated with lowered risk of mortality. *Psychological Science* 30(5): 798–803. https://www.psychologicalscience.org/news/releases/happy-spouses-longer-lives.html 2019

21. Borau, Sylvie, Couprie, Hélène, and Hopfensitz, Astrid. (2022). The prosociality of married people: Evidence from a large multinational sample. Available at SSRN: https://ssrn.com/abstract=4041294 or http://dx.doi.org/10.2139/ssrn.4041294

22. Easterlin, Richard A. (2003, September 16). Explaining happiness. Proceedings of the National Academy of Sciences of the United States of America. 100(19): 11176–11183. https://www.ncbi.nlm.nih.gov/pmc/articles/PMC196947/

23. Gardiner, Aidan. (2019, September 5). I put my own life on hold: the pain and joy of caring for parents. *New York Times.* https://www.nytimes.com/2019/09/05/reader-center/taking-care-of-elderly-relatives.html?smid=nytcore-ios-share

24. Cohen, R. (2020, October 20). What if friendship, not marriage, was at the center of life? *The Atlantic.* https://www.theatlantic.com/family/archive/2020/10/people-who-prioritize-friendship-over-romance/616779/

25. Patton, S. (2013, March 29). Letter to the Editor: Advice for the young women of Princeton: The daughters I never had. *Daily Princetonian.* http://dailyprincetonian.com/opinion/2013/03/letter-to-the-editor-advice-for-the-young-women-of-princeton-the-daughters-i-never-had/

26. Stone, P. (2007). Opting out? *Why women really quit careers and head home.* Berkeley and Los Angeles: University of California Press, p. 61.

27. Hitsch, Guenter J., Hortacsu, Ali, and Ariely, Dan. (2008, March 1). Matching and sorting in online dating. Available at SSRN: https://ssrn.com/abstract=1113243 or http://dx.doi.org/10.2139/ssrn.1113243

28. Bursztyn, Leonardo, Fujiwara, Thomas, and Pallais, Amanda. (2017). "Acting wife": Marriage market incentives and labor market investments. *American Economic Review* 107(11): 3288–3319.

29. Dhar, Diva. (2023). Indian matchmaking: Are working women penalized in the marriage market? 1. Available at SSRN: https://ssrn.com/abstract=4479657 or http://dx.doi.org/10.2139/ssrn.4479657

30. Hitsch, Guenter J., Hortacsu, Ali, and Ariely, Dan. (2008, March 1). Matching and sorting in online dating. Available at SSRN: https://ssrn.com/abstract=1113243 or http://dx.doi.org/10.2139/ssrn.1113243

31. Lippmann, Quentin, and Surana, Khushboo. (2022, November). The hierarchy of partner preferences. Available at SSRN: https://ssrn.com/abstract=4272900 or http://dx.doi.org/10.2139/ssrn.4272900

32. Klasne, Catherine. (2011, April). Wealth: Its joys and its discontents— The Boston College Survey. *The Atlantic.* Secret fears of the super-rich. https://www.uww-adr.com/blog/wealth-its-joys-and-its-discontents-the-boston-college-survey

33. Murphy, C. (2015, June 2). Interfaith marriage is common in U.S., particularly among the recently wed. Pew Research Center. https://www.pewresearch.org/short-reads/2015/06/02/interfaith-marriage/

34. Farooqi, M. (2021, April 16). I tried to filter him out. *New York Times.* https://www.nytimes.com/2021/04/16/style/modern-love-muslim-hindu-dating.html

35. Hirschel, Linda. (2019, April 4). Arranged my kids' Jewish marriages: Here's what happened. Kveller. https://www.kveller.com/i-arranged-my-kids-jewish-marriages-heres-what-.happened/

36. Reyes, N. (2022, May 27). Her mother (and his father) knew best. *New York Times.* https://www.nytimes.com/2022/05/27/style/mina-shankar-aditya-radhakrishnan-wedding.html

37. Cable News Network (2012). Arranged marriage, American-style. https://www.cnn.com/2012/05/16/living/arranged-marriage/index.html (accessed 22 October 2023).

38. Gui, Tianhan. (2021, October 14). Coping with parental pressure to get married: Perspective from Chinese "leftover women." Available

at SSRN: https://ssrn.com/abstract=3954642 or http://dx.doi.org/10.2139/ssrn.3954642

39. Vogl, Tom. (2012, August). Marriage institutions and sibling competition: Evidence from South Asia. NBER Working Paper No. w18319. Available at SSRN: https://ssrn.com/abstract=2131689

40. Mathur, Divya. (2007, November 7). What's love got to do with it? Parental involvement and spouse choice in urban India. Available at SSRN: https://ssrn.com/abstract=1655998 or http://dx.doi.org/10.2139/ssrn.1655998

41. Huang, Fali, Jin, Ginger Zhe, and Xu, Lixin Colin. (2015, February 22). Love, money, and old age support: Does parental matchmaking matter? Available at SSRN: https://ssrn.com/abstract=2568471 or http://dx.doi.org/10.2139/ssrn.2568471

42. Wilson, Nicholas. (2022). Child marriage bans and female schooling and labor market outcomes: Evidence from natural experiments in 17 low- and middle-income countries. *American Economic Journal: Economic Policy* 14(3): 449–477. doi:10.1257/pol.20200008

43. Becker, Charles Maxwell, and Steiner, Susan. (2018, June 29). How forced marriages differ: Evidence on assortative mating in Kyrgyzstani marriages. University of Central Asia—Institute of Public Policy and Administration (IPPA) Working Paper No. 45. Available at SSRN: https://ssrn.com/abstract=3807822 or http://dx.doi.org/10.2139/ssrn.3807822

44. Tierce, M. (2021, December 2). The abortion I didn't have. *New York Times*. https://www.nytimes.com/2021/12/02/magazine/abortion-parent-mother-child.html

45. Abramitzky, Ran, Delavande, Adeline, and Vasconcelos, Luis. (2011, July). Marrying up: The role of sex ratio in assortative matching. *American Economic Journal: Applied Economics* 3(3): 124–157.

46. Hardin, William G., Hu, Mingzhi, and Lin, Zhenguo. (2020, November 24). It's a buy! Culture, wealth, real estate and consumption in China. Available at SSRN: https://ssrn.com/abstract=3746080 or http://dx.doi.org/10.2139/ssrn.3746080

47. Autor, David, Dorn, David, and Hanson, Gordon. (2019). When work disappears: Manufacturing decline and the falling marriage market value of young men. *American Economic Review: Insights* 1(2): 161–178.

48. Weaver, Jeffrey, and Chiplunkar, Gaurav. (2022). Marriage markets and the rise of dowry in India. Available at SSRN: https://ssrn.com/abstract=4092332 or http://dx.doi.org/10.2139/ssrn.4092332

49. Bhat, Bilal, and Thakur, Sounak. (2022, September 9). The intergenerational effects of marital transfers: Evidence from India. Available at SSRN: https://ssrn.com/abstract=4217995 or http://dx.doi.org/10.2139/ssrn.4217995

50. Edin, K., and Kefalas, M. (2005). *Promises I can keep: Why poor women put motherhood before marriage.* Berkeley and Los Angeles: University of California Press, p. 203.

51. Chen, V. (2017, August 20). America, home of the transactional marriage. *The Atlantic.* https://www.theatlantic.com/business/archive/2017/08/marriage-rates-education/536913/

52. Butler, Alexander W., Spyridopoulos, Ioannis, Tellez, Yessenia, and Xu, Billy. (2023, July 1). Financial breakups. Available at SSRN: https://ssrn.com/abstract=4497450 or http://dx.doi.org/10.2139/ssrn.4497450

53. Cesarini, David, Lindqvist, Erik, Ostling, Robert, and Terskaya, Anastasia. (2023, March). Fortunate families? The effects of wealth on marriage and fertility. NBER Working Paper No. w31039. Available at SSRN: https://ssrn.com/abstract=4393380 or http://dx.doi.org/10.2139/ssrn.4393380

54. Edin, K., and Nelson, T. (2013). *Doing the best I can: Fatherhood in the inner city.* Berkeley and Los Angeles: University of California Press, p. 205.

55. Melissa S. Kearney, and Riley Wilson. (2018). Male earnings, marriageable men, and nonmarital fertility: Evidence from the fracking boom. *The Review of Economics and Statistics* 100(4): 678–690.

56. Finkel, E. (2019, January 8). Educated Americans paved the way for divorce—Then embraced marriage. *The Atlantic.* https://www.theatlantic.com/family/archive/2019/01/education-divide-marriage/579688/

57. Edin, K., and Nelson, T. (2013). *Doing the best I can: Fatherhood in the inner city.* Berkeley and Los Angeles: University of California Press. pp. 222–223.

58. Goldin, Claudia, and Katz, Lawrence F. (2002). The power of the pill: Oral contraceptives and women's career and marriage decisions. *Journal of Political Economy* 110(4): 730–770.

59. Gershoni, Naomi, and Low, Corinne. (2021). Older yet fairer: How extended reproductive time horizons reshaped marriage patterns in Israel. *American Economic Journal: Applied Economics* 13(1): 198–234. doi:10.1257/app.20180780

60. Grover, Shawn, and Helliwell, John F. (2014, December). How's life at home? New evidence on marriage and the set point for happiness. NBER Working Paper No. w20794. Available at SSRN: https://ssrn.com/abstract=2545179

61. Tierney, J., and Baumeister, R. (2020, January 9). How negativity can kill a relationship. *The Atlantic.* https://www.theatlantic.com/family/archive/2020/01/negativity-can-ruin-relationships/604597/

62. Smith, E. (2014, June 12). The secret to love is just kindness. *The Atlantic.* https://www.theatlantic.com/health/archive/2014/06/happily-ever-after/372573/

63. Cohen, R. (2021, September 13). The secret to a fight-free relationship. *The Atlantic.* https://www.theatlantic.com/family/archive/2021/09/delaying-conflict-better-venting-relationships-scheduled-disagreement/620057/

64. Nicolaus, P. (2021, June 21). The most effective way to thank your significant other. *The Atlantic.* https://www.theatlantic.com/family/archive/2021/06/thank-your-partner-gratitude-more/619233/

65. Cohen, R. (2021, September 13). The secret to a fight-free relationship. *The Atlantic.* https://www.theatlantic.com/family/archive/2021/09/delaying-conflict-better-venting-relationships-scheduled-disagreement/620057/

66. Wasik, J. (2022, April 15). Their cheating heart, your damaged retirement plan. *New York Times.* https://www.nytimes.com/2022/04/15/business/money-secrets-cheating-retirement.html

67. Garbinsky, Emily N., and Gladstone, Joe J. (2018, December 12). The consumption consequences of couples pooling finances. https://doi.org/10.1002/jcpy.1083 Journal of Consumer Psychology

68. Carpenter, J. (2022, December 5). Couples who combine finances are happier. So why don't more do it? *Wall Street Journal.* https://www.wsj.com/articles/couples-who-combine-finances-are-happier-so-why-dont-more-do-it-11670174525

69. Sherman, R. (2017). *Uneasy street: The anxieties of affluence.* Princeton, NJ: Princeton University Press, pp. 155–156.

70. Jackson, N. (2022, August 10). Opinion | What does "vex money" do to love? *New York Times.* https://www.nytimes.com/2022/08/10/opinion/vex-money-afro-caribbean-women.html

71. Dokko, Jane, Geng Li, and Jessica Hayes. (2015, April 29). Credit scores and committed relationships. FEDS Working Paper No. 2015-081.

Available at SSRN: http://ssrn.com/abstract=2667158 or http://dx .doi.org/10.2139/ssrn.2667158.

72. Plantinga, Auke, and DeBondt, Werner F.M. (2018, September 30). Growing apart in marriage, or coming together? The structure and dynamics of differences in risk aversion between partners. 2019 Academic Research Colloquium for Financial Planning and Related Disciplines. Available at SSRN: https://ssrn.com/abstract=3257948

73. Hsee, Christopher K., and Hastie, Reid. (2006). Decision and experience: Why don't we choose what makes us happy? *Trends in Cognitive Sciences*. Available at SSRN: https://ssrn.com/abstract=929914

74. Saxey, Matthew T. LeBaron-Black, Ashley B., and Curran, Melissa A. (2022). The sooner, the better? Couples' first financial discussion, relationship quality, and financial conflict in emerging adulthood. *Journal of Financial Therapy* 13(1), 1–19. https://doi.org/ 10.4148/1944-9771.1299

75. Ahn, So Yoon, and Koh, Yu Kyung. (2022, March 1). Spousal bargaining power and consumption of married couples in the US: Evidence from scanner data. Available at SSRN: https://ssrn.com/ abstract=4073740 or http://dx.doi.org/10.2139/ssrn.4073740

76. Sherman, Rachel. *Uneasy street: The anxieties of affluence*. Princeton, NJ: Princeton University Press. Kindle Edition, pp. 84–85.

77. White, G. (2015, June, 16). Millennials: Let's make marriage less oppressive. *The Atlantic*. https://www.theatlantic.com/business/ archive/2015/06/millennials-delaying-marriage-money-weddings/ 395870/

78. Kitchener, C. (2018, March 23). Marriage proposals are stupid. *The Atlantic*. https://www.theatlantic.com/family/archive/2018/03/ marriage-proposals-are-stupid/556403/

79. Hennecke, Juliane, and Pape, Astrid. (2020). Suddenly a stay-at-home dad? Short- and long-term consequences of fathers' job loss on time investment in the household. IZA Discussion Paper No. 13866, Available at SSRN: https://ssrn.com/abstract=3730464

80. Sherman, R. (2017). *Uneasy street: The anxieties of affluence*. Princeton, NJ: Princeton University Press, pp. 65–66.

81. Pierce, Lamar, Dahl, Michael S., and Nielsen, Jimmi. (2012, November 15). In sickness and in wealth: Psychological and sexual costs of income comparison in marriage. Available at SSRN: https://ssrn .com/abstract=2185944or http://dx.doi.org/10.2139/ssrn.2185944

82. Bertrand, Marianne, Pan, Jessica, and Kamenica, Emir. (2013, May). Gender identity and relative income within households. Twitter-LinkedIn. Email Working Paper 19023. doi:10.3386/w19023

83. Miller, C. (2018, July 17). When wives earn more than husbands, neither partner likes to admit it. *New York Times.* https://www.nytimes.com/2018/07/17/upshot/when-wives-earn-more-than-husbands-neither-like-to-admit-it.html

84. Ibid.

85. Sherman, R. (2017). *Uneasy street: The anxieties of affluence.* Princeton, NJ: Princeton University Press, p. 192.

86. Cooper, M. (2014). *Cut adrift: Families in insecure times.* Berkeley and Los Angeles: University of California Press, p. 74.

87. Ke, Da. (2018, August 4). Who wears the pants? Gender identity norms and intra-household financial decision making. Available at SSRN: https://ssrn.com/abstract=2909720 or http://dx.doi.org/10.2139/ssrn.2909720.

88. Sherman, R. (2017). *Uneasy street: The anxieties of affluence.* Princeton, NJ: Princeton University Press, p. 193.

89. https://www.nytimes.com/2020/10/24/business/millennial-personal-finance.html?searchResultPosition=24

90. Cooper, M. (2014). *Cut adrift: Families in insecure times.* Berkeley and Los Angeles: University of California Press, p. 12.

91. Lee, K. S., and Ono, H. (2012). Marriage, cohabitation, and happiness: A cross-national analysis of 27 countries. *Journal of Marriage and Family* 74, 953–972. doi:10.1111/j.1741-3737.2012.01001.x

92. Balsam, K. F., Beauchaine, T. P., Rothblum, E. D., and Solomon, S. E. (2008). Three-year follow-up of same-sex couples who had civil unions in Vermont, same-sex couples not in civil unions, and heterosexual married couples. *Developmental Psychology* 44: 102–116. doi:10.1037/0012-1649.44.1.102

93. Catron, M. (2019, July 2). What you lose when you gain a spouse. *The Atlantic.* https://www.theatlantic.com/family/archive/2019/07/case-against-marriage/591973/

94. Chen, Shuai, and van Ours, Jan. (2017, September 21). Subjective well-being and partnership dynamics: Are same-sex relationships different? CentER Discussion Paper Series No. 2017-041. Available at SSRN: https://ssrn.com/abstract=3040596 or http://dx.doi.org/10.2139/ssrn.3040596

95. Wilcox, W., and DeRose, L. (2017), March 27. In Europe, cohabitation is stable . . . right? *Brookings*. https://www.brookings.edu/articles/in-europe-cohabitation-is-stable-right/

96. Stanley, Scott, and Rhoades, Galena. (2023, April 26). What's the plan? Cohabitation, engagement, and divorce. Institute for Family Studies. https://ifstudies.org/blog/whats-the-plan-cohabitation-engagement-and-divorce

Chapter 6: Widowhood and Divorce

1. Rollin, B. (2022, November 27). Opinion | How to talk to a widow. *New York Times*. https://www.nytimes.com/2022/11/27/opinion/widows-mental-health.html

2. Bosman, Julie. (2021). "The other half of my soul": Widows of Covid-19 bond over sudden loss. *New York Times*. Men have died of the coronavirus in larger numbers than women, leaving untold thousands of spouses suddenly alone. Some have turned to bereavement groups on Facebook. https://www.nytimes.com/2020/12/31/us/covid-widows-deaths.html?action=click&module=Top%20Stories&pgtype=Homepage

3. Lee, Gary R., DeMaris, Alfred, Bavin, Stefoni, and Sullivan, Rachel. (2001, January 1). Gender differences in the depressive effect of widowhood in later life. *The Journals of Gerontology: Series B* 56(1): S56–S61. https://doi.org/10.1093/geronb/56.1.S56

4. Elwert, Felix, and Christakis, Nicholas A. (2008, November). The effect of widowhood on mortality by the causes of death of both spouses. *American Journal of Public Health* 98(11): 2092–2098. doi:10.2105/AJPH.2007.114348. PMC 2636447. PMID 18511733.

5. Bilanow, T. (2010, June 14). Life as a widow or widower. *New York Times*. https://archive.nytimes.com/well.blogs.nytimes.com/2010/06/14/life-as-a-widow-or-widower/

6. Roark, A. (2009, July 13). With friends aplenty, many widows choose singlehood. *New York Times*. https://archive.nytimes.com/newoldage.blogs.nytimes.com/2009/07/13/with-friends-aplenty-many-widows-choose-singlehood/

7. Elwert, Felix, and Christakis, Nicholas A. (2008, November). The effect of widowhood on mortality by the causes of death of both spouses. *American Journal of Public Health* 98(11): 2092–2098. doi:10.2105/AJPH.2007.114348. PMC 2636447. PMID 18511733.

8. Hurd, Michael D., and Wise, David A. (1987, July). The wealth and poverty of widows: Assets before and after the husband's death. NBER Working Paper No. w2325. Available at SSRN: https://ssrn .com/abstract=227279

9. LaGorce, T. (2018, November 17). Widows are faring better financially. Here's why. *New York Times*. https://www.nytimes.com/2018/ 11/17/business/widows-financial-independence.html

10. Munnell, Alicia Haydock, Sanzenbacher, Geoffrey T., and Zulkarnain, Alice. (2018, May). What factors explain the decline in widows' poverty? CRR WP 2018-4. file:///C:/Users/Meir%20Downloads/ PDF%20datastream.pdf

11. Shahar, D., R., Schultz, R., Shahar, A., and Wing, R. R. (2001, May). The effect of widowhood on weight change, dietary intake, and eating behavior in the elderly population. *Journal of Aging and Health* 13(2): 189–199. https://doi.org/10.1177/089826430101300202

12. Nierenberg, A. (2019, October 28). For many widows, the hardest part is mealtime. *New York Times*. https://www.nytimes.com/2019/ 10/28/dining/widows-cooking-grief.html

13. Adena, Maja, Hamermesh, Daniel, Myck, Michal, and Oczkowska, Monika. (2023). Home alone: Widows' well-being and time. IZA Discussion Paper No. 14881. Available at SSRN: https://ssrn.com/ abstract=4326605 or http://dx.doi.org/10.2139/ssrn.4326605

14. Hahn, Elizabeth A., Cichy, Kelly E., Almeida, David M., and Haley, William E. (2011). Time use and well-being in older widows: Adaptation and resilience. *Journal of Women Aging* 23(2): 149–159. doi:10 .1080/08952841.2011.561139 PMCID: PMC3485066 NIHMSID: NIHMS370126 PMID: 21534105

15. Bilanow, T. (2010, June 14). Life as a widow or widower. *New York Times*. https://archive.nytimes.com/well.blogs.nytimes.com/2010/ 06/14/life-as-a-widow-or-widower/

16. Jones, Honor. (2021, December 28). How I demolished my life: A home-improvement story. *The Atlantic*. https://www.theatlantic .com/family/archive/2021/12/divorce-parenting/621054/

17. Davis Alyssa and Jones. M Jefferey (2012, April 20) Separation, Divorce Linked to Sharply Lower Well-Being. Married American have highest well-being. https://news.gallup.com/poll/154001separation-divorce-linked-sharply-lower-wellbeing.aspx

18. Gardner, Jonathan, and Oswald, Andrew J. (2005, September). Do divorcing couples become happier by breaking up? IZA Discussion Paper No. 1788. Available at SSRN: https://ssrn.com/ abstract=826447

19. Cavapozzi Danilo, Fiore Simona, Pasini Giacomo, Divorce and well-being. Disentangling the role of stress and socio economic status, volume 16, 2020, 100212, ISSN 2212-828x, https://doi.org/10.1016/j.jeoa.2019.100212.

20. Warren, T. (2022, June 5). Opinion | I married the wrong person, and I'm so glad I did. *New York Times*. https://www.nytimes.com/2022/06/05/opinion/marriage-satisfaction-love.html hl

21. Butcher, Amy. (2021, September 30). I know all too well how a lovely relationship can descend into abuse. *New York Times*. https://www.nytimes.com/2021/09/30/opinion/gabby-petito-domestic-abuse.html

22. Camp, Anna Rachel. (2022, December). From experiencing abuse to seeking protection: Examining the shame of intimate partner violence. 13 UC Irvine L. Rev. 103. Available at SSRN: https://ssrn.com/abstract=4323805

23. Arenas-Arroyo, Esther, Fernández-Kranz, Daniel, and Nollenberger, Natalia. (2023). Can't leave you now! Intimate partner violence under forced coexistence and economic uncertainty. IZA Discussion Paper No. 13570. Available at SSRN: https://ssrn.com/abstract=3669499

24. Folke, Olle, and Rickne, Johanna. (2020). All the single ladies: Job promotions and the durability of marriage. *American Economic Journal: Applied Economics* 12(1): 260–287. https://doi.org/10.1257/app.20180435 260

25. Dunn, J. (2020, May 18). The man who coaches husbands on how to avoid divorce. *New York Times*. https://www.nytimes.com/2020/05/18/parenting/marriage-invisible-labor-coach.html

26. Whitesides, J. (2017, February 7). From disputes to a breakup: Wounds still raw after U.S. election. *Reuters*. https://www.reuters.com/article/us-usa-trump-relationships-insight-idUSKBN15M13L

27. Guven, Cahit, Senik, Claudia, and Stichnoth, Holger. (2010). You can't be happier than your wife: Happiness gaps and divorce. ZEW—Centre for European Economic Research Discussion Paper No. 10-007. Available at SSRN: https://ssrn.com/abstract=1554352 or http://dx.doi.org/10.2139/ssrn.1554352

28. Copaken, D. (2019, February 12). The DIY divorce. *The Atlantic*. https://www.theatlantic.com/family/archive/2019/02/how-i-got-divorced-without-hiring-lawyer/582508/

29. Wakabayashi, D. (2021, August 20). Who gets the L.L.C.? Inside a Silicon Valley billionaire's divorce. *New York Times*. https://www.

nytimes.com/2021/08/20/technology/Scott-Hassan-Allison-Huynh-divorce.html

30. Cunha, D. (2016, April 28). The divorce gap. *The Atlantic*. https://www.theatlantic.com/business/archive/2016/04/the-divorce-gap/480333/

31. Span, Paula. (2021, December 26). Why older women face greater financial hardship than older men. In a troubling picture, American women are looking at a rockier road to secure retirement than their male counterparts. *New York Times*. https://www.nytimes.com/2021/12/26/health/older-women-financial-hardship-retirement.html?campaign_id=12&emc=edit_my_20211227&instance_id=48810&nl=your-money&regi_id=39889985&segment_id=78036&te=1&user_id=b3f8e7355159ac19efea070b3d343015

32. Statman, Meir. (2020, Winter). Well-being advisers, *The Journal of Wealth Management Winter* 23 (Supplement 1): 2–44, p. 2. doi: https://doi.org/10.3905/jwm.23.s1.00

33. Muñoz, N. (2021, March 5). My two-house, duffel-bag life. *New York Times*. https://www.nytimes.com/2021/03/05/style/modern-love-my-two-house-duffle-bag-life.html

34. Lilienfeld, H. A., and Scott, O. (2023). Is divorce bad for children? *Scientific American*. doi:10.1038/scientificamericanmind0313-68

35. Ibid.

36. Maynard, Joyce. (2021, July 5). A "broken home" didn't break me, or my kids. *New York Times*. Ms. Maynard's newest novel, *Count the Ways*—the story of a marriage and a divorce, and the children who survived it—will be published this month. https://www.nytimes.com/2021/07/05/opinion/divorce-children.html?smid=em-share

Chapter 7: Parents and children

1. Smith, Z. (2013, January 10). Joy. *The New York Review*. https://www.nybooks.com/articles/2013/01/10/joy/#:~:text=Occasionally%20percent20the%20percent20child%20percent2C%20percent-20too%20percent2C%20percent20is,way%20percent20to%20per-cent20live%20percent20with%20percent20daily

2. Yoon, J. (2022, October 30). "How can I explain t in words?": A mother mourns the loss of her daughter. *New York Times*. https://www.nytimes.com/2022/10/30/world/asia/victim-mother-mourns-daughter.html

3. Myrskylä, Mikko, and Margolis, Rachel. (2014, October). Happiness: Before and after the kids. *Demography* 51(5): 1843–1966. doi: 10.1007/s13524-014-0321-x

4. Stanford, J. (2016, August 14). Parenting study misses the point. *HuffPost*. https://www.huffpost.com/entry/parenting-study-misses-th_b_7988462

5. Statman, Meir. (2020, Winter). Well-being advisers. *The Journal of Wealth Management* Winter 23 (Supplement 1): 2–44, p. 2. doi: https://doi.org/10.3905/jwm.23.s1.

6. Grose, J. (2020, December 30). Alone in a fancy hotel bathroom. *New York Times*. https://www.nytimes.com/2020/12/30/parenting/parents-fantasy-vacations.html

7. Herbst, Chris M., and Ifcher, John. (2016). The increasing happiness of US parents. *Review of Economics of the Household* 14: 529–551.

8. Basu, Tanya. (2014, May 8). Does having kids make parents happy after all? New research overturns the decades-old belief that having children is a downer. Business. *The Atlantic*. https://www.theatlantic.com/business/archive/2014/05/do-kids-make-parents-happy-after-all/361894/

9. Nelson, S. Katherine, Kushlev, Kostadin, English, Tammy, Dunn, Elizabeth W., and Lyubomirsky, Sonja. (2013, January 1). In defense of parenthood: Children are associated with more joy than misery. *PubMed* 24(1): 3–19. https://doi.org/10.1177/0956797612447798

10. Sawhill, I., Welch, M., and Miller, C. (2022, August 30). It's getting more expensive to raise children. And government isn't doing much to help. Brookings. https://www.brookings.edu/articles/its-getting-more-expensive-to-raise-children-and-government-isnt-doing-much-to-help/

11. Ibid.

12. Timsit, A. (2021, November 24). More Americans say they're not planning to have a child, new poll says, as U.S. birthrate declines. *Washington Post*. https://www.washingtonpost.com/nation/2021/11/21/americans-childless-pew-us-population/

13. Fokkema, T., Esveldt, I. (2008). Motivation to have children in Europe. In: C. Höhn, D. Avramov, and I. E. Kotowska (eds). *People, population change and policies: European studies of population* 16(1). Springer, Dordrecht. https://doi.org/10.1007/978-1-4020-6609-2_7

14. Koropeckyj-Cox, T., and Pendell, G. (2007). The gender gap in attitudes about childlessness in the United States. *Journal of*

Marriage and Family 69(4), 899–915. https://doi.org/10.1111/j
.1741-3737.2007.00420.x

15. Zoepf, Katherine. (2019, August 27). The unspeakable cost of parenthood money struggles are often kept quiet, but many American families are living on the edge. *New York Times*. Updated September 5, 2019. https://www.nytimes.com/2019/08/27/parenting/parents-money-stress.html

16. Wakabayashi, D., and Frenkel, S. (2020, September 5). Parents got more time off. Then the backlash started. *New York Times*. https://www.nytimes.com/2020/09/05/technology/parents-time-off-backlash.html

17. Casali, M. (2022, December 10). The connection between puberty and mental health. *Turnbridge*. https://www.turnbridge.com/news-events/uncategorized/puberty-and-mental-health/

18. Sommer, Constance. (2021, May 6). Tiffany Lee and her son, Bo Deal, a high school freshman in Metter, Ga., had conflicts over her house rules in the pandemic. *New York Times*. https://www.nytimes.com/2021/05/06/well/family/parents-teenagers-staying-at-home-coronavirus-pandemic.html

19. Banerjee, Sudipto. (2015, June 1). Intra-family cash transfers in older American households. EBRI Issue Brief, Number 415 (June 2015). Available at SSRN: http://ssrn.com/abstract=2620835

20. The Economist (2023). The bank of mum and dad as young adults' social insurance. https://www.economist.com/graphic-detail/2020/07/13/the-bank-of-mum-and-dad-as-young-adults-social-insurance

21. Eisenberg, Richard. (2018, October 2). Parents support to adult kids: A stunning $500 billion a year—Are Boomers and Gen Xers harming their retirement due to their generosity? Next Avenue. https://www.nextavenue.org/parents-support-adult-kids/

22. Statman, Meir. (2020, Winter). Well-being advisers. *The Journal of Wealth Management* Winter 23 (Supplement 1): 2–44, p. 2. doi: https://doi.org/10.3905/jwm.23.s1.

23. Schwarze, Johannes, and Winkelmann, Rainer. (2005, February). What can happiness research tell us about altruism? Evidence from the German Socio-Economic Panel. IZA Discussion Paper No. 1487. Available at SSRN: https://ssrn.com/abstract=670165

24. Murphy, S. (2023, September 2). When financial independence isn't always the goal. *New York Times*. https://www.nytimes.com/2023/09/02/business/iranian-americans-education-money.html

25. Calarco, J. M. (2018, June 1). Why rich kids are so good at the Marshmallow Test. *The Atlantic*. https://www.theatlantic.com/family/archive/2018/06/marshmallow-test/561779/

26. Fingerman, Karen L., Cheng, Yen-Pi, Wesselmann, Eric D., Zarit, Steven, Furstenberg, Frank, and Birditt, Kira S. (2012, August). Helicopter parents and landing pad kids: Intense parental support of grown children. *Journal of Marriage and Family* 74(4): 880–896. https://www.ncbi.nlm.nih.gov/pmc/articles/PMC4553417/

27. Eisen, B., and Tergesen, A. (2021, July 2). Older Americans stockpiled a record $35 trillion. The time has come to give it away. *Wall Street Journal*. https://www.wsj.com/articles/older-americans-35-trillion-wealth-giving-away-heirs-philanthropy-11625234216

28. Corrigan, K. (2021, September 5). Opinion | How to let go of your irreplaceable, unstoppable daughter. *New York Times*. https://www.nytimes.com/2021/09/05/opinion/parenting-college-empty-nest-pandemic.html

29. Fingerman, Karen L., Cheng, Yen-Pi, Wesselmann, Eric D., Zarit, Steven, Furstenberg, Frank, and Birditt, Kira S. (2012, August). Helicopter parents and landing pad kids: Intense parental support of grown children. *Journal of Marriage and Family* 74(4): 880–896. https://www.ncbi.nlm.nih.gov/pmc/articles/PMC4553417/

30. Gottlieb, Lori. (2020, December 7). Dear therapist: Should I give my adult children more money? They're both angry at me, and I want to mend our relationship. *The Atlantic*. https://www.theatlantic.com/family/archive/2020/12/dear-therapist-should-i-financially-support-my-struggling-children/617296/

31. Lee, Samuel, and Petra Persson. (2016, September). Financing from family and friends, *The Review of Financial Studies* 29(9): 2341–2386. https://doi.org/10.1093/rfs/hhw031 https://www.economist.com/graphic-detail/2020/07/13/the-bank-of-mum-and-dad-as-young-adults-socialinsurance

32. Jennie Green, Jennie. (2003, July 20). Leaning on their parents, again. *New York Times*, Business Day. http://www.nytimes.com/2003/07/20/business/leaning-on-their-parents -again.html?pagewanted=all

33. Michael Luo, Michael. (2010, January 30). Jobless turn to family for help. *New York Times*, US section. http://www.nytimes.com/2010/01/30/us/30borrow.html.

34. Blanchflower, David G., and Clark, Andrew Eric. (2019, February). Children, unhappiness and family finances: Evidence from one million Europeans. NBER Working Paper No. w25597. Available at SSRN: https://ssrn.com/abstract=3341258

35. Cetre, Sophie, Clark, Andrew, and Senik, Claudia. (2016, August). Happy people have children: Choice and self-selection into parenthood. *European Journal of Population* 32(3): 445–473. doi: 10.1007/s10680-016-9389-x. Epub 2016 Aug 22. PMID: 28713186; PMCID: PMC5505668.

36. Mr. Money Mustache. (2016). The "everybody seems wealthy" illusion—Is it really just all fueled by debt? https://forum.mrmoneymustache.com/welcome-to-the-forum/the-'everybody-seems-wealthy'-illusion-is-it-really-just-all-fueled-by-debt/

37. Myerson, A. R. (1997, May 18). Daughters do battle with a corporate King Lear. *New York Times.* https://www.nytimes.com/1997/05/18/business/daughters-do-battle-with-a-corporate-king-lear.html

38. Wood, Graeme. (2011, April). Secret fears of the super-rich. *The Atlantic.* https://www.theatlantic.com/magazine/archive/2011/04/secret-fears-of-the-super-rich/308419/

39. Wood, G. (2011, February 24). Secret fears of the super-rich. *The Atlantic.* https://www.theatlantic.com/magazine/archive/2011/04/secret-fears-of-the-super-rich/308419/

40. Nelson-Coffey, S. Katherine, Killingsworth, Matthew, Layous, Kristin, Cole, Steve W., and Lyubomirsky, Sonja. (2019, September). Parenthood is associated with greater well-being for fathers than mothers. *Personality and Social Psychology Bulletin* 45(9): 1378–1390. doi:10.1177/0146167219829174.

41. Van Kessel, P., Hughes, A., and Walker, K. (2023, November 20). The meaning of life: 100 quotes from Americans on what keeps them going. *Pew Research Center.* https://www.pewresearch.org/religion/interactives/what-keeps-us-going/

42. Machin, A. (2020, April 15). How men's bodies change when they become fathers. *New York Times.* https://www.nytimes.com/2020/04/15/parenting/baby/fatherhood-mens-bodies.html

43. Massenkoff, Maxim, and Rose, Evan K. (2022, August 22). Family formation and crime. University of Chicago, Becker Friedman Institute for Economics Working Paper No. 110, 2022. Available at SSRN: https://ssrn.com/abstract=4198344 or http://dx.doi.org/10.2139/ssrn.4198344

44. Zimmer, C. (2016, April 8). Fathered by the mailman? It's mostly an urban legend. *New York Times.* https://www.nytimes.com/2016/

04/12/science/extra-marital-paternity-less-common-than-assumed-scientists-find.html

45. Padawer, R. (2009, November 17). Who knew I was not the father? *New York Times.* https://www.nytimes.com/2009/11/22/magazine/22Paternity-t.html

46. Ibid.

47. Statman, Meir. (2020, Winter). Well-being advisers. *The Journal of Wealth Management Winter* 23 (Supplement 1): 2–44, p. 2. doi: https://doi.org/10.3905/jwm.23.s1.002

48. Peterson, R. (2017, August 25). "I'm proud of my child because. . . ." *One Good Thing.* https://onegoodthingteach.wordpress.com/2017/08/24/im-proud-of-my-child-because/

49. Chaplin, L. N. (2022, April 8). What I wish I had known about my mother. *Harvard Business Review.* https://hbr.org/2022/04/what-i-wish-i-had-known-about-my-mother

50. Parent, J. (2017, March 2). It's college acceptance season: Watch out for bragging parents! *Your Teen Magazine.* https://yourteenmag.com/teens-college/bragging-parents. https://yourteenmag.com/teens-college/bragging-parents

51. Lerner, H. (2011, August 7). Are you secretly ashamed of your kid? *Psychology Today.* https://www.psychologytoday.com/us/blog/the-dance-connection/201108/are-you-secrectly-ashamed-your-kid.

52. Smith, C. S. (2004, April 14). World Briefing | Europe: France: American facing extradition commits suicide. *New York Times.* https://www.nytimes.com/2004/04/14/world/world-briefing-europe-france-american-facing-extradition-commits-suicide.html

53. Brody, J. E. (2020, December 7). When a family is fractured. *New York Times.* https://www.nytimes.com/2020/12/07/well/family/when-a-family-is-fractured.html

54. Ibid.

55. Ibid.

56. Knowles, H., and Villegas, P. (2021, January 16). Pushed to the edge by the Capitol riot, people are reporting their family and friends to the FBI. *Washington Post.* https://www.washingtonpost.com/nation/2021/01/16/capitol-riot-family-fbi/

57. Klemko, R. (2021, January 17). Perspective | My family, like the country, split over race. Like the country, we can heal. *Washington Post.* https://www.washingtonpost.com/outlook/my-family-like-the-country-split-over-race-like-the-country-we-can-heal/2021/01/15/bfbac002-567a-11eb-a08b-f1381ef3d207_story.html

58. Marcano, Tony. (1997, May 14). Toddler, left outside restaurant, is returned to her mother. *New York Times*. https://www.nytimes.com/1997/05/14/nyregion/toddler-left-outside-restaurant-is-returned-to-her-mother.html

59. Zelizer, Viviana. (2011). *Economic lives*. Princeton, NJ: Princeton University Press.

60. Ibid., p. 50.

61. Quirke, Linda. (2016, July). "Fat-proof your child": Parenting advice and "child obesity." *Fat Studies* 5(2): 137–155.

62. Hart, Roger. (1979). *Children's experience of place*. New York. Irvington Publisher, Inc. http://cergnyc.org/files/2013/12/Hart_Childrens-Experience-of-Place.pdf

63. Murray, S. H. (2023, July 5). The gravitational pull of supervising kids all the time. *The Atlantic*. https://www.theatlantic.com/family/archive/2023/07/helicopter-parenting-child-autonomy-standards/674618/

64. Buteau, M. (2020, December 8). Helicopter mom vs. Jimmy Buffett dad. *New York Times*. https://www.nytimes.com/2020/12/08/parenting/michelle-buteau-twins.html

65. Ibid.

66. Calarco, Jessica McCrory. (2018). Family "free range" parenting's unfair double standard when poorer mothers and fathers let their children play unsupervised, they come under suspicion. *The Atlantic*. https://www.theatlantic.com/family/archive/2018/04/free-range-parenting/557051/

67. Lareau, A. (2011). *Unequal childhoods: Class, race, and family life*. Berkeley and Los Angeles: University of California Press.

68. Edin, K., and Kefalas, M. (2005). *Promises I can keep: Why poor women put motherhood before marriage*. Berkeley and Los Angeles: University of California Press.

69. Quirke, Linda. (2006, November). Keeping young minds sharp: Children's cognitive stimulation and the rise of parenting magazines, 1959–2000. *Canadian Review of Sociology* 43(4): 387–406.

70. Stone, P., and Lovejoy, M. (2019). *Opting back in: What really happens when mothers go back to work*. Berkeley and Los Angeles: University of California Press.

71. Ibid.

72. Ibid., p. 57.

73. Ibid., pp. 210–211.

74. Ishizuka, Patrick. (2019, September). Social class, gender, and contemporary parenting standards in the United States: Evidence from

a national survey experiment. *Social Forces* 98(1): 31–58. https://doi.org/10.1093/sf/soy107

75. Ibid.

76. Miller, C. C. (2018, December 25). The relentlessness of modern parenting. *New York Times.* https://www.nytimes.com/2018/12/25/upshot/the-relentlessness-of-modern-parenting.html

77. Corrigan, K. (2021, September 5). Opinion | How to let go of your irreplaceable, unstoppable daughter. *New York Times.* https://www.nytimes.com/2021/09/05/opinion/parenting-college-empty-nest-pandemic.html https://www.nytimes.com/2021/09/05/opinion/parenting-college-empty-nest-pandemic.html

78. Lorenz, T. (2018, December 1). The controversy over parents who eat lunch with their children at school. *The Atlantic.* https://www.theatlantic.com/education/archive/2018/12/should-parents-eat-lunch-their-children-school/577117/

79. Grose, J. (2021, November 17). Opinion | What if your kids never let you sleep again? *New York Times.* https://www.nytimes.com/2021/11/17/opinion/what-if-your-kids-never-let-you-sleep-again.html

80. Pearson, C. (2022, May 5). New report confirms most working parents are burned out. *New York Times.* https://www.nytimes.com/2022/05/05/well/family/parental-burnout-symptoms.html

81. Shankar, S. (2021, July 9). Opinion | A packed schedule doesn't really "enrich" your child. *New York Times.* https://www.nytimes.com/2021/07/09/opinion/culture/kids-schedule-parents.html

82. Miller, C. C. (2018, July 5). Americans are having fewer babies. They told us why. *New York Times.* https://www.nytimes.com/2018/07/05/upshot/americans-are-having-fewer-babies-they-told-us-why.html

83. Blanchflower, David G., and Clark, Andrew Eric. (2019, February). Children, unhappiness and family finances: Evidence from one million Europeans. NBER Working Paper No. w25597. Available at SSRN: https://ssrn.com/abstract=3341258

84. Cetre, Sophie, Clark, Andrew, and Senik, Claudia. (2016, August). Happy people have children: Choice and self-selection into parenthood. *European Journal of Population* 32(3): 445–473. doi: 10.1007/s10680-016-9389-x. Epub 2016 Aug 22. PMID: 28713186; PMCID: PMC5505668.

85. Cooper, Marianne. (2014). *Cut Adrift Families in insecure times.* Berkeley and Los Angeles: University of California Press.

86. Ibid., p. 78.

87. Glass, Glass, Simon, Robin W., Andersson, Matthew A. (2016, November). Parenthood and happiness: Effects of work-family reconciliation policies in 22 OECD countries. *American Journal of Sociology* 122(3): 886–929. https://doi.org/10.1086/688892

88. Edin, K., and Kefalas, M. *Promises I can keep: Why poor women put motherhood before marriage.* Berkeley and Los Angeles: University of California Press, p. 48.

89. Ibid., p. 211.

90. Ibid., p. 34.

91. Barry, E. (2022, December 27). Parents often bring children to psychiatric E.R.s to subdue them, study finds. *New York Times.* https://www.nytimes.com/2022/12/27/health/children-emergency-room-mental-health.html

92. Quillan, L. (2018, August 21). The isolating life of parenting a potential psychopath. *The Atlantic.* (August 21) https://www.theatlantic.com/family/archive/2018/08/conduct-disorder-parent-support-group/567946/

93. Miller, C. C. (2018, December 25). The relentlessness of modern parenting. *New York Times.* https://www.nytimes.com/2018/12/25/upshot/the-relentlessness-of-modern-parenting.html

94. Reichman, N. E., Corman, H., and Noonan, K. (2004). Effects of child health on parents' relationship status. *Demography* 41, 569–584. https://doi.org/10.1353/dem.2004.0026

95. Novoa, C. (2020, January 29). The child care crisis disproportionately affects children with disabilities. *Center for American Progress.* https://www.americanprogress.org/article/child-care-crisis-disproportionately-affects-children-disabilities/

96. Engber, D. (2021, October 6). Can robots heal an injured brain? *The Atlantic.* https://www.theatlantic.com/magazine/archive/2021/11/engineers-daughter-tbi-rehab/620172/

97. Ornstein, N. J. (2018, March 7). Opinion | How a bad law and a big mistake drove my mentally ill son away. *New York Times.* https://www.nytimes.com/2018/03/06/opinion/guns-mental-health-baker-act.html

98. Bertin, Mark. (2020, May 13). The extra burden for parents of children with special needs. Your child may have setbacks during the school shutdown. But remember, schools will open again at some point and help get things back on track. *New York Times.* https://www.nytimes.com/2020/05/13/well/family/coronavirus-shutdowns-children-special-needs-adhd-autism.html

99. Zhang, S. (2020, November 18). The last children of Down Syndrome. *The Atlantic*. https://www.theatlantic.com/magazine/archive/2020/12/the-last-children-of-down-syndrome/616928/

100. Cornwall, G. (2021, August 31). The two reasons parents regret having kids. *The Atlantic*. https://www.theatlantic.com/family/archive/2021/08/why-parents-regret-children/619931/

101. Wan, W. (2022, March 17). "Is this what a good mother looks like?" *Washington Post*. https://www.washingtonpost.com/dc-md-va/2022/03/17/parental-rights-mental-illness-custody/

102. Boland, R. (2016, November 16) Minding my disabled daughter: "I don't want to do this any more." *The Irish Times*. https://www.irishtimes.com/life-and-style/health-family/minding-my-disabled-daughter-i-don-t-want-to-do-this-any-more-1.2872341

Chapter 8: Elderly parents, grandparents, siblings, and pets

1. MediaCom. (2017). A background to Hofstede's cultural dimensions. https://mediacomstaging.blob.core.windows.net/pdfs/mediacom-cms.azurewebsites.net/nl/pdfs/a-background-to-hofstedes-cultural-dimensions.pdf (accessed 31 October 2023).

2. Hua, Y. (2013, July 8). Opinion | When filial piety is the law. *New York Times*. https://www.nytimes.com/2013/07/08/opinion/yu-when-filial-piety-is-the-law.html

3. Fang, Hanming, Lei, Ziteng, Lin, Liguo, and Zhang, Peng. (2021, March). Family companionship and elderly suicide: Evidence from the Chinese Lunar New Year. NBER Working Paper No. w28566. Available at SSRN: https://ssrn.com/abstract=3809529

4. Yi, W. (2016, Occtober 30). Fomenting filial piety amid changing lifestyles in China. *Nippon*. https://www.nippon.com/en/features/c02806/fomenting-filial-piety-amid-changing-lifestyles-in-china.html

5. Hua, Y. (2013, July 8). Opinion | When filial piety is the law. *New York Times*. https://www.nytimes.com/2013/07/08/opinion/yu-when-filial-piety-is-the-law.html

6. Yi, W. (2016, Occtober 30). Fomenting filial piety amid changing lifestyles in China. *Nippon*. https://www.nippon.com/en/features/c02806/fomenting-filial-piety-amid-changing-lifestyles-in-china.html

7. Jing-Ann Chou, R. (2011, February). Filial piety by contract? The emergence, implementation, and implications of the "Family Support Agreement in China." *The Gerontologist* 51(1): 3–16. https://doi.org/10.1093/geront/gnq059

8. Yi, Zeng, George, Linda, Sereny, Melanie, Gu, Danan, and Vaupel, James W. (2016). Older parents enjoy better filial piety and care from daughters than sons in China. *American Journal of Medical Research* 39(1): 75–95. https://www.ncbi.nlm.nih.gov/pmc/articles/PMC5438089/

9. Grose, J. (2020, February 11). "It's pretty brutal": The sandwich generation pays a price. *New York Times*. https://www.nytimes.com/2020/02/11/parenting/sandwich-generation-costs.html

10. Banerjee, Sudipto. (2015, June). Intra-family cash transfers in older American households. EBRI Issue Brief, Number 415. Available at SSRN: http://ssrn.com/abstract=2620835

11. Gardiner, A. (2019, September 5). "I put my own life on hold": The pain and joy of caring for parents. *New York Times*. https://www.nytimes.com/2019/09/05/reader-center/taking-care-of-elderly-relatives.html

12. *Next Avenue*. (2018). Parents' support to adult Kids: $500 billion a year. https://www.nextavenue.org/parents-support-adult-kids/

13. Gardiner, A. (2019, September 5). "I put my own life on hold": The pain and joy of caring for parents. *New York Times*. https://www.nytimes.com/2019/09/05/reader-center/taking-care-of-elderly-relatives.html

14. Span, P. (2022, December 3). Who will care for "kinless' seniors"? *New York Times*. https://www.nytimes.com/2022/12/03/health/elderly-living-alone.html

15. Spitze, Glenna, and Gallant, Mary P. (2004). "The bitter with the sweet": Older adults' strategies for handling ambivalence in relations with their adult children. *Research on Aging* 26: 387–412. https://doi.org/10.1177/0164027504264677

16. Ibid.

17. Heid, A. R., Kim, K., Zarit, S. H., Birditt, K. S., and Fingerman, K. L. (2018, March). Relationship tensions and mood: Adult children's daily experience of aging parents' stubbornness. *Personal Relationships* 25(1): 87–02. doi: 10.1111/pere.12229. Epub 2018 Feb 28. PMID: 30166932; PMCID: PMC6110395.

18. Ibid.

19. Lee, Hyo Jung, Kim, Kyungmin, Bangerter, Lauren R., Zarit, Steven H., and Fingerman, Karen L. (2020). Parents' and middle-aged children's evaluations of parents' disability and life problems. *Journal of Adult Development* 27(2): 135–146. https://doi.org/10.1007/s10804-019-09336-x

20. https://www.nytimes.com/2019/08/30/health/stubbornness-parents-elderly.html

21. Berman, Claire. (2016, March 4). What aging parents want from their kids: There's a fine line between caring and controlling—but older adults and their grown children often disagree on where it is. *The Atlantic.* https://www.theatlantic.com/health/archive/2016/03/when-youre-the-aging-parent/472290/

22. Span, P. (2019). Think Your Aging Parents Are Stubborn? Blame 'Mismatched Goals.' *The New York Times.* (August 30) https://www.nytimes.com/2019/08/30/health/stubbornness-parents-elderly.html.

23. Saxon, Leslie, Ebert, Rebecca, and Sobhani, Mona. (2019, August 13). Health impacts of unlimited access to networked transportation in older adults. *The Journal of mHealth.* https://thejournalofmhealth.com/health-impacts-of-unlimited-access-to-networked-transportation-in-older-adults/

24. Levenson, M. (2021, November 12). Husband of "Sweetheart Swindler" sentenced to 85 years for bilking older people. *New York Times.* https://www.nytimes.com/2021/11/12/us/sweetheart-swindler-sentenced.html

25. Blanton, K. (2019, March 27). Elderly report financial abuse by kids—Center for Retirement Research. Center for Retirement Research at Boston College. https://crr.bc.edu/elderly-report-financial-abuse-by-kids/

26. Horioka, Charles Yuji. (2014, May 28). Are Americans and Indians more altruistic than the Japanese and Chinese? Evidence from a New International Survey of Bequest Plans. ISER Discussion Paper No. 901. Available at SSRN: https://ssrn.com/abstract=2441008

27. Horioka, Charles Yuji, Gahramanov, Emin, Hayat, Aziz, and Tang, Xueli. (2016, May 7). Why do children take care of their elderly parents? Are the Japanese any different? ISER Discussion Paper No. 970. Available at SSRN: https://ssrn.com/abstract=2777286 or http://dx.doi.org/10.2139/ssrn.2777286

28. Almås, Ingvild, Freddi, Eleonora, and Thogersen, Oystein. (2016, May 24). Saving and bequest in China: An analysis of intergenerational

exchange. NHH Dept. of Economics Discussion Paper No. 10/2016. Available at SSRN: https://ssrn.com/abstract=2786877 or http://dx.doi.org/10.2139/ssrn.2786877

29. He, Jia, Wu, Jing, Zhang, Qi, and Zhang, Rongjie. (2021, December 3). Caring about bequest, so caring for parents? Evidence from China's housing sector. Available at SSRN: https://ssrn.com/abstract=3976927 or http://dx.doi.org/10.2139/ssrn.3976927

30. Span, Paula. (2019, May 10). Many Americans will need long-term care. Most won't be able to afford it. A decade from now, most middle-income seniors will not be able to pay the rising costs of independent or assisted living *New York Times*.

31. Henig, Robin Marantz. (2018). The age of grandparents is made of many tragedies. The proportion of children living in "grandfamilies" has doubled in the United States since 1970—and the reasons are often sad ones. *The Atlantic*. https://www.theatlantic.com/family/archive/2018/06/this-is-the-age-of-grandparents/561527/

32. Powdthavee, Nattavudh. (2011). Life satisfaction and grandparenthood: Evidence from a nationwide survey. IZA Discussion Paper No. 5869. Available at SSRN: https://ssrn.com/abstract=1906172

33. Yasir, S., and Ives, M. (2022, May 29). No grandchild? Six years after son's wedding, these parents are suing. *New York Times*. https://www.nytimes.com/2022/05/29/world/asia/india-couple-grandchild-suing.html

34. Blanton, K. (2022, December 13). Retiring to care for grandchild isn't unusual—Center for Retirement Research. Center for Retirement Research at Boston College. https://crr.bc.edu/retiring-to-care-for-grandchild-isnt-unusual/

35. Malisa, Amedeus. (2022, September 21). Grandparenthood and retirement. Available at SSRN: https://ssrn.com/abstract=4225814 or http://dx.doi.org/10.2139/ssrn.4225814

36. Joseph, M. (2022, April 7). The pandemic was a gift to this grandpa—Center for Retirement Research. Center for Retirement Research at Boston College. https://crr.bc.edu/the-pandemic-was-a-gift-to-this-grandpa/

37. Hida, H., and Yoon, J. (2022, September 1). In a Japanese nursing home, some workers are babies. *New York Times*. https://www.nytimes.com/2022/09/01/world/asia/japan-nursing-home-babies.html

38. Span, P. (2019), July 23. When grandparents help hold it all together. *New York Times*. https://www.nytimes.com/2019/07/23/well/family/when-grandparents-help-hold-it-all-together.html

39. Deaton, Angus, and Stone, Arthur. (2013, June). Grandpa and the snapper: The wellbeing of the elderly who live with children. NBER Working Paper No. w19100. Available at SSRN: https://ssrn.com/abstract=2276364

40. Henig, Robin Marantz. (2018). The age of grandparents is made of many tragedies. The proportion of children living in "grandfamiles" has doubled in the United States since 1970—and the reasons are often sad ones. *The Atlantic*. https://www.theatlantic.com/family/archive/2018/06/this-is-the-age-of-grandparents/561527/

41. Span, Paula. (2020, July 23). Generation grandparent. *New York Times*. https://www.nytimes.com/2020/07/23/well/family/estrangement-grandparents-grandchildren.html

42. Henig, Robin Marantz. (2021, April 30). The unspoken wedge between parents and grandparents. Each generation has its own norms for parenting. Arguing over the differences can be an emotional minefield. *The Atlantic*. https://www.theatlantic.com/family/archive/2021/04/when-grandparenting-clashes-parenting/618758/

43. Ibid.

44. Ibid.

45. Span, Paula. (2020, July 23). Generation grandparent. *New York Times*. https://www.nytimes.com/2020/07/23/well/family/estrangement-grandparents-grandchildren.html

46. Hax, C. (2022, December 19). Advice | Carolyn Hax: Does grandparent get second chance after nut-allergy mistake? *Washington Post*. https://www.washingtonpost.com/advice/2022/12/19/carolyn-hax-grandma-nut-allergy-grandkid/

47. Hesse, M. (2023, January 15). Perspective | Prince Harry doesn't need to explain himself anymore. *Washington Post*. https://www.washingtonpost.com/lifestyle/2023/01/13/prince-harry-spare-memoir/

48. Pearson, C. (2023, June 5). The lifelong gift of sibling friendship. *New York Times*. https://www.nytimes.com/2023/06/05/well/family/sibling-friends-relationship.html

49. Jensen, A. C., Killoren, S. E., Campione-Barr, N., Padilla, J., and Chen, B.-B. (2023). Sibling relationships in adolescence and young adulthood in multiple contexts: A critical review. *Journal of Social and Personal Relationships* 40(2): 384–419. https://doi.org/10.1177/02654075221104188

50. Borga, Liyousew Gebremedhin, and Myroslav, Pidkuyko. (2019, February 1). Whoever has will be given more: Child endowment and human capital investment. CERGE-EI Working Paper Series No. 616. Available at SSRN: https://ssrn.com/abstract=3161182 or http://dx.doi.org/10.2139/ssrn.3161182

51. Garg, Ashish, and Morduch, Jonathan. (1998). Sibling rivalry and the gender gap: Evidence from child health outcomes in Ghana. *Journal of Population Economics* 11(4). Available at SSRN: https://ssrn.com/abstract=147310 co

52. McCarthy, C. (2022, December 6). Sibling rivalry is normal—but is it helpful or harmful? *Harvard Health.* https://www.health.harvard.edu/blog/sibling-rivalry-is-normal-but-is-it-helpful-or-harmful-202212062861

53. Simmons-Duffin, S. (2010, November 26). Brotherly (and sisterly) love in the animal world. NPR. https://www.npr.org/2010/11/24/131571394/brotherly-and-sisterly-love-in-the-animal-world

54. Lucas-Thompson, Rachel, and Goldberg, Wendy A. (2011). Family relationships and children's stress responses. In: *Advances in Child Development and Behavior.*

55. Grose, J. (2021, January 13). The psychology behind sibling rivalry. *New York Times.* https://www.nytimes.com/2021/01/13/parenting/sibling-rivalry-fights-kids.html

56. Vivona, J.M. (2007). Sibling Differentiation, Identity Development and the Lateral Dimension of Psychic Life. Journal of the American Psychoanalytic Association, 55(4) 1191-1215. https://doi.org/10.1177/000306510705500405

57. Lu, F. (2023, January 12). Grudge diary: Chinese girl, 8, keeps secret journal of grievances against sister. *South China Morning Post.* https://www.scmp.com/news/people-culture/article/3206077/grudge-diary-chinese-girl-8-keeps-bitter-secret-journal-grievances-she-holds-against-16-year-old

58. Spragins, E. (2003, September 7). Love & money: When a windfall frays family ties. *New York Times.* https://www.nytimes.com/2003/09/07/business/love-money-when-a-windfall-frays-family-ties.html

59. Wang, Shun, and Zhou, Weina. (2016, February 6). Do siblings make us happy? KDI School of Pub Policy & Management Paper No. 16-04. Available at SSRN: https://ssrn.com/abstract=2772034

60. Galanes, P. (2021, June 10). How do I get my parents to stop bankrolling their adult son? *New York Times*. https://www.nytimes.com/2021/06/10/style/parents-financial-support-social-qs.html

61. Ansberry, C. (2023, February 15). When parents need care, sibling relationships face new challenges. *Wall Street Journal*. https://www.wsj.com/articles/avoid-the-sibling-resentment-trap-in-caring-for-an-aging-parent-d79c33ec

62. Klein, M. (2022, January 22). Nasty family feud over mom's will lands two retired sisters in jail—and one may lose her home. *New York Post*. https://nypost.com/2022/01/22/battle-over-estate-landed-two-sisters-on-rikers-island/

63. Jervey, G. (2004, March 28). Personal Business: A legacy of rancor: Estate fights rising. *New York Times*. https://www.nytimes.com/2004/03/28/business/personal-business-a-legacy-of-rancor-estate-fights-rising.html

64. Schmidt, G. (2022, June 16). Dog owners want more space. Here's where they're finding it. *New York Times*. https://www.nytimes.com/2022/06/16/realestate/top-cities-dog-owners.html

65. Smith, Z. (2013, January 10). Joy. *The New York Review*. https://www.nybooks.com/articles/2013/01/10/joy/#:~:text=Occasionally%20percent20the%20percent20child%20percent2C%20percent20too%20percent2C%20percent20is,way%20percent20to%20percent20live-%20percent20with%20percent20daily

66. Gerson, Michael. (2022, July 4). Why I will never live without a dog again. *Washington Post*. https://www.washingtonpost.com/opinions/2022/07/04/why-i-will-never-live-without-dog-love-again/

67. Owens, Nicole, and Grauerholz, Liz. (2018). Interspecies parenting: How pet parents construct their roles. *Humanity & Society* 1–24.

68. The power of pets: Health benefits of human-animal interactions. NIH News in Health A monthly newsletter from the National Institutes of Health, part of the U.S. Department of Health and Human Services. https://newsinhealth.nih.gov/2018/02/power-pets

69. Ibid.

70. Powell, Kate M., Edwards, Paul McGreevy, Bauman, Adrian, Podberscek, Anthony, and Neilly, Brendon. (2019). Companion dog acquisition and mental well-being: A community-based three-arm

controlled study. *BMC Public Health* 19, Article number: 1428. https://bmcpublichealth.biomedcentral.com/articles/10.1186/s12889-019-7770-5

71. Santos, F. (2021, February 2). Opinion | A snake bit my cat. Clearing out my bank accounts to save him was an easy choice. *Washington Post.* https://www.washingtonpost.com/opinions/2020/12/31/snake-bit-my-cat-clearing-out-my-bank-accounts-save-him-was-an-easy-choice/

72. Jordan, M. (2022, April 14). Ukrainians face new hurdle at U.S. border: No dogs. *New York Times.* https://www.nytimes.com/2022/04/14/us/ukrainian-refugees-dogs-us-border.html

73. Ibid.

74. Renkl, M. (2021, February 1). Opinion | A dog's place is at the White House. *New York Times.* https://www.nytimes.com/2021/02/01/opinion/champ-major-white-house-dogs.html

75. Gurley, G. (2023, January 26). Future cringe. *New York Times.* https://www.nytimes.com/interactive/2023/01/26/style/culture-regret-crocs-social-media-cringe.html

Chapter 9: Friendship

1. Van Kessel, P., Hughes, A., and Walker, K. (2018, November 20). The meaning of life: 100 quotes from Americans on what keeps them going. *Pew Research Center's Religion & Public Life Project.* https://www.pewresearch.org/religion/interactives/what-keeps-us-going/

2. Diener, E., and Biswas-Diener, R. (2008). *Happiness: Unlocking the mysteries of psychological wealth.* Malden, MA: Blackwell.

3. 22 heartwarming stories of true friendship that will make you call your bestie. If you're lucky, you'll find one person who brightens your day, lends an ear, and inspires you. RD readers share stories of their best buds. Heartwarming-Stories-of-True-Friendship. Updated May 8, 2019). https://www.rd.com/article/stories-of-friendship/

4. Young, D. (2022, December 15). Advice | Ask Damon: I can't afford to hang out with my rich friends. *Washington Post.* https://www.washingtonpost.com/advice/2022/12/16/ask-damon-rich-friends-afford/

5. Singletary, M. (2023, July 20). Advice | They do, but you don't. It's okay to RSVP "no" if you're broke. *Washington Post*. https://www.wash ingtonpost.com/business/2023/07/21/wedding-guest-money/

6. Pearson, C. (2022, July 11). Text your friends. It matters more than you think. *New York Times*. https://www.nytimes.com/2022/07/11/well/family/check-in-text-friendship.html

7. Caron, C. (2021, December 21). An overlooked cure for loneliness. *New York Times*. https://www.nytimes.com/2021/12/21/well/mind/loneliness-volunteering.html

8. Kerns K. A. (1996). Individual differences in friendship quality: Links to child-mother attachment. In: W. M. Bukowski, A. F. Newcomb, and W.W. Hartup (eds.). *The company they keep: Friendship in childhood and adolescence*. New York: Cambridge University Press, pp. 137–157.

9. Glick GC, Rose AJ. Prospective associations between friendship adjustment and social strategies: friendship as a context for building social skills. Dev Psychol. 2011 Jul;47(4):1117-32. doi: 10.1037/a0023277. PMID: 21443336; PMCID: PMC3389512. https://www.ncbi.nlm.nih.gov/pmc/articles/PMC3389512/

10. Murphy, K. (2021, April 23). The pandemic shrank our social circles. Let's keep it that way. *New York Times*. https://www.nytimes.com/2021/04/23/sunday-review/covid-friendship.html

11. Stulberg, B. (2022, April 17). Opinion | One part of your life you shouldn't optimize. *New York Times*. https://www.nytimes.com/2022/04/17/opinion/culture/making-friends-covid.html

12. Diener, E., Suh, E. M., Lucas, E. R., and Smith, H. L. (1999). Subjective well-being: Three decades of progress. *Psychological Bulletin* 125, 276–302.

13. Barrera, M., Jr. (1986). Distinctions between social support concepts, measures and models. *American Journal of Community Psychology* 14: 413–445; David, Susan, Boniwell, Ilona, and Conley Ayers, Amanda. *Oxford Handbook of Happiness*. Oxford: Oxford Library of Psychology, p. 856. OUP Oxford. Kindle Edition.

14. Helliwell, J. F., Huang, H., and Harris, A. (2009). International differences in the determinants of life satisfaction. In: B. Dutta, T. Ray, and E. Somanathan (eds.), *New and enduring themes in development economics*. World Scientific Publishing, pp. 3–40.

15. Statman, Meir. (2020, Winter). Well-being advisers. *The Journal of Wealth Management Winter* 23 (Supplement 1): 2–44, p. 2. doi: https://doi.org/10.3905/jwm.23.s1.002

16. Saleh, Lamis. (2020, June 1). A city in the Jordanian desert: Where do Syrian refugees want to live? Available at SSRN: https://ssrn.com/abstract=3778575 or http://dx.doi.org/10.2139/ssrn.3778575

17. Bailey M., Cao, R., Kuchler, T., and Stroebel J. (2018a.) The economic effects of social networks: Evidence from the housing market. *Journal of Political Economy* 126: 2224–2276.

18. McCartney, W. Ben, and Shah, Avni. (2019, May 2). The economic importance of neighbors: Evidence from hyperlocal social influence effects in mortgage markets. Available at SSRN: https://ssrn.com/abstract=2882317 or http://dx.doi.org/10.2139/ssrn.2882317

19. Banerjee, P. (2019, April 8). Want to save money on your mortgage? Have drinks with your neighbours. *The Globe and Mail*. https://www.theglobeandmail.com/investing/personal-finance/household-finances/article-being-neighbourly-might-save-you-some-money-on-your-mortgage/

20. The Financial Diaries, p. 65.

21. Fishman, B. (2022, September 3). Opinion | The post-colonoscopy male friendship test. *New York Times*. https://www.nytimes.com/2022/09/03/opinion/men-friendship-middle-age.html

22. Schmidt, S. (2020, December 4). No game days. No bars. The pandemic is forcing some men to realize they need deeper friendships. *Washington Post*. https://www.washingtonpost.com/road-to-recovery/2020/11/30/male-bonding-covid/

23. Baker, B. (2021, January 28). Why middle-aged men have trouble sustaining friendships. Literary Hub. https://lithub.com/why-middle-aged-men-have-trouble-sustaining-friendships/

24. Pearson, C. (2022, November 28). Why is it so hard for men to make close friends? *New York Times*. https://www.nytimes.com/2022/11/28/well/family/male-friendship-loneliness.html

25. Hickman, Adam. (2018, March). Why friendships among remote workers are crucial. Workplace. https://www.gallup.com/workplace/236072/why-friendships-among-remote-workers-crucial.aspx

26. https://www.theatlantic.com/family/archive/2020/07/what-pandemic-doing-work-friendships/614407/

27. Mo, Nicole. (2020, July 21). The pandemic is changing work friendships. Co-workers had little choice but to bond when they spent 40 hours a week together. But if widespread remote work sticks around, those relationships will never be the same. *The Atlantic*. https://www.theatlantic.com/family/archive/2020/07/what-pandemic-doing-work-friendships/614407/

28. Allcott, Hunt, Braghieri, Luca, Eichmeyer, Sarah, and Gentzkow, Matthew. (2019, March 25). The welfare effects of social media. Available at SSRN: https://ssrn.com/abstract=3308640 or http://dx.doi.org/10.2139/ssrn.3308640

29. Allcott, Hunt, Gentzkow, Matthew, and Song, Lena. (2022). *American Economic Review* 112(7): 2424–2463. https://doi.org/10.1257/aer.20210867 2424 Digital Addiction.

30. Carey, B. (2019, January 30). This is your brain off Facebook. *New York Times.* https://www.nytimes.com/2019/01/30/health/facebook-psychology-health.html

31. Han, S. (2021, May 20). You can only maintain so many close friendships. *The Atlantic.* https://www.theatlantic.com/family/archive/2021/05/robin-dunbar-explains-circles-friendship-dunbars-number/618931/

32. Mull, A. (2021, January 27). The pandemic has erased entire categories of friendship. *The Atlantic.* https://www.theatlantic.com/health/archive/2021/01/pandemic-goodbye-casual-friends/617839/

33. Keohane, J. (2021, August 4). The surprising benefits of talking to strangers. *The Atlantic.* https://www.theatlantic.com/family/archive/2021/08/why-we-should-talk-strangers-more/619642/

34. Sax, D. (2022, June 12). Opinion | Why strangers are good for us. *New York Times.* https://www.nytimes.com/2022/06/12/opinion/strangers-talking-benefits.html https://www.nytimes.com/2022/06/12/opinion/strangers-talking-benefits.html

35. Beck, J. (2015, October 22). How friendships change when you become an adult. *The Atlantic.* https://www.theatlantic.com/health/archive/2015/10/how-friendships-change-over-time-in-adulthood/411466/

36. Denworth, Lydia. (2020, January 28). The outsize influence of your middle-school friends. The intensity of feelings generated by friendship in childhood and adolescence is by design. *The Atlantic.* https://www.theatlantic.com/family/archive/2020/01/friendship-crucial-adolescent-brain/605638/

37. Lavy, Victor, and Sand, Edith. (2012, October). The friends factor: How students' social networks affect their academic achievement and well-being. NBER Working Paper No. w18430. Available at SSRN: https://ssrn.com/abstract=2160187; The effect of social networks on student's academic and non-cognitive behavioral outcomes: Evidence from conditional random assignment of friends in school. (2019, January). *The Economic Journal* 129(617): 439–480. https://doi.org/10.1111/ecoj.12582

38. Wu, Jia, Zhang, Junsen, andd Wang, Chunchao. (2023). Student performance, peer effects, and friend networks: Evidence from a randomized peer intervention. *American Economic Journal: Economic Policy* 15(1): 510–542.

39. Chetty, R., Jackson, M.O., Kuchler, T., et al. (2022). Social capital II: Determinants of economic connectedness. *Nature* 608: 122–134. https://doi.org/10.1038/s41586-022-04997-3

40. Offer, Shira. (2021). Negative social ties: Prevalence and consequences annual review of sociology negative social ties. *Annual Review of Sociology* 47: 177–196. https://doi.org/10.1146/annurev-soc-090820-025827

41. Statman, Meir. (2020, Winter). Well-being advisers. *The Journal of Wealth Management Winter* 23 (Supplement 1): 2–44, p. 2. doi: https://doi.org/10.3905/jwm.23.s1.002

42. The myth of the BFF and the end of female friendships. *The Guardian.* https://www.theguardian.com/books/australia-culture-blog/2013/may/29/bff-female-friendships-end

43. Makhijani, Pooja. (2020, June 25). How to handle a mom-friend breakup: those bonds forged when you have babies don't always last. *New York Times.* https://www.nytimes.com/2020/06/25/parenting/moms-friends-fight.html

44. Jargon, J. (2021, February 20). New mothers are lonely during coronavirus. Mom-shaming on social media is making it worse. *Wall Street Journal.* https://www.wsj.com/articles/new-mothers-are-lonely-during-coronavirus-mom-shaming-on-social-media-is-making-it-worse-11613829600

45. Bahadur, N. (2013, June 11). 5 women who have "broken up" with their BFFs. *HuffPost.* https://www.huffpost.com/entry/friend-breakup-stories_n_3417347

46. Pinsker, J. (2021, March 30). Trump's presidency is over. So are many relationships. *The Atlantic.* https://www.theatlantic.com/family/archive/2021/03/trump-friend-family-relationships/618457/

47. Brandon, Emily. (2009, April 20). Forget tuition: How retirees can attend college for free. A look at universities that offer free or low-cost classes. *U.S. News.* https://money.usnews.com/money/articles/2009/04/20/forget-tuition-how-retirees-can-attend-college-for-free

48. http://www.sixthtone.com/news/1840/universities-offer-lifelong-learning-to-chinas-elderly

49. Statman, Meir. (2020, Winter). Well-being advisers. *The Journal of Wealth Management Winter* 23 (Supplement 1): 2–44, p. 2. doi: https://doi.org/10.3905/jwm.23.s1.002

50. Borgonovi, F. (2008). Doing well by doing good: The relationship between formal volunteering and self-reported health and happiness. *Social Science & Medicine* 66(11), 2321–2334.

51. Silver, L., Van Kessel, P., Huang, C., Clancy, L., and Gubbala, S. (2021, November 18). What makes life meaningful? Views from 17 advanced economies. Pew Research Center. https://www.pewresearch.org/global/2021/11/18/finding-meaning-in-others/

52. Ren, Zhiying (Bella), Dimant, Eugen, and Schweitzer, Maurice E. (2021, September 8). Social motives for sharing conspiracy theories. Available at SSRN: https://ssrn.com/abstract=3919364 or http://dx.doi.org/10.2139/ssrn.3919364

53. Span, Paula. (2019, September 27). "We need each other": Seniors are drawn to new housing arrangements. Older Americans are exploring housing alternatives, including villages and home-sharing. *New York Times.* Updated October 1, 2019. https://www.nytimes.com/2019/09/27/health/seniors-housing-sharing-villages.html

54. Yiying, F. (2018, March 5). Why China's elderly "huddle to stay warm." *Sixth Tone.* https://www.sixthtone.com/news/1001858

55. Njiokiktjien, I. (2021, September 2). Where home blends with community. *New York Times.* https://www.nytimes.com/2021/09/02/style/cohousing-netherlands-belgium-community.html

56. Hypolite, L. I. (2020). People, place, and connections: Black cultural center staff as facilitators of social capital. *Journal of Black Studies* 51(1), 37–59. https://doi.org/10.1177/0021934719892238

57. Rosa, A., and Keith, S. (2020, July 8). See that fridge on the sidewalk? It's full of free food. *New York Times.* https://www.nytimes.com/2020/07/08/nyregion/free-food-fridge-nyc.html

58. Krieger, D. (2012, August 16). Cycling and socializing in Central Park. *New York Times.* https://www.nytimes.com/2012/08/17/nyregion/cycling-and-socializing-in-central-park.html h

59. Buerger, Catherine. (2020, December 14). The anti-hate brigade: How a group of thousands responds collectively to online vitriol. Available at SSRN: https://ssrn.com/abstract=3748803 or http://dx.doi.org/10.2139/ssrn.3748803

60. Span, Paula. (2019, November 8). A retirement community that comes to you in continuing care at-home programs. Members live

in their own houses for years with regular health check-ins. *New York Times*. Updated November 10, 2019. https://www.nytimes .com/2019/11/08/health/retirement-home-ccrc.html

Chapter 10: Health

1. Statman, Meir. (2020, Winter). Well-being advisers. *The Journal of Wealth Management Winter* 23 (Supplement 1): 2–44, p. 2. doi: https:// doi.org/10.3905/jwm.23.s1.002

2. Oswald, Andrew J., and Powdthavee, Nattavudh (2006, July). Does happiness adapt? A longitudinal study of disability with implications for economists and judges. IZA Discussion Paper No. 2208. Available at SSRN: https://ssrn.com/abstract=921040

3. Bostock, S., Hamer, M., Wawrzyniak, A. J., Mitchell, E. S., and Steptoe, A. (2011). Positive emotional style and subjective, cardiovascular and cortisol responses to acute laboratory stress. *Psychoneuroendocrinology* 36: 1175–1183.

4. Giuntella, Osea, Hyde, Kelly, Saccardo, Silvia, and Sadoff, Sally. (2020, August 4). Lifestyle and mental health disruptions during COVID-19. Available at SSRN: https://ssrn.com/abstract=3666985 or http:// dx.doi.org/10.2139/ssrn.3666985

5. Duan, Hongbo, Huang, Zhilin, Jiang, Jie, and Wang, Shouyang. (2020, July 19). The COVID-19 outbreak decreases residents' self-reported happiness. Available at SSRN: https://ssrn.com/abstract= 3686190 or http://dx.doi.org/10.2139/ssrn.3686190

6. Krekel, Christian, Swanke, Sarah, De Neve, Jan-Emmanuel, and Fancourt, Daisy. (2023, May). Happiness predicts compliance with preventive health behaviours during Covid-19 lockdowns. *Scientific Reports* 13(1): 7989. doi: 10.1038/s41598-023-33136-9. PMID: 37198247; PMCID: PMC10189679.

7. Brody, J. E. (2021, October 4). The devastating ways depression and anxiety impact the body. *New York Times*. https://www.nytimes.com/ 2021/10/04/well/mind/depression-anxiety-physical-health.html

8. Goodman, F. R., Doorley, J. D., and Kashdan, T. B. (2018). Well-being and psychopathology: A deep exploration into positive emotions, meaning and purpose in life, and social relationships. In: E. Diener, S. Oishi, and L. Tay (eds.), *Handbook of well-being*. Salt Lake City, UT: DEF Publishers. doi: nobascholar.com

9. Physical Activity and Incident Depression: A Meta-Analysis of Prospective Cohort Studies Felipe B. Schuch, Ph.D., Davy Vancampfort, Ph.D., Joseph Firth, Ph.D., Simon Rosenbaum, Ph.D., Philip B. Ward, Ph.D., Edson S. Silva, B.Sc., Mats Hallgren, Ph.D., Antonio Ponce De Leon, Ph.D., Andrea L. Dunn, Ph.D., Andrea C. Deslandes, Ph.D., Marcelo P. Fleck, Ph.D., Andre F. Carvalho, Ph.D., Brendon Stubbs, Ph.D. Published Online:25 Apr 2018https://doi.org/10.1176/appi.ajp.2018.17111194

10. Solomon, A. (2020, July 10). What happens when you're disabled but nobody can tell. *New York Times*. https://www.nytimes.com/2020/07/10/style/invisible-disabilities.html

11. Casali, M. (2022, December 10). The connection between puberty and mental health. Turnbridge. https://www.turnbridge.com/news-events/uncategorized/puberty-and-mental-health/ h

12. Richtel, M., and Flanagan, A. (2022, April 24). "It's life or death": The mental health crisis among U.S. teens. *New York Times*. https://www.nytimes.com/2022/04/23/health/mental-health-crisis-teens.html

13. Arenas-Arroyo, E., Fernandez-Kranz, D., and Nollenberger, N. (2023, May). High speed internet and the widening gender gap in adolescent mental health: Evidence from hospital records. IZA Institute of Labor Economics. https://www.iza.org/publications/dp/15728/high-speed-internet-and-the-widening-gender-gap-in-adolescent-mental-health-evidence-from-hospital-records

14. Braghieri, Luca, Levy, Ro'ee, and Makarin, Alexey. (2022). Social media and mental health. *American Economic Review* 112(11): 3660–3693. https://doi.org/10.1257/aer.20211218 3660

15. Wang, B., Frank, R., and Glied, S. (2022, December 20). Lasting scars: The impact of depression in early adulthood on subsequent labor market outcomes. *Brookings*. https://www.brookings.edu/articles/lasting-scars-the-impact-of-depression-in-early-adulthood-on-subsequent-labor-market-outcomes/

16. Biasi, Barbara, Dahl, Michael Slavensky, and Moser, Petr. (2021, July). Career effects of mental health. NBER Working Paper No. w29031. Available at SSRN: https://ssrn.com/abstract=3889138

17. Layard, Richard, Chisholm, Dan, Patel, Vikram, and Saxena, Shekhar. (2013). Mental illness and unhappiness. IZA Discussion Paper No. 7620. Available at SSRN: https://ssrn.com/abstract=2336397

18. Bergner, D. (2022, May 17). Doctors gave her antipsychotics. She decided to live with her voices. *New York Times*. https://www.nytimes.com/2022/05/17/magazine/antipsychotic-medications-mental-health.html

19. Currie, J., and Schwandt, H. (2021). The opioid epidemic was not caused by economic distress but by factors that could be more rapidly addressed. *The ANNALS of the American Academy of Political and Social Science* 695(1): 276–291. https://doi.org/10.1177/00027162211033833

20. Szalavitz, M. (2023, January 3). Opinion | "Entire body is shaking": Why Americans with chronic pain are dying. *New York Times.* https://www.nytimes.com/2023/01/03/opinion/chronic-pain-suicides.html

21. Persson, Petra, and Rossin-Slater, Maya. (2018). Family ruptures, stress, and the mental health of the next generation. *American Economic Review* 108(4–5): 1214–1252. https://doi.org/10.1257/aer.20141406 1214

22. Almond, Douglas, and Mazumder, Bhashkar. (2011). Health capital and the prenatal environment: The effect of Ramadan observance during pregnancy. *American Economic Journal: Applied Economics* 3(4): 56–85. doi:10.1257/app.3.4.56

23. Currie, Janet, and Walker, Reed. (2011, January). Traffic congestion and infant health: Evidence from E-ZPass. *American Economic Journal: Applied Economics* 3: 65–90. http://www.aeaweb.org/articles.php?doi=10.1257/app.3.1.65

24. Currie, Janet, Voorheis, John, and Walker, Reed. (2023, January 1). What caused racial disparities in particulate exposure to fall? New evidence from the clean air act and satellite-based measures of air quality. *American Economic Review* 113(1): 71–97.

25. East, Chloe N., Miller, Marianne, Page, Marianne, and Wherry, Laura R. (2011). Multigenerational impacts of childhood access to the safety net: Early life exposure to Medicaid and the next generation's health. *American Economic Review* 13(1): 98–135.

26. Currie, Janet. (2011). Inequality at birth: Some causes and consequences. *American Economic Review.* Papers & Proceedings 101(3): 1–22. http://www.aeaweb.org/articles.php?doi=10.1257/aer.101.3.1

27. Scid, Roberta Pollack. (1989). *Never too thin: Why women at war with their bodies.* Prentice Hall Press; Clark, Kenneth. (1956). *The nude: A study in ideal form.* Princeton, NJ: Princeton University Press, pp. 5–6.

28. Hollander, A. (1977, October 23). When fat was in fashion. *New York Times.* https://www.nytimes.com/1977/10/23/archives/when-fat-was-in-fashion-abundant-flesh-was-a-thing-of-beauty-to.html https://www.nytimes.com/1977/10/23/archives/when-fat-was-in-fashion-abundant-flesh-was-a-thing-of-beauty-to.html

29. https://www.psychologicalscience.org/publications/observer/obsonline/yoga-and-meditation-may-enhance-not-diminish-our-

sense-of-self.html https://journals.sagepub.com/doi/abs/10.1177/0956797618764621; Gebauer, J. E., Nehrlich, A. D., Stahlberg, D., Sedikides, C., Hackenschmidt, A., Schick, D., Stegmaier, C. A., Windfelder, C. C., Bruk, A., and Mander, J. (2018). Mind-body practices and the self: Yoga and meditation do not quiet the ego but instead boost self-enhancement. *Psychological Science* 29(8), 1299–1308. https://doi.org/10.1177/0956797618764621

30. Graham, Carol, and Felton, Andrew. (2005, September). Variance in obesity across cohorts and countries: A norms-based explanation using happiness surveys. CSED Working Paper No. 42. Available at SSRN: https://ssrn.com/abstract=1024823 or http://dx.doi.org/10.2139/ssrn.1024823

31. Gogoi, P. (2023, April 29). The weight bias against women in the workforce is real—and it's only getting worse. NPR. https://www.npr.org/2023/04/29/1171593736/women-weight-bias-wages-workplace-wage-gap

32. Macchi, Elisa. (2023, September). Worth your weight: Experimental evidence on the benefits of obesity in low-income countries. *American Economic Review* 113(9): 2287–2322.

33. Graham, Carol, and Felton, Andrew. (2005, September). Variance in obesity across cohorts and countries: A norms-based explanation using happiness surveys. CSED Working Paper No. 42. Available at SSRN: https://ssrn.com/abstract=1024823 or http://dx.doi.org/10.2139/ssrn.1024823

34. Lee, Wang-Sheng, and Zhao, Zhong. (2015). Height, weight and well-being for rural, urban and migrant workers in China. IZA Discussion Paper No. 9397. Available at SSRN: https://ssrn.com/abstract=2672183

35. Katzmarzyk, Peter T., and Davis, Caroline. (2001, April 20). Thinness and body shape of *Playboy* centerfolds from 1978 to 1998. *International Journal of Obesity* 25: 90–592.

36. Roberts, Alan, and Muta, Sena. (2017, March). Body image representations of female body weight in the media: An update of *Playboy* magazine from 2000 to 2014. *Science Direct* 20: 16–19. https://www.sciencedirect.com/science/article/pii/S1740144516303187?via%3Dihub

37. Flynn, Mark A., Park, Sung-Yeon, Morin, David T., and Stana Alexandru. (2015). Anything but real: Body idealization and objectification of MTV docusoap characters. *Sex Roles* 72: 173–182.

38. Beck, C. M. and M. Mazmanian, Dreams of the Overworked Living, Working, and Parenting in the Digital Age, 2020, Standard University Press, Stanford, California.

39. Ibid., p. 71.

40. Swami, V., Weis, L., Barron, D., and Furnham, A. (2018). Positive body image is positively associated with hedonic (emotional) and eudaimonic (psychological and social) well-being in British adults. *Journal of Social Psychology* 158(5): 541–552. doi:10.1080/00224545.2017.1 392278. Epub 2017 Nov 21. Erratum in: *Journal of Social Psychology*, 2020, 160(2): 264–266. PMID: 29053404.

41. Thames, A., and Abrams, J. (2022, November 10). Female college athletes say pressure to cut body fat is toxic. *New York Times*. https://www.nytimes.com/2022/11/10/sports/college-athletes-body-fat-women.html

42. Jargon, J. (2021, November 13). Boys have eating disorders, too. Doctors think social media is making it worse. *Wall Street Journal*. https://www.wsj.com/articles/boys-have-eating-disorders-too-doctors-think-social-media-is-making-it-worse-11636812000

43. Davis, D. (2018, August 21). Sex, steroids, and Arnold: The story of the gym that shaped America. *Deadspin*. https://deadspin.com/sex-steroids-and-arnold-the-gym-that-shaped-america-1828228786

44. Dwyer, K. (2021). The way we worked out. *New York Times*. https://www.nytimes.com/2021/02/24/style/vertical-club.html

45. Khan, A. M. (2017, March 10). Wellness is the new status symbol: Euromonitor. *American Marketer*. https://americanmarketer.com/2017/03/10/wellness-is-the-new-luxury-status-symbol-euromonitor/

46. Khan, A. M. (2017, March 10). Wellness is the new status symbol: Euromonitor. *American Marketer*. https://americanmarketer.com/2017/03/10/wellness-is-the-new-luxury-status-symbol-euromonitor/

47. Braff, D. (2023, March 25). Think getting into college is hard? Try applying for these gyms. *New York Times*. https://www.nytimes.com/2023/03/25/style/exclusive-gym-memberships.html

48. Lieber, C. (2023, March 10). How young women fight loneliness—Walking together in the park by the hundreds. *Wall Street Journal*. https://www.wsj.com/articles/women-walking-clubs-city-fitness-13e6dfe3

49. Kasriel-Alexander, D. (2017, October 13). Top 10 global consumer trends for 2017. *Euromonitor International*. https://kupdf.net/download/top-consumer-trends-2017pdf_59e0367c08bbc5c914e65330_pdf

50. Khan, A.M. (2017, March 10). Wellness is the new status symbol: Euromonitor. *American Marketer* https://americanmarketer.com/2017/03/10/wellness-is-the-new-luxury-status-symbol-euromonitor/

51. Berlinger, M. (2021, February 17). How Erewhon became L. A.'s hottest hangout. *New York Times.* https://www.nytimes.com/2021/02/17/style/erewhon-los-angeles-health-food.html

52. Pearson, C. (2023, January 20). New guidelines underscore how complicated childhood obesity is for patients and providers. *New York Times.* https://www.nytimes.com/2023/01/20/well/family/childhood-obesity-guidelines.html

53. Belluz, J. (2023, January 31). Opinion | What new weight loss drugs teach us about fat and free will. *New York Times.* https://www.nytimes.com/2023/01/31/opinion/ozempic-weight-loss-drugs.html

54. Lamas, D. J. (202, January 4). Opinion | As a doctor, I see aging differently. *New York Times.* https://www.nytimes.com/2023/01/04/opinion/anti-aging-science-longevity.html

55. Pinsker, J. (2022, January 7). Some questions for a man who expects he could live to 150. *The Atlantic.* https://www.theatlantic.com/family/archive/2022/01/live-to-150-life-expectancy-extension/621190/

56. Span, Paula. (2020, January 31). CPR by default when very old patients suffer cardiac arrest, doctors usually try to revive them—even if they were already near death. *New York Times.* https://www.nytimes.com/2020/01/31/health/cpr-elderly.html

57. Lamas, D. J. (2022, November 22). Opinion | When the treatment of last resort sends a life into limbo. *New York Times.* https://www.nytimes.com/2022/11/22/opinion/hospital-death-ecmo.html

58. Span, P. (2018, November 9). Dementia is getting some very public faces. *New York Times.* https://www.nytimes.com/2018/11/09/health/alzheimers-dementia-celebrities.html

59. Egan, E. (2022, February 27). When her husband said he wanted to die, Amy Bloom listened. *New York Times.* https://www.nytimes.com/2022/02/27/books/in-love-amy-bloom.html

60. Rosengren, J. (2023, November 30). A son's decision to help his father die. *Washington Post.* https://www.washingtonpost.com/magazine/interactive/2022/vsed-refuse-treatment-cruzan/

61. White, K. (2020, January 7). Suicide is not an act of cowardice. *The Atlantic.* https://www.theatlantic.com/ideas/archive/2020/01/david-foster-wallace-was-no-coward/604501/

62. Span, P. (2018, August 31). A debate over "rational suicide." *New York Times.* https://www.nytimes.com/2018/08/31/health/suicide-elderly.html

63. Kliff, S., and Sanger-Katz, M. (2021, July 20). Americans' medical debts are bigger than was known, totaling $140 Billion. *New York Times.* https://www.nytimes.com/2021/07/20/upshot/medical-debt-americans-medicaid.html

64. Span, P. (2022, June 5). In older Americans, rising debt may adversely affect health. *New York Times.* https://www.nytimes.com/2022/06/05/health/elderly-medical-health-debt.html

65. Span, P. (2018, November 9). Dementia is getting some very public faces. *New York Times.* https://www.nytimes.com/2018/11/09/health/alzheimers-dementia-celebrities.html

66. Goodman-Bacon, Andrew. (2021, August). The long-run effects of childhood insurance coverage: Medicaid implementation, adult health, and labor market outcomes. *American Economic Review* 111(8): 2550–2593.

67. Raut, Nilesh. (2018, March 11). Universal healthcare coverage and subjective wellbeing: Evidence from Massachusetts healthcare reform. Available at SSRN: https://ssrn.com/abstract=3374331 or http://dx.doi.org/10.2139/ssrn.3374331

68. Baicker, K., and Finkelstein, A. Oregon Health Insurance Experiment. National Bureau of Economic Research. https://www.nber.org/programs-projects/projects-and-centers/oregon-health-insurance-experiment

69. Solomon, Andrew. (2020). What happens when you're disabled but nobody can tell. *New York Times.* https://www.nytimes.com/2020/07/10/style/invisible-disabilities.html

Chapter 11: Work

1. Caza, Brianna Barker, Wrzesniewsk, Amy, and David, Susan. How work shapes well-being. In: *Oxford Handbook of Happiness* (Oxford Library of Psychology), p. 693. OUP Oxford. Kindle Edition.

2. Kahneman, Daniel, and Krueger, Alan B. (2006). Developments in the measurement of subjective well-being. *Journal of Economic Perspectives* 20(1): 3–24.

3. De Neve, Jan-Emmanuel, and Ward, George. (2017, February 1). Happiness at work. Saïd Business School WP 2017-07. Available at SSRN: https://ssrn.com/abstract=2943318 or http://dx.doi.org/10.2139/ssrn.2943318

4. Bryce, Andrew. (2018, May). Finding meaning through work: Eudaimonic well-being and job type in the US and UK. SERPS no. 2018004, Sheffield Economic Research Paper Series. https://www.sheffield.ac.uk/economics/research/serps/articles/2018004.

5. Helliwell, John F., and Wang, Shun. (2011, July). Weekends and subjective well-being. NBER Working Paper No. w17180. Available at SSRN: https://ssrn.com/abstract=1882157

6. Zulkarnain, A., and Rutledge, M. (2021, May 11). Do men who work longer live longer? Evidence from the Netherlands—Center for Retirement Research. Center for Retirement Research at Boston College. https://crr.bc.edu/do-men-who-work-longer-live-longer-evidence-from-the-netherlands/

7. Krekel, Christian, Ward, George, and De Neve, Jan-Emmanuel. (2019, March 3). Employee well-being, productivity, and firm performance. Saïd Business School WP 2019-04. Available at SSRN: https://ssrn.com/abstract=3356581 or http://dx.doi.org/10.2139/ssrn.3356581

8. Fisher, J., and Phillips, A. (2023). For CFOs, well-being can offer healthy returns. *Wall Street Journal*. https://deloitte.wsj.com/cfo/for-cfos-well-being-can-offer-healthy-returns-01627066927 h

9. Abelson, R. (2019, April 16). Employee wellness programs yield little benefit, study shows. *New York Times*. https://www.nytimes.com/2019/04/16/health/employee-wellness-programs.html

10. Edelheit, E. (2023). "I Didn't Make It." *Washington Post*. https://www.washingtonpost.com/graphics/2020/national/disney-layoffs-coronavirus/

11. Silver, L., Van Kessel, P., Huang, C., Clancy, L., and Gubbala, S. (2021, November 18). What makes life meaningful? Views from 17 advanced economies. Pew Research Center. https://www.pewresearch.org/global/2021/11/18/finding-meaning-in-others/

12. Werner, E. (2023, February 24). High-skilled visa holders at risk of deportation amid tech layoffs. *Washington Post*. https://www.washingtonpost.com/us-policy/2023/02/24/temporary-visa-h1b-tech-layoffs/

13. Hussam, Reshmaan, Kelley, Erin M., Lane, Gregory, and Zahra, Fatima. (2022). The psychosocial value of employment: Evidence from a refugee camp. *American Economic Review* 112(11): 3694–3724. https://doi.org/10.1257/aer.20211616

14. Harter, J. (2018, August 26). Employee engagement on the rise in the U.S. Gallup. https://news.gallup.com/poll/241649/employee-engagement-rise.aspx

15. Statman, Meir. (2017, December 16). Meet today's challenges by becoming a well-being adviser. *Journal of Financial Planning*, 22–23.

16. Cooper, M. (2014). *Cut Adrift: Families in Insecure Times*. Berkeley and Los Angeles: University of California Press, p. 124

17. Johnston, David W., and Lee, Wang-Sheng. (2013, January 1). Extra status and extra stress: Are promotions good for us? *Industrial and*

Labor Relations Review 66(1). Available at SSRN: https://ssrn.com/abstract=2221555

18. Harter, J. (2022, September 6). Is quiet quitting real? *Gallup.* https://www.gallup.com/workplace/398306/quiet-quitting-real.aspx

19. Parker, Robert, and Clark, Benjamin Y. (2022, January 27). Unraveling the Great Resignation: Impacts of the COVID-19 pandemic on Oregon workers. Available at SSRN: https://ssrn.com/abstract=4019586 or http://dx.doi.org/10.2139/ssrn.4019586

20. Ember, S. (2021, June 20. How Do They Say Economic Recovery? 'I Quit.' https://www.nytimes.com/2021/06/20/business/economy/workers-quit-jobs.html

21. Thompson, D. (2022, March 25). The myth that most Americans hate their job. *The Atlantic.* https://www.theatlantic.com/newsletters/archive/2022/03/american-great-resignation-hate-work/627761/

22. Kodé, A. (2022, August 22). How quitting a job changed my personal finances. *New York Times.* https://www.nytimes.com/2022/08/22/style/quitting-personal-finances.html

23. Frey, Bruno S. (2008, May). Being independent is a great thing: Subjective evaluations of self-employment and hierarchy. *Economica* 75(298): 362–383. Available at SSRN: https://ssrn.com/abstract=1117050 or http://dx.doi.org/10.1111/j.1468-0335.2007.00594.x

24. Reto Odermatt, Nattavudh Powdthavee, and Alois Stutzer. (2021, December), Are newly self-employed overly optimistic about their future well-being? *Journal of Behavioral and Experimental Economics* 95.

25. Appau, Samuelson, Awaworyi Churchill, Sefa, and Farrell, Lisa. (2017, July 27). Job type, identity and subjective well-being. Available at SSRN: https://ssrn.com/abstract=3012698 or http://dx.doi.org/10.2139/ssrn.3012698

26. Van Kessel, P., Hughes, A., and Walker, K. (2018, November 20). The meaning of life: 100 quotes from Americans on what keeps them going. *Pew Research Center's Religion & Public Life Project.* https://www.pewresearch.org/religion/interactives/what-keeps-us-going/

27. Bryce, Andrew. (2018, May). Finding meaning through work: Eudaimonic well-being and job type in the US and UK. SERPS no. 2018004, Sheffield Economic Research Paper Series. https://www.sheffield.ac.uk/economics/research/serps/articles/2018004.

28. Statman, Meir. (2017, December 16). Meet today's challenges by becoming a well-being adviser. *Journal of Financial Planning,* 22–23.

29. Moynihan, Donald P., DeLeire, Thomas, and Enami, Kohei (2015, May). A life worth living: Evidence on the relationship between

prosocial values and happiness. *The American Review of Public Administration* 45(3): 311–326. doi:10.1177/0275074013493657. Available at SSRN: https://ssrn.com/abstract=3484604

30. Dur, Robert, and van Lent, Max. (2018, March 30). Socially useless jobs. Tinbergen Institute Discussion Paper 18-034/VII. Available at SSRN: https://ssrn.com/abstract=3162569 or http://dx.doi.org/10.2139/ssrn.3162569

31. Chandler, Dana, and Kapelner, Adam. (2013). Breaking monotony with weaning: Motivation in crowdsourcing markets. *Journal of Economic Behavior & Organization* 90: 123–133.

32. Ariely, Dan, Kamenica, Emir, and Prelec, Drazen. (2008). Man's search for Meaning: The case of Legos. *Journal of Economic Behavior & Organization* 67(3–4): 671–677.

33. Karni, A. (2023, May 19). Why Dianne Feinstein, like many before her, refuses to let go. *New York Times.* https://www.nytimes.com/2023/05/19/us/politics/dianne-feinstein-older-lawmakers-senate.html

34. Tiffany, K. (2021, June 16). The rise and fall of an American tech giant. *The Atlantic.* https://www.theatlantic.com/magazine/archive/2021/07/kodak-rochester-new-york/619009/

35. Stone, P. (2007). *Opting out? Why Women Really Quit Careers and Head Home.* Berkeley and Los Angeles: University of California Press, pp. 144–145.

36. Van Kessel, P., Hughes, A., and Walker, K. (2018, November 20). The meaning of life: 100 quotes from Americans on what keeps them going. *Pew Research Center's Religion & Public Life Project.* https://www.pewresearch.org/religion/interactives/what-keeps-us-going/

37. Kristof-Brown, Amy L., Zimmerman, Ryan D., and Johnson, Erin C. (2005). Consequences of individual's fit at work: A meta-analysis of person-job, person-organization, person-group, and person-supervisor fit. *Personnel Psychology* 58: 281–342.

38. De Neve, Jan-Emmanuel, and Ward, George. (2017, February 1). Happiness at work. Saïd Business School WP 2017-07. Available at SSRN: https://ssrn.com/abstract=2943318 or http://dx.doi.org/10.2139/ssrn.2943318

39. Blanton, K. (2020, November 19). Blue-collar workers often retire early— Center for Retirement Research. Center for Retirement Research at Boston College.. https://crr.bc.edu/blue-collar-workers-often-retire-early/

40. Ibid.

41. Ibid.

42. Williams, Joan C. (2020). *White working class, with a new foreword by Mark Cuban and a new preface by the author.* Harvard Business Review Press, Kindle Edition, p. 42.

43. Ibid., pp. 44–45.

44. Sandel, M.J. (2020, September 2). What liberals get wrong about work. *The Atlantic.* https://www.theatlantic.com/ideas/archive/2020/09/contributive-justice-and-dignity-work/615919/

45. Acemoglu, Daron. (2021, August). Obedience in the labor market and social mobility: A socio-economic approach. NBER Working Paper No. w2912. Available at SSRN: https://ssrn.com/abstract=3901589

46. Bartik, Alexander, Cullen, Zoe, Glaeser, Edward L., Luca, Michael, and Stanton, Christopher. (2020, June 20). What jobs are being done at home during the COVID-19 crisis? Evidence from firm-level surveys. Harvard Business School Entrepreneurial Management, Harvard Business School NOM Unit Working Paper No. 20-138. Available at SSRN: https://ssrn.com/abstract=3634983 or http://dx.doi.org/10.2139/ssrn.3634983

47. Ford, Michael, Want, Yi-Ren, and Huh, Youjeong. (2018). Work, the work-family interface, and subjective well-being. In: E. Diener, S. Oishi, and L. Tay (eds.), *Handbook of well-being.* Salt Lake City, UT: DEF Publishers. doi: nobascholar.com

48. Cooper, M. (2014). *Cut Adrift: Families in Insecure Times.* Berkeley and Los Angeles: University of California Press. p. 124

49. Statman, Meir. (2017, December 16). Meet today's challenges by becoming a well-being adviser. *Journal of Financial Planning,* 22–23.

50. Hannah. (2016, January 4). Work-life balance—Readers' stories: "It was hard work, now it's paying off." *The Guardian.* https://www.theguardian.com/money/2016/jan/04/work-life-balance-readers-stories-it-was-hard-work-now-its-paying-off

51. Fuhrmans, V. (2023, February 21). After testing four-day week, companies say they don't want to stop. *Wall Street Journal.* https://www.wsj.com/articles/after-testing-four-day-week-companies-say-they-dont-want-to-stop-a06089cc

52. Jaga, Ameeta, and Bagraim, Jeffrey. (2011). The relationship between work-family enrichment and work-family satisfaction outcomes. *South African Journal of Psychology* 41(1): 52–62.

53. Bronnenberg, Bart, Klein, Tobias J., and Xu, Yan. (2022, September 16). Consumer time budgets and grocery shopping behavior. Available at SSRN: https://ssrn.com/abstract=4269614 or http://dx.doi.org/10.2139/ssrn.4269614

54. Thompson, Derek. (2019, December 23). Three theories for why you have no time. *The Atlantic.*

55. Ford, Tiffany N., Silva, Jennifer M., Welch, Morgan, and Sawhill, Isabel V. (2021, February 16). No time to spare: Exploring the middle class time squeeze. Brookings Institution.

56. Halpern-Meekin, S., Edin, K., Tach, L. et al. (2015). *It's Not Like I'm Poor: How Working Families Make Ends Meet in a Post-Welfare World.* Berkeley and Los Angeles: University of California Press, p. 33.

57. Okulicz-Kozaryn, Adam. (2017, August 12). Unhappiness is unpredictability. Available at SSRN: https://ssrn.com/abstract=3044540 or http://dx.doi.org/10.2139/ssrn.3044540

58. Kesavan, Saravanan, Lambert, Susan, Williams, Joan, and Pendem, Pradeep. (2020, July 13). Doing well by doing good: Improving store performance with employee-friendly scheduling practices at the Gap, Inc. Available at SSRN: https://ssrn.com/abstract=3731670 or http://dx.doi.org/10.2139/ssrn.3731670

59. Kuhn, Peter, and Lozano, Fernando (2008, April). The expanding workweek? Understanding trends in long work hours among U.S. men, 1979–2006. *Journal of Labor Economics* 26(2): 311–343.

60. Bazelon, L. (2019, June 29). Opinion | I've picked my job over my kids. *New York Times.* https://www.nytimes.com/2019/06/29/opinion/sunday/ive-picked-my-job-over-my-kids.html

61. Thompson, Derek. (2019, February 24). Workism is making Americans miserable. *The Atlantic.*

62. Putill, Corinne. (2020, September 1). Ideal, perfect, ultimate: What drives parents to seek the unattainable? *The New York Times.*

63. Bellezza, Silvia, Paharia, Neeru, and Keinan, Anat. (2017, June). Conspicuous consumption of time: When busyness and lack of leisure time become a status symbol. *Journal of Consumer Research* 44(1): 118–138.

64. Markovits, Daniel. (2019). The meritocracy trap: How America's foundational myth feeds inequality, dismantles the middle class, and devours the elite. New York: Penguin Press, p. 4. Kindle Edition.

65. Artz, B. M., Goodall, A. H., and Oswald, A. J. (2016). Boss competence and worker well-being. *Industrial and Labor Relations Review,* forthcoming.

66. Statman, Meir. (2017, December 16). Meet today's challenges by becoming a well-being adviser. *Journal of Financial Planning,* 22–23.

67. Ellis, L. (2022, October 20). Toxic workplaces are bad for mental and physical health, surgeon general says. *Wall Street Journal*. https://headtopics.com/us/toxic-workplaces-are-bad-for-mental-and-physical-health-surgeon-general-says-30923830

68. Pinsker, J. (2022, February 16). The dark side of saying work is "like a family." *The Atlantic*. https://www.theatlantic.com/family/archive/2022/02/work-actually-is-like-a-family/622813/

69. Fuller, T., Browning, K., Bogel-Burroughs, N., and Mazzei, P. (2021, May 28). San Jose gunman detested workplace long before rampage, police say. *New York Times*. https://www.nytimes.com/2021/05/27/us/san-jose-shooting.html

70. Ellis, L. (2022, October 20). Toxic workplaces are bad for mental and physical health, surgeon general says. *Wall Street Journal*. https://headtopics.com/us/toxic-workplaces-are-bad-for-mental-and-physical-health-surgeon-general-says-30923830

71. Michele Lamont, Graziella Moraes Silva, Jessicac S. Welburn, Joshua Guetzkow, Nissim Mizrachi, Hanna Herzog, and Elisa Reis. (2016). *Getting respect: Responding to stigma and discrimination in the United States, Brazil, and Israel*. Princeton, NJ: Princeton University Press, p. 7.

72. Statman, Meir. (2017, December 16). Meet today's challenges by becoming a well-being adviser. *Journal of Financial Planning*, 22–23.

73. Bach, Laurent, Baghai, Ramin, Bos, Marieke, and Silva, Rui. (2021, October 18). How do acquisitions affect the mental health of employees? Swedish House of Finance Research Paper No. 21-21, Available at SSRN: https://ssrn.com/abstract=3947957 or http://dx.doi.org/10.2139/ssrn.3947957

74. Taja, J. (2013, June 25). 6 inspiring stories from people who unexpectedly lost their jobs. *Business Insider*. https://www.businessinsider.com/6-stories-of-job-loss-that-will-inspire-2013-7

75. Khazan, O. (2021, March 12). Only your boss can cure your burnout. *The Atlantic*. https://www.theatlantic.com/politics/archive/2021/03/how-tell-if-you-have-burnout/618250/

76. Seppälä, Emma, and Cameron, Kim. (2015, December 1). Proof that positive work cultures are more productive. *Harvard Business Review*. https://hbr.org/2015/12/proof-that-positive-work-cultures-are-more-productive

77. Ibid.

78. Okat, Deniz, and Vasudevan, Ellapulli. (2021, March 23). Going the extra mile: What taxi rides tell us about the long-hour culture in finance. Available at SSRN: https://ssrn.com/abstract=3810864 or http://dx.doi.org/10.2139/ssrn.3810864

79. Baer, J. (2021, April 17). Bond giant Pimco attempts to change its culture. *Wall Street Journal*. https://www.wsj.com/articles/bond-giant-pimco-attempts-to-change-its-culture-11618651802

80. Ibid.

81. Korducki, K. M. (2021, June 6). Opinion | We're finally starting to revolt against the cult of ambition. *New York Times*. https://www.nytimes.com/2021/06/06/opinion/Naomi-Osaka-ambition-women.html

82. Zechmann, Andrea, and Karsten Ingmar, Paul. (2019). Why do individuals suffer during unemployment? Analyzing the role of deprived psychological needs in a six-wave longitudinal study. *Journal of Occupational Health Psychology* 24(6): 641–661. https://doi.org/10.1037/ocp0000154

83. Crabtree, S. (2014, June 9). In U.S., depression rates higher for long-term unemployed. *Gallup*. https://news.gallup.com/poll/171044/depression-rates-higher-among-long-term-unemployed.aspx

84. Statman, Meir. (2017, December 16). Meet today's challenges by becoming a well-being adviser. *Journal of Financial Planning*, 22–23.

85. Knabe, Andreas, and Rätzel, Steffen. (2011). Scarring or scaring? The psychological impact of past unemployment and future unemployment risk. *Economica* 78(310): 283–293.

86. Di Tella, Rafael, MacCulloch, Robert J., and Oswald, Andrew J. (2001). Preferences over inflation and unemployment: Evidence from surveys of happiness. *American Economic Review* 91: 335–341.

87. Oesch, Daniel, and Lipps, Oliver. (2011, July 21). Does unemployment hurt less if there is more of it around? A panel analysis of life satisfaction in Germany and Switzerland. SOEP paper No. 393. Available at SSRN: https://ssrn.com/abstract=1914249 or http://dx.doi.org/10.2139/ssrn.1914249

88. Clark, Andrew, Diener, Ed, Georgellis, Yannis, and Lucas, Richard E. (2006, December). Lags and leads in life satisfaction: A test of the baseline hypothesis. IZA Discussion Paper No. 2526. Available at SSRN: https://ssrn.com/abstract=956920

89. Newman, K. S. (1999). *Falling from grace: Downward mobility in the age of affluence*. Oakland: University of California Press.

90. Chen, V.T. (2015). *Cut Loose: Jobless and Hopeless in an Unfair Economy*. Berkeley and Los Angeles: University of California Press, p. 1.

91. Ibid., p. 4.

92. Lohr, S. (2022, January 11). Economists pin more blame on tech for rising inequality. *New York Times*. https://www.nytimes.com/ 2022/01/11/technology/income-inequality-technology.html

93. Chen, Kelly, and Islam, Samia. (2023). Declining unionization and the despair of the working class. *Journal of Law and Economics* 66(2): 279–307.

94. Akay, Alpaslan, Karabulut, Gokhan, and Yilmaz, Levent. (2021). Life satisfaction, pro-activity, and employment. IZA Discussion Paper No. 14117. Available at SSRN: https://ssrn.com/abstract=3789384

95. Galama, Titus J., van de Kraats, Coen, and Lindeboom, Maarten. (2022, October 29). Why life gets better after age 50, for some: Mental well-being and the social norm of work. CESR-Schaeffer Working Paper No. 2022_005. Available at SSRN: https://ssrn.com/ abstract=4267420 or http://dx.doi.org/10.2139/ssrn.4267420

96. De Neve, Jan-Emmanuel, and Ward, George. (2017, February 1). Happiness at work. Saïd Business School WP 2017-07. Available at SSRN: https://ssrn.com/abstract=2943318 or http://dx.doi. org/10.2139/ssrn.2943318

97. Van Kessel, P., Hughes, A., and Walker, K. (2018, November 20). The meaning of life: 100 quotes from Americans on what keeps them going. *Pew Research Center's Religion & Public Life Project*. https://www.pewresearch.org/religion/interactives/what-keeps-us-going/

98. De Neve, Jan-Emmanuel, and Ward, George (2017, February 1). Happiness at work. Saïd Business School WP 2017-07. Available at SSRN: https://ssrn.com/abstract=2943318 or http://dx.doi. org/10.2139/ssrn.2943318

99. Statman, WellBeing Advisers.

100. Amer-Mestre, Josep, and Charpin, Agnès. (2021, December 1). Gender differences in early occupational choices: Evidence from medical specialty selection. Available at SSRN: https://ssrn.com/ abstract=3976273 or http://dx.doi.org/10.2139/ssrn.3976273

101. Yu, Shuye, and Postepska, Agnieszka. (2020). Flexible jobs make parents happier: Evidence from Australia. IZA Discussion Paper No. 13700. Available at SSRN: https://ssrn.com/abstract=3695401

102. Booth, Alison L., and van Ours, Jan C. (2007, August). Job satisfaction and family happiness: The part-time work puzzle. IZA Discussion Paper No. 3020. Center Discussion Paper Series No. 2007-69. Available at SSRN: https://ssrn.com/abstract=1012293

103. De Neve, Jan-Emmanuel, and Ward, George. (2017, February 1). Happiness at work. Saïd Business School WP 2017-07. Available at SSRN: https://ssrn.com/abstract=2943318 or http://dx.doi.org/10.2139/ssrn.2943318

104. Van Kessel, P., Hughes, A., and Walker, K. (2018, November 20). The meaning of life: 100 quotes from Americans on what keeps them going. *Pew Research Center's Religion & Public Life Project*. https://www.pewresearch.org/religion/interactives/what-keeps-us-going/

105. Carpenter, J. (2022, December 5). Couples who combine finances are happier. So why don't more do it? *Wall Street Journal*. https://www.wsj.com/articles/couples-who-combine-finances-are-happier-so-why-dont-more-do-it-11670174525

106. Olien, J. (2010, November 15). Going Dutch. *Slate*. https://slate.com/human-interest/2010/11/women-in-the-netherlands-work-less-have-lesser-titles-and-a-big-gender-pay-gap-and-they-love-it.html

107. Van Kessel, P., Hughes, A., and Walker, K. (2018, November 20). The meaning of life: 100 quotes from Americans on what keeps them going. *Pew Research Center's Religion & Public Life Project*. https://www.pewresearch.org/religion/interactives/what-keeps-us-going/

108. Gerdeman, D. (2018, September 7). Welcome to retirement. Who am I now? Harvard Business School. http://hbswk.hbs.edu/item/welcome-to-retirement-who-am-i-now

109. Blanton, K. (2020, February 20). Mapping out a fulfilling retirement. Center for Retirement Research at Boston College. https://crr.bc.edu/mapping-out-a-fulfilling-retirement/

110. Chuard, Patrick. (2020, October 29). With booze, you lose: The mortality effects of early retirement. Available at SSRN: https://ssrn.com/abstract=3721505 or http://dx.doi.org/10.2139/ssrn.3721505

111. Dhaval, Dave, Inas Rashad, Kelly, and Spasojevic, Jasmina. (2007, October). The effects of retirement on physical and mental health outcomes. Andrew Young School of Policy Studies Research Paper Series No. 07-35. Available at SSRN: https://ssrn.com/abstract=1024475 or http://dx.doi.org/10.2139/ssrn.1024475

112. Picchio, Matteo, and van Ours, Jan (2019). The mental health effects of retirement. IZA Discussion Paper No. 12791. Available at SSRN: https://ssrn.com/abstract=3495768

113. Appau, Samuelson, Awaworyi Churchill, Sefa, and Farrell, Lisa. (2017, July 27). Job type, identity and subjective wellbeing. Available at SSRN: https://ssrn.com/abstract=3012698 or http://dx.doi.org/10.2139/ssrn.3012698

114. Span, Paula. (2018, March 30). Many Americans try retirement, then change their minds. *New York Times*.

115. Sharif, Marissa, Mogilner, Cassie, and Hershfield, Hal. (2018, November 15). The effects of being time poor and time rich on life satisfaction. Available at SSRN: https://ssrn.com/abstract=3285436 or http://dx.doi.org/10.2139/ssrn.3285436

116. Span, Paula. (2018, March 30). Many Americans try retirement, then change their minds. *New York Times*.

117. Ameriks, John, Briggs, Joseph, Caplin, Andrew, Lee, Minjoon, Shapiro, Matthew D., and Tonetti, Christopher. (2018, February 1). Shocks and transitions from career jobs to bridge jobs and retirement: A new approach. Michigan Retirement Research Center Research Paper No. 2018-380. Stanford University Graduate School of Business Research Paper No. 18-39. Available at SSRN: https://ssrn.com/abstract=3240808 or http://dx.doi.org/10.2139/ssrn.3240808

118. Calvo, Esteban, Haverstick, Kelly, and Sass, Steven A. (2009, January 1). Gradual retirement, sense of control, and retirees' happiness. *Research on Aging*, SAGE Publications, Ltd. 31(1): 112–135. doi:10.1177/0164027508324704. Available at SSRN: https://ssrn.com/abstract=2309483

119. Schwartz, N. D., and Marcos, C. M. (2021, July 2). They didn't expect to retire early. The pandemic changed their plans. *New York Times*. https://www.nytimes.com/2021/07/02/business/economy/retire-early-pandemic-social-security.html

120. Marcus, J. (2021, March 10). Pandemic forced millions of workers to retire early. AARP. https://www.aarp.org/work/careers/pandemic-workers-early-retirement/

121. Burn, Ian, Firoozi, Daniel, Ladd, Daniel, and Neumark, David. (2022, July). Help really wanted? The impact of age stereotypes in job ads on applications from older workers. NBER Working Paper No. w30287. Available at SSRN: https://ssrn.com/abstract=4177539

122. Engelman, Michal, and Joo, Won-tak. (2021). Retirement in the context of intergenerational transfers. WI21-02. https://cfsrdrc.wisc.edu/project/wi21-02 or https://squaredawayblog.bc.edu/squared-away/men-make-bigger-changes-after-retiring/

123. Finch, P. (2018, April 27). How to talk about moving to a retirement home: "it's a journey." *New York Times*. https://www.nytimes.com/2018/04/27/business/retirement-home-move-talk.html

124. Free, C. (2020, March 31). Newspaper deliveryman brings groceries to his older customers on morning route, no extra charge. *Washington Post*. https://www.washingtonpost.com/lifestyle/2020/03/31/newspaper-delivery-man-brings-groceries-his-older-customers-morning-route-no-extra-charge/

125. Victoria H. "Inspiring young writers" in these Heartwarming Volunteer Stories Will Totally Inspire You To Give Back. Buzzfeed. (August 28) https://www.buzzfeed.com/usbank/these-heartwarming-volunteer-stories-will-totally.

126. Lawton, Ricky N., Gramatki, Iulian, Watt, Will, and Fujiwara, Daniel. (2021). Does volunteering make us happier, or are happier people more likely to volunteer? Addressing the problem of reverse causality when estimating the wellbeing impacts of volunteering. *Fujiwara Journal of Happiness Studies* 22: 599–624.

127. Thoits, Peggy A., and Hewitt, Lyndi N. (2001, June). *Journal of Health and Social Behavior* 42(2): 115–131. https://doi.org/10.2307/3090173 https://www.jstor.org/stable/3090173

128. Dolan, Paul, Krekel, Christian, Shreedhar, Ganga, Lee, Helen, Marshall, Claire, and Smith, Allison. (2021). Happy to help: The welfare effects of a nationwide micro-volunteering programme. IZA Discussion Paper No. 14431. Available at SSRN: https://ssrn.com/abstract=3865456

129. Costello, John P., and Malkoc, Selin A. (2022, December). Why are donors more generous with time than money? The role of perceived control over donations on charitable giving. *Journal of Consumer Research* 49(4): 678–696. https://doi.org/10.1093/jcr/ucac011

130. Binder, M., and Freytag, A. (2013). Volunteering, subjective well-being and public policy. *Journal of Economic Psychology*, 34, 97–119. https://doi.org/10.1016/j.joep.2012.11.008

131. Moren, G. (2022, June 29). How volunteering helps your career goals and overall wellbeing. *Fast Company*. https://www.fastcompany.com/90763899/how-volunteering-helps-your-career-goals-and-overall-wellbeing

132. Burt, Emily L., and Atkinson, Jacqueline. (2012, March). The relationship between quilting and wellbeing. *Journal of Public Health* 34(1): 54–59, p. 56.

133. Van Kessel, P., Hughes, A., and Walker, K. (2018, November 20). The meaning of life: 100 quotes from Americans on what keeps them

going. *Pew Research Center's Religion & Public Life Project.* https://www.pewresearch.org/religion/interactives/what-keeps-us-going/

134. Statman, Meir. (2017, December 16). Meet today's challenges by becoming a well-being adviser. *Journal of Financial Planning*, 22–23.

135. Mihaly Csikszentmihalyi. (1997). *Finding flow: The psychology of engagement.* New York: HarperCollins, pp. 28–29.

136. Statman, Meir. (2017, December 16). Meet today's challenges by becoming a well-being adviser. *Journal of Financial Planning*, 22–23.

137. In a stressful time, knitting for calm and connection. *The New York Times.* https://www.nytimes.com/2020/11/02/well/family/pandemic-knitting-election-stress.html

138. Csikszentmihalyi, M. (1999). If we are so rich, why aren't we happy? *American Psychologist* 54(10): 821–827.

139. Hond, P. (2020, May). The smart person's guide to aging. *Columbia Magazine.* https://magazine.columbia.edu/article/smart-persons-guide-aging

Chapter 12: Education

1. Malesic, J. (2022, May 13). Opinion | My college students are not OK. *New York Times.* https://www.nytimes.com/2022/05/13/opinion/college-university-remote-pandemic.html

2. Bures, F. (2020, July 22). What my kids learned when they weren't in school. *The Atlantic.* https://www.theatlantic.com/family/archive/2020/07/kids-time-away-school-hasnt-been-wasted/614482/

3. Knowles, M. (2020, May 27). I never thought that I would miss school, but I do. *EdSource.* https://edsource.org/2020/i-never-thought-that-i-would-miss-school-but-i-do/631970

4. https://www.j2e.com/?id=ZVVCdTU1elpjdG9GdmRpSA==&wp&blog=2&revision=3

5. Bures, F. (2020, July 22). What my kids learned when they weren't in school. *The Atlantic.* https://www.theatlantic.com/family/archive/2020/07/kids-time-away-school-hasnt-been-wasted/614482/

6. García Bacete, F.J., Marande Perrin, G., Schneider, B.H., Blanchard, C. (2014). Effects of School on the Well-Being of Children and Adolescents. In: Ben-Arieh, A., Casas, F., Frønes, I., Korbin, J. (eds) Handbook of Child Well-Being. Springer, Dordrecht. https://doi.org/10.1007/978-90-481-9063-8_149

7. Barry, E. (2022, March 31). Many teens report emotional and physical abuse by parents during lockdown. *New York Times*. https://www.nytimes.com/2022/03/31/health/covid-mental-health-teens.

8. García Bacete, F. J., Marande Perrin, G., Schneider, B. H., and Blanchard, C. (2014). Effects of school on the well-being of children and adolescents. In: A. Ben-Arieh, F. Casas, I. Frønes, and J. Korbin (eds.). *Handbook of child well-being* (pp. 1251–1305). Springer, Dordrecht. https://doi.org/10.1007/978-90-481-9063-8_149

9. Sang Ho, Lok, and Ip, Patrick. (2018, May). What accounts for the decline of happiness of children as they grow into their teens: A Hong Kong case study. *Pacific Economic Review* 23(29): 222–243. https://doi.org/10.1111/1468-0106.12145

10. Packer, G. (2019, September 13). When the culture war comes for the kids. *The Atlantic*. https://www.theatlantic.com/magazine/archive/2019/10/when-the-culture-war-comes-for-the-kids/596668/

11. Christakis, E. (2015, December 18). How the new preschool is crushing kids. *The Atlantic*. https://www.theatlantic.com/magazine/archive/2016/01/the-new-preschool-is-crushing-kids/419139/

12. Stone, P., and Lovejoy, M. (2019). *Opting Back In: What really happens when mother go back to work*. Berkeley and Los Angeles: University of California Press, pp. 57–58.

13. Lorenz, T., and Pinsker, J. (2019, July 11). The slackification of the American home. *The Atlantic*. https://www.theatlantic.com/family/archive/2019/07/families-slack-asana/593584/

14. Levine, M. (2020, February 16). Kids don't need to stay "on track" to succeed. *The Atlantic*. https://www.theatlantic.com/family/archive/2020/02/path-success-squiggly-line/606631

15. Ibid.

16. Rosenberg, A. (2021, March 16). Opinion | What a cheerleading squad, a mom's arrest and deepfakes reveal about regulating technology. *Washington Post*. https://www.washingtonpost.com/opinions/2021/03/16/what-cheerleading-squad-moms-arrest-deepfakes-reveal-about-regulating-technology/

17. Markovits, D. (2019, August 19). How life became an endless, terrible competition. *The Atlantic*. https://www.theatlantic.com/magazine/archive/2019/09/meritocracys-miserable-winners/594760/

18. Flanagan, C. (2021, March 11). Private schools have become truly obscene. *The Atlantic*. https://www.theatlantic.com/magazine/archive/2021/04/private-schools-are-indefensible/618078/

19. Cooper, M. (2014). *Cut adrift: Families in insecure times.* Berkeley and Los Angeles: University of California Press, pp. 7–9.

20. Rosen, R. J. (2015, November 21). Why affluent parents put so much pressure on their kids. *The Atlantic.* https://www.theatlantic.com/business/archive/2015/11/pressure-affluent-parents/417045/

21. Cooper, M. (2014). *Cut adrift: Families in insecure times.* Berkeley and Los Angeles: University of California Press, p. 107.

22. Ibid., pp. 112–113.

23. Lieber, R. (2021, February 3). An invisible cost of college: Parental guilt. *New York Times.* https://www.nytimes.com/2021/02/03/well/family/college-costs-guilt.html

24. Dale, Stacy Berg, and Krueger, Alan B. (2002, November). Estimating the payoff of attending a more selective college: An application of selection on observables and unobservables. *Quarterly Journal of Economics* 107(4): 1491–1527.

25. Gladwell, M. (2005, October 2). Getting in. *The New Yorker.* https://www.newyorker.com/magazine/2005/10/10/getting-in-ivy-league-college-admissions

26. Thompson, D. (2018, December 11). Does it matter where you go to college? *The Atlantic.* https://www.theatlantic.com/ideas/archive/2018/12/does-it-matter-where-you-go-college/577816/

27. Black, Sandra E., Denning, Jeffrey T., and Rothstein, Jesse. (2023, January). Winners and losers? The effect of gaining and losing access to selective colleges on education and labor market outcomes. *American Economic Journal: Applied Economics* 15(1): 26–67.

28. Lieber, R. (2021, February 3). An invisible cost of college: Parental guilt. *New York Times.* https://www.nytimes.com/2021/02/03/well/family/college-costs-guilt.html

29. Hersch, Joni. (2019, June 12). Catching up is hard to do: Undergraduate prestige, elite graduate programs, and the earnings premium. Vanderbilt Law and Economics Research Paper No. 14-23. Vanderbilt Public Law Research Paper No. 16-17. Journal of Benefit-Cost Analysis, Forthcoming, Available at SSRN: https://ssrn.com/abstract=2473238 or http://dx.doi.org/10.2139/ssrn.2473238

30. Zumbrun, J. (2023, July 28). How Ivy League schools tilt your odds in the lottery of life. *Wall Street Journal.* https://www.wsj.com/us-news/education/how-ivy-league-schools-tilt-your-odds-in-the-lottery-of-life-590f8ec1

31. Rivera, L. (2015). *Pedigree: How elite students get elite jobs.* Princeton, NJ: Princeton University Press, p. 36.

32. Ibid., pp. 37–38.

33. Markovits, Daniel. (2019). *The meritocracy trap: How America's foundational myth feeds inequality, dismantles the middle class, and devours the elite.* New York: Penguin Press, p. 4. Kindle Edition.

34. Goodell, J. (2022, February 18). Saving their souls. *HumbleDollar.* https://humbledollar.com/2022/02/saving-their-souls/

35. Taylor, K. (2020, February 7). Former Pimco C.E.O. gets 9 months in prison in college admissions case. *New York Times.* https://www.nytimes.com/2020/02/07/us/douglas-hodge-college-admissions-scandal.html

36. Stone, P., and Lovejoy, M. (2019). *Opting back in: What really happens when mothers go back to work.* Berkeley and Los Angeles: University of California Press, pp. 57–58.

37. Ibid.

38. Sun, Ken Chih-Yan, and Smith, Jill M. (2017, February 3). Parenting, uncertainty, and expert advice: How privileged American families work with private counselors in their children's college race. https://onlinelibrary.wiley.com/doi/abs/10.1002/symb.258 https://doi.org/10.1002/symb.258Citations:

39. Jargon, J. (2021, May 1). Decision day 2021: How teens are sharing college acceptances (and rejections) after a rough year. *Wall Street Journal.* https://www.wsj.com/articles/decision-day-2021-how-teens-are-sharing-college-acceptances-and-rejections-after-a-rough-year-11619874002

40. Kirp, D. L. (2021, April 6). Opinion | Why Stanford should clone itself. *New York Times.* https://www.nytimes.com/2021/04/06/opinion/stanford-admissions-campus.html

41. Belkin, D. (2022, April 21). To get into the Ivy League, "extraordinary" isn't always enough these days. *Wall Street Journal.* https://www.wsj.com/articles/to-get-into-the-ivy-league-extraordinary-isnt-always-enough-these-days-11650546000

42. Gottlieb, L. (2020, May 11). Dear therapist: I staked my identity on attending an Ivy League school. *The Atlantic.* https://www.theatlantic.com/family/archive/2020/05/dear-therapist-my-dream-college-rejected-me/611407/

43. Paul, P. (2022, July 30). Opinion | The best extracurricular may be an after-school job. *New York Times*. https://www.nytimes.com/2022/07/30/opinion/jobs-teenagers.html

44. Binder, Amy J., and Abel, Andrea R. (2018, December 23). Symbolically maintained inequality: How Harvard and Stanford students construct boundaries among elite universities. Research Article. https://doi.org/10.1177/0038040718821073

45. Phillip, A. (2021, December 4). An Ivy League degree doesn't make you happier at work. Here's why. *Washington Post*. https://www.washingtonpost.com/blogs/local/wp/2014/05/06/an-ivy-league-degree-doesnt-make-you-happier-at-work-heres-why/

46. Bouchrika, I. (2023, July 25). Life after college: Adjusting & tips based on the Gallup-Purdue Index. Research.com. https://research.com/careers/life-after-college

47. Gottlieb, L. (2019, February 18). Dear therapist: I'm worried the college-admissions process is rigged against my son. *The Atlantic*. https://www.theatlantic.com/family/archive/2019/02/im-worried-my-son-wont-get-good-college/582979/

48. Lieber, R. (2021, February 3). An invisible cost of college: Parental guilt. *New York Times*. https://www.nytimes.com/2021/02/03/well/family/college-costs-guilt.html

49. Carey, K. (2021, September 9). Men fall behind in college enrollment. Women still play catch-up at work. *New York Times*. https://www.nytimes.com/2021/09/09/upshot/college-admissions-men.html

50. Davies, Scott, and Hammack, Floyd M. (2005). The channeling of student competition in higher education: Comparing Canada and the U.S. *The Journal of Higher Education* 76(1): 89–106. doi:10.1353/jhe.2005.0003. https://muse.jhu.edu/article/177630/pdf

51. Aurini, Janice, Missaghian, Rod, and Milian, Roger Pizarro. (2020, February 28). Educational status hierarchies, after-school activities, and parenting logics: Lessons from Canada. Research Article. https://doi.org/10.1177/0038040720908173

52. Cooper, M. (2014). *Cut adrift: Families in insecure times*. Berkeley and Los Angeles: University of California Press, p. 104.

53. Gladwell, M. (2005, October 2). Getting in. *The New Yorker*. https://www.newyorker.com/magazine/2005/10/10/getting-in-ivy-league-college-admissions

54. Karabel, Jerome. (2005). *The chosen: The hidden history of admission and exclusion at Harvard, Yale, and Princeton*. Boston: Houghton Mifflin.

55. Hoxby, Caroline M. (2009). The changing selectivity of American colleges. *Journal of Economic Perspectives* 23(4): 95–118.

56. U.S. News & World Report's College Rankings: Why do they matter?" (1999, November/December). *Change* 31(6): 42–51.

57. Ramey, Garey, and Ramey, Valerie A. (2009, August). The Rug-Rat Race. NBER Working Paper No. 15284.

58. Warikoo, N. (2022). *Race at the top: Pursuit of the American dream in suburban schools.* Chicago: University of Chicago Press, pp. 133–134.

59. Ibid., p. 135.

60. Boustain, Leah Platt, Cai, Christine, and Tseng, Tammy. (2023, July). White flight from Asian immigration: Evidence from California public schools. Working Paper 31434. doi:10.3386/w31434

61. Hsin A, Xie Y. Explaining Asian Americans' academic advantage over whites. Proc Natl Acad Sci U S A. 2014 Jun 10;111(23):8416-21. doi:10.1073/pnas.1406402111. Epub 2014 May 5. PMID: 24799702; PMCID: PMC4060715.

62. Ibid.

63. Warikoo, N. (2022). *Race at the top: Pursuit of the American dream in suburban schools.* Chicago: University of Chicago Press, p. 125.

64. Saul, S. (2022, October 17). Fencing can be six-figure expensive, but it wins in college admissions. *New York Times.* https://www.nytimes.com/2022/10/17/us/fencing-ivy-league-college-admissions.html

65. Callcott, S. (2022, October 1). Opinion | There's still one big trick for getting into an elite college. *New York Times.* https://www.nytimes.com/2022/10/01/opinion/school-private-college.html https://www.nytimes.com/2022/10/01/opinion/school-private-college.html

66. Cooper, M. (2014). *Cut adrift: Families in insecure times.* Berkeley and Los Angeles: University of California Press, p. 124

67. Chang, H. (2021, June 22). Chicken parenting is China's helicopter parenting on steroids. *The China Project.* https://thechinaproject.com/2021/06/22/chicken-parenting-is-chinas-helicopter-parenting-on-steroids/

68. Stevenson, A., and Li, C. (2021, July 30). China targets costly tutoring classes. Parents want to save them. *New York Times.* https://www.nytimes.com/2021/07/30/business/economy/china-education-tutors.html

69. Qian, J. (2022, December 26). Opinion | I've had enough of my parents' "no pain, no gain." *New York Times.* https://www.nytimes.com/2022/12/26/opinion/china-society-culture-youth-covid-protests.html

70. Belkin, D. (2022, April 21). To get into the Ivy League, "extraordinary" isn't always enough these days. *Wall Street Journal.* https://www.wsj.com/articles/to-get-into-the-ivy-league-extraordinary-isnt-always-enough-these-days-11650546000

71. Christakis, E. (2015, December 18). How the new preschool is crushing kids. *The Atlantic.* https://www.theatlantic.com/magazine/archive/2016/01/the-new-preschool-is-crushing-kids/419139/

72. Hirsh-Pasek, K., Farran, D., Burchinal, M., and Nesbitt, K. (2022, February 28). Making pre-K work: Lessons from the Tennessee study. Brookings. https://www.brookings.edu/articles/making-pre-k-work-lessons-from-the-tennessee-study/

73. Ibid.

74. Bailey, Martha J., Sun, Shuqiao, and Timpe, Brenden. (2021). Prep school for poor kids: The long-run impacts of head start on human capital and economic self-sufficiency. *American Economic Review* 111(12): 3963–4001. https://www.brookings.edu/blog/brown-center-chalkboard/2022/02/09/is-universal-preschool-worth-it/?utm_campaign=Brookings%20Brief&utm_medium=email&utm_content=203684869&utm_source=hs_email

75. Kirp, D. L. (2021, December 2). Opinion | A way to break the cycle of poverty. *New York Times.* https://www.nytimes.com/2021/12/02/opinion/politics/child-poverty-us.html

76. Garcia, Jorge Luis, Heckman, James J., and Ronda, Victor. (2021, July 16). The lasting effects of early childhood education on promoting the skills and social mobility of disadvantaged African Americans. University of Chicago, Becker Friedman Institute for Economics Working Paper No. 2021-83. Available at SSRN: https://ssrn.com/abstract=3888323 or http://dx.doi.org/10.2139/ssrn.3888323

77. List, John A., Pernaudet, Julie, and Suskind, Dana. (2021, October). It all starts with beliefs: Addressing the roots of educational inequities by shifting parental beliefs. NBER Working Paper No. w29394. Available at SSRN: https://ssrn.com/abstract=3949192 or http://dx.doi.org/10.2139/ssrn.3949192

78. Shah, Rohen, Kalil, Ariel, and Mayer, Susan. (2022, July 28). Engaging parents with preschools: Evidence from a field experiment. University of Chicago, Becker Friedman Institute for Economics Working Paper No. 2022-97. Available at SSRN: https://ssrn.com/abstract=4168257 or http://dx.doi.org/10.2139/ssrn.4168257

79. Guryan, Jonathan, Ludwig, Jens, Bhatt, Monica, Cook, Philip J., Davis, Jonathan, Dodge, Kenneth, Farkas, George, Fryer, Roland G., Mayer, Susan, Pollack, Harold A., and Steinberg, Laurence. (2021, March). Not too late: Improving academic outcomes among adolescents. NBER Working Paper No. w28531. Available at SSRN: https://ssrn.com/abstract=3799822

80. Bond, Timothy N., Carr, Jillian B., Packham, Analisa, and Smith, Jonathan. (2022). Hungry for success? SNAP timing, high-stakes exam performance, and college attendance. *American Economic Journal: Economic Policy* 14(4): 51–79.

81. Statman, Meir. (2020, Winter). Well-being advisers. *The Journal of Wealth Management* Winter 23 (Supplement 1): 2–44, p. 2. doi: https://doi.org/10.3905/jwm.23.s1.002

82. Hulbert, A. (2013). How To Escape the Community-College Trap. The Atlantic. (December 23) https://www.theatlantic.com/magazine/archive/2014/01/how-to-escape-the-community-college-trap/355745/.

83. Mountjoy, Jack. (2022, August). Community colleges and upward mobility. *American Economic Review* 112(8): pp. 2580–2630.

84. Marcotte, Dave E. (2019). The returns to education at community colleges: New evidence from the Education Longitudinal Survey. *Education Finance and Policy* 14(4): 523–547. doi: https://doi.org/10.1162/edfp_a_00267

85. Shadyvady. (2021). Community college success stories. Reddit Post.R/Education. www.reddit.com/r/education/comments/mz3j6f/community_college_success_stories/

86. Ibid.

87. Hulbert, A. (2013, December 23). How to escape the community-college trap. *The Atlantic*. https://www.theatlantic.com/magazine/archive/2014/01/how-to-escape-the-community-college-trap/355745/

89. Dynarski, Susan, Libassi, C. J., Michelmore, Katherine, and Owen, Stephanie. (2021). Closing the gap: The effect of reducing complexity and uncertainty in college pricing on the choices of low-income

students. *American Economic Review* 111(6): 1721–1756. doi:10.1257/aer.20200451

90. Ray, Ranita. (2018). *The making of a teenage service class: Poverty and mobility in an American city*. Oakland, CA: University of California Press, p. 3.

91. Powell, M. (2022, January 25). How it feels to be an Asian student in an elite public school. *New York Times*. https://www.nytimes.com/2022/01/25/us/selective-high-schools-brooklyn-tech.html

92. Nierenberg, A., and Bui, Q. (2019), December 24. Chinese restaurants are closing. That's a good thing, the owners say. *New York Times*. https://www.nytimes.com/2019/12/24/upshot/chinese-restaurants-closing-upward-mobility-second-generation.html

93. Latif, Z., and Choksi, M. (2023, January 18). Inside India's cram city. *New York Times*. https://www.nytimes.com/2023/01/18/magazine/india-cram-schools-kota.html

94. Sherman, R. (2017). *Uneasy street: The anxieties of affluence*. Princeton, NJ: Princeton University Press, pp. 62–63.

95. Bulman, George, Fairlie, Robert, Goodman, Sarena, and Isen, Adam. (2021). Parental resources and college attendance: Evidence from lottery wins. *American Economic Review* 111(4): 1201–1240.

96. Williams, J. C. (2020). *White working class: Overcoming class cluelessness*. Boston: Harvard Business School Publishing, p. 38.

97. Graham, C. (2021). America's Crisis of Despair: A Fedral Task Force for Economic Recovery and Societal Well-Being. *Brookings*. (February 10) https://www.brookings.edu/research/americas-crisis-of-despair-a-federal-task-force-for-economic-recovery-and-societal-well-being/

98. Ibid.

99. Williams, J. C. (2020). *White working class: Overcoming class cluelessness*. Boston: Harvard Business School Publishing, p. 28.

100. Lamont, M. (2002). *The dignity of working men: Morality and the boundaries of race, class, and immigration*. Cambridge: Harvard University Press, pp. 123–124.

101. Lamont, M. (1992) *Money, morals, and manners: The culture of French and American upper-middle class*. Chicago: Chicago University Press, p. 8.

102. Wyman, P. (2021, September 23). American gentry. *The Atlantic*. https://www.theatlantic.com/ideas/archive/2021/09/trump-american-gentry-wyman-elites/620151/

Chapter 13: Religion

1. Van Kessel, P., Hughes, A., Smith, G., and Alper, B. (2018, November 20). Where Americans find meaning in life. Pew Research Center. https://www.pewresearch.org/religion/2018/11/20/where-americans-find-meaning-in-life/

2. Newman, David B., and Graham, Jesse. (2018). Religion and well-being. In: E. Diener, S. Oishi, and L. Tay (eds.), *Handbook of well-being*. Salt Lake City, UT: DEF Publishers. doi: nobascholar.com

3. Jacobs, A. (2021, Nov 7). On Consolation' Searches for Solace in the Face of Grief and Misery, *The New York Times*. https://www.nytimes.com/2021/11/07/books/review-on-consolation-michael-ignatieff.html?smid=em-share

4. Lelkes, Orsolya. (2002, August 12). Tasting freedom: Happiness, religion and economic transition. LSE, Centre for Analysis of Social Exclusion, CASE Paper No. 59. Available at SSRN: https://ssrn.com/abstract=323140 or http://dx.doi.org/10.2139/ssrn.323140

5. Bryukhanov, Maksym, and Fedotenkov, Igor. (2017, November 13). Religiosity and life satisfaction in Russia: Evidence from the Russian data. Higher School of Economics Research Paper No. WP BRP 180/EC/2017. Available at SSRN: https://ssrn.com/abstract=3070238 or http://dx.doi.org/10.2139/ssrn.3070238

6. Headey, Bruce, Schupp, Jürgen, Tucci, Ingrid, and Wagner, Gert G. (2008, December 30). Authentic happiness theory supported by impact of religion on life satisfaction—A longitudinal analysis with data for Germany. SOEP paper No. 151. Available at SSRN: https://ssrn.com/abstract=1323686 or http://dx.doi.org/10.2139/ssrn.1323686

7. Vishkin, Allon, Bloom, Pazit Ben-Nun, and Tamir, Maya. (2019, February). Always look on the bright side of life: Religiosity, emotion regulation and well-being in a Jewish and Christian sample. *Journal of Happiness Studies*, Springer 20(2): 427–447. doi:10.1007/s10902-017-9956-9

8. Collins, P. (2013, October). Is God good for us? *Ovations UTSA's College of Liberal and Fine Arts Magazine*. https://www.utsa.edu/ovations/vol8/story/god.html

9. Dehejia, Rajeev H., DeLeire, Thomas, and Luttmer, Erzo F. P. (2005, August). Insuring consumption and happiness through religious organizations. NBER Working Paper No. w11576. Available at SSRN: https://ssrn.com/abstract=788441

10. Cooper, M. (2014). *Cut adrift: Families in insecure times.* Berkeley and Los Angeles: University of California Press, p. 159.

11. Iannaccone, Laurence. (1998, November). Introduction to the economics of religion. *Journal of Economic Literature* 36: 1465–1496; Kelley, Dean. (1986). *Why conservative churches are growing: A study in the sociology of religion.* Macon, GA: Mercer University Press.

12. Cooper, M. (2014). *Cut adrift: Families in insecure times.* Berkeley and Los Angeles: University of California Press, p. 179.

13. Morduch, J., and Schneider, R. (2017). *The financial diaries: How American families cope in a world of uncertainty.* Princeton, New Jersey: Princeton University Press, p. 45.

14. Glaeser, Edward L., and Sacerdote, Bruce I. (2008). Education and religion. *Journal of Human Capital* 2: 188–215. https://doi.org/10.1086/590413

15. Van Kessel, P., Hughes, A., Smith, G., and Alper, B. (2018, November 20). Where Americans find meaning in life. Pew Research Center. https://www.pewresearch.org/religion/2018/11/20/where-americans-find-meaning-in-life/

16. Saad, L., and Hrynowski, Z. (2022, June 24). How many Americans believe in God? Gallup. https://news.gallup.com/poll/268205/americans-believe-god.aspx

17. Pew Research Center. (2019, October 17). In U.S., decline of Christianity continues at rapid pace. *Pew Research Center's Religion & Public Life Project.* https://www.pewresearch.org/religion/2019/10/17/in-u-s-decline-of-christianity-continues-at-rapid-pace/

18. Silver, L., Van Kessel, P., Huang, C., Clancy, L., and Gubbala, S. (2021, November 18). Finding meaning in the bigger picture. *Pew Research Center's Global Attitudes Project.* https://www.pewresearch.org/global/2021/11/18/finding-meaning-in-the-bigger-picture/

19. Reuell, P. (2016, August 1). Belief in a deity helps humans cooperate and live in large groups, studies say. *Harvard Gazette.* https://phys.org/news/2016-08-belief-deity-humans-cooperate-large.html

20. Reuell, P. (2016, July 29). Religion as social unifier. *Harvard Gazette.* https://news.harvard.edu/gazette/story/2016/07/religion-as-social-unifier/

21. Davis, K. (2012, October). America's true history of religious tolerance. *Smithsonian Magazine.* https://www.smithsonianmag.com/history/americas-true-history-of-religious-tolerance-61312684/

22. Corichi, M., Sahgal, N., Evans, J., Salazar, A. M., and Starr, K. (2021, June 29). Religion in India: Tolerance and segregation. *Pew Research Center's Religion & Public Life Project*. https://www.pewresearch.org/religion/2021/06/29/religion-in-india-tolerance-and-segregation/

23. Grose, J. (2023, June 28). Opinion | What churches offer that "nones" still long for. *New York Times*. https://www.nytimes.com/2023/06/28/opinion/religion-affiliation-community.html

24. Pasek, M. H., and Cook, J. E. (2019). Religion from the target's perspective: A portrait of religious threat and its consequences in the United States. *Social Psychological and Personality Science* 10(1): 82–93.

25. Ibid.

26. Hamid, S. (2021, March 10). America without God. *The Atlantic*. https://www.theatlantic.com/magazine/archive/2021/04/america-politics-religion/618072/

27. Stern, Shai. (2020, June 28). The dark side of communities: Illiberal religious communities' compliance with COVID-19 public health regulations. Bar Ilan University Faculty of Law Research Paper No. 20-11. Available at SSRN: https://ssrn.com/abstract=3637335 or http://dx.doi.org/10.2139/ssrn.3637335

28. Ghosh, Arkadev. (2022, August 12). Religious divisions and production technology: Experimental evidence from India. Available at SSRN: https://ssrn.com/abstract=4188354 or http://dx.doi.org/10.2139/ssrn.4188354

29. Canaan, Serena, Deeb, Antoine, and Mouganie, Pierre. (2022). Does religious diversity improve trust and performance? Evidence from Lebanon. IZA Discussion Paper No. 15206. Available at SSRN: https://ssrn.com/abstract=4114779 or http://dx.doi.org/10.2139/ssrn.4114779

Chapter 14: Society

1. Helliwell, J. F., Layard, R., Sachs, J. D., Emmanuel De Neve, J., Aknin, L. B., and Wang, S. (2022, March 18). *World Happiness Report 2022*. https://worldhappiness.report/ed/2022/

2. Ibid., Foreword.

3. Huang, Chye-Ching. (2020, January 1). New Zealand's "Wellbeing Budget" approach. Available at SSRN: https://ssrn.com/abstract=3606841 or http://dx.doi.org/10.2139/ssrn.3606841

4. El-Jahel, Lina, and MacCulloch, Robert. (2020). It's (not) the economy, stupid: New Zealand's targeting of Gross National Happiness during the coronavirus crisis. The University of Auckland Business School Research Paper, Forthcoming. Book chapter "Management Perspectives on the Covid-19 Crisis: Lessons from New Zealand," Forthcoming, edited by Kenneth Husted and Rudolf Sinkovics. Available at SSRN: https://ssrn.com/abstract=3787171 or http://dx.doi .org/10.2139/ssrn.3787171

5. Gandelman, Nestor, Piani, Giorgina, and Ferre, Zuleika. (2012). Neighborhood determinants of quality of life. *Journal of Happiness Studies* 13(3): 547–563. doi:10.1007/s10902-011-9278-2. Available at SSRN: https://ssrn.com/abstract=2296920

6. Helliwell, John F., Huang, Haifang, Grover, Shawn, and Wang, Shun. (2018). Empirical linkages between good governance and national well-being. *Journal of Comparative Economics*, Elsevier 46(4): 1332–1346.

7. Edsall, T. B. (2022, September 14). Opinion | Why aren't you voting in your financial self-interest? *New York Times*. https://www.nytimes. com/2022/09/14/opinion/elites-populists-political-beliefs.html

8. Graham, C. (2021, February 10). America's crisis of despair: A federal task force for economic recovery and societal well-being. *Brookings*. https://www.brookings.edu/articles/americas-crisis-of-despair-a- federal-task-force-for-economic-recovery-and-societal-well-being/

9. Edsall, T. B. (2021, October 20). Opinion | Conservatives are happier than liberals. Discuss. *New York Times*. https://www.nytimes. com/2021/10/20/opinion/conservatives-liberals-happiness.html

10. Napier, J. L., and Jost, J. T. (2008). Why are conservatives happier than liberals? *Psychological Science* 19(6): 565–572. doi:10.1111/ j.1467-9280.2008.02124.x

11. Schlenker, Barry, Chambers, John R., and Le, Bonnie. (2012). Conservatives are happier than liberals, but why? Political ideology, personality, and life satisfaction. *Journal of Research in Personality* 46: 127–146. Available at SSRN: https://ssrn.com/abstract=2239819

12. Coibion, Olivier, Gorodnichenko, Yuriy, and Weber, Michael. (2021, March 19). Political polarization and expected economic outcomes. Chicago Booth Research Paper No. 20-45. Fama-Miller Working Paper. Available at SSRN: https://ssrn.com/abstract=3720029 or http://dx.doi.org/10.2139/ssrn.3720029

13. Lynch, D. J. (2020, December 28). Democrats and Republicans have traded places in their views of the economy's direction. *Washington*

Post. https://www.washingtonpost.com/business/2020/12/28/biden-trump-economy-confidence/

14. Telhami, S., and Rouse, S. (2022, May 24). Measuring the impact of partisanship on attitudes toward the US response to the Russia-Ukraine War. *Brookings.* https://www.brookings.edu/articles/measuring-the-impact-of-partisanship-on-attitudes-toward-the-us-response-to-the-russia-ukraine-war/

15. Lench, H. C., Levine, L. J., Perez, K. A., Carpenter, Z. K., Carlson, S. J., and Tibbett, T. (2019). Changes in subjective well-being following the U.S. presidential election of 2016. *Emotion* 19(1): 1–9. https://doi.org/10.1037/emo0000411

16. Pierce, Lamar, Rogers, Todd, and Snyder, Jaso. (2015, March 5). Losing hurts: The happiness impact of partisan electoral loss. HKS Working Paper No. RWP14-051. Available at SSRN: https://ssrn.com/abstract=2528709 or http://dx.doi.org/10.2139/ssrn.2528709

17. Pinto, Sergio, Bencsik, Panka, Chuluun, Tuugi, and Graham, Carol. (2020, February 14). Presidential elections, divided politics, and happiness in the U.S. Available at SSRN: https://ssrn.com/abstract=3586049 or http://dx.doi.org/10.2139/ssrn.3586049

18. Haendler, Charlotte, and Heimer, Rawley. (2021, January 14). The financial restitution gap in consumer finance: Insights from complaints filed with the CFPB. Available at SSRN: https://ssrn.com/abstract=3766485 or http://dx.doi.org/10.2139/ssrn.3766485

19. Cullen, Julie Berry, Turner, Nicholas, and Washington, Ebonya. (2021, August). Political alignment, attitudes toward government, and tax evasion. *American Economic Journal: Economic Policy* 13(3): 135–166.

20. Stuart, Michael D., Wang, Jing, and Willis, Richard H. (2021, October 1). CEO partisan bias and management earnings forecast bias. Vanderbilt Owen Graduate School of Management Research Paper. Available at SSRN: https://ssrn.com/abstract=3946547 or http://dx.doi.org/10.2139/ssrn.3946547

21. Fos, Vyacheslav, Kempf, Elisabeth, and Tsoutsoura, Margarita. (2022, June 29). The political polarization of corporate America. University of Chicago, Becker Friedman Institute for Economics Working Paper No. 2022-77. Available at SSRN: https://ssrn.com/abstract=4142685 or http://dx.doi.org/10.2139/ssrn.4142685

22. Kempf, Elisabeth, Luo, Mancy, Schäfer, Larissa, and Tsoutsoura, Margarita. (2021, August 12). Does political partisanship cross borders? Evidence from international capital flows. Available at SSRN:

https://ssrn.com/abstract=3904077 or http://dx.doi.org/10.2139/ssrn.3904077

23. Meeuwis, Maarten, Parker, Jonathan A., Schoar, Antoinette, and Simester, Duncan. (2021, September 30). Belief disagreement and portfolio choice. *Journal of Finance*, Forthcoming. Available at SSRN: https://ssrn.com/abstract=3934061

24. Bomgardner, M. (2022, September 1). Could your political views stymie your career? *Kellogg Insight.* https://insight.kellogg.north-western.edu/article/could-your-political-views-stymie-your-career

25. Elinson, Zusha. (2021, March 12). Black Rifle Coffee seeks like-minded aficonados. *Wall Street Journal.* https://www.wsj.com/articles/black-rifle-coffee-seeks-like-minded-aficonados-11615550401?st=b6nf92jshzfhcm0&reflink=article_email_share

26. Schoenmueller, Verena, Netzer, Oded, and Stahl, Florian. (2019, October 17). Polarized America: From political partisanship to preference partisanship. Columbia Business School Research Paper, Forthcoming. Available at SSRN: https://ssrn.com/abstract=3471477 or http://dx.doi.org/10.2139/ssrn.3471477

27. Ibid.

28. Edsall, T. B. (2022, July 20). Opinion | How you feel about gender roles can tell us how you'll vote. *New York Times.* https://www.nytimes.com/2022/07/20/opinion/gender-gap-partisanship-politics.html

29. Li, C., Zuckerman, M., and Diener, E. (2021). Culture moderates the relation between gender inequality and well-being. *Psychological Science* 32(6): 823–835. doi:10.1177/0956797620972492

30. Dumetz, Jérôme, Zanolini, Valentina, and Morgan, Caitlin. (2021). Too much culturally aware? When intercultural reconciliation fails in business: The case of IKEA in Saudi Arabia (September 2020). WIBF (Würzburg International Business Forum) International Business Conference 2020, Available at SSRN: https://ssrn.com/abstract=3843618

31. Motyl, Matt. (2014, November 11). Liberals and conservatives are (geographically) dividing. In: P. Valdesolo and J. Graham (eds.), *Bridging ideological divides: The Claremont Symposium for Applied Social Psychology.* Sage Press, Forthcoming. Available at SSRN: https://ssrn.com/abstract=2522999

32. Pazzanese, C. (2021, March 16). Democrats and Republicans live in partisan bubbles, study finds. *Harvard Gazette.* https://news.harvard

.edu/gazette/story/2021/03/democrats-and-republicans-live-in-partisan-bubbles-study-finds/.

33. Badger, E., Quealy, K., and Katz, J. (2021, March 17). A close-up picture of partisan segregation, among 180 million voters. *New York Times.* https://www.nytimes.com/interactive/2021/03/17/upshot/partisan-segregation-maps.html

34. Ballard, J. (2020, September 17). How Republicans and Democrats would feel if their child married across the political aisle. YouGov. https://today.yougov.com/politics/articles/32041-republicans-democrats-marriage-poll?redirect_from=%2Ftopics%2Fpolitics%2Farticles-reports%2F2020%2F09%2F17%2Frepublicans-democrats-marriage-poll: https://today.yougov.com/topics/politics/articles-reports/2020/09/17/republicans-democrats-marriage-poll

35. Vavreck, L. (2017, January 31). A measure of identity: Are you wedded to your party? *New York Times* https://www.nytimes.com/2017/01/31/upshot/are-you-married-to-your-party.html

36. Dahl, Gordon B., Lu, Runjing, and Mullins, William. (2021, December). Partisan fertility and presidential elections. CEPR Discussion Paper No. DP16821. Available at SSRN: https://ssrn.com/abstract=4026689

37. Bjørnskov, Christian, Dreher, Axel, Fischer, Justina A.V., and Schnellenbach, Jan. (2009, December). On the relation between income inequality and happiness: Do fairness perceptions matter. KOF Working Paper No. 245, KOF Swiss Economic Institute, ETH Zurich. Available at SSRN: https://ssrn.com/abstract=1527356 or http://dx.doi.org/10.2139/ssrn.1527356

38. Krijnen, Job, Ulkumen, Gulden, Bogard, Jonathan, and Fox, Craig R. (2020, September 18). Lay beliefs about changes in financial well-being predict political and policy message preferences. Available at SRN: https://ssrn.com/abstract=3695322 or http://dx.doi.org/10.2139/ssrn.3695322; Krijnen, J. M. T., Ülkümen, G., Bogard, J. E., Fox, C. R. (2022). Lay theories of financial well-being predict political and policy message preferences. *Journal of Personality and Social Psychology.*

39. Bjørnskov, Christian, Dreher, Axel, Fischer, Justina A.V., and Schnellenbach, Jan. (2009, December). On the relation between income inequality and happiness: Do fairness perceptions matter. KOF Working Paper No. 245, KOF Swiss Economic Institute, ETH Zurich.

Available at SSRN: https://ssrn.com/abstract=1527356 or http://dx.doi.org/10.2139/ssrn.1527356

40. Alesina, Alberto, Stantcheva, Stefanie, and Teso, Edoardo. (2018, February). Intergenerational mobility and preferences for redistribution. *American Economic Review* 108(2): 521–554.

41. Graham, Carol, and Felton, Andrew. (2005, January). Does inequality matter to individual welfare? An initial exploration based on happiness surveys from Latin America. Center on Social and Economic Dynamics Working Paper Number 38. Available at SSRN: https://ssrn.com/abstract=1028066 or http://dx.doi.org/10.2139/ssrn.1028066

42. Welsch, Heinz, and Biermann, Philipp. (2016, December). Poverty is a public bad: Panel evidence from subjective well-being data. SOEP paper No. 885. Available at SSRN: https://ssrn.com/abstract=2920612

43. Rothwell, J. (2020, February 13). Experiment shows conservatives more willing to share wealth than they say. *New York Times*. https://www.nytimes.com/2020/02/13/upshot/trump-supporters-experiment-inequality.html

44. Sherman, R. (2017). *Uneasy street: The anxieties of affluence*. Princeton, NJ: Princeton University Press, pp. 58–59.

45. DeSantis, Jake. (2009, March 24). Dear A.I.G., I quit. *New York Times*, Opinion. http://www.nytimes.com/2009/03/25/opinion/25desantis.html?pagewanted=all

46. Giuliano, Paola, and Tabellini, Marco. (2020, November 9). The seeds of ideology: Historical immigration and political preferences in the United States. Harvard Business School BGIE Unit Working Paper No. 20-118. Available at SSRN: https://ssrn.com/abstract=3606506 or http://dx.doi.org/10.2139/ssrn.3606506

47. Alesina, Alberto F., Glaeser, Edward L., and Sacerdote, Bruce. (2001, October). Why doesn't the US have a European-style welfare state? Available at SSRN: https://ssrn.com/abstract=290047 or http://dx.doi.org/10.2139/ssrn.290047

48. Michel, A. (2018, July 31). The paradox of diversity. *Association for Psychological Science*. https://www.psychologicalscience.org/observer/the-paradox-of-diversity

49. Khazan, O. (2018, April 23). People voted for Trump because they were anxious, not poor. *The Atlantic*. https://www.theatlantic.com/

science/archive/2018/04/existential-anxiety-not-poverty-motivates-trump-support/558674/

50. Edsall, T. B. (2022, April 27). Opinion | Where does all that hate we feel come from? *New York Times*. https://www.nytimes.com/2022/04/27/opinion/rich-poor-immigration-fear.html

51. Beerli, Andreas, Ruffner, Jan, Siegenthaler, Michael, and Peri, Giovanni. (2021, March).

52. Edsall, T. B. (2022, April 27). Opinion | Where does all that hate we feel come from? *New York Times*. https://www.nytimes.com/2022/04/27/opinion/rich-poor-immigration-fear.html

53. Van Kessel, P., Hughes, A., Smith, G., and Alper, B. (2018, November 20). Where Americans find meaning in life. Pew Research Center. https://www.pewresearch.org/religion/2018/11/20/where-americans-find-meaning-in-life/

54. Bursztyn, Leonardo, Egorov, Georgy, and Fiorin, Stefano. (2020). From extreme to mainstream: The erosion of social norms. *American Economic Review* 110(11): 3522–3548.

55. Van Kessel, P., Hughes, A., and Walker, K. (2018, November 20). The meaning of life: 100 quotes from Americans on what keeps them going. *Pew Research Center's Religion & Public Life Project*. https://www.pewresearch.org/religion/interactives/what-keeps-us-going/

56. Tabellini, Marco. (2019, April 2). Gifts of the immigrants, woes of the natives: Lessons from the age of mass migration. Harvard Business School BGIE Unit Working Paper No. 19-005. Available at SSRN: https://ssrn.com/abstract=3220430 or http://dx.doi.org/10.2139/ssrn.3220430

57. Alesina, A., Harnoss, J., and Rapoport, H. (2021). Immigration and the future of the welfare state in Europe. *The ANNALS of the American Academy of Political and Social Science*, 697(1): 120–147. https://doi.org/10.1177/00027162211055409

58. Van de Vyver, J., Houston, D., and Abrams, D. (2015, December 17). Terrorism may make liberals think more like conservatives. Association for Psychological Science. https://www.psychologicalscience.org/news/releases/terrorism-may-make-liberals-think-like-conservatives.html

59. Law, Kelvin, and Zuo, Luo. (2021, September 6). Public concern about immigration and customer complaints against minority financial advisors. *Management Science*, Forthcoming. Nanyang Business

School Research Paper No. 21-33. Available at SSRN: https://ssrn
.com/abstract=3918663 or http://dx.doi.org/10.2139/ssrn.3918663

60. Alesina, Alberto F., Miano, Armando, and Stantcheva, Stefanie. (2018,
    June). Immigration and redistribution. NBER Working Paper No.
    w24733. Available at SSRN: https://ssrn.com/abstract=3206414

61. Brooks, D. (2022, April 8). Opinion | Globalization is over. The global
    culture wars have begun. *New York Times*. https://www.nytimes.com/
    2022/04/08/opinion/globalization-global-culture-war.html

62. Glaeser, Edward L. (2002, September). The political economy of
    hatred. NBER Working Paper No. w9171. Available at SSRN:
    https://ssrn.com/abstract=330310

63. Freddi, Eleonora, Potters, Johannes (Jan) J. M., and Suetens, S. (2022,
    March 1). Brief cooperative contact with ethnic minorities reduces
    discrimination. CEPR Discussion Paper No. DP17098. Available at
    SSRN: https://ssrn.com/abstract=4069906

64. Achard, Pascal, Albrecht, Sabina, Cettolin, Elena, Ghidoni, Riccardo,
    and Suetens, S. (2022, May). The effect of exposure to ethnic minori-
    ties on ethnic preferences. CEPR Discussion Paper No. DP17294.
    Available at SSRN: https://ssrn.com/abstract=4121479

65. Qiu, Lin, Qiao, Dandan, Tan, Bernard, and Whinston, Andrew B. (2022,
    March 17). Connected in the ride: An empirical investigation into
    ride-hailing services and hate crimes. Available at SSRN: https://ssrn
    .com/abstract=4059664 or http://dx.doi.org/10.2139/ssrn.4059664

66. Bursztyn, Leonardo, Chaney, Thomas, Hassan, Tarek Alexander, and
    Rao, Aakash. (2021, February 8). The immigrant next door: Expo-
    sure, prejudice, and altruism. University of Chicago, Becker Fried-
    man Institute for Economics Working Paper No. 2021-16. Available
    at SSRN: https://ssrn.com/abstract=3781974 or http://dx.doi
    .org/10.2139/ssrn.3781974

67. Jordan, M. and Steinhauer, J. 2021. Americans Stretch Across Political
    Divides to Welcome Afghan Refugees. *The New York Times*. (Septem-
    ber 6)https://www.nytimes.com/2021/09/06/us/afghan-refugees-
    volunteers.html

68. Hornsey, M. J., Harris, E. A., and Fielding, K. S. (2018). The psy-
    chological roots of anti-vaccination attitudes: A 24-nation investi-
    gation. *Health Psychology* 37(4), 307–315. https://doi.org/10.1037/
    hea0000586

69. Amin, A. B., Bednarczyk, R. A., Ray, C .E. et al. (2017). Association
    of moral values with vaccine hesitancy. *Nature Human Behavior.*
    873–880. https://doi.org/10.1038/s41562-017-0256-5

70. https://www.nytimes.com/2021/04/29/us/vaccine-skepticism-beliefs.html?action=click&module=Top%20Stories&pgtype=Homepage https://moralfoundations.org/

71. Peng, Yilang. (2022, January 9). Give me liberty or give me COVID-19: How social dominance orientation, right-wing authoritarianism, and libertarianism explain Americans' reactions to COVID-19. *Risk Analysis*, Forthcoming. Available at SSRN: https://ssrn.com/abstract=4004357 or http://dx.doi.org/10.2139/ssrn.4004357

72. Huang, Li, Li, Oliver Zhen, Wang, Baiqiang, and Zhang, Zilong. (2020, December 8). Individualism and the fight against COVID-19. Available at SSRN: https://ssrn.com/abstract=3665493 or http://dx.doi.org/10.2139/ssrn.3665493

73. Goldstein, Noah J., Cialdini, Robert B., and Griskevicius, Vladas. (2008, October). A room with a viewpoint: Using social norms to motivate environmental conservation in hotels. *Journal of Consumer Research* 35(3): 472–482. https://doi.org/10.1086/586910

74. Bicchieri, Cristina, Fatas, Enrique, Aldama, Abraham, Casas, Andrés, Casas, Deshpande, Ishwari, Lauro, Mariagiulia, Parilli, Cristina, Spohn, Max, Pereira, Paula, Wen, Ruiling. (2021, June 4). In science we (should) trust: Expectations and compliance across nine countries during the COVID-19 pandemic. https://doi.org/10.1371/journal.pone.0252892

75. Nakayachi, Kazuya, Ozaki, Taku, Shibata, Yukihide, and Yokoi, Ryosuke. (2020). Why do Japanese people use masks against COVID-19, even though masks are unlikely to offer protection against infection. *Frontiers in Psychology* 11: 1918. doi:10.3389/fpsyg.2020.01918 PMCID: PMC7417658 PMID: 32849127.

76. Milosh, Maria, Painter, Marcus, Van Dijcke, David, and Wright, Austin L. (2020, July 31). Unmasking partisanship: How polarization influences public responses to collective risk. University of Chicago, Becker Friedman Institute for Economics Working Paper No. 2020-102. Available at SSRN: https://ssrn.com/abstract=3664779 or http://dx.doi.org/10.2139/ssrn.3664779

77. Simonov, Andrey, Sacher, Szymon, Dube, Jean-Pierre H., and Biswas, Shirsho. (2020, July 28). The persuasive effect of Fox News: Non-compliance with social distancing during the COVID-19 pandemic. Columbia Business School Research Paper, Forthcoming. Available at SSRN: https://ssrn.com/abstract=3600088 or http://dx.doi.org/10.2139/ssrn.3600088

78. Stantcheva, Stefanie. (2021). Understanding tax policy: How do people reason? *The Quarterly Journal of Economics* 136(4): 2309–2369.

79. Hope, David, Limberg, Julian, and Weber, Nina. (2021, August 17). Why do (some) ordinary Americans support tax cuts for the rich? Evidence from a randomized survey experiment. Available at SSRN: https://ssrn.com/abstract=3906631 or http://dx.doi.org/10.2139/ssrn.3906631

80. Nathan, Brad, Perez-Truglia, Ricardo, and Zentner, Alejandro. (2020, September 12). My taxes are too darn high: Tax protests as revealed preferences for taxation. Available at SSRN: https://ssrn.com/abstract=3691361 or http://dx.doi.org/10.2139/ssrn.3691361

81. DeParle, Jason. (2022, September 11). Expanded safety net drives sharp drop in child poverty. For this article, the reporter worked closely for five months with researchers from a nonpartisan group to document the decline in child poverty and the forces pushing it lower. *New York Times*. https://www.nytimes.com/2022/09/11/us/politics/child-poverty-analysis-safety-net.html

82. Galama, Titus J., Morgan, Robson, and Saavedra, Juan. (2017, November). Wealthier, happier and more self-sufficient: When anti-poverty programs improve economic and subjective wellbeing at a reduced cost to taxpayers. NBER Working Paper No. w24090. Available at SSRN: https://ssrn.com/abstract=3082273

83. Bando, Rosangela, Galiani, Sebastian, and Gertler, Paul J. (2020, December 29). Another brick on the wall: On the effects of non-contributory pensions on material and subjective well-being. Available at SSRN: https://ssrn.com/abstract=3756906 or http://dx.doi.org/10.2139/ssrn.3756906

84. Milligan, Kevin S., and Stabile, Mark. (2008, December). Do child tax benefits affect the wellbeing of children? Evidence from Canadian child benefit expansions. NBER Working Paper No. w14624. Available at SSRN: https://ssrn.com/abstract=1327246

85. Halpern-Meekin, S., Edin, K., Tach, L., et al. (2015). *It's not like I'm poor: How working families make ends meet in a post-welfare world.* Berkeley and Los Angeles: University of California Press, p. 71.

86. Boyd-Swan, Casey, Herbst, Chris M., Ifcher, John, and Zarghamee, Homa. (2016). The Earned Income Tax Credit, health, and happiness. *Journal of Economic Behavior & Organization* 126, Part A: 18–38. ISSN 0167-2681. https://doi.org/10.1016/j.jebo.2015.11.004

87. Halpern-Meekin, S., Edin, K., Tach, L., et al. (2015). *It's not like I'm poor: How working families make ends meet in a post-welfare world*. Berkeley and Los Angeles: University of California Press, pp. 76–77.

88. Dempsey, B. (2019, June 20). Parenting in poverty. *New York Times*. https://www.nytimes.com/2019/06/20/well/family/parenting-in-poverty.html

89. Bollinger, Bryan, Leslie, Philip, and Sorensen, Alan. (2011). Calorie posting in chain restaurants. *American Economic Journal: Economic Policy* 3(1): 91–128.

90. Wansink, Brian, and Chandon, Pierre. (2006, November). Can "low-fat" nutrition labels lead to obesity? *Journal of Marketing Research* 43(4): 605–617.

91. Chandon, Pierre, and Wansink, Brian. (2007). The biasing health halos of fast food restaurant health claims: Lower calorie estimates and higher side–dish consumption intentions. *Journal of Consumer Research* 34(3): 301–314.

92. Epperson, Raphael, and Gerster, Andreas. (2021, October 8). Information avoidance and moral behavior: Experimental evidence from food choices. Available at SSRN: https://ssrn.com/abstract=3938994 or http://dx.doi.org/10.2139/ssrn.3938994

93. Loibl, Cäzilia, Jones, Lauren Eden, Haisley, Emily, and Loewenstein, George F. (2016, February 20). Testing strategies to increase saving and retention in individual development account programs. Available at SSRN: https://ssrn.com/abstract=2735625 or http://dx.doi.org/10.2139/ssrn.2735625

94. Buccafusco, Christopher J., Hemel, Daniel J., and Talley, Eric L. (2021, January 1). Price gouging in a pandemic. University of Chicago Coase-Sandor Institute for Law & Economics Research Paper No. 921, Cardozo Legal Studies Research Paper No. 626, University of Chicago, Public Law Working Paper No. 762, Columbia Law and Economics Working Paper No. 652. Available at SSRN: https://ssrn.com/abstract=3758620 or http://dx.doi.org/10.2139/ssrn.3758620

95. Nicas, J. (2020, March 14). He has 17,700 bottles of hand sanitizer and nowhere to sell them. *New York Times*. https://www.nytimes.com/2020/03/14/technology/coronavirus-purell-wipes-amazon-sellers.html

96. Spruk, Rok, and Keseljevic, Aleksandar (2016, April 1). Institutional origins of subjective well-being: Estimating the effects of economic freedom on national happiness. *Journal of Happiness Studies* 17(2): 659–712. Available at SSRN: https://ssrn.com/abstract=2901872

97. Berggren, Niclas, Bjørnskov, Christian, and Nilsson, Therese. (2017, March 8). Do equal rights for a minority affect general life satisfaction? IFN Working Paper No. 1156. Available at SSRN: https://ssrn.com/abstract=2929337

98. Gehring, Kai. (2013, December 21). Who benefits from economic freedom? Unraveling the effect of economic freedom on subjective well-being. University of Heidelberg Department of Economics Discussion Paper No. 531. Available at SSRN: https://ssrn.com/abstract=2370856

99. Dorn, David, Fischer, Justina A. V., Kirchgässner, Gebhard, and Sousa-Poza, Alfonso. (2005, June). Is it culture or democracy? The impact of democracy, income, and culture on happiness. University of St. Gallen Economics Working Paper No. 2005-12. Available at SSRN: https://ssrn.com/abstract=757629 or http://dx.doi.org/10.2139/ssrn.757629

100. Batinti, Alberto, and Costa-Font, Joan. (2021). Does democracy make taller men? Cross-country European evidence. Available at SSRN: https://ssrn.com/abstract=3985780 or http://dx.doi.org/10.2139/ssrn.3985780

101. Glaeser, Edward L., Ponzetto, Giacomo A. M., and Shleifer, Andrei. (2006, April). Why does democracy need education? NBER Working Paper No. w12128. Available at SSRN: https://ssrn.com/abstract=896068

102. Sulemana, Iddisah, Iddrisu, Abdul Malik, and Kyoore, Jude A. (2015, December 9). Micro-level study of the relationship between experienced corruption and subjective well-being in Africa. *The Journal of Development Studies*, Forthcoming. Available at SSRN: https://ssrn.com/abstract=2836948

103. Eriksson, D. (2022, January 25). 2021 Corruption Perceptions Index—Explore the results. Transparency International. https://www.transparency.org/en/cpi/2021

104. Sumit Agarwal, Qian, Wenlan, Seru, Amit, and Zhang, Jian. (2020). Disguised corruption: Evidence from consumer credit in China. *Journal of Financial Economics* 137(2): 430–450.

105. Condra, Luke, and Wright, Austin L. (2021, May 14). Corruption and political mobilization: Evidence from a natural experiment. University of Chicago, Becker Friedman Institute for Economics Working Paper No. 2021-59. Available at SSRN: https://ssrn.com/abstract=3846431 or http://dx.doi.org/10.2139/ssrn.3846431

106. Lutsiv, Sofiya. (2021, June 28). Corruption as a social phenomenon: Case of Ukraine. Available at SSRN: https://ssrn.com/abstract=3875709 or http://dx.doi.org/10.2139/ssrn.3875709

107. Patrucic, M., Gillies, A., Eisen, N., and Blumenthal, L. (2002). Investigate Journalism Is Essential for Ukraine Reconstruction and Anti-Corruption. *Brookings*. (October 6) https://www.brookings.edu/blog/up-front/2022/10/06/investigative-journalism-is-essential-for-ukraine-reconstruction-and-anti-corruption/.

108. Siddique, Abu Bakkar. (2022, September 9). Does corruption culture matter for tax morale? Evidence from generation of immigrant samples. Available at SSRN: https://ssrn.com/abstract=4213991 or http://dx.doi.org/10.2139/ssrn.4213991

109. Gross, J., and Lemola, J. (2021, April 20). What makes a happy country? *New York Times*. https://www.nytimes.com/2021/04/20/world/europe/world-happiness-report-ranking.html

110. Ortiz-Ospina, E., and Roser, M. (2016, July). Trust. *Our World in Data*. https://ourworldindata.org/trust

111. Knack, Stephan, and Keefer, Philip. (1997, November). Does social capital have an economic payoff? A cross country investigation. *Quarterly Journal of Economics* 112(4): 1251–1288.

112. Helliwell, John F., Huang, Haifang, and Wang, Shun. (2016, July). New evidence on trust and well-being. NBER Working Paper No. w22450. Available at SSRN: https://ssrn.com/abstract=2813918

113. Yamamura, Eiji, Tsutsui, Yoshiro, Yamane, Chisako, Yamane, Shoko, and Powdthavee, Nattavudh. (2014, July 4). Trust and happiness: Comparative study before and after the Great East Japan Earthquake. ISER Discussion Paper No. 904. Available at SSRN: https://ssrn.com/abstract=2462352

114. Helliwell, John F., Huang, Haifang, and Wang, Shun. (2016, July). New evidence on trust and well-being. NBER Working Paper No. w22450. Available at SSRN: https://ssrn.com/abstract=2813918

115. Guven, Cahit. (2009, June). Are happier people better citizens? SOEP paper No. 199. Available at SSRN: https://ssrn.com/abstract=1422493 or http://dx.doi.org/10.2139/ssrn.1422493

116. Wu, Cary, and Dawson, Andrew. (2021, June 28). Why is trust lower in Quebec? A cultural explanation. Available at SSRN: https://ssrn.com/abstract=3957969 or http://dx.doi.org/10.2139/ssrn.3957969

117. Glaeser, Edward L., Laibson, David I., Scheinkman, José, and Soutter, Christine L. (1999, July). What is social capital? The determinants of trust and trustworthiness. NBER Working Paper No. w7216. Available at SSRN: https://ssrn.com/abstract=171073

118. Schilke, Oliver, Reimann, Martin, and Cook, Karen S. (2021). Annual review of sociology trust in social relations. *Annual. Review of Sociology* 47: 10.1–10.21. The *Annual Review of Sociology* is online at soc.annualreviews.org. https://doi.org/10.1146/annurev-soc-082120- 082850 WHAT IS TRUST?

119. Tomy, Rimmy, and Regina, Wittenberg Moerman. (2021, January 25). Community membership and reciprocity in lending: Evidence from informal markets. Chicago Booth Research Paper No. 21-09, Fama-Miller Working Paper. Available at SSRN: https://ssrn.com/abstract=3773160 or http://dx.doi.org/10.2139/ssrn.3773160

120. Bachas, Pierre, Gertler, Paul J., Higgins, Sean, and Seira, Enrique. (2017, March). Banking on trust: How debit cards enable the poor to save more. NBER Working Paper No. w23252. Available at SSRN: https://ssrn.com/abstract=2937522

121. Beckmann, Elisabeth, and Mare, Davide Salvatore. (2017, August 1). Formal and informal household savings: How does trust in financial institutions influence the choice of saving instruments? Available at SSRN: https://ssrn.com/abstract=3023711 or http://dx.doi.org/10.2139/ssrn.3023711

122. Velasquez-Manoff, M. (2022, May 25). The anti-vaccine movement's new frontier. *New York Times.* https://www.nytimes.com/2022/05/25/magazine/anti-vaccine-movement.html

123. Gilbert, K. (2020, November 4). One key trait that predicts how much people will socially distance. *Kellogg Insight.* https://insight.kellogg.northwestern.edu/article/key-trait-predicts-how-much-people-will-socially-distance

124. Jalan, Akanksha, Matkovskyy, Roman, Urquhart, Andrew, and Yarovaya, Larisa. (2022, May 3). The role of interpersonal trust in cryptocurrency adoption. Available at SSRN: https://ssrn.com/abstract=4099518 or http://dx.doi.org/10.2139/ssrn.4099518

125. Phua, Jing Wen Kenny, Sang, Bo, Wei, Chishen, and Yu, Gloria Yang. (2022, March 23). Trust, but verify: The economics of scams in initial coin offerings. Available at SSRN: https://ssrn.com/abstract=4064453 or http://dx.doi.org/10.2139/ssrn.4064453

126. Deason, Stephen, Rajgopal, Shivaram, and Waymire, Gregory B. (2015, March 28). Who gets swindled in Ponzi schemes? Available at SSRN: http://ssrn.com/abstract=2586490 or http://dx.doi.org/10.2139/ssrn.2586490

127. Giannetti, Mariassunta, and Wang, Tracy Yue. (2015, July 29). Corporate scandals and household stock market participation. *Journal of Finance*, Forthcoming. Available at SSRN: http://ssrn.com/abstract=2637559

128. Soni, Aparna, and Tekin, Erdal. (2020). How do mass shootings affect community wellbeing? IZA Discussion Paper No. 13879. Available at SSRN: https://ssrn.com/abstract=3734747

129. Fortin, J. (2018, June 8). New Jersey teacher leaves students $1 million gift in her will. *New York Times*. https://www.nytimes.com/2018/06/08/nyregion/teacher-scholarship-will-new-jersey.html

130. U.S. Bank, Member. (2018, August 28. These heartwarming volunteer stories will totally inspire you to give back. *BuzzFeed*. https://www.buzzfeed.com/usbank/these-heartwarming-volunteer-stories-will-totally a

131. Caron, C. (2018, June 24). Teenage girl helps a blind and deaf passenger and wins praise for doing "something beautiful." *New York Times*. https://www.nytimes.com/2018/06/24/us/teenager-alaska-airlines-sign-language.html

132. Aknin, Lara B., Barrington-Leigh, Christopher P., Dunn, Elizabeth W., Helliwell, John F., Biswas-Diener, Robert, Kemeza, Imelda, Nyende, Paul, Ashton-James, Claire E., and Norton, Michael I. (2010, September). Prosocial spending and well-being: Cross-cultural evidence for a psychological universal. NBER Working Paper No. w16415. Available at SSRN: https://ssrn.com/abstract=1685722

133. Liu, Wendy, and Aaker, Jennifer. (2008, October). The happiness of giving: The time-ask effect. *Journal of Consumer Research* 35(3): 543–557.

134. Jonathan Rizzo Foundation. (2023, November 5). http://www.jonathanrizzofoundation.org

135. Mizan, N. (2022, June 29). $13 million in donations collected for Uvalde families affected by Robb School shooting. *Austin American-Statesman*. https://www.statesman.com/story/news/2022/06/29/robb-elementary-school-shooting-texas-13-million-donated-help-uvalde-victims-families/7725521001/

136. Porter, E. (2007, April 29). The divisions that tighten the purse strings. *New York Times*. https://www.nytimes.com/2007/04/29/business/yourmoney/29view.html

137. DellaVigna, Stefano, List, John A., and Malmendier, Ulrike. (2012, February). Testing for altruism and social pressure in charitable giving. *The Quarterly Journal of Economics* 127(1): 1–56.

Chapter 15: Conclusion

1. Van Kessel, P., Hughes, A., Smith, G., and Alper, B. (2018, November 20). Where Americans find meaning in life. Pew Research Center. https://www.pewresearch.org/religion/2018/11/20/where-americans-find-meaning-in-life

2. Wildman, S. (2023). Opinion | My daughter's future was taken from her, and from us. (2023, May 19). *New York Times*. https://www.nytimes.com/2023/05/19/opinion/grief-childhood-cancer.html

3. Blanchflower, David G., and Oswald, Andrew J. (2007, September). Is well-being U-shaped over the life cycle? IZA Discussion Paper No. 3075. Available at SSRN: https://ssrn.com/abstract=1026895

4. March, Carey. (2021, March 12). The Pandemic Happiness Gap new surveys show that in the last year, older adults tended to be more positive than younger ones, suggesting that the ability to cope improves with age. https://www.nytimes.com/2021/03/12/health/covid-pandemic-happiness-age.html?action=click&module=Top%20Stories&pgtype=Homepage

5. Brody, B. (2020, July 28). Why it's good to be old, even in a pandemic. *New York Times*. https://www.nytimes.com/2020/07/28/well/live/aging-benefits-pandemic.html

6. Pinsker, J. (2023, August 6). If all you want is money, these financial advisers might say "no thanks." *Wall Street Journal*. https://www.wsj.com/articles/financial-advisors-money-job-satisfaction-happiness-20c40e17

7. Alter, Charlotte. Inside a 46-year-old millionaire's mission to look and feel 18 again: Bryan Johnson's quest for immortality. https://time.com/6315607/bryan-johnsons-quest-for-immortality/

8. Jarman, M. (2005). When the Light Came On: The Epic Gilgamesh [Review of GILGAMESH: A New English Version, by S. Mitchell]. The Hudson Review, 58(2), 329-334. https://www.jstor.org/stable/30044781

About the Author

Meir Statman is the Glenn Klimek Professor of Finance at Santa Clara University. His research focuses on behavioral finance. He describes people as "normal," neither computer-like "rational," nor bumbling "irrational," and attempts to understand and explain how normal people make choices and how these choices affect their well-being.

Meir's research has been published in the *Journal of Finance*, the *Journal of Financial Economics*, the *Review of Financial Studies*, the *Journal of Financial and Quantitative Analysis*, the *Financial Analysts Journal*, the *Journal of Portfolio Management*, and many other journals. The research has been supported by the National Science Foundation, the CFA Institute Research Foundation, and the Investment and Wealth Institute (IWI).

Meir is a member of the Advisory Board of the *Journal of Portfolio Management*, the *Journal of Wealth Management*, the *Journal of Retirement*, the *Journal of Investment Consulting*, and the *Journal of Behavioral and Experimental Finance*; an Associate Editor of the *Journal of Behavioral Finance* and the *Journal of Investment Management*; and a recipient of a Batterymarch Fellowship, a William F. Sharpe Best Paper Award, two Bernstein Fabozzi/Jacobs Levy Awards, a Davis Ethics Award, a Moskowitz Prize for best paper on socially responsible investing, a Matthew R. McArthur Industry Pioneer Award, three Baker IMCA Journal Awards, and three Graham and Dodd Awards. Meir was named as one of the 25 most influential people by *Investment Advisor* magazine. He consults with many investment companies and presents his work to academics and professionals in many forums in the United States and abroad.

Meir received his Ph.D. from Columbia University, and his B.A. and M.B.A. from the Hebrew University of Jerusalem.

Author Index

Subject Index